The Painter 7 Wow! Book

The Painter 7 Wow! Book

Cher Threinen-Pendarvis

Peachpit Press

The Painter 7 Wow! Book

Cher Threinen-Pendarvis

Peachpit Press
1249 Eighth Street
Berkeley, CA 94710
(510) 524-2178
(800) 283-9444
(510) 524-2221 (fax)

Find us on the World Wide Web at: http://www.peachpit.com/books/wow.html

Peachpit Press is a division of Pearson Education.

Series Editor: Linnea Dayton
Peachpit Press Editor: Cary Norsworthy
Cover design: Mimi Heft
Cover illustration: Cher Threinen-Pendarvis
Book design: Jill Davis
Art direction and layout: Cher Threinen-Pendarvis
Editing: Linnea Dayton
Proofreading: Susan Bugbee
Index: Jackie Estrada
Production and prepress manager: Jonathan Parker

This book was set using the Stone Serif and Stone Sans families. It was written and composed in Adobe PageMaker 6.52. Final output was computer to plate at CDS, Medford, Oregon.

ISBN 0-201-77362-7

0 9 8 7 6 5 4 3 2 1
Printed and bound in the United States of America.

To my husband Steven,
for his friendship,
encouragement and understanding;
and to our Creator
from whom all inspiration comes. . . .

— Cher Threinen-Pendarvis

Mark Zimmer, creator of Painter

FOREWORD

"Gee Mark. . is it Seven already?"

"Yeah. . Painter 7. . Wow!"

"Time sure does fly when we're havin' fun!"

Looking through the pages of this newest edition of the *Painter Wow!* series, it is simply amazing to observe the wide variety of art and illustration created by Painter users. A central aim of Painter has always been to allow the artist's style to come through in the final image. It becomes clear, looking through the chapters of this book, that Painter achieves this goal. Cher's refined mastery of Painter enables her to expertly guide both new and experienced users to their own personal form of self-expression.

It is often difficult, if not impossible, to examine a finished piece of art and reconstruct the process that the artist used to create it. Oftentimes, the designer can't even recall the exact order in which various tools and techniques were applied to an image. It is this spontaneous creative activity that is so often undocumented and unavailable to the viewer. The casual observer isn't likely to be interested in this creative inner structure. But the curious artist, seeking inspiration and new techniques, would love to have access to this often mysterious "inside information".

Thankfully, Cher has a developed a wonderful talent for coaxing this inside information from artists. Through her conversations, she is able to accurately create a blueprint of sorts. This blueprint

John Derry, co-creator of Painter

provides other artists with an insight into an illustration's underlying technique. Cher extends this blueprinting method with projects of her own. By designing an image around a specific set of Painter tools, she can highlight those tools' creative application.

Painter was designed for both beginners and experts alike. To the novice, this book acts as an introductory primer. For the experienced user, it is a magic book of secret formulas. For both, it can be used as a key to unlock bottled-up creativity. One time-honored method for creating great images is to look at lots of great images. This book is lushly illustrated with dozens of great images created with Painter. Just thumbing through this book can get your creative juices flowing!

Once again, Cher has mined out the new Painter features in this latest edition and produced an excellent companion to Painter 7. We hope that you will find inspiration within these pages. Now Go Forth and Create!

"Hey, is this a picture of a zebra or a teapot?"

"You're holding the book upside-down, John."

"Oh, you're right. It's a picture of a paint can!"

Mark Zimmer

John Derry

La Selva Beach, California

March, 2002

This Paint Can *illustration was created for the Painter 7 poster by Karen Carr.*

Susan Levan created Conch Shell *using Painter's Water Color brushes, Pens, Airbrushes, masks and layers.*

Capitola Woodcut *was created by John Derry using Painter 7's updated and expanded Woodcut features.*

PREFACE

"What is art?" is a question that has been debated for centuries. With the advent of the computer, that question continues to be asked but in a whole new context — is it possible to create art using the computer? *The Painter 7 Wow! Book* by Cher Threinen-Pendarvis clearly demonstrates that the answer to this question is yes.

Over the years, Mark Zimmer, John Derry and Tom Hedges have developed a program that truly delivers the art-making experience by bringing traditional, natural-media tools to the computer desktop. *The Painter 7 Wow! Book* showcases these tools in a unique, meaningful and artistic way.

Conveying the art-making process is a huge challenge. Cher addresses this challenge by teaching through example. *The Painter 7 Wow! Book* is an incredible collection of art and design created by fine artists, designers, photographers and illustrators from around the world.

Cher's personal and professional experience as an artist, designer and illustrator provides her with a complete understanding of the image-making process, which she showcases clearly in this book. Cher not only describes how to use the vast array of natural-media tools in Painter 7 but also demonstrates how to conceptualize and create compelling images, guiding the reader through the elements of composition, layout and form to medium, texture and color.

Whether you are a graphic designer, web designer, traditional illustrator, concept designer, storyboard artist, photographer, fine artist or someone who just wants to have fun with digital painting, *The Painter 7 Wow! Book* is the ideal resource for both learning and inspiration.

Tanya Staples

Program Manager, procreate Painter™

March, 2002

Mark Zimmer created the original Paint Can *image for the Painter 1.0 program.*

ACKNOWLEDGMENTS

The Painter 7 Wow! Book would not have been possible without a great deal of help from some extraordinary people and sources.

My heartfelt thanks go to Linnea Dayton, the *Wow!* Series Editor and a treasured friend and colleague. During all *five* editions, her inspiration, wisdom and encouragement proved invaluable. Thank you, Linnea, for editing *The Painter 7 Wow! Book*.

Warmest thanks go to my friends at Peachpit Press, especially Ted Nace for his inspiration, Nancy Ruenzel for her guidance, Cary Norsworthy—our *Wow!* Peachpit editor—for her advice that came when it was needed most, and the rest of the publishing team for their support. Thank you Peachpit, for giving me the opportunity to do this book.

A big "thank you" goes to the creators of Painter: Mark Zimmer, Tom Hedges and John Derry, for creating such a *Wow!* program and for their inspiration, enthusiasm and openness;

Warmest thanks go to Tanya Staples and Alice White, the Program Manager and Product Manager for Painter Products—for their support; I'm also grateful to the Painter 7 development, quality assurance and documentation teams as well as the procreate strategic alliance team.

I am grateful to each of the talented Painter artists who contributed their work and techniques; their names are listed in Appendix D in the back of the book. I would especially like to thank Daryl Wise who helped me locate artists who use Painter.

I'd also like to thank the companies who supplied the *Wow!* book team with supporting software during the development of the book—Adobe Systems for supplying me with Photoshop, Illustrator, Premiere and GoLive; and Macromedia, for contributing

John Derry created this illustration for the Painter 4 poster.

This Paint Can *illustration was created for the Painter 6 poster by John Derry.*

© COREL CORPORATION

Phoenix and Painter 7 at Mount Fuji *was created for the Painter 7 poster by Cher Threinen-Pendarvis, using the version's new Water Color brushes and layers.*

Director, Dreamweaver, Fireworks, and Flash so I could demonstrate how nicely these programs work with Painter.

Thanks to Corbis Images and PhotoDisc for their support during all five editions of the book; these two "stock on CD-ROM and Web" companies allowed us to use their photos for demonstration purposes in the book. I am also grateful to the other companies who provided images or video clips for *The Painter 7 Wow!* CD-ROM; they are listed in Appendix A in the back of the book.

Additionally, the following companies donated, loaned or gave us a good deal on hardware that helped to create the book. Thanks to Wacom, for their great pressure-sensitive tablets and to Hewlett-Packard and Epson for color printers for the testing of printing techniques.

I'm grateful to Linnea Dayton, Jack Davis, Victor Gavenda, Chris (Boz) Jennings, Donal Jolley, Shawn Grunberger and Cary Norsworthy for their helpful technical reads. My warmest thanks go to Carol Benioff for her expertise in traditional and digital printmaking, Michele Lill for sharing her knowledge about reflection maps, and Steven Gordon for his experience with terrain maps. Special thanks also go to Dorothy Krause and Bonny Lhotka for sharing their knowledge of experimental printmaking, Jon Lee and Geoff Hull of Fox Television for sharing their experience in designing for broadcast television; Cindy and Dewey Reid of Reid Creative for sharing their expertise in animation and film; and Lynda Weinman for sharing her knowledge about designing graphics for the Web.

I'd like to thank my co-workers "behind the scenes" on the Wow! book team. Warmest thanks go to Jill Davis for her brilliant book design; Susan Bugbee for her friendship and helpful copyediting and proofreading; Jackie Estrada for her careful indexing; and PageMaker whiz Jonathan Parker for his production and prepress expertise. Jonathan's calm assurance during the deadlines of all five editions of this book was much appreciated!

My very special thanks go to Victor Gavenda at Peachpit Press for his fine work on the *Painter Wow!* CD-ROM.

A heartfelt thank you to these special "co-workers:" to my husband Steve, for his encouragement, tasty meals and reminders to take breaks during the project; and to our cats Little Doll, Soshi and Pearl, the close companions who keep me company in the office and warm my office chair. A warm thanks to our sister-in-law Joy Young and dear friends Lisa Baker and Julie Klein who shared sincere encouragement and prayers. Thanks for checking in with me while I worked!

Finally, I would like to thank all the other family, friends and colleagues who have been so patient and understanding during the development of five editions of this book.

Cher Threinen-Pendarvis

CONTENTS

WELCOME TO *PAINTER 7 WOW!*

SOME PEOPLE EMPHASIZE THE DIFFERENCES between traditional and digital art tools—almost as if "real" art and the computer are not compatible. But during the early development of this book, we discovered many working artists who had bought computers specifically because they were thrilled by the promise of Painter. It seemed logical that *The Painter Wow! Book* should become a bridge connecting conventional tools and techniques with their electronic counterparts. Early chapters of the book, in particular, touch on color theory, art history and conventional media, and explain how to translate foundational art theory using Painter's tools.

This book addresses the needs of a wide variety of creative professionals: artists making the transition from traditional to digital media; photographers looking to expand their visual vocabulary; screen or print graphic designers hunting for special effects to apply to type; even creative explorers out for some fun. For those of you with a long history in a traditional art form and a short history with computers, we've done our best to guide you through Painter's interface, making it as simple as possible for you to achieve the results you want. And if you've spent more time with a keyboard and mouse than you have with an artist's palette and paintbrush, you may learn a lot about conventional art terms and techniques as you read the book.

The creative team that invented Painter—Mark Zimmer, John Derry and Tom Hedges of Fractal.com—consulted with the Corel development team during the creation of Painter 7. Both companies are famous for their innovation and dedication to improving software tools and this new release reflects that. Along with exciting new natural media tools, such as Water Color that actually drips and runs and thick, sticky Liquid Ink, as well as other new tools, the team has also made changes to the interface that make Painter easier to use.

The new Water Color brushes and layers in Painter 7 let you paint with realistic watercolor washes that can be smooth or runny, as show here in African Violet.

Hillside Lake *was created using the new Liquid Ink brushes and layers in Painter 7, with which you can create images with thick, sticky ink.*

Athos Boncompagni used Painter 7's Dry Media, Pencils and Pens variants while creating this wrapping paper design.

WHAT'S NEW IN PAINTER 7?

To make *The Painter 7 Wow! Book* complete and up-to-date for Painter 7, we've revised every page. And we've expanded the book—adding many pages of brand-new real-world tips, techniques and galleries that specifically profile features added in version 7. Here's a quick overview of some of Painter's exciting new features and a description of where in this book you can find information about them.

Among the changes that make Painter easier to use are these: Painter 7 features new **Palette Preferences** that allow you to display only the sections of an expandable palette that you need. Notably, the updated Brush architecture makes it easier to **customize brushes** to your heart's content and it makes the process of moving brush libraries, categories and variants much simpler! The helpful new continuous, variable **zoom** feature includes a scale slider and you can also specify an exact factor in the text field. Also important in the redesign, Painter makes better use of large amounts of RAM when working with big images.

An area of the program that's most likely to change the way you work is Painter 7's industry-standard **masks and layers** model, which will be familiar to users of Adobe Photoshop. With Painter, you can make selections and save them as masks into the Masks section of the Objects palette, much like saving selections as masks into the Channels palette in Photoshop. The new layers operate much more like Photoshop's layers, and are true transparent layers (with Preserve Transparency) that you can paint on with most any brush. You can also use a selection with any layer you target. And Opacity and Compositing Methods controls are included in the Layers section of the Objects palette. You can also enable **Pick Up Underlying Color** from layers underneath the one you're working on, which is useful when painting with the **Smeary Brushes**.

Painter 7 boasts two new exciting new media layers, **Water Color** and **Liquid Ink**, with dozens of new brushes to use with them. The new redesigned Water Color tools allow you to brush on transparent washes that can be smooth—or be painted to drip and run, as the pigment particles appear to be suspended in a medium—just like real watercolor! Liquid Ink is viscous and sticky and can be given a three-dimensional appearance. You can also etch or erode away Liquid Ink by painting with Liquid Ink **resist** brushes. Brushstrokes can be painted smoothly or with bristle marks, and the Liquid Ink and its 3D information are **resolution independent**. See "A Painter Water Color Primer" on page 70 and "A Painter Liquid Ink Primer" on page 110 for foundational information for using these new tools in a creative way.

Users of previous versions of the program will be pleased to find Painter's familiar Brushes palette, stocked with brand-new **brushes** that paint more naturally than ever before—and faster, too. The new **variable** Dry Media and Pencils variants add more sensitivity: For instance, the new Oily Variable Pencil can lay

Painter's brushes and industry-standard masks and layers let you paint on the Canvas and layers with realistic brush work and create layered composite images to produce results like John Derry's Imagine, *shown here.*

You'll learn real applications for Painter's tools in the Basics sections of each chapter.

Each chapter includes step-by-step technique sections.

down color or subtly smear it, and the redesigned Flattened Pencil offers an even more natural experience while sketching. The program also includes many more **realistic cloning brushes** such as the new Bristle Brush Cloner and Camel Impasto Cloner.

Painter 7 combines the dynamic text and text shapes of previous versions into one Text tool that allows you to set type directly on the image and style it, including applying the **text on a curve** and adding a live drop shadow. You'll find information about how these **type tools** work and techniques for using them in the Chapter 8, "Working with Type in Painter."

Photographers and illustrators will appreciate Painter's updated **Woodcut** and **Distress** features which allow you to create more natural-media effects. You can even save you own Woodcut presets. For a step-by-step technique see "Creating a Woodcut From a Photo" on page 220.

Designers will love adding motion to Web pages with Painter's improved export of **GIF animations**. See Chapter 10, "Multimedia and Film with Painter," and Chapter 11, "Using Painter for Web Graphics," for more information about animation, video and Web graphics using Painter.

If you need to prepare images for print, Painter 7 offers a useful updated **Kodak Color Management System**. Turn to Chapter 12, "Printing and Archival Concerns," to read about this system.

DO YOU USE MAC OR WINDOWS?

Painter works similarly on Macintosh and PC/Windows platforms. We've taken the path of least resistance by using primarily Macintosh screenshots. (Just to make sure of our techniques, though, we've tested them under Windows 2000, and we've included key commands for both Mac and Windows users.) The few differences between running Painter on Mac and PC are covered in Chapter 1.

ARE YOU A BEGINNER OR A POWER-USER?

If you're new to Painter, welcome! We've worked very hard to make this edition of *Painter Wow*! more friendly to beginners by adding more cross-references and by including complete, unabbreviated directions to the techniques in the book. We've also added more basics to the chapter introductions. For intermediate and advanced users, we've included new power-user tips throughout and added many new techniques and inspiring galleries.

We've assumed that you're familiar with the basic Mac or Windows mouse functions and that you know how to open and save files, copy items to the clipboard and navigate through the Mac's hierarchical file system or through Windows directories. We suggest reading Chapter 1, "Getting To Know Painter," Chapter 4, "Selections, Shapes and Masks," and Chapter 5, "Using Layers and Shapes," before jumping into the more advanced techniques. It's also a good idea, though it isn't essential, to have worked with the *Painter 7 User Guide* and to have completed tutorials that come with the program.

3 SAMPLING PAINT

You can temporarily switch to the Dropper tool and sample colors by holding down the Ctrl/⌘ key while you're using many of Painter's other tools.

4

Each chapter includes an inspiring gallery of professional work.

5

You'll find helpful resources in the Appendixes.

PAINTER 7.1 SOFTWARE PATCH

The Painter development team has built a software patch (Painter 7.1) that adds a few new features (which are covered in this book) and fixes problems in the Painter 7.0 program. The patch is available for free download at http://www.procreate.com/go/painter_update/

HOW TO USE THIS BOOK

In Chapters 2 through 12, the information we're presenting generally progresses from simple to complex. We've organized these chapters into four types of material: "Basics" sections, techniques, practical tips and galleries. In addition, useful hardware, software and other resources are listed at the back of the book.

1 The **Basics** sections teach how Painter's tools and functions work, and give real-world applications for the tools. *The Painter 7 Wow! Book* wasn't designed to be a replacement for the *Painter 7 User Guide* that comes with the program. We've focused on the tools and functions that we think are most useful. In some cases we've further explained items covered in the manual, and, where important, we've dug deeper to help you understand how the tools and functions work. In other cases, we've covered undocumented functions and practical applications, either shared by contributing artists or uncovered in our own research.

2 Within each **Technique** section, you'll find step-by-step, real-world methods that give you enough information to re-create the process yourself. In the *Wow!* format, pictures illustrating the stages of the process are positioned alongside the appropriate step in the project. Browse the pictures in the art column within a technique for a quick overview of the development of an image. We've done our best to give you enough information so you won't have to refer to the manual to follow the steps.

3 The **Tips** are easily identified by their gray title bar. We've placed them in the Basics and Technique sections where we thought they'd be the most helpful. But each tip is a self-contained tidbit of useful information, so you can learn a lot very quickly by taking a brisk walk through the book, reading only the tips.

4 The **Galleries** are there for inspiration, and one appears at the end of every chapter. With each gallery image, you'll find a short description of how the artwork was produced.

5 No book is an island, so in the **Appendixes** in the back of this one, we've included lists of other resources for your use. If you want to contact a vendor, an artist, or a fine art print studio, or locate an art-related book or other publication, you'll find the information you need there.

The Painter 7 Wow! Book was created to share useful techniques and tips and to provide creative suggestions for using the program. We hope that you'll use it as inspiration and a point of departure for your own creative exploration. Above all, don't be overwhelmed by Painter's richness. . . Just dig in and enjoy it!

Cher Threinen-Pendarvis
http://www.peachpit.com/about/author.bios/cher.threinen-pendarvis.html
Painter Wow! Web site: http://beta.peachpit.com/wow/painter

GETTING TO KNOW PAINTER

John Derry's illustration, Piece of Cake, *was inspired by the artist Wayne Theibaud. Derry created it for the promotion of Painter 7 using a variety of tools, including Pencils variants, colored shapes and thick Impasto.*

© COREL CORPORATION

SIT RIGHT DOWN AND POWER UP! This chapter explores Painter's basic needs and functions, as well as its unique strengths and idiosyncrasies. If you're new to Painter, you'll benefit the most from this chapter if you've already spent some time with the *Painter 7 User Guide* that ships with the program.

PAINTER'S REQUIREMENTS FOR MAC AND PC

Here are Painter's *minimum* requirements: If you use a Macintosh you'll need at least a G3 running System 8.6 or later with a minimum of 64 MB of application RAM (128 MB is recommended when running Mac OS X). To run Painter on Windows 98, 2000, Windows XT, Windows NT 4 or Windows ME, you'll need at least an IBM Compatible PC, Pentium 200 or higher with at least 64 MB of application RAM (128 MB is recommended). For both platforms you'll need a hard disk with approximately 100 MB of free space to perform a minimum installation.

When you open an image in Painter—for example, a 5 MB image—and begin working with it, Painter needs three to five times that file size in RAM in order to work at optimal speed—in our example, that would be 15–25 MB of RAM. Opening more than one image, adding layers or shapes, or increasing the number of Undos (under Edit, Preferences, Undos) adds further demands on RAM. When Painter runs out of RAM, it uses the hard

ABOUT LAYERS AND SHAPES

Layers and *shapes* are image elements that reside in layers above the Painter image canvas. Both layers and shapes can be manipulated independently of the image canvas—allowing for exciting compositing effects.

On the Mac in System 9.2 and earlier, Painter runs faster with Virtual Memory turned off in the Memory Control Panel. (It interferes with Painter's own virtual memory scheme.)

On the Mac in System 9.2 and earlier, you can use the Finder's File, Get Info window to set the memory allocation for the program.

Setting the Maximum Memory for Painter in Windows

disk chosen in Edit, Preferences, General as a RAM substitute. This "scratch disk" holds the Painter Temp file you may have seen. Since hard disks operate much slower than RAM, performance suffers accordingly—even if you have a fast hard disk.

Ideally, to work with Painter, you would use a computer with a speedy processor; a large, fast hard disk; and lots of RAM. In addition, you'll want a large, 24-bit color monitor—probably no less than 17 inches—and perhaps a second monitor on which to store palettes. Also highly recommended—some might say *essential*—is a drawing tablet with a pressure-sensitive stylus. Not only is it a more natural drawing and painting tool than a mouse, but many of Painter's brushes lose their personality without a pressure-sensitive input device.

Mac memory allocation.
Mac OS X allows Painter to use as much RAM as it needs. Painter does not have any special options for setting memory in OS X. To allot maximum RAM to Painter on a Mac running OS 9.2 or earlier, first quit all open applications. In the Finder, under the Apple menu, choose About This Macintosh and write down the number next to Largest Unused Block. This is the total amount of RAM in which you can run applications. Subtract 500 or 1000 K from this number (as a buffer). Now, in the Painter folder, click once (not twice!) on the Painter application icon and choose File, Get Info. Enter the result of your math in the Preferred Size box. This method won't let you open any other applications of significant size while Painter is running, but it assures you of the use of nearly all available RAM while you're in Painter.

Windows memory allocation. To make maximum RAM available for your Windows–based PC, choose Edit, Preferences, Windows to access the Windows Preferences dialog box. Under Physical Memory Usage click the "Maximum Memory for Painter" button. Quit all applications and relaunch Painter. Painter will run faster if you let Windows manage the virtual memory scheme.

HARD DISK TIPS

You can speed up your scratch disk by using hard disk driver software to make a separate partition just for the Painter Temp file. Additionally, use a hard disk utility program like Norton Utilities or PC Tools (from Symantec) to regularly defragment the partition. Over time, hard drives become fragmented (space is broken into smaller and smaller blocks)—and thus slower—because the file data has to be split up in order to be written to them and then reassembled when a file is opened.

FASTER STARTUP

Painter reads all open fonts and loaded plug-in filters when it starts up. For faster startup, consider organizing your fonts with a utility (Suitcase or MasterJuggler) that enables you to turn them on and off.

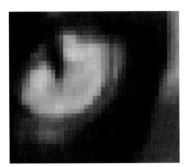

This scan of a photograph is a pixel-based image. Enlarging it to 1200% reveals the grid of pixels.

QUICK CLOSING KEYS

To quickly close a file without having to click the on-screen buttons in the warning box that appears during the closing process, use these keyboard shortcuts: press **D** for Don't Save; press **C** for Cancel to change your mind, closing the box without closing the file; or press **S** (or Return) for Save.

QUICK COPIES

Here are two ways to make quick copies without going through the clipboard and using valuable RAM. To make a copy of your entire document, use File, Clone. (This is also a quick way to make a "flat" copy with the layers in the document merged.) To quickly duplicate a layer, select the layer in the layers section of the Objects palette, choose the Layer Adjuster tool, press the Alt/Option key and click in the image to make a copy in register, or drag off a copy into another area of the document.

FILE SIZE AND RESOLUTION

If you're new to the computer, here's important background information regarding file sizes: Painter is primarily a *pixel-based* program, also known as a *bitmap*, *painting* or *raster* program, not a *drawing* program, also known as an *object-oriented* or *vector* program (see "Painter's Vector Capabilities" below). Drawing programs use mathematical expressions to describe the outline and fill attributes of objects in the drawing, while pixel-based programs describe things dot-by-dot. Because its components are mathematically described, object-oriented art can be resized or transformed with no loss of quality. Not so with Painter, Photoshop and other pixel-based programs. Increasing the size of most images in these programs means that additional pixels must be created to accommodate the larger size by filling in spaces as the existing pixels spread apart. As a result of these interpolated (manufactured) pixels, resized images can lose their crispness.

There are ways of working around this "soft image" dilemma. One solution is to do studies using a small file size (for instance, an 8 x 10-inch image at 75 pixels per inch), then start over with a large file to do final art at full size (for instance an 8 x 10-inch file at 300 pixels per inch). You can also block in the basic form and color in a small file, then scale the image up to final size (using Canvas, Resize) to add texture and details (textures seem particularly vulnerable to softening when enlarged). You'll notice that many of the artists whose work is featured in this book use another efficient method: They create the components of a final piece of art in separate documents, then copy and paste the components into a final "master" image. Painter offers yet another solution for working with large file sizes—composing with reference layers (small "stand-in" versions of larger images that are kept outside the document). Because data for the large image is not kept in the working file, performance improves. Turn to "Using Reference Layers" on page 144, to learn about this feature.

Painter's vector capabilities. Although it's primarily a pixel-based program, Painter does have some object-oriented features—shapes, shape paths and outline-based selections. Painter's shapes exist as floating elements above the image canvas; they are mathematically described outlines with stroke and fill attributes. And Painter's selections (areas of the image designated for work) are versatile; they can be used as pixel-based selections (similar to Photoshop's selections), or they can be transformed into outline-based selections or converted into shapes. (Other elements in Painter—the image canvas, masks and layers—are pixel-based.) Chapters 4 and 5 tell more about selections and shapes.

Pixel size and resolution. There are two commonly used ways of describing file sizes: in terms of their pixel measurements, or in a unit of measure (such as inches) plus a resolution (pixels per unit of

Expressing width and height in "pixels" in the New dialog box keeps the file size the same, regardless of how you change the Resolution.

Whether the Constrain File Size checkbox in the Canvas, Resize dialog box is checked or unchecked, if you're using "pixels" as the units, the file size stays the same, regardless of how you change the Resolution.

Click the Browse button in the Open dialog box to preview all of the images in a folder. The watercolor studies in Mary Envall's "Lilies" folder are shown here. (Some files may not have a preview—for example, some PICT or JPEG files created by other programs.)

measure). An image is a fixed number of pixels wide and tall—like 1200 x 1500—or a measurement combined with a resolution—4 x 5 inches at 300 ppi. (Either way it's expressed, this full-color file is 7 MB.) If you use pixels as a measurement for Width and Height in the New dialog box, notice that changing the numbers you type into the Resolution box doesn't change the file size. The pixel number does not change unless you resize the image using Canvas, Resize. Increasing or decreasing the number of pixels in the Width and Height fields in the Canvas, Resize dialog box to add (or reduce) pixel information in the picture automatically unchecks the Constrain File Size box.

OPENING FILES

Images in Painter are 24-bit color, made up of RGB (red, green and blue) components consisting of 8 bits each of color information. Painter will recognize and open CMYK TIFF and grayscale TIFF images, but it will convert both CMYK and grayscale TIFF files to Painter's own RGB mode. Layered files saved in Photoshop format must be converted to RGB mode before they can be opened in Painter. CIE LAB, Kodak Photo CD format and other color formats will need to be converted to RGB in a program such as Adobe Photoshop or Equilibrium's Debabelizer before Painter can read them.

SAVING FILES

Painter offers numerous ways to save your image under File, Save or Save As. If you've created an image with a mask (Chapter 4 tells how to create masks), some of the formats will allow you to preserve the mask (by checking the Save Alpha box in the Save or Save As dialog box), while others won't. Here's a list of the current formats that includes their "mask-friendliness" and other advantages and disadvantages:

RIFF. Thrifty (files are saved quite small) and robust (allows for multiple layers), RIFF (Raster Image File Format) is Painter's native format. If you're using elements unique to Painter, such as Wet Paint, reference layers, dynamic layers, shapes, selections or mosaics, saving in RIFF format will preserve them. (Selections, masks, layers and shapes are described in depth in Chapters 4 and 5.) If you have *lots* of free hard disk space, check the Uncompressed box in the Save dialog box when you're saving in RIFF: Files will become many times larger, but will save and open much more quickly. Few other programs recognize RIFF, so if you want to work with a Painter image in another program, save a copy in a different format.

Photoshop format. Saving files in Photoshop format gives you nearly all the flexibility of RIFF, and is ideal if you frequently move data between Painter and Photoshop. When you use Photoshop to open a file saved in this format, Painter's layers become Photoshop layers (Chapter 9, "Using Painter with Photoshop,"

You can preserve layers in files by saving in either RIFF or Photoshop format, but RIFF (even uncompressed) is usually significantly smaller. Rick Kirkman's 663 x 663-pixel image with 150 layers weighs in at 1.7 MB as a compressed RIFF, 6.1 MB as an uncompressed RIFF, and 7.1 MB when saved in Photoshop format.

A SAVING GRACE

Saving multiple versions of your art at various steps along the way makes good sense: It helps you remember how you created your art, and it could be your saving grace if a file gets corrupted.

KEYBOARD SHORTCUTS

Use these shortcuts to switch tools from the keyboard:

In the Tools palette, several tools are nested with other tools and thus don't appear in the view of the Tools palette shown above. Use these keys to select these tools: Rotate Page, e; Oval Selection, o; Quick Curve, q; Oval Shape, j; Add Point, a; Delete Point, x; Convert Point, y; Selection Adjuster, s; Shape Selection, h. In addition to choosing tools in the Tools palette, you can change settings in the Controls palette for the Brush tool using your keyboard. Press b to navigate to the brush, then press v to paint straight lines; press b to toggle back to freehand operation.

contains more information about working with Painter and Photoshop); Painter's masks (explained in depth in Chapter 4) become Photoshop channels; and Painter's Bézier paths translate perfectly to Photoshop's paths and subpaths, appearing in Photoshop's Paths palette.

TIFF. Probably the most popular and widely recognized of the bitmap file formats, TIFF allows you to save a mask with your image (check the Save Alpha checkbox). Unfortunately, unlike Photoshop, Painter's Save As dialog box gives you no option to compress the TIFF file—the Uncompressed check box is checked and grayed-out.

PICT. PICT is the format of choice for many multimedia programs and other on-screen display. Painter's PICT format lets you save a single mask (but not layers), and save a Painter movie as a sequence of numbered PICT files to export and animate in another program (described in Chapter 10, "Multimedia and Film with Painter"). Painter also opens PICT files very quickly.

JPEG. When you save a file in JPEG format, a dialog box will appear with four choices: Excellent, High, Good and Fair. You'll get the best-looking results by choosing Excellent. The advantage of saving a file in JPEG format is that you get superb space savings: a JPEG file is usually only one-tenth as large as a TIFF file of the same image if you choose Excellent, and only one-hundredth the size if you choose Fair. The drawbacks: No mask, layers or paths are saved; and the compression is a lossy compression—which means that some data (color detail in the image) is lost in the compression process. While JPEG is a good way to archive images once they're finished (especially images that have no sharp edges), many artists prefer not to use JPEG because it alters pixels. Don't save a file in JPEG format more than once—you'll lose more data every time you do so.

JPEG is also useful for preparing 24-bit images with the tiny file sizes that are needed for graphics used on the World Wide Web. (See Chapter 11 for more information on JPEG use in projects created for the Web.)

WORKING WITH CMYK

Here are some hints for working with Painter in a CMYK production environment. If you're starting with scanned images, scan them in RGB instead of CMYK—RGB has a significantly broader color gamut. If possible, avoid importing your image into another program (like Photoshop) to convert it to CMYK until you're ready to print, since you lose colors when you convert from RGB to CMYK. And, it's a good idea to save a copy of the RGB image before converting in case you want to convert it again with different RGB-to-CMYK conversion settings.

Relative sizes and extents of color gamuts

The Save As GIF Options dialog box includes GIF Animation Options. To learn about creating a GIF animation step-by-step, turn to "Making a Slide Show Animation" on page 352.

LAYER ADJUSTER TOOL TOGGLE

Painter's Layer Adjuster tool is analogous to the Move tool in Adobe Photoshop. You can use the Ctrl/⌘ key to switch temporarily to the Layer Adjuster tool when you are using the following tools: the Magnifier, Page Rotation, Crop, Lasso, Magic Wand, Brush, Paint Bucket, Dropper, Rectangular Selection, Oval Selection, Selection Adjuster and Shape Adjuster.

When you make a brushstroke in the Preferences, Brush Tracking dialog box, Painter adjusts the range of pressure-sensitivity based on the stroke.

GIF. GIF is the graphics format of choice for most non-photographic images on the World Wide Web. Like TIFF, PICT or JPEG, saving in GIF format combines layers with the background. It also reduces the number of colors to a maximum of 256, so remember to Save As in a different file format first, if you want to be able to access the original image structure again. When you save in GIF, a dialog box appears that gives you a number of options for saving your file. Click the Preview Data button to see how your choices will affect your image. For more information about using Painter's GIF format turn to Chapter 11, "Using Painter for Web Graphics."

EPS. Saving in this format drops layered elements into the background and ignores masks, so it's best to choose Save As in another format if you'll want to make changes to your document at a later time. Saving in EPS format also converts the file into a five-part DCS file: four separate files for the four process printing colors, and a fifth file as a preview of the composite image. Check Chapters 3 and 21 in the *Painter 7 User Guide* for a complete explanation of the EPS Options dialog box.

PC formats. BMP, PCX and Targa are formats commonly used on DOS and Windows platforms. BMP (short for "bitmap") is a Windows-based graphics file format, and PCX is the PC Paintbrush native format. Neither of these two formats supports shapes or masks. Targa is a popular format used for creating sophisticated 24-bit graphics; it was originally developed by the Truevision company as a proprietary format for use with its video capture boards. The Targa format is often used (in place of PICT) when preparing numbered files for import into Windows animation applications.

Movie formats. Movies in Painter (described in Chapter 10, "Multimedia and Film with Painter") are saved as frame stacks, but you can choose Save As to export the current frame of your movie, export the entire frame stack as a QuickTime or AVI (on the PC) movie, or export the entire Frame Stack as numbered PICT files. See Chapter 10 for more about multimedia formats.

SETTING PREFERENCES

Painter's Preferences (under the Edit menu) go a long way in helping you create an efficient workspace. Here are a few pointers:

Brush tracking. Before you begin to draw, it's important to set up the Brush Tracking so you can customize how Painter interprets the input of your stylus, including parameters such as pressure and speed. Choose Edit, Preferences, Brush Tracking and make a brushstroke with your stylus using a typical amount of pressure. Painter accepts this as the average stroke and adjusts to give you the maximum amount of range and pressure-sensitivity based on your sample stroke. Unfortunately, Painter doesn't remember your custom setting after you quit the program; so it's a good idea to re-establish your typical brushstroke every time you launch.

The new continuous, variable zoom function in the left corner of the Painter image window includes a Scale slider, and you can also specify an exact zoom factor using the text field. Click the arrow to its left to access a navigator, and pan around your image.

The General Preferences dialog box lets you specify default libraries, cursor type and orientation, Temp File Volume (location of the scratch disk) and Units, among other features.

To view Painter's brush footprint cursor (shown here when painting a brushstroke with the Captured Bristle variant of Brushes), turn on the "Brush ghost when possible" checkbox in the General Preferences dialog box.

In the Art Materials, Preferences dialog box, you can choose which palettes will be displayed when you start up the program by checking or unchecking the boxes and then clicking OK.

Multiple undos. Painter lets you set the number of Undos you want under Edit, Preferences, Undo. (System X users, choose File, Preferences, Undo.) It's important to note that this option applies cumulatively across all open documents within Painter. For example, if the number of Undos is set to 5 (the default) and you have two documents open, if you use two Undos on the first document, you'll be able to perform only three Undos on the second document. And, since a high setting for the number of Undos will burden your RAM and scratch disk, unless you have a good reason (such as working on a small sketch where you'll need to make many changes), it's best to leave the Undo setting at 5.

Palette Preferences. You choose which palette sections are displayed by choosing Edit, Preferences, Palettes (System X users, choose File, Preferences, Palettes.) This new feature makes it easy to configure Painter to save valuable screen real estate. For instance, if you don't currently need the Color Sets, RGB Colors and Looks sections of the Art Materials palette, it's easy to turn them off so they don't load when Painter is launched.

PAINTER BASICS

Here's a guide to some of Painter's basic operating procedures.

Navigating the expandable palettes. Painter's three expandable palettes (the Art Materials, Brush Controls and Objects palettes) have several sections that you can open so that you can see and access the tools you need easily. When closed, the expandable palettes display a stacked series of section bars. To open a section of a palette, (for instance, the Colors section of the Art Materials palette), click the left triangle on the section bar. Click the name of a section to open that section and close all other sections in the palette.

Additionally, the Art Materials and Objects palettes have pull-down menus that contain commands. To use an alternate color set, for instance, choose the Load Color Set command by clicking the right triangle on the Colors section bar.

In the Art Materials palette, a swatch on the Colors, Papers, Patterns, Gradients or Weaves section bar displays the current

You can set your own set of function keys for favorite commands, making it easier to access the commands nested in Painter's menus and palettes. Choose Edit, Preferences, Function Keys, then select a key from the Function key list. Now choose a command; we chose Select, Hide Marquee (to hide a selection marquee while keeping the area selected). Then choose the Set button and click OK.

Making a new function key using the Customize Keys dialog box

Clicking on the pushbar to open the Brushes drawer

The new expandable Art Materials palette has section swatches that display the current color, paper, gradient and pattern. Clicking on a swatch allows you to choose another material from a pop-up list.

resource choice—for instance, the current color chosen in the Colors section. Each of these swatches (except color) allows you to access a resource list. For instance, click on the Papers swatch, and you can view the list of Papers in the loaded library.

Opening drawers. The Brushes palette and some sections of the Art Materials palette (the Papers, Patterns, Gradients, Weaves, Looks and Nozzles sections), display a pushbar when they are open, with an arrowhead in the center that you can click on to open (the arrow turns green) or close a drawer. An open drawer gives you access to a wide choice of brushes, gradients, papers and so on from whatever library is active for that section at the time. A closed drawer (you see only the "front" of the drawer) shows your five most recent choices and may give you additional controls.

Screen management shortcuts. Like other programs, Painter offers lots of shortcuts designed to cut down on your trips to the menus, palettes or scroll bars. To *scroll* around the page, press and hold the spacebar (a grabber hand appears), then drag on your image. To *zoom in* on an area of your image at the next level of magnification, hold down Ctrl/⌘-spacebar (a magnifier tool appears) and click in your image. Add the Alt/Option key to *zoom out*. (You can also use Ctrl/⌘-plus to *zoom in* one magnification level and Ctrl/⌘-minus to *zoom out*.) These are the same zooming shortcuts used in Photoshop and Adobe Illustrator.

To *rotate the page* to better suit your drawing style, press Spacebar-Alt (Windows) or Spacebar-Option (Mac) the Rotate Page icon appears, and click and drag in your image

By right-clicking the mouse in Windows, or by pressing the Control key and clicking on the Mac, you can access helpful context-sensitive menus like this one, which appears when a Brush is chosen.

The Tracing Paper, Grid Overlay, Output Preview and Impasto icons reside at the top of Painter's vertical scroll bar.

A. Rafinelli Vineyard by Cher Threinen-Pendarvis. The Drawing Mode icons will pop up if you click the icon in the lower left corner of the image window. They are, from left to right: Draw Anywhere, Draw Outside and Draw Inside. To read more about them, turn to Chapter 4.

until the dotted outline preview shows you the angle you want. (The Rotate Page command rotates the view of the image only, not the actual pixels.) Restore your rotated image to its original position by holding down Spacebar-Alt or Spacebar-Option and clicking once on your image.

Two other frequently used screen-management shortcuts are Ctrl/⌘-M (Window, Screen Mode Toggle), which replaces a window's scroll and title bars with a frame of gray (or toggles back to normal view), and Ctrl/⌘-H (Window, Hide Palettes), which hides (or restores) all palettes.

Context-sensitive menus. Painter 7 boasts context-sensitive menus that make it easier to change the settings for a brush, or even quickly copy a selection to a layer. Context-sensitive menus are available for all of Painter's tools and for some modes, such as for an active selection when a Selection tool is chosen. To access a context-sensitive menu, right/Ctrl-click.

Helpful icon buttons. Just outside the Painter image window are two sets of very helpful icon buttons. At the top right on the Painter Window scroll bar are four icon buttons: the Tracing Paper icon (allowing you to toggle Tracing Paper on and off), the Grid Overlay icon (which turns the Grid View on and off), the Output Preview icon (to toggle between the full-color RGB view and a preview of what your image will look like when printed) and the Impasto icon (which you can click to hide or show the highlights and shadows on thick paint). Turn to Chapter 12, "Printing and Archival Concerns," for information about Painter's Output Preview.

To the left of Painter's bottom scroll bar are the Drawing Mode icons, which allow you to control where you paint—anywhere in the image, outside of a selection, or inside of a selection. Turn to the beginning of Chapter 4, "Selections, Shapes and Masks," to read more about the Drawing Modes.

Interactive dialog boxes. In most programs, clicking to make choices outside of a dialog box will reward you with an error beep, but Painter's interactive dialog box design encourages you to continue to make the choices you need. As an example, you can open a piece of artwork or a photo, then choose Effects, Surface Control, Apply Surface Texture and click and drag in the Preview window until you see a part of the image that you like. If

SEEING THE WHOLE PICTURE

If you're working with an image too large to fit within your screen, choose Window, Zoom To Fit Screen, or double-click on the Grabber tool in the Tools palette. Painter will enlarge the window and reduce the magnification to fit the screen. If the image is small, the window will resize to fit its canvas size, and magnification will reset to 100%.

The Apply Surface Texture dialog box Preview window, here shown Using Paper, updates when a new choice is made in the Papers section of the Art Materials palette.

Positioning the baseline of active letterform shapes with the help of the Ruler and horizontal Guides created by clicking the Vertical ruler. The circled items here are the Ruler Origin field (top) and a triangular guide marker (bottom).

you then choose Paper in the Using pop-up menu you can go outside the dialog box to choose a different paper (even a paper in another library) in the Papers section of the Art Materials palette. You can even move the Scale, Contrast and Brightness sliders in the Papers section and watch as the Preview image in the Apply Surface Texture dialog box updates to reflect your choice. When you've arrived at a result that you like, you can click OK in the Apply Surface Texture dialog box. The Effects, Surface Control, Color Overlay dialog box behaves in a similar way, allowing you to choose Uniform Color in the pop-up menu and test different colors from the Colors section of the Art Materials palette before you click OK. The Edit, Fill dialog box (Ctrl/⌘-F) is also interactive, giving you the ability to preview your image before it's filled with the current color, a pattern, a gradient or a weave.

ALIGNING SHAPES AND LAYERS AUTOMATICALLY

The Align dialog box (Effects, Objects, Align) is helpful for lining up shapes or layers (or a combination of the two). To align a series of items, start by selecting the Layer Adjuster tool, pressing the Shift key and clicking on each item's name in the Layers section (Objects palette). When all the items are selected, go to the Effects menu and choose Objects, Align, and choose your settings. The dialog box preview will update to show you how your choice of Horizontal and Vertical options will affect alignment of the objects, and you can click OK to accept, or Cancel. The elements below in the center, are aligned using Horizontal: Center and Vertical: None. The elements below on the right, were aligned using their tops. The settings were Horizontal: None and Vertical: Top.

The Objects, Align dialog box with settings for the shapes

Measuring and positioning elements. The Ruler, Guides, Grid Overlay and Perspective Grid can help you measure and position shapes and layers. The commands for these features reside in the Canvas menu. They are especially helpful for aligning text and selections.

To set up a guide using precise measurements or to change the default guide color, double-click on the Ruler to access the Guide Options. Double-click on a triangular marker on the Ruler to access options for an individual guide. Delete guides by dragging their triangles off the document window or by pressing the Delete All Guides button in Guide Options.

To easily measure the exact *width* of an item, try moving the Ruler Origin. Press and drag it from the upper-left corner of the Ruler, where the horizontal and vertical measurements meet, to

The new Perspective Grid feature allows you to set up a one-point perspective grid which is useful as a guide while drawing.

Using the Grid overlay to help when positioning text shapes

The Art Materials palette with sections closed, showing a custom stacking order for the sections

A custom Oil Painting palette with favorite brushes, textures and effects. You can use Tool Tips in the custom palette to display the name of the brush. Tool Tips are turned on by default; if you've turned them off, choose Show Tool Tips from the Help menu.

the left end of the item you want to measure. Then see where the right end falls on the ruler.

The Grid overlay is useful for aligning items. Choose Canvas, Grid, Show Grid or click on the checkered Grid icon above the scroll bar. To change the grid's appearance (for example, to create a grid of only horizontal lines), choose Canvas, Grid, Grid Options and adjust the settings.

The Perspective Grid is useful both for aligning items and for setting up a grid that is helpful when drawing. Choose Canvas, Perspective Grids, Show Grid to display a grid that you can adjust by dragging the vanishing point and horizon line. Choose Canvas, Perspective Grids, Grid Options to adjust the settings and to save your own presets.

CUSTOMIZING YOUR WORKSPACE

Painter makes it easy to customize your workspace. You can change the order of sections of the three expandable palettes (such as dragging the RGB Color section to a new position directly under the Colors section of the Art Materials palette). And the program allows you to build your own custom palettes to store favorite menu commands (brushes and textures, for instance).

Arranging palette sections. Painter lets you move palette sections up or down within the palette. To see this work easily, click on a blank area of a section bar and drag it up or down. For instance, we rearranged our Art Materials palette in this order: Colors, Papers, Patterns, Gradients, RGB Color, Color Variability, Color Set, Weaves, Looks and Nozzles. Painter will remember the changes you made to the palette. To save your palette layout permanently, choose Window, Arrange Palettes, Save Layout and when the Save Layout dialog box appears, name it and click OK. As your needs change, it's easy to rearrange the sections. To restore a saved layout, choose Window, Arrange Palettes and choose the saved layout from the menu.

Building a custom palette. You can make your own palettes to store menu commands and art materials for your work. For instance, to make a custom palette for watercolor painting, begin by selecting the Brushes icon in the Brushes palette and choose a brush variant that you prefer (we chose the Round Camelhair variant of Water Color). Drag the Brushes icon off the Brushes palette—this action will create a new custom palette with a copy of the Brushes icon in it. To add another item, select another brush variant and drag it directly over the new palette; the palette will expand automatically. (We added the Smeary Flat, and Smeary Bristle Spray variants of Brushes.) For thick paint, we clicked in the Impasto icon and chose the Opaque Round and the Wet Bristle variants. We needed blending tools to mix colors, so we added the Grainy Water variant of the Liquid brush and the Palette Knife variant of the Impasto and dragged them onto our new custom palette. Now for the texture: We clicked on the Raw Silk texture from Painter 7's default Papers library and dragged it into our palette, then clicked on the Cold Press Water Color texture and dragged it into the new custom palette.

White Rose, *a detail of which is shown here, was painted with several of Painter's Brushes variants, including the Round Camelhair and Smeary Flat, which we included in our custom Oil Painting palette (shown on page 16). The full illustration appears on the front cover of this book.*

CHER THREINEN-PENDARVIS

SAVING PALETTE LAYOUTS

You can drag a palette anywhere on your desktop, and Painter will remember the palette arrangement until you choose to return to the default palette arrangement. To save a layout permanently, choose Window, Arrange Palettes, Save Layout and when the Save Layout dialog box appears, name it and click OK. (We saved a layout that included our Pastel Painting custom palette and a favorite arrangement of the Art Materials palette, so that we could choose it by name from the Window menu.) To delete a layout, choose Window, Arrange Palettes, Delete Layout and choose the layout you want to remove from the list. To return to Painter's default palette arrangement, choose Window, Arrange Palettes, Default.

MENU ITEM CUSTOM PALETTE

To create a palette that contains a command such as Save As from the File menu, press the Alt/Option and Shift keys and choose the menu item. A new palette with the menu item will appear! To name it, choose Window, Custom Palette, Organizer and click the rename button.

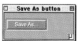

To add a menu command to a custom palette, choose Window, Custom Palette, Add Command, then select the menu item that you'd like to add to the palette. We added two commands that are useful for adding texture to paintings after the brushwork is complete: Effects, Focus, Glass Distortion and Effects, Surface Control, Apply Surface Texture. To name the custom palette, choose Window, Custom Palette, Organizer, click the Rename button and enter a name.

LIBRARIES AND MOVERS

Painter uses *libraries* and *movers* to help you manage the huge volume of custom textures, brushes and other items that the program can generate. Libraries are the "storage bins" for those items, and movers let you customize those bins by transferring items into or out of them.

How libraries work. You'll find the Load Library command at the bottom of every palette that has a resource list—for instance, the paper list on the Papers section of the Art Materials palette, or the Script list on the Scripts section of the Objects palette. Scroll down to the bottom of the list and choose Load Library to display

KEEPING FAVORITE ITEMS ON THE FRONT OF DRAWER

Clicking on an item inside a drawer may be an easy way to select a new tool, but if you want *total* control over the arrangement of items on the front of the palette's drawer, don't click—instead, drag the item from the drawer directly to the desired positions on the front. (Dragging to the front of the drawer—or clicking on an item inside the drawer—causes the previous occupant of the space to be displaced by a new occupant.)

To keep a frequently used item on the front of a palette's drawer, click and hold the item for one second. When the tiny green light appears below the item, it's locked, meaning it's kept out of the drawer-to-front cycle. Click and hold again for a second to unlock and return the item to the rotation.

A green light indicates a locked item.

CHANGING A CUSTOM PALETTE

You can add items to an existing custom palette, delete items from it or change the palette's layout. To *add* an art material (such as a brush, a texture or a gradient), drag it directly into the palette. And a bonus: You can also drag to copy items from one custom palette to another. To *add* a menu command choose Window, Custom Palette, Add Command, then select the menu item. To delete *any* item, select it, press the Alt/Option keys, and when the trash can cursor appears, click on the item to delete it. To move an item, press the Ctrl/⌘, and when the four-arrowed cursor appears, drag the item to a new location in the palette.

We arranged our pastel painting palette horizontally, so we could keep it along the bottom of our image canvas. We included the Square Chalk, Sharp Chalk and Oil Pastel variants of Dry Media and the Ribbed Pastel, Hand-Made and Basic Paper textures.

You'll find the Load Library command at the bottom of the resource list on the Brushes palette and on some sections of the expandable Art Materials and Objects palettes.

Dragging an item into the Pastel Paper Textures library

The open Papers section's drawer showing the newly created Pastel Paper Textures library, stocked with five interesting textures

a dialog box that lets you can search through folders on any hard disk until you find the library you want; then double-click to open it. (Although you can load libraries directly from a CD-ROM—like the Painter 7 CD-ROM or the Wow! CD-ROM—it's more reliable to copy the libraries from the CD-ROM, into your Painter application folder.) Fortunately, Painter is smart enough to show only libraries that can be opened in the palette of origin. For instance, if you choose Load Library button in the Papers section, you'll see Paper libraries only, not the Gradients or Brushes libraries.

Using movers to customize your libraries. If you find that you're continually switching Paper texture libraries, it's probably time to use the Paper Mover to compile several textures into a single custom library for your work. For instance, you can create a Paper texture library containing favorite textures that work well with Painters's grain-sensitive Dry Media brushes and the Chalky Brushes library on the Wow! CD-ROM—such as Sanded Pastel Board and Laid Pastel Paper (from Painter's default paper texture library), Big Canvas and Small Canvas (from the More Paper Textures library) and Ribbed Deckle (from the Drawing Paper Textures library) in the Paper Textures folder on the Painter_CD2 CD-ROM).

Here's how to build this custom paper library: On the Art Materials palette, click the right triangle on the Papers section bar to open the pull-down menu and choose Paper Mover. In the Paper Mover, create a new, empty Paper library by clicking on the New button on the right side of the mover, then name your Paper Texture file and save it. (We named ours Pastel Paper Textures.) To copy a texture from the left side of the mover (your currently active library) into the new

You can make new script libraries to store some of your automated special effects (and reduce the size of the Painter Script Data file, where the default scripts are stored). On the Objects palette's Scripts section bar, click the right triangle to open the menu and choose Script Mover. The Painter Script Data file will open on the left side of the mover. Click the New button on the right side of the mover to make a new library and name it when prompted. Select the scripts you want to copy and drag and drop them into the new library. When you've finished copying, delete the items you've copied from the Painter Script Data file to keep file size trim. (For more information about effects scripts, see Chapter 10.)

Using the Script Mover to import scripts saved in the Painter Script Data file (left side) into a custom library of special effects scripts (right side)

The Script library containing special effects "macros" that can be applied to images

For this illustration of a Queen Parrotfish, we used brushes included in the custom Oil Painting and Pastel Painting palettes (described on pages 17 and 18). We laid in color for an underpainting with the oil-painting brushes (including the Round Camelhair), then we added texture to areas of the image by painting with grain-sensitive brushes (the Square Chalk variant of Dry Media, for instance), which was included in the Pastel Painting palette.

library, select a texture's icon on the left side of the mover: The name of the selected texture will appear in the center of the mover window; drag the texture icon from the original library (left side) and drop it into the new library (right side).

Continue adding textures to the new library in this fashion. We selected the two textures from the More Paper Textures library and dropped their icons into the new Pastel Paper Textures library. Next, we added the Ribbed Deckle texture from the Drawing Paper Textures library to our new library. To add a texture from another library to your new library, click on the left-hand Close button, then click again when it changes to an Open button and open the next library that you want to draw from. (Don't forget the libraries on the Wow! and Painter 7 Application CD-ROMs!) We selected the Sandy texture and dragged and dropped it to our new library. When you've finished, click Quit. Now open your new library by choosing Load Library from the Papers section's paper list menu. If you want your new library to open every time you launch Painter, choose Edit, Preferences, General and type its exact name in the Papers box.

All movers work in the same way, so you can follow the above procedure to, say, create a new Patterns library that contains the only five patterns that you ever use. (See "Creating a Pattern" in Chapter 7 on page 347, for an example of building a new pattern and using the Pattern Mover.)

3RD PARTY FILTERS & PAINTER

You can use third-party filters with Painter by installing them in the Painter application folder within the Plugins folder. Painter will automatically load them the next time you launch the program. To use third-party filters that are stored outside the Painter application folder, you can set up a Shortcut (Windows) or an Alias (Mac) for the plug-in folder to access it: To create a Shortcut, choose the folder containing the plug-in in My Computer or Windows Explorer. Then choose File, Create Shortcut. To create an Alias on the Mac, select the folder on the desktop and choose File, Make Alias. Move the Shortcut or Alias into the Plugins folder in the Painter application folder and restart Painter to see the new filters, which will appear at the bottom of the Effects menu.

LOADING AN ALTERNATE BRUSH LIBRARY IN PAINTER 7

To load a different brush library in Painter 7, first copy it into the Brushes folder within the Painter application folder, then choose Load Library from the bottom of the resource list on the Brushes palette. When the Brush Libraries dialog box appears, click the Import button, navigate to the brush library and click Open. (We chose the 7 Wow! Chalks). When the Brush Libraries dialog box reappears, click the Load button. The new brushes will now be visible in the Brushes palette.

Clicking Import in the Brush Libraries dialog box; choosing the 7 Wow! Chalks library in the Select Brush Library dialog box; selecting the library in Brush Libraries dialog box and then clicking the Load button.

IMPORTING OLDER BRUSHES

In Painter 7 you can import favorite brushes that were created in earlier versions of Painter. These brushes must be converted to the new brush model, and this is done by choosing Import Brush Library from the Brush menu at the top of the Brushes palette. Early Water Color brushes were not built to work with Painter 7's new Water Color layers. They can be imported, but will not perform the same as in the earlier version because they were designed to work with the old Wet Painter layer on the Canvas.

THE POWER
OF COLOR

Don Stewart used reds, oranges and yellows to depict fall afternoon light in Hunting Dad, *as shown in this detail. To see more of Stewart's work, turn to the gallery at the end of Chapter 3.*

Colors section bar

Color (Hue) ring

Color triangle

Color rectangles

HSV/RGB color readout

The Standard Colors picker with Hue ring, opened by expanding the Colors section bar

Hue bar

The Colors section command menu opens so you can switch between the Standard and Small Colors pickers

"COLOR, THE FRUIT OF LIGHT, is the foundation of the painter's means of painting—and its language." Abstract painter Robert Delaunay's observation mirrors our own appreciation of color as an expressive and essential element of the visual arts. Getting the most out of Painter's powerful color tools is an important first step for those of us who work with "the fruit of light."

HUE, SATURATION AND VALUE

Painter's interface for choosing color is built around a model that uses *hue, saturation* and *value* (HSV) as the three basic properties of color. The program is designed so that you'll typically first choose a hue, then alter it by changing its saturation or value. Painter's Standard Color picker and Small Color picker are designed to work with these properties, but the program also allows you to work in RGB (red, green, blue) color space if you prefer. Clicking the triangle on the left end of the Colors section bar in the Art Materials palette (Window, Show Art Materials) opens the HSV Colors section. To switch between Standard and Small Colors pickers, click the triangle at the top right of the Colors section bar to access the pull-down menu. To specify RGB rather than HSV, open the RGB Color section of the Art Materials palette by clicking the triangle on the RGB Color section bar.

Hue. The term *hue* refers to a predominant spectral color, such as red or blue-green. Hue indicates a color's position on the color wheel or spectrum, and also tells us the color's temperature. A red-orange hue is the warmest color; a blue-green hue is the coolest. (Keep in

QUICK SWITCH TO RGB

Click on the HSV color readout on the Standard or Small Colors picker to show color readings in RGB mode. Click again to switch back to HSV.

The RGB Color section with Red, Green and Blue sliders. (We moved the RGB Color section nearer to the Colors section in Art Materials. To move it, drag the RGB section bar.)

A pigment-based color wheel

PRIMARY/SECONDARY COLORS

Two overlapping rectangles display the current Primary and Secondary colors. To exchange the Primary and Secondary colors in the Colors section of the Art Materials palette, click the "Swap" icon, or press the Shift and X keys.

Saturating a color

Desaturating a color

Creating a shade of a color

Creating a tint of a color

mind, though, that temperatures are relative. Blue-violet is a cool color, but it warms up when it's placed next to blue-green.)

In the traditional pigment-based color system, red, yellow and blue are *primary* hues—colors that cannot be obtained by mixing. *Secondary* hues—green, orange and violet—are those colors located midway between two primary colors on the color wheel. Yellow-green, blue-violet and red-orange are examples of *tertiary* hues, each found between a primary and a secondary color.

Analogous hues are adjacent to each other on the color wheel and have in common a shared component—for instance, blue-green, blue and blue-violet. *Complementary hues* sit opposite one another on the color wheel. Red and green are complements, as are blue and orange. (Painter's Hue ring and bar are based on the RGB components of the computer screen, so it doesn't exactly match a traditional pigment-based color wheel.)

To change hues in Painter's Standard Color picker, drag the little circle on the Hue ring or click anywhere on the ring. Dragging and clicking also work with the Hue bar in the Small Color picker.

Saturation. Also known as *intensity* or *chroma*, *saturation* indicates a color's purity or strength. The most common way of changing a color's saturation is by adjusting the amount of its gray component. In the Color triangle, move the little circle to the left to desaturate a color, or to the right to saturate it. Fully or very saturated colors—those at or near the tip of the Color triangle—won't print the way they look on the screen. If you want to see colors closer to their printed equivalents while you paint, the Canvas, Kodak Color Correction command can help. (See the "Color Management" tip on page 28 of this chapter and Chapter 21 of the *Painter 7 User Guide*.)

SAMPLING PAINT

While you're using many of Painter's other tools, you can temporarily switch to the Dropper tool and sample colors by holding down the Alt/Option key.

A COLOR PREVIEW

As you drag the circle in the HSV triangle or Hue ring (or slider on the Hue bar), Painter compares the previous color you'd clicked on (right) with the new color (left) in the front Color rectangle. The entire Color rectangle updates when you release the mouse button or lift the stylus. The front rectangle in the RGB Colors section also updates as you drag in the Color section, but not if you drag the RGB Color sliders.

Dragging to choose a new color in the Small Colors picker; the RGB Color picker updates automatically in response.

An example of atmospheric perspective. The illusion of distance is enhanced in this detail of Along Tomales Bay *because the distant hills are painted with reduced saturation and less value contrast.*

As you can see in this detail of 1872, Richard Noble used saturated color, clear detail and strong contrast to paint a bright morning. To see more of Noble's work turn to the galleries at the end of Chapters 2 and 3.

A study in value contrast, based on a drawing by Michelangelo

Value. A color's lightness or darkness is its *luminance* or *value*. To create a *tint* of a color (lightening it, or increasing its value), move the little circle higher in the Color triangle. To create a *shade* of a color (darkening it, or decreasing its value), move the little circle lower in the Color triangle.

PUTTING HSV TO WORK

Here are several practical suggestions and creative solutions for solving artistic problems using hue, saturation and value.

Reduce saturation and value to indicate distance. Artists have been creating *atmospheric* (or *aerial*) *perspective* in their work for thousands of years. The wall paintings of Pompeii in the first century B.C. show this technique. Hills we see in the distance have less intensity than nearer hills, and they also have less variation in value. This effect increases in hazy or foggy conditions. To depict this in your art, you can reduce the color saturation and value range as the landscape recedes from the foreground.

Use saturation to indicate time of day. At dawn or dusk, colors appear to be less saturated, and it becomes more difficult to distinguish colors. At noon on a bright sunny day, colors seem saturated and distinct.

Use color temperature to indicate distance. The eye puts warm colors in front of cool colors. For example, orange flowers in the foreground of a hedge appear closer than blue ones.

Create drama with light-to-dark value contrast. Baroque and Romantic period artists as diverse as Caravaggio, Zurbarán, Géricault and Rembrandt are known for their use of extreme light-to-dark contrast. They accomplished this by limiting their palette to only a few hues, which they either tinted with white or shaded by adding black. A close look at the shadows and highlights that these artists created reveals complex, modulated tone. Digital artists can use Painter's Apply Lighting feature (from Effects, Surface Control) to add a dramatic splash of contrast to an image and also to unify a painting's color scheme, although achieving genuine tonal complexity requires additional painting.

Use complementary colors to create shadows. The Impressionists Monet, Renoir and Degas frequently avoided the use of black in the shadow areas of their paintings. They embraced a more subjective view of reality by layering complementary colors to create luminous shadows.

Neutralize with a complement or gray. One way to tone down a hue is to paint on top of it with a translucent form of its complement. El Greco painted his backgrounds in this manner to draw attention to more saturated foreground subjects. Try painting with a bright green hue, then glaze over it with a reduced opacity of red. The result will be an earthy olive. You can also

To paint dramatic billowing clouds in View From Point Loma, *shown here as a detail, we blended color by using the Grainy Water variant of the Liquid brush.*

neutralize a hue using shades of gray, as did the French artist Ingres. Although he often limited his palette to red, blue, gold and flesh tones, he created the illusion of a larger palette by adding varying proportions of gray and white.

Blending, pulling and thinning colors. Subtle changes in hue and saturation take place when colors are blended in a painting. You can use the Just Add Water, Grainy Water or Smudge variant of the Liquid brush (from the Brushes palette) to blend, for instance, two primary colors (red and blue) to get a secondary color (violet). For a more dramatic blending, you can pull one color into another by using the Smear variant of the Liquid brush. Artists using traditional tools often thin paint by mixing it with an extender. In Painter, you get a similar effect by reducing a brush's Opacity in the Controls:Brush palette.

Draw attention with simultaneous contrast. If two complementary colors are placed next to one another, they intensify each other: Blue looks more blue next to orange, and white looks more white next to black. In the 1950s, Op artists used the principle of simultaneous contrast to baffle the eye. Advertising art directors understand the power of simultaneous contrast and use it to gain attention for their ads.

Simultaneous contrast at work. Notice how the gold looks brighter next to the dark blue than it does next to pink.

Use a family of colors to evoke an emotional response. You can create a calm, restful mood by using an analogous color theme of blues and blue-greens. Or develop another family of hues using reds and red-oranges to express passion and intensity. You can also use a color family to unite the elements of a composition.

Create your own color world. Post-Impressionist Paul Gauguin (among others) created a powerful, personal color language by combining several of the above techniques. He used warm, bright colors to bring a subject forward in his composition, and used cool, dark colors to convey distance and mystery. He also made the bright foreground colors seem brighter by surrounding them with darker, more subdued colors.

A landscape with figures, based on Mahana no atua (The Day of the God) *by Paul Gauguin*

PAINTING WITH MULTIPLE COLORS

Painter's Brushes palette has several brushes that can paint with more than one color at a time if you use the settings in the Color Variability section of the Art Materials palette (Window, Show Art Materials). Brushes with the Rake or Multi stroke type or the new Bristle Spray, Camel Hair or Flat dab types have the capability to paint with multiple colors. The Van Gogh variant of the Artists brush and the Round Camel Hair variant of the Brushes are examples.

Randomize colors with Color Variability. To see how multicolor works, open the Color Variability section of the Art Materials palette by clicking the triangle on the Color Variability bar. (Make sure that "in HSV" is chosen in the pop-up menu.) In the Brushes palette, choose the Round Camelhair variant of the Brushes; its Camel Hair dab type has the potential to carry a different color on each brush hair. Choose a color in the Colors section and begin painting. Then experiment by adjusting the Hue (± H), Saturation (± S) or Value (± V) slider in the Color Variability section and painting again.

These brushstrokes were painted with the Round Camelhair variant of the Brushes with the following settings in the Color Variability section of the Art Materials palette: top brushstroke, Hue slider only set to 50%; middle, Saturation slider only set to 50%; bottom, Value slider only set to 50%.

For transparent Water Color washes with variable color, try the Diffuse Grainy Camel and the Wash Bristle. Both of these brushes have the potential to carry a different color in each brush hair.

Also try the Scratchboard Rake variant of the Pens. The Scratchboard Rake incorporates the Rake stroke type; each "tine" of a Rake brush can paint with a different color. In the Color Variability section, set Hue to 10% (for a subtle variation) or much higher (for a rainbow-like effect) and make brushstrokes on your image.

KEEPING TABS ON DABS

By keeping the Brush Controls: General section open as you choose variants from the Brushes palette, you can see if they have a Dab Type (Bristle Spray, Camel Hair, or Flat) or Stroke Type (Rake or Multi) that allows multicolor painting. To open the General section, choose Window, Show Brush Controls, and click the triangle on the General section bar.

COLOR VARIABILITY CAUTION

Painter remembers the changes when you try out Color Variability, and this may cause confusing results later. After you've finished using added Color Variability, set the Color Variability pop-up menu to "in HSV" and restore the Hue, Saturation and Value sliders to 0.

These brushstrokes were painted with the Diffuse Grainy Camel (top) and the Wash Bristle (bottom) variants of Water Color with a Hue variability of 10%.

These brushstrokes were painted with the Scratchboard Rake variant of the Pens with an increased Hue variability of 10% (top) and 50% (bottom). Each "tine" of this Rake brush can carry a different color.

Using Color Variability based on a gradient. With Painter 7, you can paint with multiple colors from a gradient instead of using completely random Color Variability. To begin, set all the Color Variability sliders to 0; open the Colors section of the Art Materials palette and set up the colors for a two-point gradient by clicking on the front color rectangle and selecting a color, then clicking on the back color rectangle and selecting a color. In the Gradients section, choose Two-Point from the pop-up menu. From the Brushes palette select the Opaque Bristle Spray variant of the

Brushstroke painted with the Opaque Bristle Spray variant of the Brushes using Color Variability based on the current gradient. Note that the front rectangle in the Color picker updates to include both colors from the active two-point gradient.

Brushstrokes painted with the Smeary Flat (above) and the Dry Ink (below) variants of the Brushes using Color Variability based on the Color Set shown here.

Brushes. In the Color Variability palette, choose From Gradient from the pop-up menu, then make brushstrokes on your image. If the brush does not immediately paint using the Color Variability from the gradient, click the little circle in the Color picker to help it to update.)

Using Color Variability based on a color set. You can create a special Color Set containing a few colors and then use those colors when painting. Begin by opening the Color Variability section of the Art Materials palette; set Color Variability to "in HSV" and the ± H, ±S, and ±V sliders to 0. Open the Color Set section and click on the New Color Set button (the one with the picture of the Grid). A very small empty Color Set palette will appear. Choose a color in the Color picker. Click on the Add Color to Color Set button (the "Plus"), to add the current color to the Color Set. Continue to select and add more colors by using the Color picker and clicking the "Plus" button. Choose the Smeary Flat variant of the Brushes, and in the Color Variability section, set Color Variability to "from Color Set." Paint brushstrokes on your image. To learn more about color sets turn to "Keeping Colors in Color Sets," on page 29 and to "Capturing a Color Set," later in this chapter.

Change colors with stylus pressure. Use your pressure-sensitive stylus to paint in two colors. Start by choosing the Captured Bristle variant of the Brushes. In the Expression section of the Brush Controls palette choose Pressure from the Color pop-up menu. In the Standard or Small Color picker, click on the front color rectangle and choose a bright blue color. Click the back Color rectangle and select a rose color. If you paint with a light touch, you'll be painting in rose. If you press heavily, the stroke turns blue. (If the balance between the two colors seems uneven, choose Edit, Preferences, Brush Tracking. Make a typical brushstroke in the Scratch Pad area, click OK, and try the graduated version of the Captured Bristle variant again.)

MORE COLOR VARIABILITY

Painter's Color Variability controls include RGB variability and variability based on the current Gradient or Color Set. These options are chosen from the pop-up menu in the Color Variability section of the Art Materials palette.

Choosing Color Variability from Gradient

MORE COLORFUL STROKES

To paint with two colors using criteria other than pressure, open the Brush Controls:Expression palette and move the Color pop-up menu to Velocity. Once you get started, if you move slowly, you paint using the color in the front Color rectangle; speeding your strokes paints with the back color. Now change the Color menu to Direction. Start drawing horizontal brushstrokes (front color) and then gradually turn the strokes vertical (back color).

Before and after: Sampling in the image with the Dropper to determine the color cast of a bright highlight on the aluminum foil reveals these values: Red: 227, Green: 241, and Blue 213 (left); the corrected image (right) with pure white highlights shows Red, Green and Blue values of 255.

Pulling the Green color curve in the Color Correction dialog box to lessen the green cast in the image above. Light colors are represented at the upper right and dark colors in the lower left. The biggest change in color occurs at the point where you pull the curve. If you pull the dot, the color you sampled will be affected most. The Effect slider controls how much of the curve will change when you pull on it. Move the slider to the right to affect a broad range of tones. Move the slider to the left to affect a narrower range of tones.

MAKING COLOR ADJUSTMENTS

Painter offers several ways to modify color in scanned photos or in your art work *after* you have created it. To see the results of your choices in many of the dialog boxes that are involved in color adjustments, you'll need to click and drag in the Preview window.

Correct Colors. Do you see an unnatural color cast in your image? The Correct Colors, Curve feature can help you fix this problem. This feature is especially useful when working with scanned photos, for instance.

To adjust an image so that the brightest highlights are pure white, begin by analyzing the color cast. (To ensure that the front Color rectangle in the Color picker will show the color you are about to sample, make sure that "in HSV" is chosen from the pop-out menu in the Color Variability section of the Art Materials palette.) Use the Dropper tool to sample a bright highlight in your image. In the

Colors section, click on the HSV values box to toggle to RGB values. Check the RGB values in the Color palette. In our example (shown at the left), the color and numbers show that the unwanted color cast is green, because the G value is higher than the R and B values. A bright white should have R, G and B values of 255 in the Color picker. Choose Effects, Tonal Control, Correct Colors and choose Curve from the pop-up menu in the Color Correction dialog box. Curve will allow you to adjust the individual RGB values. Click on the small square icon for the color that you want to adjust. (We clicked on the Green color icon—to constrain the adjustment to *only* the green values in the image.) Then, position the crosshair cursor over the diagonal line, and when you see the hand cursor appear, pull down and to the right. Pulling down (as shown) will decrease the selected color in the image. Click the Reset button to try out another adjustment without leaving the dialog box.

Adjust Colors. To change the hue, saturation or value of all of the colors in an image, choose Effects, Tonal Control, Adjust Colors. Experiment with the sliders and view the changes in the Preview window. Adjust Colors is also useful for quickly desaturating a full-color image—making it look black-and-white. To desaturate an image, move the Saturation slider all the way to the left.

Adjust Selected Colors. You may want to make color adjustments in particular color ranges of your image. Painter's Adjust

Using Adjust Selected Colors to neutralize a bright blue

Selected Colors feature lets you make dramatic changes (turning a blue sky yellow) or more subtle ones (removing the red cast from a subject's face). Choose Effects, Tonal Control, Adjust Selected Colors. When the dialog box opens, click in your image (*not* in the Preview window) on the color you want to change. Adjust the Hue Shift, Saturation and Value sliders at the bottom of the dialog box. When the targeted color is changed to the color you want, use low settings on the Extents sliders to limit the range of colors that are adjusted. Use the Feather sliders to adjust transitions between colors: 100% produces soft transition, 0% gives abrupt ones.

Color Overlay. Found under Effects, Surface Control, the Color Overlay dialog box lets you tint an image with a color using either a Dye Concentration model (which applies *transparent* color) or a Hiding Power model (which covers the image with the *opaque* color). With either model you can add texture by choosing Paper in the pop-up menu, as we did in the illustration at the left. When using the Dye Concentration model, adjust the Amount slider to control the density of the color: 0% for no effect; to 100% or –100% for full transparent coverage. The Hiding Power model operates differently. You can add color using a plus value, or pull color out of an image using a minus value. Try this to see how it works: open a new image and use the Rectangular Selection tool to make a selection. Choose a yellow-green in the Color picker (approximately H 58%, S 92%, V 43%). Fill the selection using Effects, Fill, Current Color. Choose yellow in the Color picker (ours was H 50%, S 94%, V 70%) then choose Effects, Surface Control, Color Overlay, Using Uniform Color and Hiding Power. Move the Opacity slider to 100% to see the yellow completely cover the yellow-green. Finally, move the Opacity slider to –100% to the see some of the yellow disappear from the original green.

We added colored texture to this photo with Color Overlay.

PHOTO: PHOTODISC

> **LAYER COMPOSITE COLOR**
>
> With Painter's Composite Methods you can change how a layer interacts with the image underneath, affecting the color in your image. For more about layers and to see examples of how Painter's 21 Composite Methods affect color, turn to the beginning of Chapter 5, "Using Layers and Shapes."
>
>
>
> *In this image, we applied the Darken composite method to the leaf layer.*

Dye Concentration. With Effects, Surface Control, Dye Concentration you can add or remove pigment from your image. Setting the Maximum slider above 100% increases the density of the existing pigment. When you choose Paper in the Using menu, the Maximum slider controls the amount of dye on the peaks and the Minimum slider controls the amount of dye in the valleys of the texture.

Susan LeVan used Effects, Tonal Control, Negative on the left side of the background of Guardians *as shown in this detail. After creating the negative side of the image, she drew over portions of the left side to make the character unique.*

Negative. Creating a negative of all or part of an image can have dramatic, artistic purposes—such as in the detail of Susan LeVan's illustration, at left. Choose Effects, Tonal Control, Negative to convert your image or a selected part of it.

Output Preview and Video Colors. Your monitor can display more colors than can be reproduced in the four-color printing process, and if you are creating images for video, some highly saturated colors will not make the transition from computer to video. It's a good idea to convert your out-of-gamut colors while you're in Painter so there won't be any surprises. Choose Canvas, Kodak Color Correction or Effects, Tonal Control, Video Legal Colors, depending on whether your image is destined for paper or video. For more information about output for printing, turn to Chapter 12, "Printing and Archival Concerns."

COLOR MANAGEMENT

Painter 7 ships with a color management system that can help to ensure color consistency and the quality of output. Earlier versions of Painter have supported color management through the Kodak Color Management System (KCMS), but the controls have been greatly expanded with Painter 7.

The new color management system allows you to move files between Painter, Photoshop and other programs while keeping the color consistent and to see an on-screen preview of how your color will look when printed on a specific device. Once it's been set up, the preview can be toggled on and off as you work. Access the Color Management dialog box by choosing Canvas, Kodak Color Correction. You'll find controls that will help you to set up color matching between devices including a scanner, digital camera, your monitor and composite printer or proofer. To learn more about Painter's color management system, turn to "Color for Printing" in Chapter 12.

MORE COLOR TOOLS

Adding color with Gradations. Painter's powerful Gradients palette lets you fill selected areas with preset gradations or ones that you've created. (See "Adding Color and Gradations to Line Art" later in this chapter.) You can also colorize an image with a gradation using Express In Image from the pop-up menu at the right side on the Gradients section bar in the Art Materials palette. To see an example of this technique, turn to "Making a Sepia Tone" in Chapter 6.

The gradient editor is a powerful tool for creating custom color ramps. You can't use this tool to alter all of Painter's existing gradations. However, it is used primarily for creating new ones. On the Art Materials palette, click the left triangle on the Gradients section bar to open the section, then click the right triangle, and choose Edit Gradient from the pop-up menu to bring up the gradient editor. Select one of the triangular color control points and choose a color from the Color picker. The color ramp will update to reflect your choice. Add new color control points by clicking directly in the color bar; the triangular control points are sliders

This is how Painter 7's Spectrum gradient appears in the Gradient Editor. When you click a square hue box above the Gradient the Color Hue pop-up menu appears, here it's set to Hue Clockwise, resulting in a tiny spectrum below the square hue box.

Linda Davick uses gradient fills to give her illustrations depth, as shown here in Mice. *Read about Davick's technique in "Adding Color and Gradations to Line Art" on page 30 of this chapter.*

Read about Davick's technique in "Adding Color and Gradations to Line Art" on page 30 of this chapter.

that can be positioned anywhere along the ramp. To delete a control point, select it and press the Delete key; click on the gradient bar to add a new control point. Clicking on any of the squares above the gradient displays the Color menu; experiment with the options available there to get quick rainbow effects in the section of the gradient indicated by the square. To store the new gradient in the Gradients section, choose Save Grad from the pop-up menu on the right end of the Gradients section bar.

Coloring images. You can color images or selected parts of images using either Effects, Fill (Ctrl/⌘-F) or the Paint Bucket tool. The Fill command lets you fill your image with a color, a gradient, a clone source (if one is available), a pattern (if no clone source is available) or a weave. The Paint Bucket gives you the same fill options. (The Paint Bucket options appear on the Controls palette when you select the Paint Bucket tool.) Cartoonists and others who fill line art with color will want to explore the Lock Out Color feature (to preserve black line art, for example) made available by double-clicking on the Paint Bucket tool icon in the Tools palette. For more information about Lock Out Color and Cartoon Cell fills, turn to page 113 in the *Painter 7 User Guide*.

Keeping colors in Color Sets. Painter can store your most frequently used colors in the Color Set section of Art Materials. Painter Colors is the default set. Switch Color Sets by clicking on the Library button in the Color Set section. You'll find more Color Sets (including several Pantone sets) in the Color Sets folder on the Painter 7 application CD-ROM. For more about Color Sets, turn to "Capturing a Color Set" on page 38.

turn to "Capturing a Color Set" on page 38.

CONSTRAINING BUCKET FILLS

You can use the Paint Bucket to fill an entire area of your image by clicking the Paint Bucket within the area, or you can constrain the fill into a rectangle. To create a rectangular filled area, press, hold and drag a marquee with the Paint Bucket. When you release the mouse or lift up on your stylus, the area will fill with color.

In H is for Hell-bent Haddocks *(shown here as a detail), Keith MacLelland used the Paint Bucket to create a background of filled squares. To see more of MacLelland's work, turn to the galleries in Chapters 2 and 3.*

To see more of MacLelland's work, turn to the galleries in Chapters 2 and 3.

NAMING AND FINDING COLORS

To name your colors so you can search for them by name, double-click on the color in the Color Set palette that you want to name, type a name and click OK. To view color names, click on the Display Text button at the bottom of the Color Set section in the Art Materials palette. To search for a named color in a set, click the Find Color in Color Set button (the binoculars near the top of the Color Set section).

A Set with names displayed

RESTORING DEFAULT COLORS

To restore the default Color Set (called Painter Colors) after you've used or created another Color Set, click the Library button and find the Painter Colors file in your Painter 7 folder on your hard disk.

The Color Set section of the Art Materials palette with Painter Colors as the current color set

Adding Color and Gradations to Line Art

Overview *Draw line art with the One-Pixel Pen variant; use the Paint Bucket to fill areas with flat color and gradations; add highlights with the Airbrushes.*

Line art created with the 1-Pixel variant of the Pens brush, shown here as a detail

Filling the drawing with flat color

FILLING LINE ART WITH COLOR AND GRADATIONS is slick and efficient in Painter, using what children's book illustrator Linda Davick calls "the coloring-book technique." Davick employed the Paint Bucket tool when creating the illustration *Fish Fry* for Debbie Smith's *Beauty Blow-Up*.

1 Creating a black-and-white line drawing. In the Brushes palette, choose the Pens brush, 1-Pixel variant, and choose the Flat Cover subcategory from the General section of the Brush Controls palette. Flat Cover lets you draw a solid-color line, creating the necessary barriers for this technique that fills all neighboring pixels of the same color. Choose black in the Colors section of the Art Materials palette and draw your line art, making sure all your shapes are completely enclosed with black lines. If you need to correct your work, switch the color to pure white in the Colors section and erase.

2 Filling with flat color. To test color choices and tonal values, you can fill areas of your illustration with flat color. First open the Color Variability section of the Art Materials palette, choose "in HSV" from the pop-up menu and set the ± H, ± S and ± V sliders to 0. Choose the Paint Bucket tool, and in the Controls:Paint Bucket palette (Window, Show Controls), choose Image under What To Fill and Current Color under Fill With. Turn off Anti-Alias. Choose a color, then click in the area of your drawing that you want to fill. Since the Paint Bucket fills all neighboring pixels of the same color, you can refill by choosing another color and clicking again. If you're filling small areas, it's important to know that the Paint Bucket's "hot spot" (where it fills from) is the tip of the red paint in the icon. Davick filled all areas except Zuba's face using this method.

3 Adding color ramps. To fill the background with a gradation, open the Gradients section of the Art Materials palette. Click the

3a

Setting up the Two-Point linear gradient for the sky behind Zuba

3b

Filling the background with the gradient

4a

4b

4c

Sampling the gradient across from the top of the area to be filled (a); sampling across from the bottom of the area to be filled (b); filling the area with the gradation (c). Repeat this process for each flat color (negative) area to be filled.

5

Adding dimension to Zuba's hair using the Digital Airbrush inside a selected area

Two-Point icon in the top left corner of the section (or choose Two-Point from the pop-up menu). Click the Linear Grad button (from the four Types buttons to the right of the direction ring), and set an angle for your fill by rotating the red ball around the direction ring. In the Art Materials:Colors section, choose colors for both the front and back Color rectangles. (Click on the front Color rectangle and select a color, then click on the back Color rectangle and select a color.) With the Paint Bucket chosen, in the Controls palette, from the What to Fill menu, choose Image, and from the Fill With menu, choose Grad. Finally, to apply the gradation, click in the area that you want to fill. Davick filled the largest background sky area with a linear gradation.

4 Duplicating color ramps. To duplicate the large background gradation in each of the smaller background shapes—to the right of Zuba, and under the ants—Davick created a new gradation using color sampled from areas in the background gradation. She then filled the smaller background shapes with the new gradation. If you need to do this on the "negative" shapes in your image, first check the Colors section to make sure that the Color rectangle that contains the starting color of your original gradation is selected. Choose the Dropper tool and position it over the gradation in your image at approximately the same height as the top of the negative area that you want to fill. Click in the gradation to sample the color. To sample the bottom portion of the gradation, select the other Color rectangle, then position and click the Dropper at about the same height as the bottom of the area to be filled. Click in the negative area using the Paint Bucket to fill with the new sampled gradation. (If you need to refill, undo the fill—Edit, Undo Paint Bucket Fill—before you fill again.)

5 Painting airbrush details. Davick finished the piece by painting with the Digital Airbrush variant of the Airbrushes within roughly circular selections to add details to Zuba's face and fur. You can make roughly circular selections using the Lasso tool by choosing the Lasso tool and dragging in your image. (To read more about selections, turn to the beginning of Chapter 4, "Selections, Shapes and Masks.") Now use the Digital Airbrush in the Brushes palette to add dimension. Paint along the edge of the animated selection marquee. Davick used the same Airbrush with unrestricted strokes to add other details in other areas, such as on the cat's face and paws. 🖌

> **A TOLERANT PAINT BUCKET**
>
> If you need to fill an area of modulated color with the Paint Bucket, use the Tolerance slider on the Controls:Paint Bucket palette to increase the amount of Tolerance. To sample a narrower color range, decrease the Tolerance setting.

Coloring a Scanned Illustration

Overview *Scan a traditional black-and-white pen drawing; clean up the scanned line art; use the Paint Bucket to fill areas with flat color; create texture and energy with a variety of brushes.*

WENDY MORRIS

The raw scan of the Rapidograph pen drawing

WENDY MORRIS'S WHIMSICAL DRAWING STYLE appears to be a quick, spontaneous expression; but her illustrations begin by drawing carefully with traditional pen and ink. In Morris's *Beeman*, the sky is vibrant and charged with frenetic bee energy. *Beeman* was colored with Paint Bucket fills and a variety of brushes.

1 Creating a pen drawing and scanning. Morris chose a bright white recycled drawing paper with a smooth finish and created a black-and-white line drawing using a conventional Rapidograph pen. She intended to use the *Beeman* illustration for a 6 x 8-inch greeting card design that would be printed with offset lithography so she scanned the line drawing using grayscale mode at 100% magnification with a resolution of 300ppi. She saved the scan as a TIFF file and opened it in Painter, which automatically converted the grayscale art to RGB. To learn more about scanning and resolution, see Chapter 1, "Getting To Know Painter" and Chapter 12, "Printing and Archival Concerns."

2 Cleaning up the scan. Morris adjusted the contrast of the scanned line work using Brightness/Contrast. To make the adjustment on your scan, choose Effects, Tonal Control, Brightness/

2a

Adjusting the Brightness and Contrast "beef up" the line work

2b

Cleaning up specks of black on the scan

3a

Setting up the Controls:Paint Bucket palette and the Mask Threshold dialog box to make Cartoon Cel fills

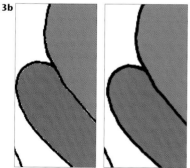

3b

Color fills with halos (left), and color fills made with the Cartoon Cel method, showing no halos (right)

Contrast. When the dialog box appears, you can thicken or thin the line work by moving the Brightness slider (the bottom one of the two) to the left or to the right, respectively. Then, to get rid of any fuzziness along the edge that resulted from the Brightness change, increase the Contrast by moving the top slider to the right. (Keep in mind that moving it too far to the right can create a pixelated edge rather than a smooth one.) Each time you move one of the sliders, you can see the tonal adjustment on your image.

Then Morris cleaned up the specks of black on the scan by choosing white in the Colors section of the Art Materials palette, and touching up areas with the Pen and Ink variant of the Pens found in Ver 5 Brushes, in the Brushes folder on the Painter 7 Application CD-ROM. (To read about loading libraries, turn to "Libraries and Movers" in Chapter 1, "Getting To Know Painter.") She switched to black color, and used the pen to repair any breaks in the black lines. (The lines must be completely solid to constrain the Paint Bucket fills that follow in step 3.)

3 Filling areas with flat color. After Morris had adjusted the contrast of the line art, to establish the color theme, she used the Paint Bucket tool to fill the flower petals, stems and sky with flat color. When the Paint Bucket is used to fill areas within scanned black-and-white line art, halos (partially unfilled areas) can appear along the edges of the anti-aliased black lines. In Painter 7 there are at least two ways to prevent these halos: One approach involves layering a copy of your original line work over a thinned version of the lines and filling the thinner version with color. This way any halos that develop on the layer below will be hidden by the original, thicker lines in the layer above. This method is easy to understand and carry out, and it makes it easy to change colors later if you want to. The technique is described in the "Trapping Fills Using a Transparent Layer" tip on page 35. However, if you feel that using extra layers would get in the way of the "painterly" experience of applying color to a single layer of canvas, the Cartoon Cel method may be the technique for you. It works by allowing the fill color to "seep into" the anti-aliasing pixels at the edge of the line work, leaving no halo. This method is described next.

There are three essential parts to the Cartoon Cel fill method: (1) making a selection based on luminance, (2) setting the Paint Bucket's Mask Threshold and filling criteria and (3) choosing a color and filling.

First select the black lines in the image using Select, Auto Select, Using Image Luminance, and click OK.

Second, in the Tools palette, double-click the Paint Bucket to open the Lock Out Color dialog box and set the Mask Threshold low—moving the slider to a point between 7% and 14% usually works well. Click OK to close the dialog box. In the Controls:Paint Bucket palette, under What to Fill choose Cartoon Cel, and under Fill With, choose Current Color.

3c

The petals and stems filled with color

3d

After filling the sky with a flat color fill

4

Using the Magic Wand to select the sky

Third, open the Color Variability section of the Art Materials palette, choose "in HSV" from the pop-up menu and set the (± H), (± S) and (± V) sliders to 0, this will allow you to choose a flat color in the Colors section. After choosing a color, click with the Paint Bucket in one of the white spaces enclosed by the black lines. Then examine the resulting color fill. (To get a better look at the edge, you can choose Select, Hide Marquee. You can also zoom in by clicking on the image with the Magnifier tool.) If the fill has overrun the lines, the Mask Threshold is set too low. On the other hand, if you see a halo at the edge, the setting is too high. If you need to refill, first undo the fill—Edit, Undo—and then change the Mask Threshold setting and fill again. Once you have a satisfactory fill, you should be able to use the same Mask Threshold setting throughout your drawing.

Morris filled the flower petals with three shades of a purple-pink color. Then she filled the stems and sky with other colors.

4 Making a selection with the Magic Wand. In preparation for the next step, when she planned to paint lively brushstrokes across the sky, Morris isolated the entire sky area (based on its color) by making a selection using the Magic Wand. To select all of the blue sky areas at once, she chose the Magic Wand in the Tools palette, unchecked the Contiguous check box on the Controls:Magic Wand palette, and clicked on a blue sky area in her image. To read more about the Magic Wand and selections, turn to the beginning of Chapter 4, "Selections, Shapes and Masks."

5 Painting with brushes. Morris used the Dropper tool to sample sky color in her image, then she used the Variable Flat variant of the Brushes to paint "helter-skelter style" brushstrokes across the sky. The Variable Flat incorporates enhanced Color Variability, which allowed the value of the color to change subtly as she painted. For more subtle brushstrokes, she lowered the opacity using the Opacity slider on the Controls:Brush palette.

6 Adding texture and details. After completing the flat color fills and the brushwork in the sky, Morris used the Dirty Marker variant of the Felt Pens to modulate color in the plant stems, then she used a low-opacity Digital Airbrush variant of the Airbrushes to paint soft shadows on the leaves and stems. To add texture to the ground, she used the Scratchboard Rake variant of the Pens.

Next, Morris added movement and energy to the bee swarm and the beeman's stinger. She chose black in the Colors section and used the Pixel Dust variant of the Pens to paint spiraling strokes behind the bee's stinger and above the hive. (The Pixel Dust pen is located in the Ver 5 Brushes library, on the Painter 7 Application CD-ROM.)

5

Painting on the sky with free brushstrokes

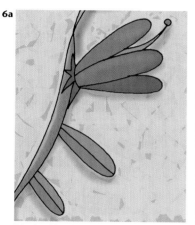

6a

Morris airbrushed soft shadows along edges of the foliage.

6b

The image with fills and brushwork texture, prior to adding Pixel Dust to the bee swarm

Morris finished the piece using the Digital Airbrush to add more highlights and shadows to the bee, plants and flowers. She airbrushed a soft drop shadow along some of the edges on the beeman and the flowers. For more subtle brushstrokes, she lowered the opacity of all of the brushes (except the Pixel Dust pen), using the Opacity slider on the Controls:Brush palette.) The completed illustration can be seen at the top the page 32.

TRAPPING FILLS USING A TRANSPARENT LAYER

This method of coloring line art uses a transparent layer that contains slightly thicker lines to trap, or hide the edges of, the fills on the image canvas below. First, correct the contrast of your line art using Effects, Tonal Control, Brightness/Contrast, and retouch any black specks, as described in step 2 of "Coloring a Scanned Illustration" on pages 32 and 33.

Select the black line art by choosing Select, Auto Select, Using Image Luminance. When the selection marquee appears, hold down Alt/Option (to copy), and choose Select, Float to make a transparent layer containing only the line art. (Layer 1 will appear in the Layers section of the Objects palette.) In the Layers section, turn off the visibility of the Layer 1 by clicking its eye icon off, then target the Canvas layer by clicking on its name. Make the lines thinner on the canvas, by choosing Effects, Tonal Control, Brightness/Contrast, and moving both sliders to the right enough to thin the lines but not enough to make breaks in them (you may have to experiment with settings, depending on the thickness of your lines).

Now choose the Paint Bucket tool, and in the Controls:Paint Bucket palette, choose Image under What To Fill and Current Color under Fill With. Open the Colors section of the Art Materials palette. Choose a new color, then click the Paint Bucket in a white area of the canvas. To complete the "trap" on your fill, toggle Layer 1's visibility back on by clicking its eye icon, and choose Multiply in the pop-up Composite Method menu at the top of the Layers section. You can inspect the result with the Magnifier tool. (To read more about Layers, turn to Chapter 5, "Using Layers and Shapes.")

The Objects:Layers section

Image canvas showing the flat color fills with "halos"

Image with Layer 1 in Multiply mode and with its visibility turned on

Coloring a Woodcut

Overview *Create black-and-white art; tint the art with sepia; float it and apply the Gel Composite Method; view the black-and-white art as you add a colored texture and brush work to the original canvas layer.*

1

Phillips' black-and-white drawing

2a

Setting up the gradient

2b

Applying Express in Image

CHET PHILLIPS

HERE'S A CREATIVE WAY TO ADD COLOR to black-and-white art, a favorite technique of artist Chet Phillips. To paint *Wild Life*, Phillips used the Gel Composite Method, which makes the white areas of a layer appear transparent. He colored the image using a limited palette of browns and warm grays, with accents of green and gold.

1 Creating black-and-white art. Phillips created a black-and white drawing in Painter as follows: Start a new document with a white background. Choose black for the front color square in the Colors section of the Art Materials palette, then choose Effects, Fill (Ctrl/⌘-F) using Current Color. Click OK. Use white and the Scratchboard Tool variant of the Pens brush to "etch" into the black fill, with the look of a rough woodcut in mind.

2 Tinting the line art sepia. Phillips tinted the black lines with a subtle dark brown to warm up the line drawing. To give your drawing a sepia color in Painter, choose a very dark brown in the Colors section of the Art Materials palette, and set up the Gradients section to apply a two-point gradient to your image as follows: If the Gradients section of the Art Materials palette is not open, click the left triangle on the Gradients section bar. Choose the Two-point gradation from the resource list menu. On the palette section front, click the Linear Grad button and choose the bottom left direction button. To apply the gradient, click the right

3a

The Layers section showing the active line drawing layer

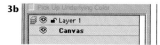

3b

The Canvas layer is selected

4a

Using the Paint Bucket tool to fill the selected area of the Canvas

4b

Applying Color Overlay to add a colored texture to the Canvas

5

Using the line art as a guide, Phillips added color to the animals on the Canvas.

triangle on the Gradients section bar and choose Express in Image. Accept the default settings and click OK.

3 Making a layer with transparent white areas. Select All (Ctrl/⌘-A), choose the Layer Adjuster tool and click once on the image to float it. The black-and-white image is now floating over a white background. In the Layers section of the Objects palette, choose Gel from the Composite Method pop-up menu. This method makes the white areas of the layer transparent, which will allow any color you will add to the background in steps 4 and 5 to completely show through without affecting the black in the layer.

4 Adding color and texture to the background. Phillips created a textured ground with an irregular edge to use as a basis for applying color with pastels.

Before beginning to color your background, click the Canvas layer's name in the Layers section of the Objects palette. This makes sure that you'll be working on the background. (To view either layer without the other, toggle the eye icon to the left of the layer name.)

To make an irregular-edged area, choose the Lasso tool from the Tools palette and press, hold and drag to create an irregular selection boundary, which will constrain the colored fill. (For more about selections, turn to Chapter 4, "Working with Selections, Paths, and Masks.")

Choose a very light cream color in the Colors section, and select the Paint Bucket tool in the Tools palette. In the Controls: Paint Bucket palette, under What to Fill, choose Image under Fill With choose Current Color; and turn on Anti Alias (for a smooth edge on the edges of your filled area). Click inside the selected area with the Paint Bucket.

After applying the cream color, Phillips added a transparent colored texture. Begin by choosing a dark brown color in the Colors section and a texture in the Papers section of the Art Materials palette (Phillips used the Nice Surface texture from the Etched and Eroded library on the Painter 7 Wow! CD-ROM). Choose Effects, Surface Control, Color Overlay. In the Using menu choose Paper, click the Dye Concentration button and set the Opacity at about 16%. Click OK. Now, deselect the area by choosing Select, None. (Ctrl/⌘-D)

5 Painting on the background. To render the background, Phillips chose a color palette that included rich browns, golds and grays. Using the Artists Pastel variant of Dry Media, he took advantage of the brush's texture-sensitive ability to bring out the Nice Surface texture (see step 4), which was chosen in the Papers section. Choose the Artist Pastel variant in the Brushes palette. Choose Restore Default Variant from the Variant menu on the Brushes palette to restore the variant to its default. Now choose a color in the Colors section and begin painting. If you need to edit the black areas, click on the black-filled layer's name in the Layers palette and then paint. 🖌

Capturing a Color Set

Overview *Capture color from a reference image using the Dropper; build and customize a Color Set; use the Color Set to paint a new image.*

1a

The reference photograph

1b

The Color Variability section of the Art Materials palette showing ± H, ± S and ± V set to 0

1c

Using the Dropper to sample color from the image

2

Choosing Create New Empty Color Set in the Color Set section

IF YOU'RE PLANNING A SERIES OF ILLUSTRATIONS based on the same color theme, you'll find Painter's Color Sets invaluable. Use this technique of sampling color from a photo or painting to quickly build a selective palette of colors as we did here prior to creating the pastel painting *Tienda Verde.*

1 Sampling the color. Open the image that contains the color range you want. Before you begin to sample the color, open the Color Variability section of the Art Materials palette, choose "in HSV" from the pop-up menu and set the (± H), (± S) and (± V) sliders to 0. (This will assure that the colors sampled will be pure color instead of variegated.) Now choose the Dropper tool and click it on a colored pixel in the image. The Colors section of the Art Materials palette will display the color. If the displayed color isn't the one you want, you can click or drag the Dropper around your image. The Colors section will update to show the new color.

2 Creating a Color Set. In the Art Materials palette, click on the Color Set section name to open the Color Set section, and click on the New Color Set button (the Grid). From the pop-up menu choose Create New Empty Color Set. A very small empty Color Set palette will appear. Click on the Add Color button (the "Plus" in the Color Set section) to add the selected color to the Color Set. Continue to sample and add more colors by clicking the Dropper and the Plus button. To save your colors, click on the Library button in the Color Sets palette, navigate to the Painter 7 application folder to store your set, then click Save, name the set and Save. We named ours "Autumn Color." To use your new Color Set after saving, you must reopen it by selecting it in the Painter application folder and clicking the Open button.

3 Arranging the Color Set display. You can change the layout of your colors in the Color Set to fit your drawing environment. To change the shape of the individual color squares, click

3a

The Autumn Color Set layout settings

3b

The completed Autumn Color Set

4

Applying colored brushstrokes with the Square Chalk using the Autumn Color Set

on the Color Square Size arrow buttons in the Color Set section, or click on Color Set Size arrow buttons to change the shape of the layout. We built our Color Set of 32-pixel-wide squares with 2 rows and 11 columns.

4 Using your new colors. To paint with the new Color Set, start a new file, click on a color in the set, choose a brush and begin painting. We drew a sketch using a dark blue-gray from our set with the Cover Pencil variant of Pencils, and added brushstrokes in other colors using the variants of the Dry Media brush.

NEW AUTOMATIC COLOR SET TOOLS

Painter 7 offers three new automatic color set building features: Create Color Set from Image, Create Color Set from Selection and Create Color Set from Layer. Using these new tools, you can quickly build a color set by extracting every color from an image, selection or layer. (These features are useful if you want to sample every color, but they don't offer quite the same control as sampling individual colors with the Dropper.) To make a color set based on a selected area of your image, begin by opening the Color Set section of the Art Materials palette by clicking the Color Set section bar name. Open an image, and make a selection (as we did here with the Rectangular Selection tool). In the Color Set section, click the New Color Set button (the Grid) to display the pop-up menu and choose Create Color Set from Selection. Painter will generate the color set. After our color set was made, we adjusted its appearance by increasing the Color Square Size by clicking the arrows on the lower left of the Color Set section. We also displayed the colors in dark-to-light order by clicking the LHS (Light, Hue and Saturation) button. Automatically generated color sets often have several colors that are very similar. To remove a color, click on it in the working Color Set and then click the Delete Color From Color Set button (the "Minus") in the Color Set section. To save your colors, click on the Library button in the Color Set section, navigate to the Painter 7 application folder to store your set, then click Save, name the set and click Save again. To use the new Color Set it must be reopened by selecting it in the Painter application folder and clicking the Open button.

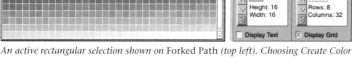

An active rectangular selection shown on Forked Path *(top left). Choosing Create Color Set from Selection in the Color Set Section of the Art Materials palette (top right); clicking the LHS button in the Color Section, and Display Grid (bottom right); and the brightly colored color set (bottom left.)*

CHER THREINEN-PENDARVIS

■ Artist **Richard Noble** successfully re-creates the look of traditional acrylic using Painter. He generally begins by importing a reference photograph into Painter to use as a template. For these two paintings of Mendocino, he roughed in the color with the Sargent Brush variant of the Artists brush and the Round Camelhair variant of the Brushes. Both of these brushes allowed Noble to move paint around on the canvas; he also blended color using the Palette Knife variant of the Brushes. He added details with Artist Pastel Chalk (Dry Media) and a tiny Digital Airbrush (Airbrushes). Noble prints his pieces on canvas, then stretches and finishes them with a clear glaze and touches of acrylic paint.

In *Fog* (above), Noble used a rustic, low-saturation palette and expressive brush work to create the foggy atmosphere. He painted highlights and shadows with subdued color and with looser detail.

In *1872* (right), Noble depicted the bright light of a sunny morning. Using the Sargent Brush and the Round Camelhair, he developed strong light-to-dark contrast. Then he used a small brush to paint fine detail in the shaded areas of the foreground flowers as well as in the sunlit areas of the painting.

■ **Dennis Orlando's** sensitive use of light combined with layered color in the shadowed areas in his paintings has earned him the name "The Modern Impressionist."

Inspired by a Chinese painting on silk, Orlando painted *The Pond with Low Branches* with the Artist Pastel Chalk variant of Dry Media. To establish a mood of late day, he used muted colors and an analogous palette with deep shadow colors but without bright highlights. He laid color in with the Artist Pastel Chalk using increased Color Variability to create activity in the color, then he pulled and blended colors into one another using the Grainy Water variant of the Liquid brush. In areas where he wanted to preserve more of the modulated color, he reduced the Opacity of the Grainy Water variant, then continued to blend and pull the color.

"I want people to see the intricacies of lines, color variations, and the subtle texture patterns that inhabit my paintings," says illustrator **Keith MacLelland**. In his illustrations he communicates the fun he has when creating his art. He began both images by making a sketch in Painter with the Flattened Pencil variant (Pencils), then refined the drawings using the Scratchboard Tool variant of the Pens.

In *H is for Hell-bent Haddocks* (right), MacLelland used warm colors for the background and cool colors for the fish. Usually cool colors recede into a background. To give his image depth, he used much more crisp detail and a larger scale with the foreground fish. The background fish were copies that he flipped, scaled and then blurred using the Depth of Field Blur (Effects, Focus, Depth Of Field). After drawing the sketch, MacLelland created the background design of overlapping rectangles with the Paint Bucket, clicking and dragging to make each small rectangle of color. Then he recolored the rectangles with the range of hues in a yellow-to-orange gradient by choosing Express in Image in the Gradients section of the Art Materials palette. The initial "H" and curved text were created in Painter using live text dynamic layers.

For *Scooter Fish* (below), MacLelland chose more pastel colors, accented by thick and thin outlines that he treated with colored texture. To add texture to the lines, he selected the lines based on their color using the Magic Wand, then he lightened them using Effects, Surface Control, Dye Concentration, and applied texture (Effects, Surface Control, Apply Surface Texture, Using Paper). The fish was painted with Brushes and Dry Media variants.

■ Creative use of saturated color, loose, illustrative strokes and an eclectic mix of brushes and paper textures let **Susan LeVan**, of LeVan/Barbee Studio, create a strong emotional quality in her work.

For the illustrations *Guardians* (above), and *Bad Dogs* (right) LeVan used a palette composed primarily of saturated colors, including many warm reds, oranges and yellows, accented by creams, greens, blues and pinks. LeVan sketched both images with the 2B variant of Pencils and the Scratchboard Tool variant of the Pens, then she added more color and brush work with the Oil Pastel and Square Chalk variants of Dry Media. For the speckled textures, she used the Coarse Spray variant of Airbrushes. To build the negative side of the illustration in *Guardians*, she began by adding more pixels to the left side of the image (Canvas, Canvas Size), selecting the right side of her image with the Rectangular Selection tool, copying it and pasting it, then flipping it (Effects, Orientation, Flip Horizontal). Then she made it negative (Effects, Tonal Control, Negative). LeVan painted and redrew areas of the figure on the left side with the Square Chalk (Dry Media) and the Scratchboard Tool (Pens) tools. Then she added details to the entire image, switching between a variety of subtle and coarse paper textures.

3

PAINTING
WITH
BRUSHES

This detailed illustration for Scholastic Press shows Karen Carr's refined digital oil painting technique, achieved by using Dry Media, Liquid and Brushes variants. See more of Carr's work in the gallery at the end of this chapter.

PAINTER'S BRUSHES ARE THE PROGRAM'S HEART: Without them, Painter would be a lot like other image editors. What sets Painter apart is the way it puts pen to paper and paint to canvas—the way its brushes interact with the surface below them. Here's a primer on getting the most from Painter's brushes.

Painting basics. If you're new to Painter, follow these steps to jump right in and begin painting. Create a new file (File, New). If the Brushes palette is not open, choose Window, Show Brushes to open it; or double-click the Brush tool in the Tools palette. (For more brush choices, you can choose a new brush from the pop-up menu on the bottom left corner of the Brushes palette or click the Brushes palette's push-bar to open the brush drawer.) Choose Dry Media from the pop-up menu or click the Dry Media icon. Then to select a color, choose Window, Show Art Materials and toggle the triangle at the left of the Colors section bar to open a Colors section. Click in the Colors section's Hue ring or bar and in its triangle to choose a color for your painting. In the Art Materials palette, you'll also find the Papers section bar. Click its left triangle to open the Papers section, click the push-bar to open the drawer, then click a paper swatch to change the texture from Painter's default. Paint a few strokes on the image canvas. Experiment by changing brushes, colors and paper textures as you paint. It's also possible to paint on a layer or a mask instead of the Canvas.

Brush style icons on the front of the drawer

Push-bar

Open drawer

Brush style menu

Brush variants

Dry Me... ▾   Artist Pastel Chalk ▾

The Brushes palette with its drawer open

Brushes:Dry Media
Brush Variant Control Nozzle Stroke

This detail of Roses *shows brushstrokes painted with custom variants based on the Captured Bristle, Round Camelhair and Opaque Flat variants of the Brushes.*

Above: Script drawn with a pressure-sensitive stylus using the Calligraphy variant of the Pens. Below: Choosing the Calligraphy variant of the Pens from the variant pop-up menu.

Painting on masks is covered in the introduction of Chapter 4; painting on layers is covered in Chapter 5 "Using Layers and Shapes."

Brush styles. Brush *styles* are shown as the mark-making tool icons on the Brushes palette, both on the front of the drawer and inside it. To choose a brush style, you can click one of the icons, such as the Pens. (As described on page 44, you can also choose a style from the pop-up menu in the bottom *left* corner of the Brushes palette). Brush styles are at the top level of organization for mark-making tools in Painter; they are like the *containers* that hold the individual brushes, pens, chalk and other painting and drawing implements.

Brush variants. Every brush *style* has its own *variants* or varieties, so every time you choose a different brush style, the list of variants changes. Brush variants appear in the pop-up menu in the bottom *right* corner of the Brushes palette drawer. For instance, within the Pens are several variants, such as Calligraphy, Smooth Ink Pen and Scratchboard Tool. To choose the Calligraphy variant of the Pens, click the variant pop-up menu and choose Calligraphy.

Saving and restoring variants. While many artists will be content to use a few of the many brush variants that come standard with the program, others will create dozens of their own. Even if you're an intuitive artist, you'll probably find yourself wanting a custom brush. (In-depth information can be found in "Building Brushes" on page 58.)

When you make modifications to a brush, Painter remembers the custom settings. Still, it's a good idea to save your custom brushes under their own names and to preserve Painter's default brushes. If you've changed settings and want to switch back to the default, choose Restore Default Variant from the Variant menu at the top of the Brushes palette. To *replace* a default brush with your custom settings, choose Variant, Set Default Variant. **Caution:** After this choice, the only way to restore Painter's original default variant is by reinstalling the Painter Brushes file as described in "Restoring Default Brushes," below.

RESTORING DEFAULT BRUSHES

To delete *all* cached variants and restore brushes to their original state, hold down the Alt/Option key and from the Brushes palette menu choose Variant, Restore Default Variant. (Keep in mind, if you've used Set Default Variant to save your own defaults, this command will restore to the *new* default you set.) To preserve your Painter Brushes with modifications and also have access to the original default set, open your Painter application folder and open the Brushes folder. Rename the Painter Brushes folder. We named ours "Painter Brushes 2." Then to restore the default Painter Brushes from the Painter 7 Application CD-ROM, open the Default Content Files folder on the CD-ROM, open the Brushes folder and copy the Painter Brushes folder into the Brushes folder within your Painter 7 application folder. To replace only a specific brush category, you would open the Painter Brushes folder within your Painter 7 application folder instead of renaming it, then select the category on the Painter 7 Application CD-ROM and copy it into your Painter Brushes folder.

A lower-opacity brush will allow you to build up color slowly with more sensitivity. This technique was used to paint the coastal hills in Punta San Antonio.

Switch Methods to make dramatic changes in brush characteristics. Here we've applied the Waxy Crayons variants of Dry Media over a gradient using the default Buildup method (top), Cover method (center) and Eraser method (bottom).

The Gritty Charcoal variant of Dry Media was applied using various Subcategory settings: the antialiased default Grainy Hard Cover (top); the pixelated Grainy Edge Flat Cover (middle); and the soft-edged Soft Cover (bottom).

Controls on the Papers section of the Art Materials palette allow adjustment of the Scale, Contrast and Brightness of textures, as shown here.

If you've made changes to a brush variant, and you'd like to store it in the Brushes palette, first check that all your settings are the way you want them. Then choose Save Variant from the Variant pull-down menu on the Brushes palette, name the variant and click OK. Your new variant will appear in the variant list for that brush style and will stay there, even after you leave the program, until you remove it by selecting it and then choosing Variant, Delete Variant.

Methods. *Methods* are the backbone of many brush variants, including brushes that users of earlier versions of Painter know and love. To see the method for a specific brush variant, such as the Artist Pastel Chalk, open the Brush Controls palette's General section by choosing Window, Show Brush Controls and then clicking the left triangle on the General section bar. A brush variant's Method setting controls how the paint will interact with the background and with other paint. For instance, by default the Felt Pens variants use the Buildup method, meaning that overlapping strokes will darken. The Chalk variants of Dry Media use the Cover method by default, which means that strokes—even light-colored ones—will cover other strokes. You can, however, switch the method for the variant that you design. For example, you can save a Cover method variant of the Felt Pens.

Subcategories. While each method gives a radically different effect to a brush, the *subcategories*, or submethods, make more subtle changes, affecting the edges of brush strokes. Subcategories that include the word *Flat* produce hard, aliased strokes with pixelated edges. Those that include the word *Hard* give smoother strokes. Strokes made using *Soft* subcategories appear with feathered edges. Strokes with the word *Grainy* in their subcategory setting will be affected by the active paper texture. Strokes that contain the word *Edge* give a thicker, stickier look; *Variable* refers to strokes that are affected by tilt and direction.

Paper textures. "Grainy" brush methods will reveal the paper texture you've selected in the Papers section of the Art Materials

Soft Charcoal default settings. Settings not available for this brush are grayed out.

Janet Martini added interest to her India *painting—maximizing the interaction between brush and virtual texture in Painter—by exaggerating the size of the texture. Before painting with Water Color and Pens variants, she adjusted the Scale slider in the Papers section of the Art Materials palette.*

palette. You can use Painter's standard papers or create your own (see "Applying Scanned Paper Textures," on page 96). Adjust the Grain slider on the Controls:Brush palette to vary the intensity of the grain revealed by your brushstrokes. For most of Painter's brushes, a lower Grain setting means that *less of the color will penetrate the grain*, so your strokes will actually look grainier (See "Grain Penetration" below.)

GRAIN PENETRATION

For almost all of Painter's brushes, the lower the Grain setting, the "grainier" your strokes will look. That's because the Grain setting actually describes *grain penetration*. A lower Grain setting means that less of the color will penetrate into the valleys of the grain. The paint is hitting only the "peaks" of the paper surface.

The Grain slider in the Controls: Brush palette

CONTINUOUS-STROKE BRUSHES

Using *continuous-stroke* technology, many of Painter's brushes paint faster than dab-based brushes. These brushes render brushstrokes using a bundle of continuous, anti-aliased one-pixel lines. Because the stroke is composed of continuous lines instead of overlapping dabs, the computed brushes can produce smoother, more realistic brushstrokes than dab-based brushes can. Additionally, each brush hair has the ability to carry its own well of color. When an artist uses a traditional brush, the bristles often get contaminated by the colors of wet paint on the canvas. When the brush touches a neighboring color, it affects the paint along the edges of the new brushstroke. When using traditional media, artists often use this technique to mix color on a conventional color palette, or on the canvas itself. In Painter this technique is known as *brush loading*. Some new brushes (the Round Camelhair variant of the Brushes, for instance) have this capability built into them. When painting with dab-based brushes without the built-in loading capability, you can activate Brush Loading in the Well section of the Brush Controls palette by enabling the Brush Loading checkbox. (You can also activate Brush Loading for brushes created in earlier versions of Painter.)

In addition to speed and brush-loading enhancements, Painter incorporates advanced input technology (such as tilt and bearing) from pressure-sensitive tablet manufacturers such as Wacom. Most brushes in Painter are able to take advantage of this capability.

Rendered dab brushes. These brushes are very responsive and smooth and they have the ability to paint with a source other than color, such as a gradient or a pattern. The Smooth Ink Pen and Grad Pen variants of the Pens use rendered dabs. For more detailed information about using rendered dab types turn to "Building Brushes" on page 58.

Detail of Agave Shawii, *painted with the Round Camelhair variant. The Round Camelhair allows for more color "activity" when painting because each brush hair can paint with its own color. For more information turn to "Painting an Expressive Color Study" later in this chapter.*

Wisteria flowers created using Painter's Pattern Pen

These quick sketches of Little Doll were drawn using the Cover Pencil variant on Cold Press Water Color paper with a Wacom pressure-sensitive tablet and stylus and a laptop.

Pattern Pen brushes. In addition to painting with color, Painter includes several new kinds of media application—for instance, brushes that paint with gradients or patterns. To make a sketch like the Wisteria example at the left, in the Brushes palette choose the Pattern Pens style and the Pattern Pen Masked variant. Load the Watercolored Patterns library. You'll find the Load Library command at the bottom of the pop-up Pattern list in the Patterns section of the Art Materials palette. Scroll down to the bottom of the list and choose Load Library to display the Open dialog box. Navigate to the Pen Patterns folder on the Painter 7_CD2 CD-ROM; choose the Watercolored Patterns library; then double-click to open it. (For more information about special-effects brushes that paint using a pattern or other source, turn to "Building Brushes" on page 58, and to Chapter 7, "Exploring Special Effects.")

EMULATING TRADITIONAL TECHNIQUES

Here's a brief description of several traditional art techniques and how to re-create them in Painter. One or two techniques for each medium are outlined as a starting point for your own experimentation. But there are a number of ways to obtain similar results.

Pencil. Pencil sketches using traditional materials are typically created on location. Tools include soft-leaded graphite pencils (HB to 6B), various erasers and white paper with a smooth to medium grain. To create a pencil sketch in Painter, select an even-textured paper texture such as Basic Paper and choose the Pencils category, 2B Pencil variant. Select a black or dark gray and begin sketching. To paint a light color over dark—for instance, to add highlights—choose a white color and draw with the Cover Pencil variant. For more about working in pencil, see "Sketching with Pencils" on page 64.

Colored pencil. Conventional colored pencils are highly sensitive to the surface used: Layering strokes with light pressure on a smooth board will create a shiny look, while a rougher surface creates more of a "broken color" effect (strokes that don't completely cover the existing art). To closely match the grainy, opaque strokes of a soft Prismacolor pencil on cold-pressed illustration board with Painter, select a fine-or medium-grained paper such as Plain Grain (found in the Drawing Paper Textures library in the Paper Textures folder on the Painter 7_CD2 CD-ROM). Choose the Colored Pencils variant of Pencils. Switch the

Artists who used earlier versions of Painter will be happy to hear that Auto Build Brush is a default in Painter 7. To toggle Auto build on and off, choose Brush, Auto Build Brush from the Brushes palette menu.

The Artist Pastel Chalk and Large Chalk variants of Dry Media were used on a rough texture to paint Coastal Meadow.

For this Harp Shell *study, a custom Conté crayon was used to draw on Laid Pastel Paper.*

This charcoal study after Raphael Sanzio, was drawn with the Charcoal and Soft Charcoal variants (Dry Media), then blended with the Just Add Water variant (Liquid).

Method from Buildup to Cover and change the Subcategory to Grainy Edge Flat Cover. See "Drawing with Colored Pencils," later in this chapter for a full description of this technique.

Pastel. Pastels encourage a bold, direct style: Edgar Degas preferred pastels for his striking compositions because they simultaneously yield tone, line and color. A great variety of hard and soft pastels are used on soft or rough-grain papers. Pastel artists often use a colored paper stock to unify a composition.

Use Painter's Sharp Chalk, Large Chalk, Artist Pastel Chalk, Soft Pastel and Oil Pastel variants from the Dry Media style to mimic traditional hard or soft pastels, and if you want to use a colored paper, click on the Paper Color box as you open a new document and choose a color. The Chalk and Pastel variants are among Painter's most popular; turn to "Blending and Feathering with Pastels," and "Painting with Pastels" later in this chapter for two different techniques for using them.

Conté crayon. Popular in Europe since the 1600s and used today for life drawing and landscapes, Conté crayons have a higher oil content than conventional chalk or pastel; as a result, they work successfully on a greater variety of surfaces.

To get a realistic Conté crayon look in Painter, start with the Sharp Chalk variant of Dry Media. Reveal more paper grain in the brushwork by moving the Grain slider in the Controls:Brush palette to 14%. On the Brush Controls palette (Window, Show Brush Controls), open the Spacing section by clicking its name. Set the Spacing at 25%. Now open the Size section of the Brush Controls palette and choose the upper right brush tip. Begin drawing. This custom Conté variant works well over the Laid Pastel Paper texture. To blend color while revealing the paper texture, choose the Smudge variant of the Liquid brush.

Charcoal. One of the oldest drawing tools, charcoal is ideal for life drawing and portraiture in *chiaroscuro* (high value contrast) style. Renaissance masters frequently chose charcoal because images created with it could be transferred from paper (where corrections could be made easily) to canvas or walls in preparation

To resize your brush on-the-fly, press Ctrl-Shift-Alt (Windows) or ⌘-Shift-Option (Mac). You will see the cursor change to cross hairs. Drag to create a circle the size of the brush you want.

Brushstrokes made using the Graphic Paintbrush Soft variant of the Brushes. In the upper left, its default size; upper right, the resized brush "ghost" cursor; lower right, a stroke made with the resized brush.

To draw Crab, *a spot illustration, Mary Envall used the Smooth Ink Pen and Scratchboard Tool variants of the Pens. Both of these Pens use Painter's rendered dabs.*

Kathy Blavatt created Heart *using Painter 7's new Liquid Ink brushes.*

In Baseball Memories, *a detail of which is shown here, Chet Phillips used the Scratchboard Tool variant of the Pens. To see the full image, turn to the gallery at the end of Chapter 5.*

for painting. To create a charcoal drawing in Painter, select a rough paper (such as Sanded Pastel Board) and the Charcoal variant of the Dry Media brush. Create a gestural drawing, then blend the strokes—as you would traditionally with a tortillion, a tissue or your fingers—with the Smudge variant of the Liquid brush. For a smoother result with less texture try blending with the Just Add Water variant of Liquid. Finish by adding more strokes using a Charcoal brush, this time using the Gritty Charcoal variant of the Dry Media brush.

Pen and Ink. Many artists use Painter's Pens variants to draw editorial and spot illustrations. To create a black-and-white pen-and-ink drawing in Painter, choose the Fine Point variant of the Pens and choose 100% black in the Colors section. Sketch your composition. To draw with lines that are expressively thick and thin based on the pressure you apply to your stylus, switch to the Smooth Ink Pen. To etch white lines and texture into black areas of your drawing, select pure white in the Colors section and draw with the Fine Point or Smooth Ink Pen. For a sense of spontaneous energy try drawing with the Nervous Pen.

Thick ink and resists. When you start to paint with Painter 7's new Liquid Ink, a special Liquid Ink layer is created. With Liquid Ink you can use the thick, viscous ink to paint graphic flat-color art and to paint thick, impasto-like brushstrokes as well. For smooth-edged strokes try the Smooth Camel variant. To paint textured brushstrokes, experiment with the Sparse Bristle and Coarse Camel variants. To erode Liquid Ink you've already laid down, choose a Resist variant, such as the Graphic Camel Resist. Brush over the area of ink you want to erode. You can also apply a resist and then paint over it. The resist will repel brushstrokes made with a regular Liquid Ink variant, until repeated strokes scrub the resist away. To see how to add volume to a Liquid Ink drawing, target the Liquid Ink layer in the Layers section of the Objects palette (Window, Show Objects) and press the Enter key. Move the Amount slider to 50%, and click OK. For more information about using Liquid Ink, turn to the "Liquid Ink Primer" later in this chapter.

Scratchboard illustration. Scratching white illustrations out of a dark (usually black) background surface became popular in the late 1800s. Illustrations created in this manner often contained subtle, detailed tone effects, making them a useful alternative to photographic halftones in the publications of that era.

A glazing technique was used for a watercolor portrait study of Sabina Gaross.

Cloudy Day on Kauai was painted with the Runny Wash Bristle, Wash Camel, Fine Camel and Diffuse Camel variants of Water Color. On the trees, highlights were brought out using the Eraser Dry variant and foreground texture was added with the Eraser Salt.

Study of a Nude after Rembrandt van Rijn. We sketched with the Fine Point variant of Pens, then added translucent washes using the Wash Camel variant of Water Color.

Modern scratchboard artists use knives and gougers on a variety of surfaces, including white board painted with India ink. To duplicate this look in Painter, start with the Flat Color variant of the Pens and increase its size in the Controls:Brush palette. Choose black from the Colors section and rough out the basic shape for your illustration. To "scratch" the image out of the shape with hatch marks, switch to white and change to the Scratchboard Tool variant. Use the Scratchboard Rake to draw several lines at once. Turn to Chapter 5's gallery to see Chet Phillips's Painter-generated scratchboard work, or check out John Fretz's blending of traditional and digital scratchboard in the gallery at the end of Chapter 4.

Calligraphy. With the exception of "rolling the nib" and a few other maneuvers, you can imitate nearly all conventional calligraphic strokes in Painter. To create hand lettering similar to the example on page 45, choose the Calligraphy variant of the Pens and begin your brush work. To make guides for your calligraphy, select Canvas, Rulers, Show Rulers and drag guides out from the rulers, or you can use Painter's Grid overlay (choose Canvas, Grid, Show Grid). If you want a rougher edge to your strokes, try switching the subcategory to Flat Cover or Grainy Edge Flat Cover in the General section of the Brush Controls palette. To fine-tune the "nib," in the Brush Controls palette click on Angle to open the Angle section. Create a flatter nib by setting a smaller value on the Squeeze slider; if you want to adjust the orientation of the brush, drag the Angle slider until you like what you see in the preview in the Size section of the palette.

Watercolor. Landscape artists like Turner and Constable helped popularize watercolors in the nineteenth century. The medium's portability lends itself nicely to painting on location. Traditional watercolor uses transparent pigment suspended in water, and the paper is often moistened and stretched prior to painting.

Painter 7 lets you achieve many traditional watercolor effects—without paper-stretching! Choose the Wash Bristle variant of Water Color, a rough paper (such as Cold Press Water Color) and a light-to-medium color, and begin painting. (If the color painted with the Wash Bristle is too intense, reduce the Opacity in the Controls:Brush palette.) To blend color, choose a new color in the Colors section, switch to the Diffuse Camel variant and make a new brushstroke. To remove only the color painted with Water Color variants, use the Eraser Dry variant of Water Color. For more about Water Color turn to "A Painter Water Color Primer" on page 70 and the step-by-step Water Color techniques later in this chapter.

Pen and wash. Tinted, translucent washes over pen work has been a medium of choice of Asian painting masters for many centuries. Painter's Water Color layers let you add a wash to any drawn (or scanned) image without smearing or hiding the original image. Choose the Soft Camel or Wash Camel variant of Water Color and

To paint Porcelain Morning Glory, *Kathy Blavatt used several Airbrushes variants.*

pick a color (it works best to build up color beginning with very light-colored washes). Choose an even, medium-textured paper (such as Basic Paper) and begin painting on top of line work.

Airbrush. The trademark of most traditional airbrush work is a slick, super-realistic look; photo retouching is a more subtle use of the tool. A traditional airbrush is a miniature spray gun with a hollow nozzle and a tapered needle. Pigments include finely ground gouache, acrylic, watercolor and colored dyes, and a typical support surface is a smooth illustration board. Airbrush artists protect areas of their work from overspraying with pieces of masking film, or flexible friskets cut from plastic.

In Painter, choose one of the Airbrushes variants and begin sketching or retouching. To get the most from the tool, make selections with the Lasso tool and use them to limit the paint just as you would traditional airbrush friskets.

Several of Painter's Airbrushes (such as the Fine Spray, Pixel Spray and Graffiti variants) spray paint onto the image canvas differently than earlier Airbrushes. These Airbrushes take advantage of new input technology available from tablet-and-stylus manufacturers such as Wacom. They respond to angle (tilt) and bearing (direction). For instance, as you paint, particles of color land on the image canvas reflecting the way the artist tilts the stylus. And with Painter's Fine Wheel Airbrush variant, you can adjust the flow of paint by adjusting the wheel on a special Airbrush stylus. For those accustomed to the Airbrushes in earlier versions of Painter, the Digital Airbrush variant is most similar to these. Turn to "Selections and Airbrush" in Chapter 4 and the gallery in Chapter 8 to see John Dismukes's masterful airbrush work using selections and layers.

Gouache. Roualt, Vlaminck, Klee and Miro were a few of the modern artists who experimented with this opaque watercolor, used most frequently in paintings that call for large areas of flat color. Gouache contains a blend of the same type of pigment used in transparent watercolor, a chalk that makes the medium opaque, and an extender that allows it to flow more easily.

Artist Nancy Stahl has modified several brushes in Painter to emulate traditional gouache applied to cold-pressed illustration board. Read about her techniques in "Gouache and Opaque Watermedia" later in this chapter.

This detail of Nancy Stahl's Mercury *shows her gouache technique. To see the full image, turn to "Gouache and Opaque Watermedia," later in this chapter.*

This detail from Amaryllis *was painted with the Opaque Bristle Spray and Smeary Bristle Spray variants of Brushes, then blended with the Smudge variant of Liquid.*

Coast *by Richard Noble is an example of the artist's digital acrylic technique.*

Chelsea Sammel used Impasto brushes to add thick paint to Dying Orchids, *a detail of which is shown here. To read about her painting process step-by-step, turn to* "Working with Thick Paint," *on page 107.*

Oil paint and acrylic. These opaque media are "standards" for easel painting. Both can be applied in a thick impasto with a palette knife or stiff brush, or they can be *extended* (thinned) with a solvent or gel and applied as transparent glazes. They are typically applied to canvas that has been primed with paint or gesso.

Try the following methods to get the look of oil or acrylic in Painter. For a technique that incorporates the texture of brush striations and a palette knife, begin by choosing the Raw Silk paper texture and the Opaque Round variant of the Brushes and then start painting. To paint brushstrokes with varied color, switch to the Variable Flat variant. Blend colors using short strokes with the Distorto variant of Liquid. To scrape back or move large areas of color on the image canvas, use the Palette Knife variant of the Brushes. When working on smaller areas of your image, adjust the size of the Palette Knife using the Size slider on the Controls: Brush palette.

For an oil painting technique with the feel of wet paint on canvas, use the Sargent Brush variant of the Artists brush. The Sargent Brush allows you to move color as well as apply it. As you pull the Sargent Brush through pools of color on the image canvas, the brush carries some of the neighboring color with it as you paint.

For a painting method that emphasizes the texture of canvas, begin by choosing the Canvas 2 texture from the More Paper Textures library (in Paper Textures, on the Painter 7_CD2 CD-ROM). Now choose the Opaque Bristle Spray variant of the Brushes and lay color into your image. To smear existing paint as you add more color, switch to the Smeary Bristle Spray variant. To reveal the texture of the image canvas, while you blend colors, switch to the Smudge variant of Liquid. For yet another digital oil method, see Dennis Orlando's version of a traditional oil look in "Painting With Oils," later in this chapter; to see more examples of Richard Noble's digital acrylic paintings, turn to the gallery in Chapter 2 "The Power of Color."

To get textured brushstrokes (a "3D paint" look) with any of these methods when you're finished, choose Effects, Surface Control, Apply Surface Texture. Choose Image Luminance from the pop-up menu, and an Amount setting of 20–30%. If you want to mimic the look of acrylic paint extended with a glossy gel medium, drag the Shine slider to 100%. To get a semi-matte finish, move the Shine slider to between 20% and 30%.

Painting with realistic Impasto. Impasto gives you the power to show the texture of brushmark striations and the thickness of paint itself with realistic highlights and shadows as you paint. Impasto brings thick paint to the tip of your stylus! When you choose a variant of the Impasto brush (such as the Opaque Round) in Painter 7's Brushes palette, the Impasto effect is automatically enabled. You can use Impasto on the image Canvas, or on added layers.

In Three Trees, *Chelsea Sammel mixed media while painting. As shown in this detail, she used modified Chalks (Dry Media); oil paints—the Smeary Bristle Spray and Palette Knife (Brushes); blenders—the Coarse Smear (Liquid); and finally the Oil Pastel and a modified Sharp Chalk variant to define details.*

In Harley, *Richard Noble blended color with a variant of Liquid to get the look of conventional acrylic.*

To complete Speedy Persimmon, *Janet Martini mixed media using the Calligraphy variant of the Pens on top of Water Color variants and Oil Pastel strokes (Dry Media).*

Here's an Impasto primer: Create a new blank file (File, New). To activate Impasto, choose an Impasto brush (such as the Round Camelhair variant) from the Brushes palette. Make brushstrokes on the image canvas. To toggle the Impasto effect on and off, you can click the small paint splat icon in the upper right of Painter's scroll bar. (This toggle does not affect the dimensionality created with the Apply Surface Texture command described on page 53.) To read more about painting with Impasto, turn to "Brushing Washes Over Live Canvas" and "Working With Thick Paint," later in this chapter.

Mixed media. You can create media combinations in Painter that would be impossible (or at least very messy!) in traditional media. Try adding strokes with a Water Color or Pencils variant atop oils, or use a Pens variant on a base of chalk and gouache. See how artists Phil Howe and Janet Martini combined media in the two paintings at the left.

Mixed media painting with a liquid feel. Painter offers several brushes that are reminiscent of wet paint on canvas—for instance, the Sargent Brush variant of the Artists brush, which can both lay down color and smear it, and the Palette Knife variant of the Brushes, which can move large areas of color. Painting with these new brushes is a very tactile experience, as you learned if you experimented as described on page 53.

In the *Paths to Water 4* study shown on page 55, we sketched in color with the Square Chalk variant of Dry Media on a rough paper. Then we switched to the Sargent Brush variant of the Artists brushes to apply more painterly strokes. To blend areas of the foreground and mid-ground we used the Grainy Water variant of Liquid, then we used the Palette Knife variant of the Brushes to expressively pull color in the sky. To paint and blend using these brushes, choose the Sargent Brush and a color, and begin painting. When you are ready to pull and blend paint, switch to the Palette Knife. Try reducing its Opacity in the Controls:Brush palette for a more subdued effect.

Liquid variants are also helpful blending tools. To create *Zinnias,* shown on page 55, we used the Bulge variant of the Liquid brush to enlarge the pink flowers, and the Coarse Smear to pull pixels and add diffused texture to the edges. Then we used the Marbling Rake variant of Liquid to add linear texture and to pull pixels up and

BRUSHSTROKES WITH DEPTH

Using Impasto, you can add brushstrokes that have 3D texture but that don't alter the color in the image—like painting with thick, clear varnish. Select any Impasto variant and in the Draw To pop-up menu in the Impasto section of Brush Controls, select Depth.

LIQUID BRUSH STRENGTH

To control the strength of the Bulge, Pinch, Smear and Turbulence variants of the Liquid brush, adjust the Opacity slider in the Controls:Brush palette.

In this detail from a study for Paths to Water 4, the Palette Knife variant of the Brushes was used to pull and spread color in the clouds and sky.

IMPASTO COMPOSITE DEPTH

You can paint Impasto on layers and then set Composite Depth on each layer (in the Layers section of the Objects palette), to raise or excavate the paint, as described on pages 53–54. (The Composite Depth option will have no effect if you've used Impasto on the Canvas instead of on added layers.)

We painted each rust brushstroke on a separate layer with the Opaque Round variant of Impasto. Then we used Composite Depth controls, Subtract (left) and Add (right), to excavate the left stroke and raise the right stroke.

For Zinnias, we painted over a photo with Dry Media variants, completely covering it with colored strokes. Then we used Liquid variants to distort the flowers, add texture and emphasize the focal point.

around the image to create a sense of movement.

Erasing techniques. Painter provides several ways to simulate traditional erasing and scratch-out techniques. *Lighten* an area of an image by using the Bleach variant of the Erasers, lowering the Opacity slider in the Controls:Brush palette to 10% for improved control. (You can also use the Dodge variant of the Photo brush to lighten color.) Use the Calligraphy variant of the Pens brush and white or a light color to *scratch out* pigment from a pastel or oil painting; to create strokes with more subtle texture, switch to Grainy Soft Cover for the subcategory in the General section of the Brush Controls palette. Use the Eraser Dry variant of the Water Color brush to pull up pigment from a "wet" painting done with Water Color variants (similar to *sponging up* a traditional watercolor). For a more subtle result, lower the Opacity slider (in the Controls:Brush palette) to 40%. Try the Bleach Runny variant of Water Color to leach color from an area, while creating a drippy texture.

Painting with texture. The Add Grain variant of the Photo brush is just as useful for painting as it is for photo manipulation, because it literally puts texture on the tip of your brush. You can switch textures at any time during the painting process by changing the selection in the Papers section of the Art Materials palette. For best results, use very light pressure on the stylus. Make a few marks in the document to preview the effect. For a more subtle look, try lowering the Opacity and Grain penetration in the Controls:Brush palette.

Painting with special effects. Painter offers intriguing special-effects brushes that allow you to paint with fire, glows, fur,

CHANGING THE IMPASTO LOOK

When you work with Impasto, the depth and lighting information is stored in a way that allows you to change it for the entire image—as many times as you like, for both past and future Impasto brushstrokes. To demonstrate this flexibility, select an Impasto variant (such as Texturizer-Heavy) and a color, and paint on your image. Next, choose Canvas, Surface Lighting, and when the dialog box opens, increase the Shine (for more glossy paint); increase the Amount (to make the paint look thicker) and experiment with other settings in the Appearance of Depth and Light Controls sections. Also try toggling Impasto off and on using the Enable Impasto checkbox. To clear (delete) the effect entirely, choose Canvas, Clear Impasto. Clearing Impasto is useful if you want to completely start over with new Impasto. Also, if you decide not to keep the Impasto effects in your image, clearing can save memory.

The Impasto Lighting dialog box allows you to dynamically set Appearance of Depth and Light Controls for Impasto brushstrokes in the entire image.

Brian Moose used the Glow brush variant of the F/X brush to make the brush tips burn in his painting Creative Journey, *a detail of which is shown here. See his complete painting in the gallery at the end of Chapter 7, "Exploring Special Effects."*

We used the Fire brush variant of the F/X brush to paint semi-transparent flames on the bottom of these letters.

WANNA TRY MY BRUSH?

With Painter 7, brushes are now multi-platform xml files, which makes it easier to share the brushes you create with your friends! For directions on how to create a new brush category in the Painter Brushes library see the "Brushes From Scratch" tip on page 99. To send brushes to a friend, the package should consist of a folder with a JPEG file (for the category icon) and the brush xml files. To use the new brushes in the Brushes palette, copy the folder into the Painter Brushes folder, in the Painter 7 application folder.

sparkly fairy dust, hair spray, neon, striped strokes, shattered glass and more! In the detail of *Creative Journey* shown at the left, Brian Moose used the Glow variant of the F/X brush to make the paint-brush tips in his image smolder with a fiery glow.

Painting with the Fire and Glow variants works best on a dark area of your image. To paint semi-transparent flames, choose the Fire brush variant of the F/X brush. For a subdued fire effect that you can build up gradually, with a light pressure on the stylus, choose a very dark orange color with a value (V) of l0–15% in the Colors section (Art Materials). Make short strokes in the direction you want the flames to go. For realism, vary the size of the brush-strokes. Change the size of the brush using the Size slider in the Controls:Brush palette, then paint more brushstrokes using a light pressure on the stylus.

EASIER ACCESS TO CUSTOM CONTROLS

In Painter you can add important brush modification commands to the Controls:Brush palette. That way all your important controls will be in one single palette and you won't have to work back and forth between the Controls:Brush palette and the various sections of the Brush Controls palette. From the Brushes palette's Control pull-down menu choose Custom Controls. The Custom Controls Palette dialog box will appear showing available settings for the current brush. To make it easy to customize our Smeary

Round (a Brushes variant) as we worked, we added two controls from the Customize Controls Palette dialog box. We selected Well from the Category menu and checked the Resaturation and Bleed checkboxes and clicked OK. To save the brush variant with these custom controls added in the Controls:Brush palette, we chose Variant, Save Variant. If you want to delete the added controls later, you can choose Control, Custom Controls, Well, and uncheck the Resaturation and Bleed checkboxes.

The Controls:Brush palette with added settings (Resat and Bleed). These added settings made it easier to control the amount of pigment that would blend as we used the Smeary Round variant to paint the study shown above of Needle's Eye, Sunset Cliffs.

PAINTING ON LAYERS

Painter lets you paint (and erase) not only on the program's canvas, but on transparent layers above it. A *transparent layer* is similar to a piece of clear acetate that hovers above the image canvas. When you paint on a transparent layer with a brush, in the clear areas you can see the canvas underneath, as well as color on other

To paint this study for Cutting Back at Rincon, *we used the Pens, Brushes and Airbrushes variants to paint on transparent layers. After drawing the line sketch on its own layer, we created a second layer for the color work. Using low-opacity color, we painted on the "color" layer to build up brushstrokes without altering the image canvas or the layer with the line sketch. We finished by dragging the line sketch layer to the top of the Layers palette, placing it on top of the color layer.*

layers that you may have stacked up. You can also change the stacking order of the acetate sheets. If you work with Adobe Photoshop, you'll find Painter's transparent layers familiar.

To add a new layer to an existing file, open the Objects palette (Windows, Show Objects) and click the left triangle on the Layers section bar to open this section. Click the right triangle on the section bar to access the Layers palette's pop-up menu, and choose New Layer. To paint on the new layer, choose any brush except a Water Color or Liquid Ink variant, target the layer in the Layers section and begin painting.

Layers offer great flexibility to digital illustrators. Some artists prefer to draw each item in an image on its own layer, which isolates the item so that it can be repositioned or painted on as an individual element. Transparent layers are also useful when creating *glazes*—thin, clear layers of color applied over existing color. (Turn to Chapter 5, "Using Layers and Shapes" to read more about painting and compositing techniques.)

PICKING UP COLOR

To bring color from underlying layers into a upper layer that you're painting on (and mix color on the active layer), turn on Pick Up Underlying Color in the Layers section.

IMPASTO AND CLONING

Here's a speedy Impasto illustration method. If there's not time to paint from scratch, choose a photo you'd like to use for reference. Make a clone (File, Clone). In the Brushes palette, choose an Impasto brush, such as the Smeary Round variant. Apply color and depth to the Impasto image based on color in the clone source by turning on the Clone Color option in the Colors section of the Art Materials palette.

ORIGINAL PHOTO: CORBIS IMAGES

Painting with Impasto using a custom Round Camelhair variant on a cloned file

THE LOOKS YOU LIKE

If you like the look of a particular brush-and-paper combination (for instance, the Square Chalk variant of Dry Media on Laid Pastel Paper), save the combo as a Brush Look so you can quickly call it up when you want to use it again. Before you can save a new Look, in Painter 7 it's necessary to select an area of an image that can be used as an icon for the Brush Look. In the Tools palette, choose the Rectangular Marquee tool and drag in the image to make a selection. Select the texture from the Papers section of the Art Materials palette and the brush variant from the Brushes palette. In the Brushes palette, from the Brush menu, choose Brush Looks, New Look. (You can also choose New Look from the pop-out menu on the right side of the Looks section bar in the Art Materials palette.) Naming your New Look saves it to the current Brush Look library, which is located in the Art Materials palette's Looks section. Open the section by clicking the left arrow on the Looks section bar. To paint with your new Brush Look, select it from the pop-up menu at the bottom of the Looks section.

Brush Looks are also useful with brushes that can paint with a source, such as the Graphic Paintbrush variant of the Brushes because you can save Brush Looks that include unique brush-and-pattern (or gradient) combinations. To try it out, choose the Graphic Paintbrush variant. In the Brush Controls:General section set the Source to Pattern With Mask. In the Art Materials:Patterns section, choose the Cherry Blossoms pattern.

A brushstroke painted with the Graphic Paintbrush (over a blue background) using the Cherry Blossoms pattern as the Source.

Building Brushes

Overview *Creating these custom brushes will give you insight into the workings of the palette sections that control them.*

Mixing color on the image canvas using the custom Camelhair Blender brush described on page 62

Brush Controls	
▶ General	Opacity 44%
▶ Size	Size 52.4
▶ Water	
▶ Spacing	
▶ Angle	
▶ Bristle	
▶ Impasto	
▶ Expression	Direction 0°
▶ Well	Bleed 0%
▶ Airbrush	Flow 672
▶ Rake	
▶ Random	Jitter 0.80
▶ Cloning	Clone Color Off
▶ Mouse	Pressure 100%
▶ Liquid Ink	

The Brush Controls palette contains most of the controls for customizing brushes. When closed, the palette displays important information about settings for the current brush—in this case, the Fine Spray variant of the Airbrushes.

PAINTER SHIPS WITH MANY NEW BRUSHES, and makes customizing them even easier than before. If you like trying new brushes but don't want to build them, check out the Brush libraries on the Wow! CD-ROM in the back of this book—you'll find the brushes shown on these pages and more. But if you enjoy creating your own brushes, read on. *Roses*, above, was painted with several of the custom brushes described here.

DAB TYPES

In Painter, brushstrokes are built from *dabs*. Painter 7 has 23 dab types, which fall into two general classifications: *Dab-based* brushes (such as the brushes in earlier versions of Painter) and brushes created with *Continuous Stroke* dab types. The main difference lies in how brushstrokes are created from the dabs as described in "Dab-Based Dab Types" (below) and "Continuous Stroke Dab Types" on pages 59–60. You can switch dab types by using the pop-up menu in the General section of the Brush Controls palette, opened by choosing Window, Show Brush Controls (Ctrl/⌘-7).

Dab-Based Brushes

For brushes that are *dab-based,* you can think of the dab as the footprint for the brush—a cross-section of its shape. The brush lays down a series of dabs of color to make a stroke. If the spacing is set tight the stroke will appear to be a continuous mark. If the spacing is loose, the stroke will be a series of footprints with space between them.

Circular. Many of Painter's brushes use this round dab type. (Don't be fooled by the term *Circular*; even if you change a brush's Squeeze setting in the Angle section of the Brush Controls palette so that its footprint looks elliptical, it's still a Circular brush.)

Choosing the Circular dab type in the General section of the Brush Controls palette

When you paint a stoke with a brush that has an airbrush-like conical spray (Airbrush, Pixel Airbrush or Line Airbrush dab type), you can tilt the stylus to apply paint more densely along the edge closest to the stylus. To switch the direction of the spray without changing the tilt of the stylus, hold down the Control/⌘-Alt/Option keys as you paint.

The Fine Spray variant of the Airbrushes is sensitive to tilt and bearing and sprays conic sections—similar to a beam of light projected onto the canvas—just like a traditional airbrush. Holding the stylus upright sprays a smaller, denser area of color (top right). Tilting the stylus sprays color wider and farther (top left). And holding down Alt/Option redirects the spray (bottom).

Single-Pixel. Just as it sounds, this is a 1-pixel-wide brush.

Static Bristle. Since Bristle brushes are made up of several "hairs," they have a rich potential. You can make adjustments in Bristle Thickness, Clumpiness and other settings in the Spacing and Bristle sections of the Brush Controls palette.

Captured. You can capture any area of a document to act as the footprint for a Captured brush. Use the Rectangular Selection tool and draw a marquee (press the Shift key if you want to constrain the selection to a perfect square) around a mark or group of markings. Go to the Brushes palette and choose Brush, Capture Brush; the brush footprint will appear in the Size section of the Brush Controls palette.

Continuous-Stroke Brushes

Brushes using *Continuous Stroke* dab types produce smoother-edged, more responsive brushstrokes because the strokes are computed as continuous anti-aliased 1-pixel lines during the stroke. Each line represents an individual brush hair.

Camel Hair. With Camel Hair dabs, you can build brushes with circular-shaped dabs that paint brushstrokes with obvious bristle marks. Brushes using the Camel Hair dab type (the Round Camelhair variant of Brushes, for example) are capable of painting very smoothly, and they can carry a different color on each brush hair.

Flat. Like it sounds, a flat dab is used to create a flat-tipped brush. With brushes using the Flat Dab Type, you can paint wide or narrow strokes, depending on the way you hold and move the stylus. The Opaque Flat variant of Brushes is an example.

For many brushes with continuous stroke dab types (Camel Hair, Flat, Palette Knife and Bristle Spray) you can control how many bristles apply paint. Simply move the Feature slider in the Size section of the Brush Controls palette. High Feature settings have a thinning effect.

For brushes with Airbrush dab types, you can use the Feature slider in the Size section of the Brush Controls palette to control the size of droplets. With a higher Feature setting, Airbrush dabs spray larger droplets.

Palette Knife. With Resat set low in the Well section of the Brush Controls palette, you can use brushes with Palette Knife dabs to scrape paint or move it around on the canvas. The Loaded Palette Knife and Palette Knife variants (Brushes) are examples.

Bristle Spray. Many brushes that use Bristle Spray dabs (such as the Opaque Bristle Spray variant of Brushes) paint like a cross between a real bristle brush and an airbrush. Use the controls in the Airbrush section of the Brush Controls palette to change the Spread and Flow of brushstrokes.

Click on the brush footprint in the Size section's Preview window to switch the view between "hard" (showing the maximum and minimum sizes) and "soft" (showing bristles).

The Size section of the Brush Controls palette showing a "soft" view of a Static Bristle dab used to create the Feathering Brush described on page 62.

Choosing the Rake stroke type in the General section of the Brush Controls palette

Brush Loading enables a brush to carry a unique color in each brush hair. Many of Painter's brushes have this capability already built into them—for instance, the Variable Round variant of the Brushes. (When Brush Loading is built into a brush, the Brush Loading checkbox is grayed out in the Well section of the Brush Controls palette.) To allow a static bristle brush (such as the Captured Bristle variant of the Brushes) or a dab-based brush from an earlier version of Painter to use Brush Loading, open the Well section of the Brush Controls palette and turn on Brush Loading.

Airbrush. Like Bristle Spray, Pixel Airbrush and Line Airbrush dab types, Airbrush dabs spray conic sections and they "understand" Bearing (which direction the stylus is leaning) and Angle (amount of tilt). (See "Redirecting the Spray" on page 59.)

Pixel Airbrush. Brushes using this dab type work like brushes using the Airbrush dab type. With the Pixel Airbrush dab type, however, the individual droplets *cannot* be adjusted using the Feature slider.

Line Airbrush. Brushes using the Line Airbrush dab type (such as the Furry Brush variant of F/X) spray lines instead of droplets.

Projected. The Projected dab-type brushes spray conic sections, similar to the Airbrush dab type, but without the responsiveness. For now, we recommend constructing brushes with the Airbrush and Pixel Airbrush dab types rather than a Projected dab type.

Rendered. In addition to painting with color, brushes built using Rendered dabs can contain a pattern or gradation as a Source. The Graphic Paintbrush variant of Brushes is an example. To change the Source used by a Rendered dab brush, use the Source pop-up menu in the General section of the Brush Controls palette.

Water Color dab types. The ten Water Color dab types were created for painting on Water Color media layers. These dabs are based on several of the rendered dab types discussed earlier—the Camel Hair, Flat, Bristle Spray, Palette Knife and Airbrush. For more information about working with Water Color, turn to "A Painter Water Color Primer," on page 70 of this chapter.

Liquid Ink dab types. Designed for painting on Liquid Ink media layers, there are ten Liquid Ink dab types. They're based on several of the rendered dab types: the Camel Hair, Flat, Bristle Spray, Palette Knife and Airbrush. To read more about Liquid Ink, turn to "A Liquid Ink Primer," on page 110.

STROKE TYPES

The *stroke* is the way a dab is applied over a distance. You can switch Stroke Types using the pop-up menu in the General section of the Brush Controls palette.

Single. Just as it sounds, Single stroke-type brushes have only one stroke path. Because of this, they're fast. If you use a Static Bristle, a Flat or Camel Hair dab type, you can create a fast Single stroke-type brush with a lot of complexity. Most Painter brushes incorporate the Single stroke type.

Multi. Painter's computation-intensive Multi stroke-type brushes can paint sensitive multicolored strokes, but are the least spontaneous of the program's brushes. The continuous-stroke brushes provide a much more responsive way to paint with multiple colors. Try drawing a line with the Gloopy variant of the Impasto.

TYPING THE SETTINGS

When changing settings for a brush, sometimes typing numerals into the fields is easier than trying to hit a point on the slider.

Most of the settings in the Brush Controls palette's sections can be typed in, as shown here in setting Brush Scale in the Rake section.

BUILDING AN IMPASTO BRUSH

You can add settings to any brush that will allow it to paint with thick Impasto paint. To set up a brush for Impasto, begin by choosing a brush (such as the Dry Ink variant of the Brushes). We used these settings in the Impasto section of the Brush Controls palette to build a Dry Ink Impasto brush: Draw To: Color and Depth; Depth Method: Uniform; Depth, 180%; Smoothing, 120% and Plow, 100%. To save your variant, from the Brushes palette's Variant menu choose Save Variant. To read more about Impasto turn to "Painting with Realistic Impasto" on page 53 and to "Working with Thick Paint," later in the chapter.

Painting thick Impasto brushstrokes with the custom Dry Ink Impasto brush

Instead of a stroke, you'll see a dotted "preview" line that shows its path; the stroke appears a moment later. Multi brushes are built from several randomly distributed dabs that may or may not overlap. The Gloopy variant of Impasto is the only example of a Multi stroke brush in the Painter 7 default brush library. But lovely, variable strokes can be made using custom Multi brushes. To spread the strokes of a Multi-stroke brush, increase the Jitter setting in the Random section of the Brush Controls palette.

Rake. The Rake stroke type is like a garden rake; each of the evenly spaced tines is a bristle of the brush. Painter gives you a lot of control over the bristles; for instance, you can make them overlap, which makes it possible to create wonderfully complex, functional brushes. And you can change the number of Bristles (keeping in mind that fewer bristles make faster brushes). In the Rake section of the Brush Controls palette, you can also adjust the way the bristles interact. To try out an existing Rake brush, paint with the Van Gogh variant of the Artists brush.

Hose. The Hose stroke type sprays a variety of images when you paint each stroke. To read about painting with the Image Hose turn to "Creating a Tidepool" in Chapter 7 of this book and to Chapter 9, "The Image Hose," in the *Painter 7 User Guide*.

BUILDING CUSTOM BRUSHES

For the custom brushes that follow, we start with an existing Painter brush and radically modify its appearance by making adjustments that affect brush behavior. After you've created the brush (and perhaps made further modifications on your own), you will want to choose Variant, Save Variant from the Brushes palette's menu to save it into your current palette. After saving your custom variant under a new name, restore the default settings for the Painter brush by selecting the variant you began with and choosing Variant, Restore Default Variant.

Try these brushes on images of 1000 pixels square or less. If you work with larger files, you'll want to proportionally increase the Size slider settings that we list here. When a Circular or Static Bristle dab type is used, you'll also want to optimize the Spacing

BRUSHES THAT SMEAR

Do you want a brush to pull and smear color? A low Resat and a high Bleed setting (in the Well section of the Brush Controls palette) will work with Brush Loading to allow the brush to smear pigment while applying it. Choose the Variable Flat variant of the Brushes, and in the Well section, set Resat at 5% and Bleed at 80%. To see the colors mix, choose a new color in the Colors section and drag the brush through existing color on your image.

SCRUBBING EXISTING COLOR

To make a brush that applies color when you use a light touch and scrubs underlying color when you use heavier pressure, in the Well section of Brush Controls, set Resat low and in the Expression section, turn on the Invert box for Resat.

Modulating color on the background with the Soft Oils brush

Using the Feathering brush to layer color on the flower petals and background

Using the Camelhair Blender brush to mix color on the petals and in the background

and Min Spacing in the Brush Controls palette's Spacing section to accommodate the larger size. If you have trouble setting exact numbers with the sliders, try typing the number into the field to the right of the slider. Hit the Enter key to accept the number you've typed. And don't think your computer has crashed if nothing happens for a while when you try to paint: Painter is working away, building a very complex brush.

To make room for more brushes, we've shortened our descriptions of how to make the brushes. For instance, "*Well:* Resat, 80%" means, "In the Brush Controls palette's Well section set Resat to 80% but leave all other sliders where they are." The palette sections you will use are found in the Brush Controls palette. For a full description of the functions of the controls in each of the sections, you can refer to Painter's *User Guide*, although painting with the brush after you make each adjustment will teach you a lot, too. **Caution:** Before starting a brush recipe with a suggested brush, restore its default settings by choosing Variant, Restore Default Variant from the Brushes palette's menu.

Soft Oils Brush. This Single stroke-type brush was created to feel like a traditional soft, flat brush with long bristles.

Start with the default Opaque Flat variant of the Brushes. *Size:* Size, 31.2; Min Size, 42%; Feature: 5.1. *General:* Opacity, 100. *Well:* Resat, 70; Bleed, 40. *Expression:* Size/Pressure; Opacity/Pressure. *Random:* Jitter .05. In the Art Materials palette, *Color Variability:* ±H, 1; ±V, 3.

Feathering Brush. Created for feathering over existing color to add interest and texture, this Single stroke, Bristle brush paints tapered strokes quickly. Increase pressure to widen the stroke.

Start with the default Captured Bristle variant of the Brushes. *Size:* Size, 23.0; Min Size, 30%. *General:* Opacity, 9. *Spacing:* Spacing, 9. *Well:* Resat and Dryout, maximum; Bleed, 0; *Bristle:* Thickness, 40; Clumpiness, 0 (for smooth strokes), Hair Scale, 515. *Expression:* Size/Pressure; in the Art Materials palette, *Color Variability:* ±H, 1; ±V, 2.

Camelhair Blender Brush. The *Well* section settings for this Single-stroke, Camel Hair brush let you pick up existing color and blend with it. The brush hairs spread with more pressure, because Feature is set to Pressure in the Expression section.

Start with the default Round Camelhair variant of the Brushes. *Size:* Size, 23; Min Size, 37%; Feature, 4.1. *General:* Opacity, 100. *Well:* Resat, 4%; Bleed, 96%. *Expression:* Feature/Pressure.

Soft Runny Wash Water Color. This round Water Color brush paints smoother runny washes with soft edges.

QUICKER CAPTURES

When you want to design and capture a brush, start by opening a variant that's close to the effect you want. That way you'll have fewer adjustments to make.

Brushstrokes made with the Soft Runny Wash Water Color brush

Brushstrokes made with the Thick Bristle Liquid Ink brush

A footprint and brushstrokes made with the Tiny Spattery Airbrush

A footprint and brushstroke made with the Graduated Hairy brush

Footprints and brushstrokes made with the Random Leaves brush

Start with the default Runny Wash Bristle variant of Water Color. *Water:* Pickup, 11%; Dry Rate, 10%; Evap Thres, 83%; Cap Factor, 0. Turn on Accurate Diffusion.

Thick Bristle Liquid Ink. This Liquid Ink brush paints a large volume of Liquid Ink with thick bristles. To access the volume setting, double-click on the Liquid Ink layer in the Layers section and increase the Amount setting to about 80%.

Start with the default Smooth Bristle variant of Liquid Ink. *Liquid Ink:* Volume, 403; Bristle Frac, 60; Rand Br Vol, 86.

Tiny Spattery Airbrush. This spatter brush with the Airbrush dab type sprays small droplets with subtle Color Variability.

Start with the default Variable Splatter variant of the Airbrushes. *Size:* Size, 34.5; Min Size, 0%; Feature, 2.9. *General:* Opacity, 75. *Expression:* Size/Pressure. *Random:* Jitter 0.50. In the Art Materials palette, *Color Variability:* ±H, 5; ±S, 5; ±V, 10.

Graduated Hairy Brush. With this special-effects brush you can paint fur or grass effects that have graduated color. First, choose a multicolor gradient (such as the Golden Sunset gradient) in the Gradients section of the Art Materials palette. Start with the Furry Brush variant of the F-X brush. *Size:* Min Size, 33%. *General:* Source, Gradient. *Spacing:* Turn off Continuous Time Deposition. *Expression:* Opacity/None. *Random*, Jitter 3.00. In the Art Materials palette, *Color Variability:* ±V, 0.

Random Leaves Brush. This Captured, Single-stroke brush with variable color and random size and direction is useful for texturizing—adding a natural look of random fallen leaves to a painting. It looks richest when used over a rough paper texture.

To create the brush dab, use the Fine Point variant of the Pens to make a few simple leaf shapes—similar to the footprint shown—then switch to the Flat Color variant and capture the brush (see "Captured," on page 59). *Size:* Size, 25.3; Min Size, 60%. *General:* Subcategory, Grainy Hard Cover; Opacity, 90%; Grain 14%. *Spacing:* Spacing, Maximum; Min Spacing, Maximum. *Expression:* Size/Random; Opacity/Random. In the Art Materials palette, *Color Variability:* ±H, 20; ±V, 7.

> **CONTINUOUS MEDIA FLOW**
>
> Thanks to Continuous Time Deposition, you can set up any brush to apply media at the first touch; if you continue to press the stylus, media will pool. Most of Painter's Airbrushes incorporate Continuous Time Deposition, but you can also turn on this feature for a variant that does not. For example, select the Digital Airbrush variant of the Airbrushes, and in the Spacing section of the Brush Controls palette, turn on Continuous Time Deposition.

Sketching with Pencils

Overview *Draw a loose sketch with Pencils variants; scribble and crosshatch to develop tones; brighten highlights with an Eraser.*

CHER THREINEN-PENDARVIS

Making a stroke in the Brush Tracking window

The loose composition sketch

Adding tones to the background and values to the faces

Darker tones and more texture have been added to the background and the faces.

LOOSE, EXPRESSIVE SKETCHES CAN BE DRAWN with the Painter's Pencils variants, with a look that's similar to traditional tools, as shown in this drawing of *Soshi and Pearl.*

1 Setting Brush Tracking. Pencil sketching often involves rapid, gestural movements with the stylus so it's important to set up Brush Tracking before you begin to sketch. With Brush Tracking you can customize how Painter interprets the input of your stylus, including parameters such as pressure and how quickly you make a brushstroke. Choose Edit, Preferences, Brush Tracking and make a representative brushstroke in the window.

2 Beginning to sketch. Create a new image file (File, New). (Ours measured 1100 x 600 pixels). Click OK. In the Papers section of the Art Materials palette, select an even-textured paper such as Basic Paper and select the Pencils category, 2B Pencil variant in the Brushes palette. The default 2B Pencil uses the Buildup method, which means that color you draw is semitransparent and will darken to black, just like when you draw with a conventional 2B graphite pencil. Select a dark gray in the Colors section and draw a line sketch that will establish the negative and positive shapes in your composition.

3 Building tones and modeling form. To bring the subjects forward in the picture frame, add dark values behind them. Make crosshatched strokes with the 2B Pencil to create the darker tones. Keep your strokes loose, and gestural. Lively stroke patterns will add texture interest to your drawing. To model the faces and bodies of the cats, we used the Oily Variable Pencil, which smeared the pencil slightly as we scribbled and crosshatched. The Oily Variable Pencil incorporates the Cover method, which means that the color you draw is opaque; a lighter color will paint over a darker color.

For highlights, choose white in the Colors section and switch to the Cover Pencil variant in the Brushes palette. The Cover Pencil is ideal for adding highlights because it covers previous strokes without smearing. To clean up areas, choose the Eraser variant (Erasers). A tiny Eraser also works well for brightening highlights.

Drawing with Colored Pencils

Overview *Create a sketch with the Colored Pencils variant; customize the brush to further develop the drawing; adjust Color Variability settings for a more active color effect.*

CHER THREINEN-PENDARVIS

The line sketch drawn with Colored Pencil

Developing values   Adding color

Building dimension using increased settings in the Art Materials:Color Variability section and strokes that follow the form

YOU CAN MODIFY THE COLORED PENCIL variant and get a broken color effect (where the color only partially covers the background or underdrawing) by brushing lightly across a textured surface.

1 Starting with a sketch. To work at the same size we did, open a new 883 pixel-wide file with a white background, then choose the Basic texture from the Art Materials, Papers section. Choose a dark brown color in the Colors section, select the Colored Pencils variant of the Pencils and sketch the portrait.

2 Developing value and adding color. In the Brush Controls, General section, change the Colored Pencil's method to Cover and the subcategory to Grainy Edge Flat Cover. In the Size section, set Size to 3.4 and Min Size to 42%. Use this brush and a lighter brown to develop values throughout the sketch. Choose a skin color (we chose a tan for this portrait of Steve Pendarvis) and apply strokes with a light touch to partially cover some of the brown sketch. Follow the form with your strokes, switching colors and brush sizes as you draw.

3 Building dimension. To give a shimmery look to the color as it's applied, drag the Hue (± H) and Value (± V) sliders in the Art Materials, Color Variability section to 3%. Using a light touch to allow the underpainting to show through, apply a fresh layer of strokes in the areas of strongest color (in our drawing, the forehead and nose shadows and the hair).

COLORED PENCIL WASHES

If you're using Colored Pencils on rough paper, you can create a wash effect. Choose the Grainy Water variant of the Liquid brush, reducing Opacity and Grain penetration in the Controls:Brush palette to 40% or less. Stroke over your pencil work to blend colors while maintaining texture on the "peaks" of the paper grain.

Blending and Feathering with Pastels

Overview *Set up a still life, sketch from life with pastels; build color and form; blend the painting; add feathered brushstrokes to finish.*

FEATHERING—THIN, PARALLEL STROKES over a blended underpainting—is a traditional pastel technique that yields texture and freshness. Because the feathered finishing strokes remain unblended on the painting's surface, the viewer's eye must work to blend the colors. Here is an example of optical color blending.

1 Starting with a sketch on colored paper. We set up a still life on a table in the side light of a window, arranging the cloth so that diagonal folds would lead the eye into the composition and give the painting more depth.

When we were satisfied with the still life design, we opened a new file (File, New: 3 x 3.3 inches x 300 ppi) with a rust-colored background. To set the Paper Color, click the Paper Color preview in the New window and choose a color in the Select Paper Color dialog box. To select a new hue, or adjust its saturation, click or drag in the color wheel. To make the color darker or lighter, adjust the value slider near the bottom of the window. When you have a color that you like, click OK to accept it. Now select Sanded Pastel Board paper texture from the Papers section of the Art Materials palette. Pick a color to sketch with from the Colors section of the Art Materials palette (we began with a golden yellow). Select the Artist Pastel Chalk variant of Dry Media. For a more sensitive response when using your stylus, choose Edit, Preferences, Brush Tracking, make a representative brushstroke in the window, and click OK. Begin to roughly sculpt the shape of the

1a

Choosing a paper color

1b

Loosely sketching with the Artist Pastel Chalk variant of Dry Media

2

Painting angled strokes of varied color on the background

3

Blending color on the apple using the Grainy Water

4

Using feathered strokes to bring out highlights and color variations on the apple

apple and suggest a horizon line (in our case, the angled table top) and then rough in the background, choosing new colors as needed.

2 Blocking in color over the sketch. Still working with the Artist Pastel Chalk, lay in more color over your sketch, allowing your strokes to follow the direction of the form.

3 Softening brush work. Select the Grainy Water variant of Liquid, and blend areas of color, again following the direction of the form. To blend while revealing more paper texture, blend colors with the Smudge variant of Liquid.

4 Building the underpainting. Using the Artist Pastel Chalk variant add color and value to your sketch. To smear existing paint as you add new color, try the Oil Pastel variant of Dry Media. We also used the Grainy Water variant of Liquid again to selectively blend areas. Layer the color and blend the underpainting until you're pleased with the form. We quickly added brown and purple colors to the background using angled brushstrokes. Then we painted more varied greens on the table cloth, and gave the wrinkles in the cloth more dimension.

5 Adding feathered strokes and detail. To create thin, textured strokes on top of the blended forms, decrease the Size of the Artist Pastel Chalk variant to 4.2 in the Brush Controls palette's Size section, and in the Expression section, set Size to Pressure. Stroke with this brush in the direction of the form. In our example, feathering is most noticeable in the highlight areas of the apple, in the reddish color overlaid over the apple's golden color, and in the foreground table cloth. Finish the piece by using Grainy Water to soften the feathering in the shadow areas. (To do the final blending touches, we lowered the Grainy Water variant's Opacity to 40% in the General section of the Brush Controls palette.) We also used a tiny Sharp Chalk to deepen the shadow under the apple.

5a

Adding more texture and shadow to the table cloth

5b

The apple with the shadows more defined and with deeper reddish colors added

Painting with Pastels

Overview *Rough out a color composition; add layers of color with a custom Large Chalk; blend colors with Liquid brushes; add highlights and details with the Sharp Chalk; use "scumbling" for texture to finish.*

CHER THREINEN-PENDARVIS

1a

Sketching in color with the Sharp Chalk variant of Dry Media

1b

Blending the hill and sky using the Smudge variant of the Liquid brush

2a

Adjusting the settings in the Controls: Brush palette

2b

Painting the sunlight shining over the ridge with a custom Large Chalk and yellow color

INSPIRED BY THE SPARKLING LIGHT on a moist, breezy morning, *Agave Meadow* was painted from memory using Painter's Dry Media, although we occasionally referred to pencil sketches made on location. To achieve the soft atmosphere, we painted layers of color with Chalk variants, blended color with Liquid brushes, and added details and broken color to finish the piece.

1 Starting with the drawing. Choose a photo or a sketch of a landscape to use as a reference and open a new file. We started with a 30 x 19.5-inch file at 120 ppi.

Open the Art Materials palette by choosing Window, Show Art Materials and choose a color in the Colors section. In the Papers section of the Art Materials palette, choose a medium-grained paper, such as Sanded Pastel Board. Select Dry Media in the Brushes palette, choose the Sharp Chalk variant and begin sketching. To keep the freshness and energy of a sketch while you draw, don't get bogged down with details. We also used the Artist Pastel Chalk to add cross-hatching to the hills and the Smudge variant of Liquid to blend colors.

2 Building a custom Pastel variant. When you've finished sketching your composition and you're ready to layer color in the underpainting, create a midsized, soft Pastel variant: First choose the Large Chalk variant of Dry Media. In the Controls:Brush palette, set the Size to 12.0, and lower the Opacity to 30%. A lower opacity will allow you to build up color slowly with more sensitivity. To save this custom brush as a variant, choose Variant, Save Variant from the Brushes palette, name your variant and click OK. The new name will appear in the Brushes palette under the Dry Media category. Choose a color and begin painting. We adjusted our new variant's size and opacity as we worked, switching to a 50% opacity, for instance, when painting the sunrise light shining over the ridge of the hill.

3

Using the Grainy Water variant to "melt" the hill separation, and create a subtle line

4

Using the custom Large Chalk variant to paint "windy" hatching strokes on the hills

5

Scumbling on the path with the Square Chalk variant

6a

Drawing the foreground grass blades and details on the acacia with the Sharp Chalk

6b

Painting the highlights on the agave plants using the Artist Pastel Chalk variant

3 Blending colors. To achieve a smooth look with traditional pastels, you rub them with precise blending tools like a tortillion or a blending stump. Use the Just Add Water, Grainy Water, and Smudge variants of the Liquid brush to mimic these traditional tools. A few hints about these blenders: The Just Add Water uses the Soft Cover subcategory, and blends smoothly without texture; Grainy Water use Grainy Flat Cover and blends showing a hint of texture; Smudge uses Grainy Hard Cover and reveals more texture as it blends color. Begin blending, and experiment with these brushes and various brush sizes while you work.

4 Achieving a feeling of movement. Select the Pastel variant you created in step 2. Imagine the wind blowing over your landscape, and apply light strokes over the hills in your painting, as if your strokes were blown by the wind. We switched to a rougher paper texture, (Big Canvas texture, loaded from the More Paper Textures library, in the Paper Texture Libraries folder on the Painter_CD2 CD-ROM), then added gold, rust-colored and blue strokes to the mid-ground hills and lighter blues to the sky. We covered most of the rolling coastal hills with soft, linear brushstrokes.

5 Scumbling for more texture. Artists using traditional media will often finish a pastel drawing by brushing the side of the pastel lightly along the peaks of the rough art paper. This technique, called *scumbling*, causes colors to blend optically and adds texture. To scumble electronically, select the Large Chalk variant and adjust Opacity to 25% (Controls:Brush palette). Choose a rough paper (Big Canvas). In the Brush Controls' Size section, (opened by clicking the left triangle on the Size section bar) select the lower left brush tip profile. Apply strokes lightly using a color sampled from your image with the Dropper. We used scumbling to complete the sky and clouds and to show subtle reflected light on the foreground path. To add a semi-transparent texture to the plant life in the foreground, we switched to the Grainy Soft Cover subcategory.

6 Finishing with fine details. After adding the scumbling, we added fine details, such as the thin foreground grass blades and the planes of the agave leaves that were illuminated by full sunlight.

To draw grass blades we chose the Sharp Chalk variant and a light greenish-gold color in the Colors section. Before we began to paint, we opened the Color Variability section of the Art Materials palette and adjusted the Value (± V) to 4% so the color would vary slightly as we painted. We painted thin, slightly curved strokes (keeping the wind direction in mind). We made a few strokes overlap and adjusted the size of the strokes using the Size slider on the Controls:Brush palette.

To enhance the focal point of the painting, we painted bright highlights on the sides of the agave leaves that were catching the direct morning sun. For the highlights we chose a light golden yellow, and painted curved strokes with the Artist Pastel Chalk, using it at its full opacity.

A Painter Watercolor Primer

Overview *Here you'll find the basics for painting with Painter 7's new Water Color brushes and layers.*

CHER THREINEN-PENDARVIS

Two brushstrokes painted with the Diffuse Grainy Camel variant of Water Color: 100% Contrast, the default (top), and painting with 0% Contrast (bottom)

PAINTER 7'S NEW WATER COLOR MEDIA LAYERS not only allow more realistic representation of watercolor but also allow an artist to enjoy a more natural watercolor experience. The Water Color layer is a simulation of a transparent wet medium containing suspended pigment. This makes it possible to create smooth, transparent washes and then diffuse color into existing wet paint to blend, as a traditional watercolorist would.

Red Hibiscus (above), is one of a series of flower studies painted using the technique presented step-by-step in "Combining Wet-into-Wet and Glazing on Layers" on page 78. But before you start using Water Color, reading these four pages will help you to understand how to achieve the results you desire.

Controlling Water Color. You can control the wetness, drying time, direction of where your wash will run and many other technique that you're able to achieve using conventional watercolor tools. The most important settings for Water Color are in several palette sections: the General, Size, and Water sections of the Brush Controls palette; the Papers section of the Art Materials palette; and the Layers section of the Objects palette. When you make a brushstroke with a Water Color brush, a Water Color layer is automatically generated in the Layers section. Water Color layers can be targeted in the Layers section and edited like other layers. Chapter 5 tells more about working with layers.

AN ANIMATED WATER DROP

When you use a Water Color brush to create a new Water Color layer in the Layers section of the Objects palette, you'll notice a water drop icon (to the left of the Layer name) that identifies the layer. When you paint a brushstroke, the animated water drop "drips" until the Water Color pigment has settled.

These two brushstrokes were painted with the Dry Bristle brush. The top stroke uses the default brush settings. For the bottom stroke, the Feature size was increased to 8.0 in the Size section of the Brush Controls palette, which resulted in a brushstroke with fewer brush hairs.

The Water section of the Brush Controls palette contains controls for modifying Water Color brushes.

The menu on the right side of the Layers section bar offers useful options for working with Water Color layers: New Water Color Layer, Lift Canvas to Water Color Layer, Wet Entire Water Color Layer, and Dry Entire Water Color layer.

In the General section of the Brush Controls palette, the Water Color dab types are displayed in the Dab Type pop-up menu. A dab type determines the shape of the brush—for instance, Water Color Flat and Water Color Camel (round). Most of the Water Color brushes use continuous-stroke technology, which means that brushstrokes are painted using brush hairs that are a set of anti-aliased 1-pixel lines. You'll find more information about dab types in "Building Brushes" on page 58 of this chapter.

In the Size section of Brush Controls, you'll find the Feature slider, which determines the density of the brush hairs in the continuous-stroke brushes. **Note:** A very low Feature setting (producing more densely packed brush hairs), takes greater computing power and this can slow down the performance of a Water Color brush.

In the Water section of the Brush Controls palette, *Wetness* works with Evaporation Threshold to control the amount and spread of the *water* and *dye*. A low Evaporation Threshold will allow more spread; higher values will cause less spread. A high Wetness setting will blur the individual bristle marks and (with a high Diffusion Amount setting) increase the spread of the stroke, but it may make the performance of the brush lag. *Pickup* controls the amount of existing paint that gets moved when a new brushstroke paints over existing pigment. High Pickup rates cause wet edges or puddles, which can be desirable. The *Dry Rate* controls the length of time the water and pigment take to settle. A high Dry Rate will keep a brush with high Diffusion Amount settings from spreading as far, because the stroke will dry before it has had time to diffuse. A low Dry Rate value will allow more time for spread. *Evaporation Threshold* controls the amount of *water* that can diffuse. (In traditional watercolor, evaporation is the rate in which liquid is sublimated into the atmosphere.) *Diffusion Amount* controls the amount of *pigment* that can diffuse. *Capillary Factor* and *Grain Soak-In* affect the amount of pigment that settles in the valleys of the paper grain. Setting both of these controls to 0 will

With Accurate Diffusion off, larger cells are visible when a brushstroke is made. Accurate Diffusion allows finer detail and a more natural-looking diffusion of pigment into the Water Color layer. But it may cause a slight decline in brush responsiveness. Accurate Diffusion is off by default.

Two brushstrokes painted with the Diffuse Camel variant of Water Color (brushstrokes shown at 200%). Accurate Diffusion was turned off when the top stroke was painted and turned on for the bottom stroke.

A smooth wash (top), and thick and thin flower petal shapes (bottom), painted with the Wash Camel variant of Water Color

A smooth stroke painted The Wash Bristle (top) and diffused strokes with wet edges, painted with the Wet Bristle (bottom). The variation in color is caused by pigment build-up.

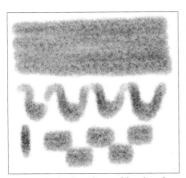

These soft-edged washes and brushstrokes were painted with the Diffuse Flat.

These crisper, expressive strokes were painted with the Wash Pointed Flat.

minimize grain effects. Also, very low Capillary Factor and Grain Soak-In settings will allow a runny wash to spread more smoothly. A high Capillary Factor (with a low Grain Soak-In setting) will create a "stringy" drip texture in the runny wash.

GETTING TO KNOW THE WATER COLOR BRUSHES.

Here are some suggestions for how to paint traditional-looking brush work using Painter 7's new Water Color brushes. Even if you're familiar with using a stylus and Painter's other brushes, try these exercises and experiment with all of the water color brushes. You may enjoy discovering a new kind of expressive brushstroke!

Versatility with Camel brushes. The most versatile of all the Water Color brushes, the Camel brushes, are round. In addition to painting various kinds of washes, most Camel brushes allow you to paint brushstrokes that can be thick and thin, depending on the pressure applied to the stylus. Other Camel brushes allow you to apply drippy washes (Runny Wash Camel and Runny Wet Camel), while the Diffuse Camel paints strokes that have soft, feathery edges.

Choose the Wash Camel variant of Water Color and paint a smooth wash area. Apply even pressure to your stylus, and make a horizontal stroke, then carefully paint a second horizontal stroke below it, just slightly overlapping the first stroke. The diffusion in the stroke edge will help make a smooth transition between the strokes. Before painting thick to thin strokes, set Brush Tracking (Edit, Preferences, Brush Tracking). Using the Wash Camel, press harder to paint the thicker area of the shape, then gradually reduce pressure on the stylus, finally lifting your stylus as you complete the stroke.

Expressive brush work with Bristle brushes. These Water Color brushes paint just like brushes with real bristles because they're sensitive to tilt and rotation of the stylus. As you tilt your stylus, the bristles of the brush spread or splay out as you rotate your hand through the stroke. To paint a wash that has the texture of soft bristle marks, try the Wash Bristle brush. For a wet-into-wet effect with subtle bristle marks and pools at the stroke edges experiment with the Wet Bristle.

Thick and thin strokes with the Flat brushes. Look for brushes with the word Flat in their name; the Diffuse Flat and Wash Pointed Flat are examples. With Flat-tipped brushes, you can paint wide or narrow strokes, depending on the way you hold the stylus and how much pressure you apply. When trying the strokes below, position your stylus with the button facing up (away from you). To paint a fuzzy wash with the Diffuse Flat (as in the image on the left), pull the brush straight across your image using even pressure. To make the thin lines, pull down. To make a curved, thin-to-thick wavy line, use light pressure on your stylus for the thin top areas, and more pressure as you sweep down and rotate the brush.

For flat brushstrokes with crisper edges and more thin-to-thick control, try the Wash Pointed Flat. For a thin-to-thick sweeping

The Fine variants are useful when painting expressive, linear brushstrokes, as in the sketches of the eye and grasses shown here.

We painted this cloud study using the Runny Wash Bristle and Runny Wet Camel to paint the clouds, the Wash Camel and Fine Camel variants to paint the water and the Diffuse Camel to soften a few edges.

For this foliage study we created texture in the foreground with a small Splatter Water brush.

As a final touch to Pink Orchid, *we used the Eraser Salt variant of Water Color to sprinkle light speckles on the tops of the petals*

curved stroke, begin the thin portion with very light pressure on your stylus, and as you sweep downward rotate your stylus slightly (changing the button orientation) and apply more pressure. To make a thick, even stroke, pull the stylus sideways relative to the button, using even pressure. For the thin lines, apply even pressure and pull in a direction toward or away from the button.

Adding detail with the Fine brushes. The Fine variants of the Water Color brush are good for painting details, and for calligraphic line work. The Fine Camel and Fine Bristle are similar to "rigger" or "line" brushes, which are used to paint expressive line work in traditional watercolor.

Painting runny washes using the Runny brushes. The *Runny* variants (the Runny Wash Bristle and the Runny Wash Camel, for instance), are useful for painting drippy wet-into-wet washes, where the colors run together and blend, but they don't displace the underlying color. The *Runny Wet* variants, however, will run and move existing color as the new pigment travels. The Runny Wet brushes are useful if you want to add a darker wet-looking edge to the bottom of a cloud, for instance.

For all of the Runny Wash and Runny Wet brushes, the Wind Direction and Force settings determine the direction of the run and how far a wash will run, much like tipping your watercolor board when working in the field. To paint a Water Color Runny wash that only moves a little ways, lower the Force setting.

While painting the clouds in the illustration on the left, we laid varied sky colors in using the Runny Wash Bristle and Runny Wet Camel. To soften some of the runny edges, we dotted in more color using the Diffuse Camel, applying color with short dabbing strokes. Then we painted the water with the Wash Camel and Fine Camel variants, again softening areas with the Diffuse Camel.

Adding spatter effects. With the Splatter Water variant, you can add dots of diffused color interest to your paintings. This is especially effective when painting foliage. Paint some wash areas using the Wash Camel or Wash Flat, and varied colors of green. Now choose the Splatter Water variant and a slightly different color. Paint a few dots of color, then change the color slightly in the Colors section and add a few more diffused color dots, changing the size of the brush as you work.

Also, you can add varied, light speckles to your images (as we did in the image on the left), with the Eraser Salt variant of Water Color. To follow the step-by-step technique used for painting the orchid, turn to Wet-Into-Wet Water Color on page 74.

To follow the step-by-step technique used for painting the orchid, turn to Wet-Into-Wet Water Color on page 74.

ERASING WATER COLOR

You can lighten areas of color using the Eraser variants of Water Color. To smoothly erase color, choose white in the Colors section of the Art Materials palette and choose the Eraser Dry variant of Water Color. Stroke over the area that you'd like to remove.

Wet-into-Wet Watercolor

Overview *Make a "pencil sketch"; loosely paint smooth washes with Water Color brushes to build up varied color; add subtle wet-into-wet bristle marks; add details to the image and create a speckled texture using Salt.*

CHER THREINEN-PENDARVIS

Starting a new file for the Orchid painting

The pencil sketch drawn in Painter using the 2B Pencil variant of Pencils

PINK ORCHID, A LOOSE DIGITAL WATER COLOR STUDY, was painted from life in Painter 7 with a Wacom Intuos pressure-sensitive tablet and stylus. Water Color wet-into-wet techniques were used, then details and texture were added. *Wet-into-wet* is a traditional technique that can be simulated using Painter 7's new Water Color technology. Wet-into-wet is the most fluid way to apply color, as it involves keeping the paper wet while new color is applied, so new colors blend with existing moist paint. Painter 7 offers the flexibility of new Water Color media layers, making the medium much more versatile than in previous versions of the program.

1 Setting up and opening a new file. For the best performance, Macintosh users may need to increase the RAM that is allotted to Painter when working with Water Color.

Begin by creating a new file with a white background (File, New). In the New dialog box, click the Image button. For a square format, set the Width and Height at 675 x 675 pixels. Click OK. (The brush sizes that you'll use will depend on the pixel size of the document.)

2 Making a pencil sketch. Choose a natural-looking grain (such as Cold Press Water Color) from the Papers section of the Art Materials palette. Choose a neutral gray color in the Colors section of the Art Materials palette and select the 2B Pencils variant of Pencils (in the Brushes palette) to draw your line sketch. We set up our blooming orchid plant next to the computer and sketched from life.

3a

Painting smooth washes using the Wash Camel variant

3b

An active Water Color layer shown in the Layers section of the Objects palette

3c

The smooth, light-colored washes

4a

Using the Wash Camel variant to add deeper colors

It's a good idea to set up Brush Tracking before you begin a Water Color session because it will increase expressiveness in Painter's brushes and make smoother strokes. With Brush Tracking you can customize how Painter interprets the input of your stylus, including parameters such as pressure and how quickly you make a brush stroke. You'll notice the more sensitive control of the Water Color brushes, especially with brushes such as the Diffuse Camel and Fine Camel variants. Choose Edit, Preferences, Brush Tracking, make a representative brush stroke in the window, then click OK.

Making a brush stroke in the Brush Tracking window

3 Painting the first washes. The brush work in the *Pink Orchid* study is loose and spontaneous. As you prepare to begin adding color, make a few loose, practice brushstrokes. (You can always undo the brushstrokes by pressing Ctrl/⌘-Z, or you can delete your practice Water Color layer by selecting it in the Layers section of the Objects palette and clicking the Delete button on the palette).

Plan to work from light-to-dark as you add color washes to your painting. Choose a light color in the Colors section of the Art Materials palette (we chose a light lavender-pink). In the Brushes palette, choose the Wash Camel variant of Water Color. (When you select a Water Color brush and make a brush stroke on your image, Painter will automatically create a new Water Color layer in the image.) When you apply a light, even pressure on your stylus, the Wash Camel will allow you to lay in the wash areas smoothly. The slight bit of diffusion built into the brush will help the brush strokes to blend subtly as you paint. When you make a new stroke, place it next to the previous stroke so that it barely overlaps. Try not to scrub with the brush or paint over areas too many times, unless you want to darken the area. Painter's Water Color operates like traditional transparent Water Color.

Paint with strokes that follow the direction of the forms in your subject. Complete the lightest wash areas, leaving some of the "white of the paper" showing through for the highlights.

4 Building up the midtones on the flower. Using medium-value colors, begin to develop your midtones, painting lighter colors first, then adding darker tones to continue to develop the form. Keep your light source in mind and let your strokes follow

4b

Continuing to develop the mid tones with the Wash Camel variant

4c

Painting bristle marks with the Dry Camel variant. The reddish color was added with the Wash Camel variant.

5

The drippy washes on the lower petals were painted with the Runny Wash variants of Water Color

the direction of the forms. To resize the brush, or change its Opacity as you work, use the slider on the Controls:Brush palette (Window, Show Controls, or press Ctrl/⌘-5). We added deeper colors of lavender-pink, while keeping the brush work loose.

We continued to gradually build up deeper color. As we completed the midtones stage, we switched to the Dry Camel variant of Water Color, which allowed us to add a little more brush stroke texture over some of the wash areas and at the ends of the strokes, while still allowing the new strokes to blend as wet-into-wet.

5 Painting wet-into-wet runny washes. Painter 7 offers dynamic brushes that allow you to emulate various traditional Water Color *run* effects. For a smooth runny wash that will not displace the underlying color, use one of the Runny Wash variants. Choose a slightly different color in the Colors section and dab the new color on to areas with existing color. Using the Runny Wash Camel and Runny Wash Bristle, we applied brighter pink and magenta colors (using short dabbing strokes) on the deeper color areas of the flower petals. Then we added deeper pink and reddish colors to the interior of the orchid. The Runny Wash variants allowed the new color to mix with existing color without moving the existing color.

6 Editing a Water Color layer or the sketch. It's not possible to use a variant of the

The *Runny* variants of Water Color (the Runny Wash Bristle and the Runny Wash Camel, for instance), are useful for painting *wash runs*, where colors run together and blend, but don't displace the underlying color. This is similar to a glazing effect. The *Runny Wet* variants, however, will run and displace existing color on the image as the new pigment travels. Often the Runny Wet brushes will leave a lighter area because the Wet variants cause leaching of the existing pigment. The Runny Wet brushes are useful if you want to add darker wet-looking edges to foliage or when painting a sky with rain clouds.

The default Runny Wet Bristle variant of Water Color paints strokes that run vertically down the image and move existing color. The Dry Rate is set at 10%, allowing lots of time for the pant to run, the Wind Direction is set to 270,° and the Force setting (71%), makes the washes drip a long way. The high Pickup rate allows the brush strokes to move existing color.

ON WATER COLOR TIME

Keep in mind that Painter 7's Water Color is based on traditional Water Color painting. With traditional water color, an artist plans on time for the paint to spread, run and dry, and this time is often used to analyze and improve the composition of the painting. Painter's new Water Color technology uses a lot of computing power. It takes time for the digital pigment to diffuse and settle on the image, not unlike traditional water color.

6

Lightening an area in the center of the flower with the Eraser Dry variant of Water Color

7

Adding soft detail to flower stamen and highlights and shadows to the stem with the Fine Camel variant of Water Color

8

Sprinkling "salt" on the upper area of the orchid using the Eraser Salt variant of Water Color

Erasers brush on a Water Color layer, and you can't use a Water Color Eraser or Bleach variant on the Canvas, or on an image layer. To softly remove color on a Water Color layer, choose the Eraser Dry variant of Water Color and choose white in the Colors section. In the Layers section, click on the name of the Water Color layer you wish to edit and brush over the area you'd like to lighten. We used the Eraser Dry variant to brighten the highlights on the flower petals and the stamen.

If you'd like to edit your pencil sketch, target the Canvas in the Layers section and switch to the Eraser variant of the Erasers and brush over the area that you'd like to erase.

7 Painting details. If you want very crisp details, it's a good idea to paint detail work on a separate layer, but in this case we stayed on the same Water Color layer because we wanted to preserve the softer wet-into-wet look. Add crisper edges to areas that need definition using a small Fine Camel variant (6–8 pixels). To reduce the Size of the Fine Camel variant, use the Size slider in the Controls:Brush palette. If the Fine Camel seems too saturated for your taste, lower the Opacity to about 20%, using the slider in the Controls:Brush palette. If you'd like softer edges, experiment with the Wash Camel and the Diffuse Camel variants, using a small size (about 6–8 pixels). Make expressive strokes, varying the pressure on the stylus. To paint expressive details, we used the Fine Camel variant to add curved brush strokes and to paint small areas of color on the interior of the orchid. To deepen color and break up a few of the edges, we dabbed a little more color on using the Runny Wash Camel variant. We also painted highlights and shadows on the stem using the Fine Camel variant.

8 Adding color modulation and texture. To add a little more activity in the color, we loosely added a few more bristle marks using the Dry Bristle variant. Finally, we added a light speckled texture using the Eraser Salt variant of Water Color. To add bleached speckles on your image, choose the Eraser Salt variant and scrub the brush over the area you want to add speckles to. For smaller salt particles, reduce the brush Size using the Size slider in the Controls:Brush palette. To keep a spontaneous hand-done look, we retained the original sketch drawn with the 2B Pencil in the image.

Combining Wet-Into-Wet and Glazing on Layers

Overview *Draw a tight pencil sketch; brush in soft wet-into-wet washes; paint glazes on separate layers; add texture and crisp details.*

CHER THREINEN-PENDARVIS

The pencil sketch drawn using the 2B Pencil variant of Pencils

The Layers section showing the "sketch" layer and the active new Water Color layer

TWO COMMON TRADITIONAL WATERCOLOR techniques that can be simulated with Painter 7 are *wet-into-wet* and *glazing*. Wet-into-wet creates a softer-edged look—the painting surface is kept wet as new color is applied, so new paint blends easily with old. Glazing involves applying transparent washes of watercolor; colors are usually built up in layers from light to dark.

Before beginning *Two Green Apples*, we arranged the apples in the natural light of a window near the computer, and chose a close-up view of our subject to emphasize subtle details. We began the painting with a tight pencil sketch in Painter and used transparent glazes to build layers of color and value, progressing from light to dark. As the painting progressed, we added more Water Color layers so that we could edit the wet-into-wet brush work separately without disturbing underlying color.

1 Drawing a tight pencil sketch. Create a new file with a white background by choosing File, New. (Our image measured 1200 x 850 pixels.) Before beginning your sketch, choose an even-textured paper (such as Cold Press Water Color or Basic Paper) from the Papers section of the Art Materials palette and choose a dark gray in the Colors section of the Art Materials palette. Now select the 2B Pencil variant of Pencils from the Brushes palette and begin sketching. While drawing, we carefully explored the shapes and forms of the apples and we established the light source. (Turn to "Sketching With Pencils" on page 64 to read more about working with Pencils in Painter.)

Because we planned to use the sketch as a guide, we wanted to be able to turn its visibility on and off and adjust its opacity as needed, so we decided to float the sketch onto a layer. (Although

The background showing the in-progress wash painted with the Diffuse Bristle

The first very light washes

The left apple, showing brushstrokes that wrap around its form

The apples with light washes established and midtones in-progress

you can adjust the Opacity slider for the Canvas, the opacity doesn't actually change.) To put your sketch onto a layer, choose Select, All (Ctrl/⌘-A), and Select, Float. To lower the opacity of the layer, open Objects palette (Window, Show Objects) and open the Layers section by clicking the left triangle on the Layers section bar. Click on the layer name in the Layers section, then adjust the Opacity slider to about 25%. (For more information about layers, turn to Chapter 5, "Using Layers and Shapes.")

2 Painting the background. When you choose a Water Color brush and touch your stylus to the tablet, a Water Color layer will automatically appear in the Layers section of the Objects palette. You can choose to paint your entire painting using only one layer (which is beneficial if you want a natural wet-into-wet look). Or you can choose to paint different stages of the painting on separate layers as we did. When creating a tight illustration (such as the apples shown here), using several layers can give you better control over separate brush work, but some of the effect of overall wet-into-wet may be sacrificed.

When painting the background, we carefully painted around the shapes of the apples. Choose the Diffuse Bristle variant of Water Color in the Brushes palette. When you apply a light pressure on your stylus, the Diffuse Bristle will allow you to smoothly lay in soft-edged washes. The Diffuse Bristle incorporates diffusion, which helps overlapping brushstrokes to subtly blend. Try not to cover every inch of your background with color. Leaving areas of white will add texture and interest to your painting. (We left some white paper showing in the top areas of the painting.)

3 Painting the first light washes. Add a new Water Color layer by choosing New Water Color layer from the menu that pops out from the upper right corner of the Layers section. As you add color washes to your painting, plan to work from light to dark as much as you can. Choose a very light color in the Colors section of the Art Materials palette and use the Diffuse Bristle variant of Water Color. Using the light color, block in large areas and begin to establish the roundness of the forms. Establish the cast shadows and foreground also by painting light washes.

4 Adding richer color and tonal values. For the deeper tones, add another new Water Color layer, as you did in step 3. Working on the new layer, build up medium-value colors, then gradually add darker tones that will sculpt volume. Keep your light source in mind as you paint, and let the brushstrokes follow the direction of the forms. Resize the brush, or change its Opacity as needed using the sliders on the Controls:Brush palette. Remember to preserve the white areas that will be kept as bright highlights. To render the volume of the left apple, we painted curved vertical strokes in the shadowed areas. Then we added a few

4c

The midtones and some darker tones in the shadows

5

The speckled texture is visible in this detail of the two apples

6

The fine details on the apple stems and their cast shadows added.

7a

Setting up the custom two-point gradient

7b

In this example, the painted blue background layer is hidden. The gradient is applied to the Canvas (left); the texture applied is applied (right).

curved horizontal brushstrokes. We also used medium tones of brown to begin to paint the stems.

5 Adding subtle wet-into-wet texture. Working on the Water Color layer that contains the midtones, we used a grain-sensitive brush to paint subtle texture in the shadow areas of the apples. The Diffuse Grainy Camel paints soft-edged washes while bringing out the texture chosen in the Papers section. Choose the Diffuse Grainy Camel. Now sample color from the image by pressing the Alt/Option key to temporarily switch from the Brush to the Dropper, then paint using short dabbing strokes to "bleed" color variation and subtle values into the shadows. We sampled color several times while we painted over the shadow areas. For the light-colored speckles on the apples, we used a small Splatter Water variant of Water Color.

6 Painting details. To keep detail crisp, add a separate layer for your detail work (as described in step 3). In areas that need more definition, paint crisper edges using a small Fine Camel brush (4–5 pixels). If the Fine Camel seems too saturated for your taste, lower its Opacity to about 20% using the slider in the Controls: Brush palette. For more subtle edge effects, try experiment with the Soft Camel and the Diffuse Camel variants, using a small size (about 6-8 pixels). To complete the study, we used the Fine Camel variant to darken the edges of the shadows under the apples.

7 Adding a gradient with water color texture. Our painting needed more depth. To quickly add deeper color to the image background, as detailed below, we filled the Canvas with a blue-to-white gradient, then we floated it to a Water Color layer and applied a Water Color texture effect.

To fill the Canvas with a gradient, target the Canvas by clicking on its name in the Layers section. Choose the Dropper and click on a rich blue in the background area behind the apples. Open the Gradients section of the Art Materials palette by clicking on the left triangle on the Gradients section bar and choose Two-Point from the resource list menu. To edit the gradient so that the blue is concentrated near the top of the image, with white below, choose Edit Gradient from the menu that pops out from the right side of the Gradients section bar. In the Edit Gradient dialog box, click on the colored ramp to add another color control point where you'd like it. With the new control point active, choose white in the Colors section. Click OK. For more information about gradients turn to Chapter 2, "The Power of Color." In the Gradients section, drag the Gradient Ring to position the Gradient Preview with the blue at the top. When the gradient is the way you like it, choose Effects, Fill, Fill With Gradient.

To give the gradient on the Canvas a water color texture, lift it to a Water Color layer by choosing Lift Canvas to Water Color

Choosing Wet Entire Water Color Layer from the Layers section menu

Blocking in the cast shadows using the Wash Bristle

The in-progress cast shadows showing some of the brush work added with the Grainy Wash Bristle

The final cast shadows after the Wet Entire Water Color layer effect was applied

Layer from the menu on the right side of the Layers section bar. You can now apply a Water Color-like texture to the new layer that is based on the characteristics of the Water Color brush chosen in Brushes palette. If the brush chosen is texture-sensitive, the paper texture chosen in the Papers section will also contribute to the effect. Select the Grainy Wash Camel variant. With the new Water Color layer active, choose Wet Entire Water Color Layer from the menu on the right side of the Layers section bar.

8 Completing the cast shadows. We carefully studied the subtle graduated tones in the cast shadows created by the light from the window. In areas where they overlapped, darker-toned curved shapes were created. The shadows gradually became lighter as they progressed toward the foreground.

Working on a new Water Color layer so that we could edit the shadows separately from the rest of the image, we gradually developed the deeper tones in the cast shadows as follows: Add a new Water Color layer using the process in step 3. Choose the Wash Bristle variant and a blue-gray color in the Colors section, which will work well with the blue you've chosen for your background. Block in the basics shapes, then to add more texture in the deeper-colored areas, switch to the Grainy Wash Bristle and gradually add to the deeper tones.

To melt the new work into the old, wet the cast shadow layer: With the Grainy Wash Bristle still selected, choose Wet Entire Water Color Layer from the menu on the right side of the Layers section bar.

LIFTING ART ON THE CANVAS TO A WATER COLOR LAYER

With Painter's new Water Color technology, any existing artwork or photograph on the Canvas layer can be turned into Water Color, as follows:

1 Open an image that contains artwork on the Canvas layer. From the pop-out menu on the right side of the Layers section bar, choose Lift Canvas to Water Color Layer

2 Choose a texture in the Papers section of the Art Materials palette. Some brushes (such as the Grainy Wash variants) are grain-sensitive and apply nice texture effects.)

3 In the Brushes palette, choose a Water Color brush whose characteristics you'd like to apply to your image.

4 Choose Wet Entire Water Color layer from the pop-out menu on the right side of the Layers section bar, and watch as Painter applies Water Color to your image! In the Layers section, when the animated water drop to the left of the Water Color layer name stops dripping, the effect is complete.

After lifting this pastel drawing to a Water Color Layer, we added to the texture on the image by using the Grainy Wash Camel variant of Water Color to "wet" the Water Color Layer.

Painting an Expressive Color Study

Overview *Open a new file and sketch using the Pens; create an underpainting; finish the study with the Round Camelhair and Palette Knife brushes.*

CHER THREINEN-PENDARVIS

We drew the loose sketch with the Fine Point and the Scratchboard Tool variants of the Pens.

SATISFYING TO USE WHEN CREATING expressive color studies, Painter's new brushes encourage spontaneity and quick gestural drawing because they make smoother, more continuous strokes and thus make possible a more tactile painting experience. For this color study of *Agave Shawii* (a threatened native in the California Maritime Succulent Scrub habitat) we sketched using Pens and Water Color variants. Then we painted with the Round Camelhair and Palette Knife variants of the Brushes, tools that can mix paint by dragging through existing pools of color on the image canvas.

1 Making a sketch. Open a new file (our file measured 1180 x 1741 pixels). Before you begin your sketch, open the Art Materials palette (Window, Art Materials). Open the Papers palette by click-

2

Painting color over the sketch

3a

Painting soft afternoon light on the water

3b

Using a low-opacity Round Camelhair brush to modulate color in areas above the plants and develop atmosphere

3c

Mixing the paint on plant leaves by pulling the Round Camelhair brush through existing color on the study

4

Defining the edge of an agave leaf

ing the left arrow on the Papers section bar, and click the push bar to open the paper drawer. Click on a paper texture to choose it. We chose Regular Fine from the default Paper Textures library. Click the left arrow on the Colors section bar to open the Colors section, and select a dark color to make your sketch. Open the Brushes palette (Window, Show Brushes), click on the Pens icon and choose the Scratchboard Tool variant from the Variant menu. We chose the Scratchboard Tool because of the sensitivity of this tool when used with a stylus—with it you can make expressive, thick and thin strokes. Begin sketching. As you sketch, develop the darks and lights in your image.

2 Developing the underpainting. We established a general color theme by laying in color—blues and greens—directly over the sketch. Using the Opaque Round and Opaque Bristle Spray variants of the Brushes, we loosing blocked in color overall the composition. We purposely left some of the black from the sketch to retain a hand-drawn quality in the study.

The brush we planned to use to complete the painting, the Round Camelhair, has unique qualities. By varying pressure on the stylus, you can add new color, or subtly mix color as you paint. To begin, choose the Round Camelhair variant of the Brushes and a color. Using your stylus, paint a few brushstrokes on your image using firm pressure, then select a new color and apply more brushstrokes over the original strokes using very light pressure. As you drag this brush through a pool of color, you'll notice the edges of the brush pick up a small amount of the existing color from the canvas. Resize the brush as you work using adjust the Size slider in the Controls:Brush palette.

3 Building atmosphere. After painting the sky, water and foreground, we created a sense of steamy afternoon light by building a subtle separation between the mid-ground plants and the water. We used a small low-opacity version of the Round Camelhair brush to modulate lighter blues, grays and yellows into the area. To lower the opacity of the brush, move the Opacity slider on the Controls:Brush palette to the left.

4 Adding details. To finish, we blended areas of the sky and water using the Round Camelhair and a low-opacity Palette Knife variant; we used a tiny Round Camelhair brush to define the edges of the plants and to brighten areas where sun was shining on the leaves; we built up more detailed, striated shadows. Finally, to spread paint and add more texture, we used a small, low-opacity Palette Knife. To build this knife, select the Palette Knife variant of the Brushes. Using the sliders in the Controls:Brush palette, make it smaller by moving the Size slider to 15 pixels, then reduce its Opacity by moving the Opacity slider to 40%.

Gouache and Opaque Watermedia

__Overview__ Create a finely grained surface; build custom brushes; begin with a scanned sketch; sculpt highlights and details using the custom variants; blend colors with a Liquid brush.

NANCY STAHL

1

Scaling the Micro Grain texture to 25%

2a

Stahl's traditional pencil drawing

2b

Sketching with the Smooth Ink Pen variant

ARTIST NANCY STAHL HAS WORKED WITH TRADITIONAL gouache on illustration board since 1976. When she began to work with the computer, her clients would accept her digital art only if the quality matched her conventional style. After much experimentation with Painter's brushes and surfaces, she has been able to fully re-create the effect of traditional gouache, evident in the painting *Mercury*, above.

1 Emulating a traditional gouache surface. Stahl's favorite traditional gouache support is a Strathmore kid finish illustration board. The kid finish is soft and allows for a smooth application of paint. To create Stahl's surface for gouache, begin by choosing Load Library (it's located at the bottom of the pop-out list of papers in the Papers section of the Art Materials palette) to retrieve the Micro Grain paper texture from the More Wild Textures library (located in the More Wild Textures library in the Paper Textures folder on the Painter_CD2 CD-ROM). To make the surface even smoother, scale it to 25%. This finely textured surface is most noticeable when used with Stahl's Gouache brush in step 4.

2 Beginning with sketches. Stahl began by using traditional pencils and paper to draw a black-and-white study to establish the composition and work out values.

In Painter, she created a new file that measured approximately 1500 x 1200 pixels. Using the Flat Color variant of Pens, Stahl roughed a brown color into the background, then drew a russet-colored outline sketch with the Smooth Ink Pen (Pens). Begin creating a new file similar to the size of Stahl's, select the Smooth Ink Pen variant and set the Size to 2.0 in the Controls:Brush palette. Choose a russet color and begin sketching.

3

Using the Camelhair Medium to paint teardrop shapes suggesting the feathers

4a

Painting textured highlights on the helmet

4b

Wings painted with the Camelhair Medium and Gouache brushes

5

Using the Coarse Smear variant of Liquid to mix and pull color on the neck

6

Adding details to the eyes, lips and nose using the Smooth Ink Pen variant of the Pens and a russet color

3 Painting teardrop shapes. To paint smooth teardrop shapes suggesting feathers on the wings and to sculpt the facial features, Stahl created a new variant based on the Round Camelhair variant of the Brushes. All of the controls needed to build Stahl's brush are located in various sections of the Brush Controls palette.

In the Brushes palette, choose the Round Camelhair variant, and in the General section of Brush Controls, set Feature to 1.3. (Lowering the Feature setting "tightens" the bristles in the brush, giving the strokes a smoother, crisper edge with fewer bristle marks, similar to using a soft traditional brush loaded with paint on a smooth surface.) In the Size section of Brush Controls, set Size to 10 and Min Size to 29%. In the Well section set Resat to 65% and Bleed to 8% (increasing the Resat setting allows the brush to paint with more of the current color, with less mixing of colors on the image canvas.) In the Expression section, set Size to Pressure, and set Opacity, Resat and Bleed to None, making sure to turn off the Invert box for Bleed. From the Brushes palette's Variant menu, choose Save Variant, name your variant (Stahl named hers Camelhair Medium) and click OK. Stahl varied the size of her brush while she worked.

> **OPERATING BRUSH CONTROLS**
>
> The Brush Controls palette can be opened by choosing Window, Show Brush Controls. Then you can open one of its sections by clicking the left triangle on a section bar. Or press the Shift key and click one of the left triangles to open all of the sections at once.

4 Building a fast, grainy Gouache brush. Stahl wanted a fast, sensitive brush with grainy edges to use on the helmet, staff and background. To build a brush like Stahl's, start with the Graphic Paintbrush variant of the Brushes. In the Size section of Brush Controls, change Size to 25; set the Min Size slider at 40%. In the General section of Brush Controls, set Grain to 25%. Also in the General section, check to make sure that the Source is set to Pattern as Opacity and the Subcategory is set to Grainy Edge Flat Cover. In the Expression section, make sure that both Size and Opacity are set to Pressure and all others to None. Save the variant. To achieve Stahl's look—before painting with your new brush—make sure that Micro Grain is still chosen in the Papers section. When the stylus is used with light pressure, this grainy Gouache brush is sensitive to texture.

5 Pulling color. To blend colors in the background and on the shoulders, Stahl used varying sizes of the Coarse Smear variant of Liquid. Since this brush uses the Diffuse Motion Brush subcategory, she was able to soften color transitions while adding texture.

6 Finishing touches. Using a small Smooth Ink Pen (Pens), Stahl added linear accents on Mercury's eyes, lips and nose. She used a low-opacity version of the Dry Ink (Brushes) to paint a few brushstrokes with thick bristle marks on the background, shoulders and helmet. 🖌

Painting with Oils

Overview *Create a sketch with a Pencils variant; add color to the underpainting with the Smeary Bristle Spray brush; use an Impasto brush to build up the look of oils.*

DENNIS ORLANDO

Orlando's pencil drawing

INSPIRED BY THE WILD WATER FLOWERS OF SUMMER that seem to emerge magically in the natural ponds of Bucks County, Pennsylvania, artist Dennis Orlando captures an exquisite harmony between the circular shapes of the lily pads, the flowers and water reflections in *Lily Pads*. Strong intersecting horizontal and vertical thrusts, color harmony that leads the viewers eye to follow the composition around the image, and sensitivity to light and shadow all combine to give this well-designed composition its power.

1 Drawing the sketch. Orlando set up a new 6 x 7-inch document with a resolution of 300 ppi and a white Paper Color. He modified a Pencils variant and used it to trace the lily pads and flowers. To create his custom variant, select the Thick and Thin Pencil variant of the Pencils. In the Brush Controls palette's General section, change to Cover method and Grainy Soft Cover subcategory. In the Size section, drag the Size slider to 2.0. Select Basic Paper in the Papers section of the Art Materials palette, choose a color in the Colors section (Orlando started with a neutral gray) and begin sketching.

2 Developing the underpainting. Before you begin to paint in color, open the Color Variability section of the Art Materials palette, and set Hue (± H), Saturation (± S) and Value (± V) to 0.

Laying the first color with the Smeary Bristle Spray

Laying in, pulling and blending color

Creating color activity while painting the reflections

Adding brushstrokes with highlights and shadows using an Impasto brush

Once Orlando felt the composition worked nicely, he began to loosely block in color (on top of the pencil drawing) using the Smeary Bristle variant of the Brushes. The Smeary Bristle Spray variant allowed him to quickly lay in color while moving it around on the image, like wet-into-wet oil paint. (The smeary quality of the brush is produced by low Resat settings and high Bleed settings in the Well section of the Brush Controls palette.) Orlando continued to work color around the entire composition and to define elements and give the painting its overall tonal value and weight. When the underpainting was complete, the color palette and the direction of light were established.

3 Using Color Variability in the water. One of Orlando's "electronic oil" trademarks is activity in the color. He achieves this by adjusting the Color Variability settings for certain brushes. To recreate the active color look he achieved in the water reflections, start with the Smeary Bristle Spray variant of the Brushes. Choose a dark gray-green, then open the Color Variability section in the Art Materials palette and adjust the Color Variability sliders: set Hue (± H) to 10, Saturation (± S) to 5 and Value (± V) to 10. Name and save this variant (on the Brushes palette, choose Variant, Save Variant, enter a name and click OK). After saving the custom variant, restore the default Smeary Bristle Spray brush to its original settings, by choosing Variant, Restore Default Variant from the menu on the Brushes palette. Begin painting. Using the Size slider in the Controls:Brush palette, Orlando changed to a smaller brush size when working close to the lily pads in order to preserve their shapes.

4 Emulating thick, traditional oils. Painter's Round Camelhair variant of Impasto lets you smear existing "pixel paint" to get the same look that you would get by pushing thick, conventional oils around a canvas. As the painting continued to evolve in the final step, Orlando switched to the Round Camelhair. He used the this variant to paint over the loose color (applied in steps 2 and 3), choosing colors and pulling the visible brushstrokes to follow the natural curves and rhythms of the flowers, pads and water. He used the Impasto brush work to add texture and dimension, as well as to unify the quality of the entire composition.

To apply thick paint while subtly blending strokes with existing color on the image, begin by selecting the Round Camelhair variant of Impasto. In the Size section of the Brush Controls palette, adjust the Size slider to the size brush you need (Orlando chose 18.5, then varied his brush size slightly by changing stylus pressure as he painted.) With the Dropper tool, sample a color from the area you want to paint, or hold down the Alt/Option key while you're using the brush to temporarily switch to the Dropper. Use the brush to make short, crisp strokes that pull color from one area of your painting into another. 🖌

Sculpting a Portrait

Overview *Make a sketch; block in color with Dry Media variants; sculpt the forms; refine the composition.*

RICHARD BIEVER

The sketch on a warm-toned paper color

Loosely blocking in mid-tone color

Sculpting the facial features

RICHARD BIEVER LOVES THE EXPRESSIVE FREEDOM he enjoys while working with Painter and a pressure-sensitive tablet and stylus—the natural brushstrokes, the sensitivity, the happy accidents of two colors blending together or a bit of canvas showing through. If he doesn't like a brushstroke, it's easy to "Undo" it by typing Ctrl/⌘-Z, or by simply using the chalk to draw over the area again. Biever's painting *The Parable,* a portrait of Jesus Christ, was painted using Painter's Dry Media and Liquid variants.

1 Sketching on a colored ground. To begin the portrait with a warm tone, Biever began a new file (about 3000 x 3500 pixels) with a sand-colored paper color. He chose the Sharp Chalk variant of Dry Media in the Brushes palette (Window, Show Brushes), a dark neutral color in the Colors section of the Art Materials palette (opened by clicking the left triangle on the Colors section bar) and Basic Paper in the Papers section. Using the Sharp Chalk, he sketched loosely, indicating the general position of the facial features and shape of the head.

2 Blocking in color and blending. Next, Biever blocked in the base tones using the Square Chalk variant (Dry Media). Using the Size slider on the Controls:Brush palette, he enlarged the Square Chalk to make thicker strokes. Using broad strokes of color, he established the planes of the face and set the general tone of the painting and the angle and color of light on the face. (Biever wanted the feeling of natural sunlight, outdoors.) He worked from dark to light, roughing in general shapes using mid-toned color to sculpt the facial structure, letting his brushstrokes follow the direction of the forms. (He planned to add the highlights last.) Using the Marbling Rake

4a

Roughing in the left hand

4b

The left hand and more canvas added

5

The completed face after the contrast was adjusted

variant of Liquid, he began to blend color and build up form.

3 Blending and sculpting.

Continuing to use the Marbling Rake, Biever began to develop the feeling of oil paint. To achieve a smoother stroke, in the Brush Controls palette, he reduced Size in the Size section, Opacity in the General section, lowered Resat in the Well section (for more smear) and reduced Brush Scale in the Rake section. The Marbling Rake gives an illusion of oil paint texture. You can lose the paper texture with the Rake, but through careful stroking Biever left bits and pieces of the canvas showing through. He continued to refine the face using the Large Chalk (Dry Media), while mixing and pulling color with the Marbling Rake.

4 Painting the hands and emphasizing the face. To

emphasize the telling of a story, Biever roughed in the hand on the left. To balance the composition and give the picture more room, he added to the canvas using Canvas, Canvas Size. After he had rendered the right hand also, he selected them using the Lasso tool, floated them (Select, Float) and repositioned them using the Layer Adjuster tool. Then, he dropped the layer by clicking the Drop button on the Layers section of the Objects palette. (To learn about using selections and layers, turn to Chapters 4 and 5.)

Using lighter colors, Biever brought out highlights in the face and hands using small Chalk variants (Dry Media). To emphasize the face even more, he painted over the tunic with the Large Chalk and lighter color, again blending with the Marbling Rake.

5 Adding final details and more texture. To enhance the

highlights and shadows in the portrait, Biever increased the contrast using Effects, Tonal Control, Brightness/Contrast.

Then for *more* atmosphere, he added a papyrus texture from an Art Beats CD-ROM, copying and pasting the texture into the file as a layer. Using the pop-up menu in the Layers section of the Objects palette, he set the Compositing Method to Soft Light. He blended the texture into the hair and beard, creating a dusty feel. To blend a texture into your painting, target the texture layer in the Layers section, then click on its mask in the Masks section. Choose the Digital Airbrush (Airbrushes) and white color. Spray over the area of the mask that you want to remove. (To read more about working with masks and layers, see Chapters 4 and 5.)

Cloning
and Tracing

Overview *Open a reference image; make a clone; delete the contents of the clone; use tracing paper to aid in tracing the original image; add detail using Cloning brushes.*

CHER THREINEN-PENDARVIS

PHOTO: CORBIS

The original photo

Sketching in the clone using Tracing Paper

Selecting the sky with the Magic Wand

WHEN THERE ISN'T TIME to draw from scratch—or if drawing from life isn't your fancy—Painter's cloning and tracing paper features make it easy to use a photo or other existing art as a reference for a new illustration.

1 Selecting an image and making a clone. In Painter, start by opening a reference image (such as a painting or photo). To make a clone, choose File, Clone. The new clone will be linked to the original file—its clone source. The cloning process maps the clone (the destination image) directly to the original (the source image), pixel-by-pixel. Leave the original image open.

2 Tracing and sketching. Working with Tracing Paper in Painter is similar to using a conventional light table. In preparation for using the Tracing Paper function, select all (Ctrl/⌘-A), and delete the contents from the clone canvas (Backspace/Delete). Turn on Tracing Paper by clicking the Tracing Paper icon at the top of the scroll bar or choose Canvas, Tracing Paper (Ctrl/⌘-T). The original image will appear "screened back," ready to be traced with a brush.

Open the Art Materials palette (Window, Show Art Materials) and click on the Papers section's name to open the Papers section. Click on a paper texture or choose it from the pop-up list. We alternated between Basic Paper and Smooth Water Color textures. Open the Colors section (by clicking the Colors section's name), click in the Hue ring or Hue bar to choose a hue, and in the color triangle to select a tint or shade of the color. We chose a warm gray for our sketch.

Open the Brushes drawer (Window, Show Brushes), and click on a brush to select it. (You do not need to use a cloning method brush to sketch using Tracing Paper.) Begin

USING CLONE COLOR

To paint brushstrokes on an image using color from another image, check the Clone Color checkbox on the Colors section.

3b

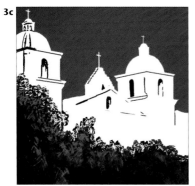

Filling the sky with imagery from the source image

3c

Adding grainy strokes to the sky and foliage using the Chalk variants

4

To add crispness to the soft illustration we cloned in a few details from the original.

5

Cloning the border. Notice the crosshair denoting the sampled area.

painting using the clone source image as a guide. To toggle Tracing Paper on and off as you work, press Ctrl/⌘-T. We drew a solid line to outline the building, using the Fine Point variant of Pens.

3 Making a selection and filling. Next, we selected the white sky above the solid line with the Magic Wand. (In the Controls: Magic Wand palette, we set the Tolerance to 1 and turned on Contiguous, so that only the white pixels would be selected in the sky area.) We saved the selection by choosing Select, Save Selection, New, to save it as a mask that we could use later. Then we chose Effects, Fill, Clone Source to bring the color from the original image into the selected sky. (For more information about selections, turn to Chapter 4.) With the selection still active, using shades of blue, we painted grainy strokes over the filled sky with the Large Chalk variant of Dry Media, and then dropped the selection (Ctrl/⌘-D).

4 Adding details with brushes. After painting the foreground foliage with greens and black using the Smooth Ink variant of Pens, we switched to the Large Chalk to add loose curved strokes of white to denote highlights on the foliage. Then, changing the brush size in the Controls:Brush palette as we worked, we added more strokes to the foliage in various shades of green, some imported from the original image using Clone Color. To brush detail from the original image onto your illustration, choose a cloning brush variant. We used the Chalk Cloner variant of the Cloners to add detail to the door of the mission. You can change any Painter brush into a cloning brush by switching its method to Cloning. For a smoother look, try cloning using the Soft Cover Cloning subcategory available in the General section of the Brush Controls palette.

5 Cloning a border with a chalky edge. In preparation for adding a rough-edged border, we increased the canvas size of the file (Canvas, Canvas Size) by 20 pixels on all four sides. (When you change the size of your canvas, Tracing Paper will no longer be available unless you also change the source image to the same pixel size.) We added the border by sampling imagery and making rough strokes along the edge using the Chalk Cloner. To clone from one point to another within an image (much like using the Rubber Stamp in Photoshop), select a source point in your image (Alt/Option-click). Reposition the cloning brush in your document and stroke to bring the imagery into the area. Reload the cloning brush as necessary as you work around the edge. 🖌

CLONING FROM ONE UNRELATED IMAGE TO ANOTHER

To clone from one unrelated image to another (to map pixel for pixel, or to use the Tracing Paper function), the two images must have exactly the same pixel dimensions. Open two images that are the same size and choose one image for your destination image. Choose File, Clone Source, and designate the second image as the clone source. Use a Cloning brush to bring imagery into the destination image, in exactly the same position as in the source. To continue to clone or use Tracing Paper, the source image must be left open.

Coloring Pencil Illustrations

Overview *Scan a pencil sketch; clone it; tint it and add texture; restore from the original; add color with the Airbrush, Dry Media and Water Color brushes.*

PHILIP HOWE

MUCH OF THE BEAUTY of illustrator Philip Howe's work lies in his seamless, creative blending of the traditional with the digital. In a spread for *Trailblazer* magazine—a detail of which is shown here—Howe combined hand-drawn calligraphy, a photo of two slides, a photo of a watercolor block (for the background), and his own pencil sketches, colored to simulate traditional watercolor.

1 Starting with a sketch. Howe began by sketching the various birds in pencil on watercolor paper. He scanned the images on a flatbed scanner, saving them as grayscale files in TIFF format. Each bird image was 4 to 5 inches square and 300 ppi.

2 Modifying a clone. Open a grayscale scan in Painter. Choose File, Clone, to clone your scan, giving you an "original" and a clone. Keep the original open—you'll want to pull from it later. Howe added a color tint and a texture to the clone of the scanned bird. To add a tint, choose a color in the Art Materials:Colors section (Howe chose a reddish brown), then choose Effects, Surface Control, Color Overlay. Select Uniform Color from the pop-up menu, set Opacity to 30%, click the Dye Concentration button and click OK. To add texture, select a paper texture (Howe chose Basic Paper) from Art Materials:Papers, and choose Effects, Surface Control, Apply Surface Texture. Select Paper from the Using menu, set Amount to 50% and set Shine to 0%. Click OK.

3 Restoring from the original. Howe used Painter's cloning capabilities to replace most of the tint and texture in the bird's body with the light gray tones of the original. You could use a standard cloning brush to do this, but Howe chose the Digital Airbrush variant of the Airbrushes and made an Airbrush cloner. To make Howe's cloner, select the Digital Airbrush, open the General section of the Brush Controls palette and change the method to Cloning and the subcategory to Soft Cover Cloning. Also in the General section, try lowering this cloning brush's Opacity for more sensitivity. Once you've changed the brush, paint on the portion of your image that you want to restore. The original will automatically be revealed in the area covered by your strokes.

4 Adding color tints with an Airbrush. To achieve the effect of traditional airbrushing with transparent dyes or watercolor

The original pencil illustration, scanned

Adding a tint and a texture to the clone

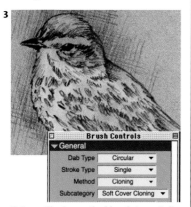

Using a Cloning method brush to partially restore the gray tones of the original

4

Applying color tints with the Digital Airbrush in Buildup method

5

Using a modified Large Chalk variant to add color to the background

6

Applying watercolor accents with the Splatter Water variant

Another spot illustration from the Trailblazer spread. Howe used the same brushes and technique for all illustrations.

pigments, Howe used two versions of the Digital Airbrush variant. In the Brush Controls:General section he switched back to Cover method, Soft Cover subcategory, and reduced the Opacity setting to between 5% and 10%. He used these settings to carefully lay in the golden brown tones on the bird's back. Next, he switched to the Buildup method, Soft Buildup subcategory, and added the more saturated yellow and rust hues. The Buildup method allowed him to use a slightly higher Opacity (between 10% and 20%) to achieve richer color while preserving the intensity of the pencil sketch.

5 Cloning again and brushing with Chalk. Howe uses the Clone feature like a flexible "Save As" command. When he's ready to move on to the next phase of an illustration, he often makes a clone and uses the original as "source material." Here, when he had colored the bird to his satisfaction, he chose File, Clone. If he over-worked an area in the new clone, he restored it by cloning in imagery from the previous version by opening that version and designating it as the "source" by choosing File, Clone Source. Then he painted with a cloning brush to restore the area.

Howe switched to the Large Chalk variant of Dry Media and began to paint loose, gestural strokes on the image background around the bird using two similar green hues. He changed the size of the brush as he worked by making adjustments in the Brush Controls:Size section. To make the brush elliptical, he set Angle to 116° and Squeeze to 60% in the Brush Controls:Angle section.

6 Adding tints and texture. To add a finishing touch without muddying his existing color work, Howe used transparent washes to add more depth to the color on the bird's head and other areas. To paint washes, use the Wash Camel variant of Water Color. (As you paint, a Water Color layer will be generated in the Layers section of the Objects palette, keeping these brushstrokes separate from the Canvas). Now, sample color from the bird and background using the Dropper tool, switch to the Splatter Water variant and paint a "water drop" effect on the background. To combine the selected Water Color layer with the Canvas, choose Drop from the Layers section menu.

Merging the files. Using the Lasso, Howe drew a loose selection around the bird, then he chose Select, Feather and feathered it 30 pixels. Then he opened the 17 x 11-inch main image and used the Layer Adjuster tool to drag and drop the bird into the main image. To blend the bird layer with the background, he set its Composite Method in the Objects:Layers section to Multiply.

Spontaneous Mixed Media

Overview *Add a colored gradient to a new document; block in color with Brushes variants; blend and smear the paint; add textured brushstrokes and detail with Chalk variants.*

Setting up the Colors section

The gradient background

Painting pastel colors onto the sky

Adding more color with Brushes variants

THE BRUSHES AND DRY MEDIA VARIANTS are among Painter's most responsive tools, and mixing the media is a natural match for artist Chelsea Sammel's spontaneous style. She painted *Three Trees* from her imagination while working in her studio.

1 Building a colored background. Pastel artists sometimes prepare a support by painting first with acrylic or oil paints. Sammel created a colored background by filling the image with a dark-to-light purple gradation to suggest a sky. To start as Sammel did, create a new document (1200 x 800 pixels) with a white paper color. Open the Art Materials palette (Window, Show Art Materials). In the Colors section of the Art Materials palette, choose a dark purple color for the Primary Color Square. Click on the Secondary Color Square and set it at a lighter purple color. Open the Gradients section of the Art Materials palette by clicking the left triangle on the Gradients section bar. Choose Two-Point from the resource list menu and set the Preview Window wheel to 90°. To fill the canvas with the gradient, choose Effects, Fill, Using Gradient. (For more information about using Gradients, turn to Chapter 2.)

2 Adding colored brushstrokes. Sammel quickly roughed cream, peach and light green colors on to the image—directly over the gradient—using the Smeary Bristle Spray and Round Camelhair variants of the Brushes. Then she blocked in the distant trees and meadow using rich greens and browns, and added a few strokes of darker color to suggest shadow.

3 Blending paint and adding more color. Traditional artists often use palette knives to move paint around on the canvas surface. To scrape back and blend areas, Sammel used a small version of the Palette Knife variant of the Brushes. To make the knife smaller, reduce its size using the Size slider in the Controls:Brushes palette. Switching between the Smeary Bristle Spray and Palette

3

Pulling and blending paint

4

Adjusting the settings for Tapered Chalk

5a

Adding color to the meadow with the custom Tapered Chalk variant

5b

The painting with the trees in progress

5c

Using the Tapered Chalk to add deeper color to the sky

Knife variants of the Brushes, she painted and scraped back, pulled and blended colors, adding expression and movement to the sky and background hills.

For the look of grainy pigment, Sammel also blended areas with the Coarse Smear variant of Liquid. Then she chose the Laid Pastel Paper texture in the Art Materials:Papers section. To bring out the paper texture, she blended areas of her image using the Smudge variant of Liquid.

4 Building custom chalk variants. Sammel likes Painter's default Chalk variants of Dry Media and makes only minor adjustments to their settings. She works quickly and spontaneously, creating a few variants on the fly and switching frequently among them. To create her Tapered Chalk, choose the Artist Pastel Chalk variant of Dry Media. Open the Brush Controls palette by choosing Window, Show Brush Controls (or type Ctrl/⌘-7); open the Size section by clicking the left triangle on the section bar; set Size to 36.5 and Min Size to 40%. Open the Expression section of the Brush Controls palette by clicking the left triangle on its Expression section bar and set Size to Pressure. This setting, combined with a moderate Min Size setting, creates more taper at the end of each stroke. To save the variant, choose Variant, Save Variant from the Brushes palette, then name your brush and click OK. To create Sammel's Conté Crayon, start with the Sharp Chalk variant. In the Size section, change Size to 9.4 and Min Size to 50%. In the Brush Controls: Expression section, set Size to Pressure. For a grainier stroke, drag the Grain slider in the Controls:Brush palette to 13%. Save the variant.

5 Adding color and texture with the chalks. Sammel added color to the grass with the Tapered Chalk variant. She used the same variant to begin the foreground trees, drawing dynamic, angled

5d

Adding more highlight color to the branches using the Conté Crayon variant.

strokes, in a very dark brown-black color so that the trees would contrast with the rich-colored background. Next she brushed a deeper blue onto the sky. Then she switched to the Conté Crayon variant and added a few strokes of complementary blues, greens, golds and oranges to the distant foliage.

Finally, she chose the Smudge variant of Liquid and smudged areas of the background and meadow. She finished the image by using the Oil Pastel variant of Dry Media to add a few lighter brushstrokes on the trees and grass. 🖌

Applying Scanned Paper Textures

Overview *Scan a textured paper; open the file in Painter and capture the texture; use a grain-sensitive brush and Painter's special effects to apply the texture to your image.*

CORRINE OKADA

The scanned paper textures: rice paper (left) and maple leaf (right)

1b

Increasing the contrast of the paper scan

2a

Capturing a selected area of the paper scan

2b

Saving and naming the new paper texture

WHILE PAINTER OFFERS A SEEMINGLY ENDLESS assortment of paper grains, many artists still choose to create their own surfaces. They draw from many sources: video grabs, scanned photos, texture collections on CD-ROM, scans of natural objects (leaves or richly grained wood), scans of papers or patterns and images drawn in Painter. They also generate their own seamless textures with Painter's Make Paper and Make Fractal Pattern features.

When Corrine Okada first began using Painter, she scanned her extensive paper collection, capturing the images in Painter and saving them into her own texture libraries. Her skill in applying these custom textures is evident in *Crane Maiden,* a CD-ROM cover commissioned by Silicon Graphics.

1 Scanning the papers. Okada scans her papers on a flatbed scanner in grayscale mode. She scans an 8 x 10-inch area at 300 ppi. If you're scanning a thin, light-colored sheet—like the piece of lacy rice paper that Okada scanned for this job—you may want to place a sheet of black paper behind it to create more contrast. Okada also scanned a sheet of Japanese maple leaf paper.

You'll have more flexibility when you apply the texture if the scan you apply has good contrast and a broad tonal range. So open your scanned texture and choose Effects, Tonal Control, Brightness/Contrast. Drag the top slider to the right to increase contrast. If necessary, adjust the lower slider (Brightness) and then click Apply.

2 Capturing the texture. Use the Rectangular Selection tool to isolate an area of your image. Start by selecting an area of about 200 x 200 pixels (read the Width and Height dimensions in the

3a

Detail of the Rice Paper texture brushed behind the head

3b

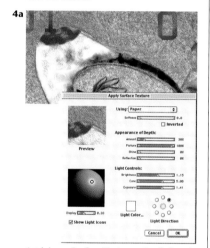

Detail of the Rice Paper texture brushed onto the kimono

4a

Applying a Surface Texture using Painter's Rice Paper texture

4b

The Maple Leaf texture on the brushstroke (applied with Surface Control effects) and the computer monitor (applied with the Charcoal variant of Dry Media)

Controls:Selection palette). The repetition of your pattern may be too obvious if your selection is much smaller. Choose Capture Paper in the Art Materials, Papers pop-up menu (opened by clicking the triangle on the right side of the Papers section bar). For the smoothest results, leave the Crossfade setting at 16. Name your paper and click OK. A picture of the texture will appear in your current Paper library.

3 Applying grain with brushes. Painter lets you apply textures in two ways: with a brush or as a special effect. Okada used both of these methods (within selections and on layers), in this piece. To brush the Rice Paper texture behind the woman's head, she first inverted the texture by checking the Invert Paper box in the Papers section. She selected the area behind the head, then brushed the texture into the selected area using the Charcoal variant of Dry Media and a white color. Okada selected a purple color to brush the same texture (with Invert Paper turned off) onto the woman's kimono. Near the end of the project, she used the same brush to apply the Maple Leaf texture onto the computer screen in blue, yellow and white.

4 Special effects with grain. To create a subtle woven look across the entire image, Okada overlaid texture on the image. She began by selecting the Rice Paper texture from in the Papers section of the Art Materials palette. Then she chose Effects, Surface Control, Apply Surface Texture. In the Using menu she selected Paper, and set the Amount at 30% and the Shine at 0 and clicked OK.

To add color, value and texture to the brushstroke that sweeps across the lower half of the image, Okada applied multiple special effects using the Maple Leaf texture. She selected, then floated the brushstroke, and used Color Overlay, Apply Lighting, and Apply Surface Texture (all under Effects, Surface Control) a few times each with various settings to get the effect she wanted. 🖌

Creative Custom Brushes

Overview *Build custom brushes before painting; create a drawing; brush in soft color; build up details and texture.*

JUDY MILLER

1a

Miller's drawing for the Leaves dab

1b

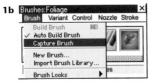

Choosing Capture Brush from the Brushes palette menu

1c

The captured leaves dab shown in the Brush Dab Preview Window

CUSTOM BRUSHES were created by Judy Miller especially for her painting *Ronnie's Joy*, which is a tribute to Miller's father-in-law, an inspired Scottish Christian. To render the foliage and stone textures in the painting, the Nova Scotia–based artist built custom brush variants and textures in advance.

1 Creating a captured brush. To design new brushes, open the Brush Controls palette by choosing Window, Show Brush Controls. Open the Size section of the Brush Controls palette by clicking the left triangle on the Size section bar.

To paint the tree leaves and grasses in her image, Miller created custom variants of Dry Media that incorporated captured dabs. To draw a dab similar to Miller's Leaves brush, begin by creating a new square file 180 x 180 pixels. Choose the Artist Pastel Chalk variant of Dry Media in the Brushes palette, and choose black in the Colors section of the Art Materials palette and draw a group of leaves. Before adding detail to the leaves, reduce the size of the Artist Pastel Chalk by adjusting the Size slider in the Size section. When you've finished drawing the dab, choose the Rectangular Selection tool and Shift-drag to make a square selection around the image. With the cursor inside the selection boundary, click. Increase the size of the Artist Pastel Chalk the size that you want for your new captured dab. Choose Capture Brush from the Brush menu on the Brushes palette. If you see a hard-edged round shape (instead of the captured dab) in the Brush Dab Preview Window, click to switch from *hard* view to *soft* view, to preview it. After capturing the dab, Miller opened the General section of Brush Controls and set the Subcategory to Soft Cover. Then she saved the variant by choosing Save Variant from the Variant menu on the Brushes palette. When the dialog box appeared, she named it and clicked OK.

1d

Brush Controls	
▼ General	
Dab Type	Captured ▼
Stroke Type	Single ▼
Method	Cover ▼
Subcategory	Soft Cover ▼
Source	
Opacity	100%
Grain	

Settings in the General section for the new captured Leaves chalk variant

2

Testing the new clouds airbrush

3

The completed drawing of the composition

4a

The painting with basic color blocked in, with the drawing visible underneath

2 Building an airbrush to paint the clouds. Miller envisioned swirling clouds in her painting, as if a storm was approaching. She chose the Fine Wheel Airbrush and modified it to get a random, wispy look as follows: In the General section of the Brush Controls palette, she changed the Airbrush's Dab Type to Bristle Spray because she likes the dab type's striated texture. In the Size section, she set the Max size to 45.8; Min size to 30% and Feature to 6.7. In the Expression section of Brush Controls, Miller set Size to Pressure, Opacity to Wheel (she uses an Intuos Airbrush stylus, and prefers to control opacity using the wheel). She set both Flow and Feature to Pressure. In the Well section of Brush Controls, she set Resat to 23% and Bleed to 95% so the brush would subtly smear existing color as she painted. Finally, so the texture would be applied with more of a random look, in the Random section of Brush Controls, she increased Jitter to .80. In the Airbrush section of Brush Controls, she set Spread at 36 degrees, Min Spread at 21%, Flow at 786 and Min flow at 31%. She saved this variant as she had in step 1.

3 Designing the composition. For inspiration while planning the color palette and atmosphere for the painting, Miller looked at many photos of Scotland. Then she made sketches using pencil and paper to lay our the compositional elements. She scanned a final pencil drawing, opened it Painter and used a modified Charcoal variant of Dry Media to add to the sketch. Miller's edited sketch image was approximately 6 x 4-inches at 300 ppi.

4 Laying in basic color and clouds. When she had finished editing the drawing, Miller began to add color to her painting on a separate layer. She opened the Objects palette (Window, Show Objects) and opened the Layers section by clicking the left triangle on the Layers section bar. From the pull-down menu on the right side of the Layers section bar, she chose New Layer. When the new layer appeared in the Layers section, she turned off Preserve Transparency (so she could paint on the layer) and Pick Up Underlying Color (so no underlying color from the drawing would be brought up into the new layer.) Using the drawing as a guide, she blocked in color on the new layer using various Charcoal and Chalk variants of Dry Media.

As she painted the clouds, Miller used a variety of lights and dark grays to create depth.

BRUSHES FROM SCRATCH

If you want to create custom brushes from scratch instead of basing them on pre-existing brushes, begin by making an icon for the brush. Select a square area of your image with the Rectangular Selection tool. Now choose Brush, New Brush from the Brushes palette menu. Name your brush style and click OK. You'll see your selection appear in the Brushes palette with no variants available. You've just created an empty "variant holder," ready to be filled with custom variants.

4b

Detail of the clouds in-progress

5

The trees were painted using Color Variability and are nearly complete in this detail of the painting.

6a

The nearly completed rocks are shown in this detail

6b

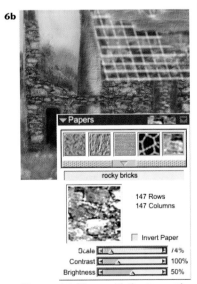

The completed house with the stone work and shadows added

When the clouds were nearly complete, she added a second new layer and added a few lighter cloud details, which helped to enhance the feeling of depth in the sky.

5 Painting the tree foliage and bark. When she was ready to paint the tree foliage, Miller added another new layer. She selected a dull gray-green in the Colors section and chose the Leaves brush in the Brushes palette. To establish depth, she painted the darkest background foliage first. Then she gradually added lighter areas, adjusting the Size of the brush as she worked. After the darkest foliage was laid in, she chose a brighter green and painted the closer leaves.

To modulate color and add more interest to the foliage, she painted the last details using increased Color Variability. To add Color Variability to the Leaves brush, open the Color Variability section of the Art Materials palette and adjust the Color Variability sliders: set Hue (± H) to 5, Saturation (± S) to 7 and Value (± V) to 36. Experiment with the settings to suit your taste. For lighter areas of the foliage that were lit by the sun, Miller painted using a lighter, warmer green.

For the tree trunks, Miller began by loading a bark paper texture (from one of her own paper libraries) into the Papers section. Then she painted the trunks using a variety of gold, brown and gray colors. Before she added darker colors, she decreased the size of the texture to 60% using the Scale slider on the Papers section of the Art Materials palette. Then she inverted the paper texture (by clicking the Invert box on the Papers section) and brushed in the lighter colors to enhance the bark texture.

6 Adding more details and texture. When completing the painting, Miller wanted to add a natural relief to the rock walls. She chose the Artist Pastel Chalk and reduced the Grain setting to 7% to reveal more grain as she painted. Then she loaded a custom rock texture into the Papers section. To achieve the look of blended pastels and vary the amount of smear when painting, Miller set Resat at 80, Bleed at 20 and Dryout at 752 in the Well section (Brush Controls). With Brush Loading turned on in the Well section, Miller laid down color and blended, then laid down more colored brushstrokes. When she wanted to blend more as she painted, she lowered the Resat and increased the Bleed settings.

To paint the detailed striations on the wood and stone walls of the building, she used a tiny 1.2-pixel brush. Then she carefully cleaned up the edges of the boards on the roof.

Miller had created the cross in a source file, so she selected it, copied and pasted it into the composite file, where she positioned it. Then, using the Digital Airbrush, she painted the shining light beams around the cross. Finally, she added a three-dimensional texture to the entire painting using Painter's Effects, Surface Control, Apply Surface Texture feature.

Applying Rich Textures with Custom Brushes

Overview *Scan a traditional pencil sketch; modify brushes to include enhanced color and grain settings; paint rich color with varied textures using the custom brushes.*

DON SEEGMILLER

The scanned pencil sketch

BY SKILLFULLY USING COLOR WHILE PAINTING with custom brushes and textures, Don Seegmiller created a dark and comically ominous atmosphere for *Strange High House*, painted from the imagination. He used somber colors in the highlight and shadow areas of the painting and developed a rich layering of multiple textures, applied with modified brushes that included increased color variability and enhanced grain settings.

Seegmiller, whose traditional oil paintings can be found in both private and public collections, is art director of Saffire Corporation, an innovative gaming development company. He also teaches illustration at Brigham Young University.

1 Sketching, scanning and equalizing. Seegmiller began by sketching with conventional pencil in his sketchbook. He scanned the pencil drawing at 300 ppi, a resolution suitable for offset printing. Because he likes working with a high-contrast version of the sketch, he removed the grays from the scan. To increase the contrast in your sketch, as Seegmiller did, choose Effects, Tonal

Using Equalize to give the sketch more contrast

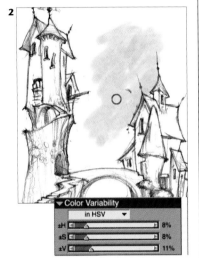

Painting the sky in the clone with a modified Water Color brush, using these Color Variability settings. Tracing Paper if turned on to view the original scan of the pencil sketch

The study with soft watercolor background and the embellished sketch

Control, Equalize. When the Equalize dialog box appears, move the black point marker and the white point marker under the histogram closer together to eliminate the gray tones. Move them right or left to affect the line thickness and quality. You'll be able to preview the adjustment in your image before you click OK to accept.

2 Painting the background. Prior to painting with color, Seegmiller made a quick duplicate of his sketch to preserve the original, using Painter's cloning process. To make a clone, choose File, Clone.

Seegmiller planned to paint washes on the sky using a modified Water Color variant. He chose Pavement texture in the Papers section of the Art Materials palette because he likes its coarse, uneven look. Then he chose a soft blue in the Colors section of the Art Materials palette and a modified Water Color brush in the Brushes palette. The custom brush included enhanced Color Variability and Grain settings so that he could subtly paint the sky with varying colors of blue while revealing the texture.

To make a brush similar to Seegmiller's, choose the Simple Round Wash variant of Water Color, then open the Color Variability section of the Art Materials palette by clicking on its section name. Adjust the sliders using these settings: ±H8 %, ±S8 %, and ±V11 %. In the General section of the Brush Controls palette move the Grain slider to 75%, to allow more grain to show as brushstrokes are applied. In the Size section increase the Size to 59.1. To avoid seeing circles (individual brush dabs as you paint) when using the larger brush size, decrease the spacing between the brush's dabs. In the Spacing section, move the Spacing slider to 14% and the Min Spacing slider to 0.5. To save your new Water Color brush (instead of leaving the new settings in the default Simple Round Wash brush), choose Save Variant from the Variant menu on the Brushes palette. When the Save Variant dialog box appears, type in a name for your brush and click OK. To restore the Simple Round Wash brush to its default settings, select the variant and from the Brushes palette menu choose Variant, Restore Default Variant.

Using a soft touch on the stylus, Seegmiller painted brushstrokes over the sky. He changed color as he worked, choosing low-saturation blues, purples, browns and grays in the Colors section. (When you paint with a Water Color brush, a Water Color layer is generated, keeping the Wet Paint separate from the image Canvas. To read more about painting with the Water Color brushes and layers, turn to "A Painter Water Color Primer," earlier in this chapter.)

3 Strengthening the sketch. After establishing the sky, Seegmiller used a modified Pencils variant to embellish areas of the pencil sketch in his working study. (Drawing with the Pencils variants will not interrupt the wet Water Color brushstrokes.) His modified Pencil incorporates the Grainy Hard Buildup subcategory, and enhanced Grain settings, making it very sensitive to the Paper grain chosen in the Papers section. To build a Sketching Pencil

4a

Seegmiller switched between custom-made Cobblestones and Bark textures

4b

Using a modified Square Chalk variant to paint layers of custom-made Cobbles and Bark texture onto the cliff areas

5a

Adding warmer, lighter tones to the top house and its windows

similar to Seegmiller's, begin by choosing the 2B Pencil variant. In the General section of the Brush Controls palette, change its Dab Type to Single-Pixel, then set the Opacity slider at 69% and the Grain slider at 24%. Open the Random section of the palette and increase Jitter to 0.95 to make the brushstrokes uneven. Increasing Jitter also broadens the stroke slightly. Now choose a fine, even-textured paper (such as Cold Press Water Color) in the Papers section of the Art Materials palette.

After drawing over certain areas, Seegmiller added more intensity to the pencil sketch by selecting the drawing in the original image, then choosing Select, All, and copying and pasting it into the working study. In the Layers section of the Objects palette, he set the Composite Method for the layer to Multiply, then he dropped it to the image canvas by clicking the Drop button in the Layers section of the Objects palette. (Multiply mode makes the white areas of the image clear, while preserving the dark areas.) To read more about Layers and Composite Methods, turn to the beginning of Chapter 5, "Using Layers and Shapes."

4 Using a custom chalk to build up textures on the cliffs. Seegmiller used a modified Square Chalk to paint custom textures (primarily the Cobblestones and Bark textures) onto the cliffs. (Seegmiller creates custom textures from scans of his own photos or by painting in Painter, then capturing the elements as paper textures. To read more about paper textures, turn to "Applying Scanned Paper Textures," earlier in this chapter.) He built up layers of texture subtly. While painting with the custom Chalk, he strengthened and lightened areas in both the sky and cliff areas. While he worked, he continually changed paper textures in the Papers section and applied the textures using slightly different colors.

To build Seegmiller's custom Chalk, begin by selecting the Square Chalk variant of Dry Media in the Brushes palette. In the Color Variability section of the Art Materials palette, move the sliders to these settings: ±H5 %, ±S7 %, and ±V10 %. Now set the Grain very low in the Controls:Brush palette: Move the Grain slider to 8%, to allow the Chalk to reveal more grain. To save your new custom Chalk without modifying settings for the default Square Chalk, choose Variant, Save Variant on the Brushes palette. Restore the Square Chalk

5b

Using the custom Warm Fuzzy brush to add soft tones to the cliffs and path

6

Modifying the Gradual light

7a

The glow added to the window

7b

The highlights added to the roofs, and glows to the lights and the moon

variant to its default settings (select the Square Chalk, and from the Brushes palette menu choose Variant, Restore Default Variant).

5 Adding lights and establishing the center of interest.
Seegmiller began to develop the feeling of light he envisioned for the house and high cliffs. He used another custom brush, the Warm Fuzzy, to achieve a softer feeling on the some of areas of the cliffs and edges of the path. Seegmiller's Warm Fuzzy brush paints with natural, "fuzzy-looking" strokes that made it a good choice for suggesting texture of vegetation on the cliffs. To build the Warm Fuzzy, begin by choosing the Opaque Round variant of the Brushes. In the Size section of the Brush Controls palette, change Size to 6.7, Min Size to 100% and Feature to 4.4 (to spread the Bristles). In the General section change Opacity to 68%. In the Expression section change Size and Jitter to None and Opacity to Pressure; set Resat, Bleed, and Feature to None. Finally, an important ingredient that adds a more natural look: In the Random section, increase Jitter to 0.43.

Using his Warm Fuzzy brush, Seegmiller added warm oranges and yellows to the two small windows to act as a balancing element against the purples, blue, grays and browns. He also added rusty-brown highlights to the roofs on the higher house to create the center of interest. He worked his way down the cliffs and added more subtle colors and texture to the houses and rocks.

6 Adding to the atmosphere and focal point. Seegmiller believes that Apply Lighting is one of the finest tools that Painter offers to change the complexion of an image without painting over underlying work. He used lighting to add atmosphere (for a more ominous feeling) and to create a soft vertical gradation from dark-to-light in the image (to strengthen the focal point). To create a custom light similar to Seegmiller's, choose Effects, Surface Control, Apply Lighting. When the dialog box appears, choose the Gradual light. Make these changes to the light: Click on the Light Color square and in the Select Light Color dialog box, choose a light blue-gray. Reduce Brightness by moving its slider to 0.18. Leave other settings at their defaults. To save your light, click the Save button, name your light and click OK. Then click OK to apply the light. To learn more about Apply Lighting, see the beginning of Chapter 7, "Exploring Special Effects."

7 Refining the painting. Seegmiller continued to add fine color detail over the entire image, particularly on the buildings, cliffs and path, while maintaining color harmony throughout the image. He added a small lamp outside the tunnel by the bridge, then embellished the lights in the windows and the lantern using the Glow variant of the F/X brush. He also used the Glow brush to lighten the moon. Using a tiny version of the Warm Fuzzy brush, he also added highlights along the roof edges of the buildings to give them a feeling of light from the moon. (For more about the F/X brushes see Chapter 7.)

Brushing Washes Over "Live" Canvas

Overview *Open a new file and use an Impasto brush to emboss texture into the image canvas; paint color washes over the canvas with brushes.*

STANLEY VEALÉ

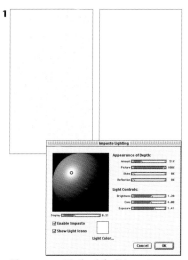

The canvas with the default Impasto Lighting settings (left) and with the reduced Amount and Shine (right), as set in the Impasto Lighting dialog box.

Choosing the Wet Bristle variant of Impasto in the Brushes palette

ON TRADITIONAL CANVAS YOU CAN USE OIL PAINT mixed with linseed oil and turpentine to brush washes over the surface without obliterating the canvas grain. With Painter's Impasto feature you can do something very similar, with the added advantage of being able to emphasize or de-emphasize the grain by changing the angle or intensity of lighting on the canvas. Using the Impasto feature to "emboss" the canvas will keep the grain "live" and changeable throughout the painting process. To paint *Ashanti,* a still-life study of an African wood carving, artist and designer Stanley Vealé used a unique method that allows the canvas texture to always show through the brushstrokes.

1 Embossing the canvas. Begin by creating a new file the size and resolution you need. (Vealé's file was 800 pixels square.) In the Papers section of the Art Materials palette, choose the Raw Silk texture. (Considering the 800-pixel file size, Vealé left the Scale of the Raw Silk texture at 100% in the Papers section.)

Vealé used the Grain Emboss variant of Impasto to "emboss" the Raw Silk texture values into the image canvas without adding color. Select the Grain Emboss variant of Impasto and paint wide strokes all over the image so that the paper texture is embossed into the image. You can reduce or increase the effect of the texture by choosing Canvas, Surface Lighting, and adjusting the Amount slider to your liking. Because the default Impasto Lighting settings seemed too coarse and shiny, Vealé reduced the Amount to 51%, and for a matte finish on the canvas, he set the Shine at 0.

2 Customizing a brush. Vealé likes the Wet Bristle variant of Impasto because of its bristle marks and how it scrubs existing paint when you apply pressure on the stylus. However, if he used the

2b

Changing the Impasto section settings for the Wet Bristle variant copy

3

Applying glazes to the image canvas

4a

The figure study in progress

4b

Vealé painted reflected light on the face of the Ashanti figure.

default Impasto Wet Bristle, the brush would paint with depth as well as color, eventually covering the embossed texture applied in step 1. So he modified a copy of the Wet Bristle so that it would apply only color to his image, as follows: Select the Wet Bristle variant of Impasto and copy it to the Brushes category by choosing Copy Variant from the Variant menu on the Brushes palette. When the Copy Variant dialog box appears, choose the Brushes category from the pop-up menu and click OK. Now choose the Wet Bristle copy from the Brushes category. In the Impasto section of the Brush Controls palette, change the Draw To pop-up menu to Color. Then choose Set Default Variant from the Variant menu in the Brushes palette to make the change permanent for the new Wet Bristle variant.

3 Painting colored washes. Using a light touch on the stylus, and the new Wet Bristle brush, Vealé freely brushed loose washes of color over the image canvas, suggesting a subtle horizon line and a glowing campfire in the background.

Choose your new Wet Bristle variant and paint brushstrokes on the image. The brush applies paint when you press lightly, but scrubs underlying paint when you press hard (because in the Expression section of the Brush Controls palette, Resat is set to vary inversely with Pressure and Bleed is set to vary with Pressure). These settings help the canvas texture to always show through the paint. (You can also achieve good washes with other brushes, such as the Smeary Round and the Variable Flat variants of the Brushes.)

4 Setting up a still life and painting the figure. Vealé set up a conventional light to shine from behind the figure that served as his model and another to reflect light onto its face. Then he carefully studied the Ashanti figure's form, and painted it directly on the image canvas with a smaller version of the Wet Bristle variant. He built up values slowly, gradually adding more saturated, darker tones to the still life study. Vealé brought out orange tones that were reminiscent of firelight in the background. He added deeper red and brown colors to the sky, and brighter colors and more detail to the bonfire in the background. Then he added stronger highlights and cast shadows to the foreground and to the carving. Finally, to relieve some of the rigidity of the centered composition, he repainted areas of the background to move the horizon up.

Variations. A slightly different effect (shown at right) can be achieved if you choose the new Wet Bristle, and in the General section of the Brush Controls palette, reduce the Opacity of the brush to between 20–40%. In the Expression section, set the Opacity menu to Pressure. 🐾

Figure study, by Stanley Vealé

Working with Thick Paint

Overview *Paint a color study; use Impasto brushes to add 3D brushwork to the study; use Impasto Lighting to adjust the appearance of the highlights and shadows on the thick paint.*

CHELSEA SAMMEL

Sammel's black-and-white pencil study

IMPASTO BRINGS THE TEXTURE OF THICK, LUSCIOUS PAINT to the tip of your stylus. When painting *Dying Orchids,* artist Chelsea Sammel used Painter's Impasto brushes to add the texture of brush marks with realistic highlights and shadows to a color study. Then she scraped back and added more expressive brushwork, bringing more texture and activity to the painting.

1 Designing the still life and making a sketch. Sammel envisioned a composition with strong side lighting in which the orchids appeared to be suspended in space. She designed an airy, asymmetrical flower arrangement with interesting negative space, set up in the natural light of a window.

To begin the sketch, she created a new file that measured 1200 x 1600 pixels. In the Brushes palette, she chose the Colored Pencil variant of the Pencils, and in the Papers section of the Art Materials palette, she clicked on Basic Paper. Then she drew a tight, black-and-white sketch. To sketch as Sammel did, choose the Colored Pencil

The color underpainting

A detail showing scraped back canvas

Adding texture to the background with the Loaded Palette Knife variant of Impasto

variant and check in the General section of the Brush Controls palette to make sure that the method for the Colored Pencil is set at Buildup and the subcategory at Grainy Hard Buildup.

2 Creating the color underpainting. She began to lay color directly over the sketch using Round Camelhair variant of the Brushes. She painted using warm autumn colors—browns, burnt sienna, golds—and other rich hues.

Traditional artists often add texture and complexity to the surface of their paintings by scraping areas of paint off the canvas. To scrape back areas, Sammel chose the Loaded Palette Knife variant of the Brushes. To make a tiny version of the brush, she reduced its size using the Size slider in the Controls:Brushes palette. Switching between the Round Camelhair and Loaded Palette Knife variants of the Brushes, she painted and scraped back, pulled and blended colors, creating an expressive painting with a lot of movement.

3 Adding textured brushwork. Then Sammel added more interest and activity to the composition by adding textured brushstrokes that did not necessarily follow the lines of the colored paint. She modified the Loaded Palette Knife variant of Impasto, so that it would paint with negative depth, but not color, and she made it smaller. To make Sammel's custom palette knife, choose the Loaded Palette Knife variant of Impasto and set the Size slider in the Controls:Brush palette to 11.0. In the Brush Controls palette's Impasto section set the Draw To menu to Depth and the Depth slider to 35%, leaving other settings at their defaults: Smoothing, 77% and Plow, 100%. Save the variant by choosing Save Variant from the Brushes palette's Variant menu, giving it a new name. Then choose the original Loaded Palette Knife and restore its default settings by choosing Variant, Restore Default Variant.

When she wanted the new palette knife to paint with both color and depth, she modified it to pick up and smear underlying colors. To make this modification, select the new palette knife, and in the Impasto section of Brush Controls, set the Draw To menu back to Color and Depth. To pick up and mix underlying colors more—in the Brush Controls palette's Well section—set Resat to 20%. Save and name the new variant, then reselect the first modified palette knife.

Using warm creamy colors, Sammel painted loose, gestural brushstrokes over the background. At this point, she exaggerated the strong side lighting and enhanced the negative space in the painting by using

4a

Painting details on the orchids

4b

Pulling and blending paint on the flowers with a small Variable Flat Opaque brush (Impasto)

5a

Adding more texture to the foreground using the Texturizer-Fine (Impasto)

the Variable Flat Opaque variant of Impasto with Draw To set to its default Color And Depth to apply more white brushwork to the right side of the image.

4 Painting details on the flowers, vase and table.

Once the background was painted in, Sammel painted over the orchids using the Variable Flat Opaque (Impasto). She added bright highlights to the right side of the orchids and deeper, richer colors to areas in shadow on the flowers, vase and table. As she worked, she frequently modified settings in the Impasto section of Brush Controls for the Variable Flat Opaque variant. To paint with color and texture, she left the Draw To menu set at Color And Depth; to add textured brushstrokes without adding color, she chose Draw To Depth setting. To paint brushstrokes with texture based on the current paper texture, she kept the Depth Method set to Paper.

5 Refining the painting. Sammel used a small Loaded Palette Knife (Impasto) to drag color through the image (especially in the vase), then she added more colored paint using the Dry Ink variant of the Brushes. To allow the Dry Ink to mix and pull colors on the canvas, she made sure that Brush Loading was turned on in the Brush Controls palette's Well section. And to enhance the effect of pulling and mixing colored paint, she lowered the Resat (to about 20%) and raised the Bleed setting (to about 80%).

5b

Painting final details on the vase and flowers using the Loaded Palette Knife (Impasto) and Dry Ink (Brushes) variants

She added spattery Impasto texture to the image foreground with the Texturizer-Fine variant of Impasto. Then she brushed over areas that were too "impastoed" using the Depth Equalizer variant (Impasto) at a low Opacity (Controls:Brush). Finally, she reduced the overall effect of the Impasto by choosing Canvas, Impasto Lighting. For a more subtle Impasto look she reduced the Amount to 75%.

A Painter Liquid Ink Primer

Overview *Here you'll find the basics for painting with the new Liquid Ink brushes and layers in Painter 7.*

We began this Liquid Ink study of Little Doll *by creating a black line drawing with the Fine Point variant of Liquid Ink on a Liquid Ink layer. Then we added a new layer (by choosing New Liquid Ink Layer from the Layers section menu), dragged it below the sketch layer in the Layers section, and added color to the table and background with the Graphic Camel variant. For the cat's fur we created another new layer between the two we already had, and painted using gold and tan colors. For the look of thicker paint on the layer with the fur, we double-clicked the layer's name in the Layers section and adjusted the Amount slider in the Liquid Ink Layer Attributes dialog box. Then we painted with the Coarse Camel Resist to erode some of the colored ink.*

WITH THE NEW LIQUID INK BRUSHES AND MEDIA LAYERS in Painter 7, you can paint bold, graphic brushstrokes of flat color, then erode ink with resist brushes or build up thick ink that has three-dimensional highlights and shadows. Like traditional viscous media (printer's ink or the enamel used in jewelry making, for example), Liquid Ink is sticky.

Yellow Pitcher (above), one in a series of studies of 1930s California pottery, was created with the Graphic Camel and Graphic Camel Resist variants on several Liquid Ink layers, so that each color could be kept separate without mixing. Before you start a Liquid Ink painting of your own, reading the next five pages will help you to understand how to achieve the results you desire.

Controlling Liquid Ink. The most important settings for Liquid Ink are in several palette sections: the General, Size, Expression and Liquid Ink sections of the Brush Controls palette; the Layers section of the Objects palette; and the Surface Lighting dialog box, found under the Canvas menu. Painting with a Liquid Ink brush automatically generates a Liquid Ink layer, which is then listed in the Layers section. Liquid Ink layers can be targeted in the Layers section and edited like other layers. (Chapter 5 tells more about working with layers.)

> **RESOLUTION-INDEPENDENT INK**
>
> A new graphic medium, Liquid Ink is resolution-independent. It's possible to create a Liquid Ink illustration at half size, then double the resolution of the file and retain the crisp edges on the brush work.

In this example, the "e" was drawn after the "S," and the new Liquid Ink stroke melted into the existing ink. The lettering was drawn using the Smooth Flat variant of Liquid Ink. The rough strokes were added using the Graphic Camel.

The Volume setting in the Expression section of the Brush Controls palette allows you to specify which factor controls the Volume of a stroke.

The Liquid Ink section of Brush Controls, showing the Type pop-up menu

The Liquid Ink section, showing the default settings for the Graphic Camel

In the General section of the Brush Controls palette, the Liquid Ink dab types are displayed in the Dab Type pop-up menu. A dab type determines the shape of the brush tip—for instance, Liquid Ink Flat and Liquid Ink Camel (Camel brush tips are round). The Liquid Ink brushes use continuous-stroke technology, which means that brushstrokes are painted using brush hairs that form a set of anti-aliased 1-pixel lines. You'll find more information about dab types in "Building Brushes" on page 58.

In the Size section of Brush Controls, you'll find the Feature slider, which determines the density of the brush hairs in the continuous-stroke brushes. **Note:** A very low Feature setting (producing more densely packed brush hairs), takes greater computing power, and this can slow down the performance of a Liquid Ink brush.

In the Expression section of Brush Controls, if the Volume controller is set to Pressure, the height of the brushstroke will increase as pressure is applied to the stylus.

Liquid Ink has two basic components: Ink and Color. *Ink* consists of the shape and dimension of the Liquid Ink, giving the medium its sticky, plastic quality and form. The *Color* component is independent of the ink form. In the Liquid Ink section of Brush Controls, the Type pop-up menu includes nine important Color-and-Ink options that dramatically affect the performance of the Liquid Ink brushes. The Type settings themselves are complex and are also affected by slider settings in the Liquid Ink section of the Brushes palette (described below). A brush of the *Ink Plus Color* type adds new ink using the current color in the Colors section. While the *Ink Only* type affects only the shape of the brushstroke, the *Color Only* type affects only the color component. *Soften Ink Plus Color* alters existing brushstrokes so that the ink changes shape and the colors blend into one another. The *Soften Ink Only* reshapes the ink without changing its color, and *Soften Color Only* blends the Color without reshaping.

Painting with a *Resist* type brush will cause brushstrokes applied over the resist to be repelled. (Scrubbing with a non-resist brush can erode the resist until it is eventually removed.) Using the *Erase* type will remove existing ink and color. *Presoftened Ink Plus Color* works in conjunction with the Volume control settings to build up height as additional brushstrokes are applied.

INK AND COLOR COMPONENTS

Liquid Ink has two basic components: Ink and Color. *Ink* controls the shape and dimensionality of the strokes and gives the medium its sticky, plastic quality. *Color* controls color without affecting the shape.

INTERACTIVE SETTINGS

Many of the various settings that control Liquid Ink interact with one another in complex ways. This is what produces the magic of this medium, but mastering the complexity can present quite a challenge. It's a good idea to experiment with the different brushes and types until you get a feel for how Liquid Ink performs.

An active Liquid Ink layer as it appears in the Layers section of the Objects palette. To create a new Liquid Ink layer, click the right triangle on the Layers section bar and choose New Liquid Ink Layer or click the Create New Layers button at the bottom of the Layers section and choose New Liquid Ink Layer.

For Ocean Waves, the Coarse Bristle variant of Liquid Ink was used to draw curved strokes with a thick, bristly texture. We used the Coarse Airbrush Resist to add a foamy texture to the water and to suggest atmosphere in the sky.

Sumo Ink Man. We drew this study using a Wacom pressure-sensitive tablet and stylus on a laptop (while watching Sumo wrestlers on TV), with the Graphic Camel and Graphic Bristle variants of Liquid Ink.

The eight sliders in the Liquid Ink section work in conjunction with each other to create many kinds of Liquid Ink brushstrokes. Because these controls are very complex and interdependent, they're difficult to clearly define. Experiment—dig in and try out the Liquid Ink variants, while keeping an eye on the Liquid Ink section controls. The *Smoothness* slider controls how sticky the ink is. Lower values will create coarser brushstrokes with less self-adhesion. A high Smoothness setting will help to hide the individual bristle marks and will increase adhesion, but it may make the performance of the brush lag. *Volume* controls the height of the brushstroke. Use this setting in conjunction with the Volume setting in the Expressions section of Brush Controls to add height to brushstrokes. (**Note:** To view volume on your image, the Amount setting must be adjusted in the Liquid Ink Layer Attributes dialog box. See the "Turning on 3D Highlights and Shadows" tip below.) The *Min Volume* controls the amount that the volume can vary. (This slider is used in conjunction with the Volume setting in the Expression section.) *Rand Vol* controls the randomness of the volume in a stroke. A low value will create a smoother, less variable stroke. *Random Size* controls randomness of brush hair size within the stroke; again, a lower value will help to create a smoother stroke. *Bristle Frac* controls the density of the bristles. *Rand Bristle Vol* controls the variation in volume of ink laid down by individual bristles, and a low value will make the bristle marks a more even thickness. *Rand Bristle Size* controls variation in the widths of individual bristles. A very low setting will make the bristles of more similar in width.

TURNING ON 3D HIGHLIGHTS AND SHADOWS

To view Liquid Ink brush work with three-dimensional highlights and shadows, double-click the name of the Liquid Ink layer in the Layers section of the Objects palette and increase the Amount (thickness) setting. Click OK. The Liquid Ink medium has no thickness limit. After you have increased the Amount setting, you can use your stylus to paint more Liquid Ink onto the layer, continuing to build up the pile of ink. You can adjust the thickness at any time using the Amount slider in the Liquid Ink Layer Attributes dialog box. (There is no preview in this dialog box. You have to adjust the slider and click OK, then observe the effect on the image.) To change the direction, intensity, or other properties of the lighting, choose Canvas, Surface Lighting, and adjust the settings in the Impasto Lighting dialog box.

Increasing the Amount setting (left) increased the thickness of the brushstrokes (right). We left the settings in the Surface Lighting dialog box at their defaults.

After drawing black line work using the Fine Point variant, John Derry created a new Liquid Ink layer, and dragged it below the line work layer in the Layers section. Working on the new layer, he used the Smooth Knife variant to paint broad areas of color onto the background. He created interesting texture by eroding paint with the Coarse Airbrush Resist. For the smooth-edged highlights on the stool, he painted with the Smooth Camel variant.

Brushstrokes painted with the Smooth Flat variant of Liquid Ink

Thin-to-thick sweeping curved strokes painted with the Pointed Flat variant of Liquid Ink

WORKING WITH THE LIQUID INK BRUSHES.

Here are some suggestions for how to paint using the new Liquid Ink brushes in Painter 7. Even if you're familiar with Painter's other brushes, try out these ideas and experiment with all of the Liquid Ink variants.

Painting coarsely textured brushstrokes. To paint brushstrokes with a coarse bristly texture, choose the Coarse Bristle variant. You can control the paint coverage by applying more or less pressure to the stylus—a lighter pressure will create a stroke with less paint. The Graphic variants also paint coarsely textured brushstrokes and with better performance, for more spontaneous painting. The Graphic Camel is one of our favorites because it paints expressive, thin-to-thick strokes, with finer texture on the edges of the brushstrokes.

Blended color with smooth brushes. Any Liquid Ink variant with Smooth in its name has a high smoothness setting and will paint just like a brush loaded with very thick, sticky ink or paint. The Smooth Bristle variant's bristles will spread or splay out as you rotate your hand through the stroke, while the Smooth Camel performs like a big, round brush with longer bristles. As you press harder on the stylus, the Smooth Camel will paint a broader stroke. As you paint a new color over existing ink with a Smooth brush, the edges of the colors will subtly blend.

Thick and thin strokes with the Flat brushes. Look for brushes with the word Flat in their name; the Coarse Flat and Pointed Flat are examples. With Flat-tipped brushes, you can paint wide or narrow strokes, depending on how you hold the stylus relative to the stroke direction and how much pressure you apply. When trying the strokes below, position your stylus with the button facing up (away from you). To paint a broad flat area of color with the Smooth Flat (as in the example on the left), pull the brush straight across your image using even pressure. To make the thin lines, pull down. To make a curved, thin-to-thick wavy line, use light pressure on your stylus for the thin top areas, and more pressure as you sweep down and rotate the brush. For flat brushstrokes with sensitive thin-to-thick control, try the Pointed Flat. With this brush, bristle marks will be more visible when heavy pressure is applied to the stylus. For a thin-to-thick sweeping curved stroke, begin the thin portion with

We drew the sketch for Yellow Pitcher *using the Velocity Sketcher variant.*

The Graphic Camel Resist variant was used to erode ink and create highlights in Yellow Pitcher. *A detail is shown here.*

very light pressure on your stylus, and as you sweep downward rotate your stylus slightly and apply more pressure. To make a thick, even stroke, pull the stylus sideways relative to the button, using even pressure. For the thin lines, apply even pressure and pull in a direction toward or away from the button.

Sketching and line work. You can also sketch or draw line work with Liquid Ink. Quick performance makes the Velocity Sketcher ideal for spontaneous sketching. On the edges of the brushstrokes, you'll notice grainy texture.

The *Fine* variants of Liquid Ink are good for painting details and for calligraphic line work. The Fine Point draws like a steel pen with a pointed nib, and the Fine Eraser is ideal for cleaning up edges and for removing small patches of ink.

Painting resists. A *resist* is a substance that can be painted onto a Liquid Ink layer with a Liquid Ink Resist type brush. A resist is capable of repelling ink when the area is painted over by a standard Liquid Ink brush. You can also "scrub away" existing Liquid Ink using a Resist type brush. The Coarse Bristle Resist and the Graphic Camel Resist, for instance, are useful for painting coarse, eroded areas on a Liquid Ink painting. For a smoother resist, try the Smooth Bristle, Smooth Flat or Smooth Camel Resist variant. To erode existing ink and create an interesting speckled texture, use the Coarse Airbrush Resist.

Using the Soften Edges and Color variant of Liquid Ink, you can subtly blur areas of ink and color.

Detail of Hillside Lake. *We used Soften Edges and Color to blend the top edge of the purple hill in the midground.*

You can nondestructively make Liquid Ink brushstrokes appear to expand or contract by adjusting the Threshold slider in the Liquid Ink Layer Attributes dialog box. To see how Threshold works, in the Layers section of the Objects palette, target the layer that you'd like to change and access the Liquid Ink Layer Attributes dialog box by double-clicking the layer's name in the Layers section (or press the Enter key). To thicken the appearance of the brushstrokes, lower the Threshold value by moving the slider to the left. To give the ink a thinner appearance, raise the Threshold value by moving the slider to the right.

Adjusting the Threshold slider very low (to −49%) thickened the blue ink.

Adjusting the Threshold very high (to 160%) dramatically thinned the blue ink on the sugar bowl.

Encaustic Painting with Liquid Ink

Overview *Use a Liquid Ink brush to paint textured color on a layer; duplicate the layer; make a custom coloring brush; recolor the layer and erode areas; add more layers with new color and texture.*

JOHN DERRY

Painting the yellow square with the Sparse Camel variant of Liquid Ink

The new active Liquid Ink layer shown in the Layers section of the Objects palette

ENCAUSTIC PAINTING INCORPORATES PIGMENTS suspended in wax. It was used by the ancient Greeks who painted the brightly colored statues in the Acropolis and by the Romans for wall murals in Pompeii. Traditional encaustic technique involves heating the wax-based medium and then painting quickly while the wax is still malleable. Delicate layering of transparent color as well as heavy impasto techniques are possible. In Painter 7, you can create the look of encaustic painting with the new Liquid Ink brushes and media layers.

To create *Chess*, John Derry used Liquid Ink brushes and media layers to emulate encaustic painting. He painted bright colors on Liquid Ink layers, then eroded and scratched out areas to reveal the color and textured brush work on the underlying layers. For the look of thick encaustic paint, he added subtle three-dimensional highlights and shadows to the layers.

1 Creating textured brush work. Begin your Liquid Ink painting by opening a new file with a white background (File, New). To work at the scale of this painting, set the Width and Height at 800 x 800 pixels and click OK.

To paint a background consisting of large, textured strokes, choose the Sparse Camel variant of Liquid Ink in the Brushes palette and choose a bright yellow color in the Colors section of the Art Materials palette. When you've chosen a Liquid Ink brush and

The completed first layer, showing the highlights and shadows on the brush work and the settings in the Liquid Ink Layer Attributes dialog box

The active, duplicate layer in the Layers section

Choosing Color Only for the Type setting in the Liquid Ink Section of the Brush Controls palette

The square reddish areas added to the image on the duplicate layer, then partially eroded using a resist brush; shown with both layers visible (left) and with the yellow layer hidden (right).

you touch your stylus to the tablet, a Liquid Ink layer will automatically be generated and will be listed in the Layers section of the Objects palette. Loosely block in a square shape using the Sparse Camel. Derry purposely painted an irregular edge and left part of the white background as an informal border, which would add to the textural contrast in his image.

2 Turning on thick paint. To add realistic highlights and shadows to the brush work on the yellow layer, double-click its name in the Layers section of the Objects palette. When the Liquid Ink Layer Attributes dialog box appears, increase the Amount setting to about 20% and click OK.

3 Duplicating a Liquid Ink layer. Derry wanted to add different colors while keeping the brushstroke pattern that he had already created. So, he duplicated the active yellow layer by choosing the Layer Adjuster tool in the Tools palette, pressing the Alt/Option key and clicking once on the layer in the image. (To read more about working with layers, turn to Chapter 5 "Using Layers and Shapes.") Once you've duplicated the layer, choose the Brush again in the Tools palette.

4 Making a custom brush for coloring. With some Liquid Ink brushes, you can recolor elements without disturbing the ink (shape, volume and lighting) component that you've painted on a layer. After the layer duplicate was created, Derry modified the Sparse Camel brush so that it would change the color without changing the shape and thickness of the existing strokes. To modify the Sparse Camel as Derry did, open the Brush Controls palette by choosing Window, Show Brush Controls, or by pressing Ctrl/⌘-7. Open the Liquid Ink section by clicking the left triangle on the Liquid Ink section bar and in the section's Type pop-up menu, choose Color Only. To save this custom Sparse Camel brush, choose Save Variant from the Variant menu on the Brushes palette, name the new brush and click OK to save it. In addition to saving your new brush, Painter will remember the changes that you've made to the default Sparse Camel brush, so it's a good idea to restore it to its default settings. To return the original Sparse Camel variant to its default, choose Restore Default Variant from the Variant menu.

5 Coloring and eroding the duplicated layer. With the duplicate layer active in the Layers section, choose a new color (Derry chose a bright reddish-pink) and paint over

ERASING LIQUID INK

To completely remove Liquid Ink from a Liquid Ink layer, choose the Eraser or Fine Eraser variant of Liquid Ink. Click on the name of the layer you wish to edit in the Layers section of the Objects palette and brush over the area that you'd like to remove. If you have a thick buildup of Liquid Ink on the layer, you may have to scrub over the area a few times to completely remove all of the ink.

6a

The smaller blue squares are added to the image, breaking each of the original four squares into four.

6b

The small green squares are added, so that now each of the four original squares has sixteen parts.

6c

The Layers section showing the renamed Liquid Ink layers

the areas that you want to recolor. To scrape away areas of the layer so that the color from the underlying layer will show through, you can use a Resist type variant or an Eraser type variant of Liquid Ink. Because he likes the texture it creates, Derry scrubbed with the Sparse Camel Resist variant to scrape away the pink upper right and lower left areas to reveal the yellow. Then, to add an eroded texture into areas within the pink squares that he planned to keep, he brushed lightly over them using the Sparse Camel Resist variant.

6 Adding the blue and green squares. To add the blue and green colors to his image, Derry repeated the duplicating, revealing and eroding process in steps 2 and 3. The blue squares were smaller, so the effect was to break each pink square into four. The green squares were even smaller, the effect was to break up each original square into sixteen.

7 Painting the chess piece. So the castle would look as if it were thicker paint sitting on top of the painted chess board, Derry wanted the direction of the brushstrokes to be different. He created a new Liquid Ink layer by choosing New Liquid Ink Layer from the pop-out menu on the right side of the Layers section bar. On the new layer, he blocked in the basic shape of the chess piece with the default Sparse Camel using white color, then used the Sparse Camel Resist to erode some of the white paint. For the black areas on the chess piece, Derry duplicated the white layer as he had done for the yellow in step 3. Then he chose his custom Sparse Camel brush (which used Color Only) and painted black onto the right half of the castle. To finish, he used the Sparse Camel Resist to erode areas of the black layer to expose the white underneath. 🖌

7a

The white shape was painted on a new Liquid Ink layer

7b

The black brush work shown in this detail was painted on a duplicate of the white layer

■ "I approach painting in Painter the same way I paint conventionally," says **Karen Carr**, an accomplished illustrator who often creates natural history illustrations for educational publishers.

Carr was commissioned by *Scholastic Press* to create the undersea illustration above. She began by sketching with the Dry Media variants, then roughed in color using Brushes variants. She painted glazes of color over the top of her underpainting just as she does with oil paints. Carr prefers to keep the use of layers to a minimum, because she likes the tactile feel of moving paint around on the Canvas. To achieve the illusion of light shining down in the upper left, she set up a custom colored light using Effects, Surface Control, Apply Lighting. After blocking in basic color on the dolphin, the fish, and coral using a modified Charcoal variant, she used the Just Add Water variant of Liquid to smoothly blend and render the sea life. She worked back and forth, adding color and blending as she refined the volume of their forms. When she wanted to smudge paint and reveal texture, she used the Coarse Smear and Smudge variants of Liquid.

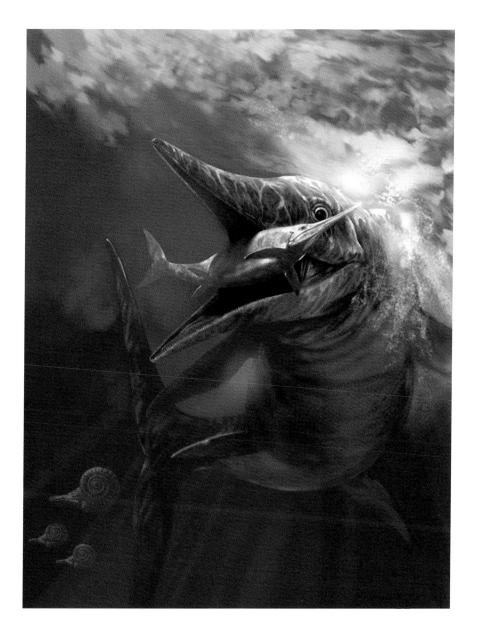

■ **Karen Carr** was commissioned by
Scientific American magazine to create
Temnodontosaur, a cover illustration
representing the work of Dr. Ryosuke
Motani, a researcher in the paleobiology
department at the Royal Ontario Museum
of Toronto. Carr worked closely with Dr.
Motani when painting this cannibal of the
Jurassic Sea. To begin *Temnodontosaur,*
Carr chose an ocean blue color in the
Colors section of Painter's Art Materials
palette and then chose Effects, Surface
Control, Color Overlay to establish the
color theme for the painting.

Then, using modified Charcoal variants
of Dry Media, she roughed in color.
While painting, she used a wide variety
of textures, and she changed the size
and opacity of the brushes often as she
worked. As Carr began to build up the
volume of the animals, she used the Just
Add Water (and other Liquid variants) to
blend and pull color around on the
image. To create the patterns in the
water in the upper area, she blended
and pulled paint using the Distorto
variants of Liquid as well her own
custom Liquid variants.

■ An accomplished commercial illustrator who specializes in book illustration, **Don Stewart** worked on gessoed illustration board with airbrush and colored pencil before he began using Painter. Today he draws on the computer using Painter's tools and brushes that match his traditional ones.

Barbour Books commissioned Stewart to create the *Abe Lincoln Collage* for the cover of the youth history book *American Heroes*. Stewart began the illustration by choosing a fine-textured paper and

drawing a detailed sketch in Painter using Pencils variants. To isolate areas of the image (such as Lincoln's head), he made freehand selections using the Lasso tool and then saved the selections as masks (Select, Save Selection), in case he needed to use them later. Then he blocked in basic color using Water Color brushes. He dropped the Water Color layer to the Canvas so he could paint on it with other brushes. (With the Water Color layer selected, in the Layers section of the Objects palette, choose Drop from

the pop-out menu in the right corner of the section). To build up tones and value, he used the Digital Airbrush variant of Airbrushes and several Brushes variants. Then he added highlights, deeper shadows and fine detail using the Colored Pencil variant of Pencils. Stewart sprayed texture on the skin and clothing using the Coarse Spray Airbrush. For the texture on the grass in the foreground, he used Chalk variants (Dry Media) and the Coarse Spray and Variable Splatter Airbrushes.

■ *Snowman Assistance* was commissioned by *LifeWise* magazine for article entitled, "Extending Your Heritage," by J. Otis Ledbetter. **Don Stewart** began the illustration by sketching in Painter using Pencils variants on fine-textured paper. He isolated areas of the image (for example, the girl's skin tones) so that he could freely paint within the selected areas. He uses selections in the same way that he used friskets in traditional airbrush illustration. To lay in colored washes he used Water Color variants. Stewart combined the Water Color layer with the Canvas by choosing Drop from the Layers section menu on the Objects palette. Next, he used the Digital Airbrush variant of Airbrushes to paint smoother areas (such as the skin), and to begin to build up tone and value. When the figures were modeled the way he wanted them, he added highlights and detail using the Colored Pencil variant of Pencils. For more texture on the hat and gloves, he used the Fine Spray and Coarse Spray variants of the Airbrushes. To add a chunky texture to the snow, he painted with subtly different colors using Chalk variants over a rough texture.

■ **Richard Noble** has been an accomplished traditional painter and designer for many years. Today he paints most of his fine artwork in Painter, using techniques that simulate traditional acrylic painting. He typically begins a painting by shooting reference photos and making sketches on location.

For *Garden* (right) and *Coast* (below), two paintings from his Mendocino series, Noble roughed in vibrant, saturated color with the Sargent Brush variant of the Artists brush and the Round Camelhair variant of the Brushes. Both of these brushes allowed Noble to move paint around on the canvas. He also blended color using the Palette Knife variant of the Brushes and the Distorto variant of Liquid. Using a small Round Camelhair variant, he painted fine details in the shady areas of the foreground foliage as well as in the sunlit areas of the paintings. Noble usually prints his paintings on canvas with light-fast inks and finishes them with touches of acrylic paint. To see two other paintings from his Mendocino series, turn to the gallery at the end of Chapter 2.

■ **Cher Threinen-Pendarvis** often makes several color studies for a painting on location, carefully observing how light and atmosphere affect color in highlights and shadows.

An isolated, breathtaking view and unique plant life provided the inspiration for *Agaves on the Edge*. For this painting, Pendarvis began by making several colored pencil sketches—details of the agave plants, the cliffs and the overall seascape—in a traditional sketchbook that she'd carried in her backpack. Later, back at the studio she created a new file in Painter. Using the 2B Pencil variant of

the Pencils and Basic Paper texture, she sketched the composition. She loosely blocked in color directly over the sketch with a Round Camelhair brush, which she had modified to include a small amount of Color Variability to help to modulate the color. To build up layers of color interest on the hills, cliffs and water, she dabbed small strokes of paint on top using a smaller Round Camelhair brush, then she blended areas of the cliffs, hills and water using the Grainy Water variant of Liquid. Pendarvis added softly colored clouds to the sky using the Square Chalk variant of Dry Media, then smoothed and

blended color using the Grainy Water. To add textured highlights to the beach and color interest to the cliffs, she used the Square Chalk and Artist Pastel Chalk (Dry Media). To balance the composition, she reworked some of the foreground plants and added soft brushstrokes to the path using the Round Camelhair variant. She also used the Artist Pastel Chalk to feather subtly colored strokes over the painted leaves, to further define their forms and to add color complexity and movement. Finally, she applied highlights to some of the leaves using the Artist Pastel Chalk.

■ **Dennis Orlando** is well known for his Impressionist-style landscape and still life paintings. To create the vibrant look of oil paints in *Martinique Beach*, he layered color with the Artist Pastel Chalk (Dry Media) and the Smeary variants of the Brushes.

Using saturated colors, he roughed out a study for the composition in Painter using the Chalk variants of Dry Media, then layered more color to build up an underpainting. He used the Sharp Chalk

variant to define the edges of the sailboats and figure. Switching back and forth between the Artist Pastel Chalk and the Grainy Water variant of Liquid, he continued to add color and smudge it. He painted the foreground sand by making short, curved strokes with a modified Smeary Flat variant of the Brushes. (To help to modulate color, Orlando increased Color Variability for the Smeary Flat variant, moving the (± H) (hue) slider to about 15% in the Color

Variability section of the Art Materials palette.) To pull and mix color in the water, sky and sand, he used a large Smeary Bristle Spray variant (Brushes). Then he added accents of more saturated color to the sails, the man's shorts and sunlit areas of the water using a smaller Smeary Bristle Spray variant. Finally, he used tiny Grainy Water and Distorto variants of Liquid to blend and finesse the highlights on the boat rails and on the shiny fabric of the sails.

■ **Cher Threinen-Pendarvis's**
experience with traditional style in pastel, watercolor and acrylic translates easily to digital pastel in Painter.

Paths to Water 1 (above), is one in a series of paintings of Sunset Cliffs Natural Park in San Diego, California. Pendarvis began the painting by making location studies using a Powerbook laptop computer, Painter and a Wacom pressure-sensitive tablet. Sitting in the shade near the trees, she began by creating a new file with a beige background paper color. She chose Sandy paper texture (loaded from the Drawing Paper Textures library in the Paper Textures folder on the Painter_CD2 CD-ROM), and sketched using the Sharp

Chalk variant of Dry Media and a dark brown color. Observing the afternoon light and shadows she worked on location using the laptop until she had established the composition, general color theme and cast shadows in the study. Later on her studio computer, Pendarvis added more layers of color using modified Square Chalk and Large Chalk variants of Dry Media, working over the entire piece. She blended areas with the Grainy Water variant of Liquid and added more textured, directional strokes with the Chalk variants. As a last step, she used Effects, Surface Control, Apply Surface Texture to apply Sandy paper texture to the entire painting, using subtle settings.

BABY BLUES **14** SCRAPBOOK

MOTHERHOOD

IS NOT FOR WIMPS

BY RICK KIRKMAN
AND JERRY SCOTT

■ A freelance illustrator for over 15 years, **Rick Kirkman** divides his time between producing cartoons for commercial clients and creating the King Feature Syndicate comic strip *Baby Blues* with partner Jerry Scott.

Kirkman began the cover illustration for *Motherhood Is Not for Wimps* (above) in Painter with black linework using Pencils variants on Basic Paper texture. Kirkman planned to add color using the Airbrushes variants. To protect areas of his image from overspray when he used the Airbrushes, Kirkman first drew Bézier paths using the Pen tool, converted the paths to selections and then saved each selection as a mask, in case he needed to use it later. (To convert a path to a selection and save it, click the Make Selection button on the Controls:Shape Design palette and then choose Select, Save Selection.) To load each mask as a selection, he chose Select, Load Selection, then he sprayed color using Spray variants of the Airbrush. For a more textured look in the foreground and the shadow, he used the Coarse Spray and Variable Splatter variants.

After the Painter Illustration was complete, Kirkman saved it as a TIFF file and placed it into an Adobe Illustrator file, where he added the blue panel and type. (Illustrator accepts both RGB and CMYK TIFF files, which makes direct export from Painter possible.)

■ **Keith MacLelland** was chosen by *Philly-Tech* magazine to create **Worker Yawn** (left) and **Technology Roulette** (below). Both illustrations began with a rough pencil sketch, which was redrawn with flowing black ink lines with the Scratchboard Tool variant of the Pens. After blocking in the basic color areas using the Chalk variants of Dry Media, MacLelland refined the color using Smeary variants of the Brushes.

After the basic colored brush work was roughed in for *Worker Yawn*, MacLelland added brushstrokes to the hair using a modified Dry Ink variant of Brushes, which incorporated finer bristles. To add volume to the woman's shoulders and apply highlights and shadows to her sweater, he used the Digital Airbrush. Then he painted the pattern on the sweater with the Scratchboard Tool. The rough edges along the bottom of the clothing were added with the Square Chalk variant of Dry Media. To finish, MacLelland set the curved text for the newspaper using the Text tool, using the Curve Style feature in the Text section of the Objects palette. (For more information about using Painter's text features, turn to Chapter 8.)

After he had drawn a sketch and laid in the basic color for *Technology Roulette*, MacLelland wanted to add custom textures to the colored areas only, so he selected each colored area with the Magic Wand and then saved the selection as a mask (Select, Save Selection). To add a smooth paper texture to each of the selected areas, he chose Effects, Surface Control, Apply Surface Texture, Using Paper. This left the line work smooth. Then he used the Square Chalk variant of Dry Media to apply more texture around the gadgets (for instance the cell phones and Palm devices). MacLelland also painted a custom "Casino-like" paper texture (which included retro shapes), onto the background with the Square Chalk. To finish, MacLelland used the Smeary Round variant of the Brushes to paint a motion trail (a wet paint smear effect) behind the ball to make it look as though it was traveling around the roulette wheel.

■ When Heidi North, Art Director for Random House Publishing, commissioned **Marc Brown** to paint a cover illustration for *The New York Times Book Review*, Brown created an inviting image with comfortable emotional appeal. For *Woman Reading*, he painted a restful color scheme of predominantly blue and green with smoothly blended highlights and shadows.

Brown began the illustration in Adobe Illustrator and rasterized the layered file in Photoshop. He saved it in Photoshop format and opened it in Painter. He used Painter's brushes to render details on each layer, working from the background to the foreground. Using the Round Camelhair variant of the Brushes, he modeled the forms of the landscape and the figure. To smoothly pull and blend color, he used the Just Add Water variant of Liquid. He added more detailed highlights and shadows to the illustration by painting with a small version of the Round Camelhair variant, again blending areas with Just Add Water. Finally, he sharpened a few highlights with the tiny Round Camelhair.

■ Based in Normandy, France, **Kathy Hammon** is an accomplished artist and educator who works both traditionally and digitally. Hammon's current work with traditional media consists of very large oil paintings on canvas. Her digital paintings also give the viewer the feeling of vast spaces. When she uses Painter she paints directly on-screen, without the use of photographs or scanning. Hammon loves the realistic textures that can be achieved with Painter's Dry Media, Brushes and Liquid variants. She began *The Whale* by using the Oil Pastel variant of Dry Media and the Dry Ink variant of Brushes to paint sweeping brushstrokes and large areas of color. When she wanted to blend one color into another, she used the Just Add Water variant of Liquid. Spontaneously painting, then blending, she worked back and forth, changing the sizes of the brushes as she worked. To complete the seascape, Hammon used a modified Artist Pastel Chalk variant to add texture and redefine the edge of the whale's tail. She also added a few small highlights to the distant hills by brushing softly with the custom Chalk variant.

SELECTIONS, SHAPES AND MASKS

Horsepower Heart. *Artist Chet Phillips began by making a black-and-white drawing with the Scratchboard Tool variant of the Pens. Then, working on top of the scratchboard drawing, he used the Pen tool to draw shapes and converted each shape to a selection (Shapes, Convert to Selection). After making each selection, he saved it as a mask (Select, Save Selection). Next, Phillips turned the entire scratchboard drawing into a separate layer by choosing Select, All and Select, Float, and set its Composite Method to Gel. Working on the image canvas, he loaded each of his masks (Select, Load Selection), and applied colored tints to the selected areas using Effects, Fill. Then he painted colored details with the Airbrushes.*

TO GET THE MOST FROM PAINTER, you need to invest some time in understanding how the program isolates portions of images so that you can paint them, apply special effects or otherwise change them without affecting the rest of the image. Much of the program's power is tucked into the complex area of *selections*, *shapes (*which are also called *paths), and *masks*.

A *selection* is an area of the image that has been isolated so changes can be made to the contents only, or so the area can be protected from change. There are two kinds of selections in Painter: outline-based and pixel-based. Like a cookie cutter, an *outline-based* selection (called a *shape* or *path*) defines the area inside a sharply defined outline. But unlike cookie cutters in the real world, an outline-based selection border in Painter can be freely scaled or reshaped. If Painter's shapes are like the outlines produced by cookie cutters, then *pixel-based* selections are more like painted resists. Pixel-based selections make the selected areas fully or partially available for change or copying, with the degree of availability determined by the nature and "thickness" of the "resist material."

SELECTING THE CANVAS

Selections are typically used to isolate areas of the image canvas. However, in Painter 7 they can also be used to isolate areas of specific layers. To learn about how to use selections with layers, turn to Chapter 5.

The perimeter of an active selection is indicated by an animated border, the selection marquee. There can be only one active selection at a time. Selections are temporary. If you choose Select, None (Ctrl/⌘-D) or accidentally click outside the selection marquee, the selection will be lost, unless you have stored it in Selection Portfolio section of the Objects palette, or have saved it

The selection and shape tools are located in the four right columns of the Tools palette. Some tools share a space in the palette with other tools, as shown here in pop-out view. In columns from left to right these tools are: Lasso (**l**), Rectangular Selection (**r**) and Oval Selection (**o**); Magic Wand (**w**); Layer Adjuster (**f**), Selection Adjuster (**s**) and Shape Selection (**h**); Shape Design (also called Quick Curve) (**q**) and Pen (**p**); Oval Shape (**j**) and Rectangular Shape (**i**); Scissors (**z**), Remove Point (also called Delete Point tool) (**x**), Add Point (**a**) and Convert Point (**y**).

USING THE OBJECTS PALETTE

In Painter, selections, masks and shapes are stored in three sections of the Objects palette: the Masks section, the Layers section and the Selection Portfolio. To open any one of these sections, click the left triangle on its section bar. To open all sections of the Objects palette at once, press the Shift key and click the left triangle on any closed section in the Objects palette. To close all sections, Shift-click the left triangle of any open section.

To isolate areas of the canvas for filling, the Oval Selection tool was used to create an antialiased selection (left); the selection made by the Rectangular Selection tool needs no antialiasing (right).

as a mask in the Masks section of the Objects palette, or have converted it to a shape.

A *shape,* or *path,* is a mathematically described outline that can be stroked and filled. Shapes can be created with the Rectangular Shape, Oval Shape, Text, Pen or Shape Design tool (The Shape Design tool is listed in the manual as the Quick Curve tool). Shapes are automatically stored in the Layers section of the Objects palette. They can be used as independent elements in an illustration, or they can be converted to selections and used to isolate areas of the image. When you convert a shape to a selection (Shapes, Convert To Selection), its name disappears from the Layers section and an animated marquee appears on the image canvas. **Beware:** If you convert a shape to a selection using Painter, it will be permanently lost if you deselect it before you either convert it back to a shape, save it as a mask, drag it into the Selection Portfolio with the Selection Adjuster tool, or choose Undo (Ctrl/⌘-Z) or Reselect (Ctrl/⌘-R). (This chapter tells about drawing shapes and their relationship to selections. The stroke and fill attributes of shapes, their layering capabilities and their relationship to layers, are covered in Chapter 5).

Unlike a shape, which is stored *outline* information, a *mask* is stored *pixel-based* information. Masks can store 8-bit grayscale information so that a painting, a photo, or a complex graphic can be saved and then loaded as a selection. Painter's 8-bit masks allow 256 levels of opacity. When a mask is loaded as a selection, in areas where it is fully opaque, it completely protects the pixels underneath from change; where it is fully clear it fully selects them and exposes them to brushstrokes. Gray areas are partially selected. The protective mask can be thinned or even completely removed pixel by pixel. Painter allows up to 32 masks in a single document stored in the Masks section. Besides allowing complex image information to be used as a selection, masks provide a way of converting selection information to "permanent" storage until you need to use it.

The Masks and Layers sections of the Objects palette not only store masks and shapes, but they also control operations such as

The context-sensitive menu for an active selection appears at the spot where you right/Ctrl-click

PHOTO: CORBIS IMAGES

To vignette this photo, we began by making an Oval selection. We scaled the selection using the Selection Adjuster tool, then applied a feather of 15 pixels (Select, Feather) to soften the edge. Next, we reversed the selection by choosing Select, Invert. Working on the image canvas, we chose Edit, Clear to delete the background, leaving the vignetted edge.

The original rectangular selection was filled with blue, then feathered 20 pixels and filled with a rose color (left). Then the selection was transformed and filled with yellow, revealing the new rounded hard edge (right).

turning them on and off so they can be used as selections. (The Masks section is described on page 135, and the Layers section is described in Chapter 5.) The Selection Portfolio (opened by clicking the left triangle on the Selection Portfolio bar in the Objects palette) is useful for storing outline-based selections. (The Selection Portfolio is described on page 139.)

TWO KINDS OF SELECTIONS

The tool used to make a selection determines whether the selection is outline-based or pixel-based. Selections made with the Lasso, Rectangular, and Oval Selection tools, as well as selections converted from shapes, are outline-based selections. (For more information about outline-based selections, turn to "Creating Selections and Shapes," below.) Two procedures under the Select menu—Color Select and Auto Select—can be used to create pixel-based (or 8-bit) selections. Painter's Magic Wand tool also creates either a pixel-based selection or mask. (To read about the Magic Wand, turn to "Selecting and Masking by Color," on page 136.)

Using antialiasing. *Antialiasing* renders a smooth selection edge by making the pixels along the selection boundary semi-transparent. This prevents jagged, pixelated edges. All of Painter's selection tools make smooth-edged selections. The Magic Wand is the one tool that gives you a choice—just uncheck the Anti-Alias checkbox on the Controls:Magic Wand palette if you want to make a jaggy-edged, aliased selection.

CREATING SELECTIONS AND SHAPES

You can make outline-based selections and shapes in a number of ways: Create them with the Lasso or the Oval or Rectangular Selection tool or with the Pen, Shape Design (Quick Curve), or Oval or Rectangular Shape tools. Or drag a stored selection from the Selection Portfolio section of the Objects palette into your image. You can also import EPS paths as shapes from a PostScript drawing program and convert them to selections. You can create a selection from a mask (Select, Load Selection) or change a mask-

These type shapes were set with the Text tool and converted to shapes (choose Convert Text to Shapes from the pop-up menu on the right side of the Layers section bar). They were then selected with the Layer Adjuster tool (top), converted to active selections (Shapes, Convert To Selection) and then used to fill areas of the image canvas by choosing Effects, Fill (bottom).

These shapes were started by setting type with the Text tool, then converting it to shapes. To convert the text to shapes, we clicked the right triangle on the Objects palette's Layers section bar, and chose Convert Text to Shapes from the pop-up menu. The shapes at the top (with no fill or stroke and selected with the Shape Selection tool) show selected Bézier anchor points and curves. The lower letter shape, not selected, has been given a white fill using the Fill checkbox and color square in the Shapes, Set Shape Attributes dialog box.

based selection to an outline-based selection (Select, Transform Selection). When a soft-edged selection is transformed, it loses its soft edge. For instance, if the selection has a 10-pixel feathered edge, the feather is built inward and outward from the border. When the selection is transformed, the new boundary will fall in the middle of the feathered edge.

Rectangular and Oval Selection tools. Drag to make selections with these tools. To constrain the Oval or Rectangular Selection tools so they select perfect squares or circles, begin dragging and then hold down the Shift key to complete the drag.

Text tool. With Painter 7, the Text tool has been modified to create Dynamic Text. A dynamic text layer can be converted to shapes by choosing Convert Text to Shapes from the pop-up menu on the right side of the Layers section bar. For more information about Dynamic Text, turn to Chapter 8 "Working With Type in Painter."

Lasso tool. The Lasso tool is good for making quick, freehand selections. Choose the Lasso and carefully drag around the area that you want to isolate.

Rectangular and Oval Shape tools. Drag with these tools to create rectangular and elliptical shape objects. Hold down the Shift key as you drag with the tool to draw a perfect square or circle shape.

Pen and Shape Design (Quick Curve) tools. Choose the Pen tool for precise drawing using a combination of straight lines and curves. Click to create straight line segments; to draw curves, press to create a curve point and drag to pull out handles that control the curves. Or drag with the Shape Design (Quick Curve) tool to draw freehand shapes. To complete an outline drawn by the Pen or Shape Design tool, close the shape by connecting to

---

PATH MANIPULATION

To manipulate a path while drawing it, press the Ctrl/⌘ key to switch from the Pen to the Shape Selection tool so you can adjust the anchor points and control handles.

PRECISION DRAWING SETUP

If you're drawing paths and you find that the default stroke and fill obscure your path and make it hard to see its outline, then change the Shape Attributes to a skeletal line: Choose Edit, Preferences, Shapes; check the Big Handles drawing option and uncheck all the Fill and Stroke preferences. You'll be able to see the path outline with anchor points and handles so you can draw more precisely.

The Shape Preferences dialog box

Choosing a heart-shaped path in Painter's Selection Portfolio section, located in the Objects palette.

When this bird, drawn in Adobe Illustrator, was copied and pasted into Painter, it came in as a compound shape. To read about how the drop shadow was added turn to page 152.

To read about how the drop shadow was added turn to page 152.

NOW YOU SEE 'EM

With Painter, when you paste Post-Script outlines into Painter, the outlines may not appear to be in the document but you'll notice their names in the Layers section of the Objects palette. To force the outlines to draw on-screen, click to open the eye icon to the left of the imported layer's name. (When using File, Acquire, Adobe Illustrator File, the outlines automatically appear in the image, and their names also appear in the Layers section of the Objects palette.)

the origin point or by pressing the Close button on the Controls: Shape Design palette. To convert a shape drawn with the Pen or Shape Design tool to a selection, click the Make Selection button on the Controls:Shape Design palette, or choose Shapes, Convert To Selection.

Selection Adjuster, Layer Adjuster and Shape Selection tools. These tools share a space in the bottom row of the Tools palette. The Layer Adjuster tool is useful for working with shapes and layers. Read more about it in the beginning of Chapter 5. Use the Selection Adjuster to move or transform selections. Read more about this tool in "Transforming Selections," on page 138.

The Shape Selection tool (hollow arrow) allows you to select and adjust individual anchor points and control handles to modify shapes. This tool works much like its counterpart in Adobe Illustrator.

Shape Edit tools. The Scissors, Add Point, Remove Point (or Delete Point) and Convert Point tools will also be familiar to Illustrator users. Like the Shape Selection tool, they are used for changing shape paths. The Scissors tool allows you to cut a segment of a shape path selected with the Shape Selection tool. To add a new anchor point, select a path segment with the Shape Selection tool and click with the Add Point tool. To delete an anchor point, click on it with the Remove Point tool.

EPS IMPORTING ALERT!

A word of warning: As of this writing, we encountered problems when importing Illustrator files created in early versions of Freehand and Illustrator (prior to version 5 of the programs), using both of the import methods. When importing compound objects, we obtained the best results with drawings completely created in Illustrator 5 or newer (simply resaving an older file created in the new format resulted in some compound objects not making the transition). When working in Illustrator 9, for best results, save as an EPS file with Illustrator 8 compatibility.

The Selection Portfolio. To use an outline selection stored in the Selection Portfolio section of the Objects palette, drag it from the palette into your image. If you use a lot of custom paths in your work, use the Selection Mover (accessed by clicking the right triangle on the Selection Portfolio bar), to create custom libraries (see the "Libraries and Movers" section in Chapter 1).

Importing EPS outlines. Painter supports two ways to reliably import shapes, such as type set on a curve and converted to outlines created in a PostScript drawing program, or preexisting EPS clip art. The first option (File, Acquire, Adobe Illustrator File) creates a new file, importing the EPS outlines—with their strokes and fills—into Painter as shapes. To add the shapes to an existing Painter file, copy and paste the shapes from the new file into your working composition.

Susan LeVan used Painter's Auto Mask, Current Color feature to make rough-edged masks for brushstrokes shown in this illustration Covering Home, *created for* Becoming Family *magazine.*

The second option allows you to copy outlines with strokes and fills from a PostScript program to the clipboard and paste them into your Painter file. The outlines will be imported into your document as shapes and will appear in the Layers section of the Objects palette. Objects such as the converted letters "O" and "A" that have a *counter,* or hole, in them will come into Painter as compound shapes, preserving the holes. Like other shapes, imported EPS shapes (as long as they are closed, rather than open), can be converted to selections (Shapes, Convert To Selection) so you can use the outlines to modify the image canvas.

AUTOMATIC SELECTING AND MASKING

Two powerful functions—Auto Select and Auto Mask—create a selection or mask based on the criteria that you choose to sample, such as Paper, 3D Brush Strokes, Image Luminance, Current Color, Original Selection or Original Luminance. The two dialog boxes are identical, with the exception that one creates a pixel-based selection whereas the other creates and stores a mask. Auto Select is located under the Select menu. To use Auto Mask, choose Auto Mask from the pull down menu accessed by clicking the right triangle on the Masks section bar in the Objects palette or use the shortcut (Ctrl/⌘-Shift-M).

To generate a mask based on the brightness values in an image, try this: Create a new file with a white background. In the Colors section of the Art Materials palette, select black, and from the Brushes palette, choose the Scratchboard Tool variant of the Pens. Make a sketch, and then generate a mask for your sketch by choosing Auto Mask (Ctrl/⌘-Shift-M) using Image Luminance. In the Masks section of the Objects palette, click on the mask name to target the mask, and open the eye icon to the left of the mask name to view the mask as a red overlay. Highlighting the mask name will target the mask, allowing

Killdeer *by Mary Envall. To create this wildlife illustration—featuring a black-and-white ink drawing floating on top of colored, textured paper—Envall began by making a black-and-white scratchboard drawing in Painter. To drop the white background out behind the drawing she made an automatic selection, choosing Select, Auto Select, using Image Luminance. She floated the active selection by clicking on it with the Layer Adjuster and then deselected the layer. Next, she filled the background (the Canvas) with a colored texture, using Effects, Surface Control, Color Overlay using Paper and Dye Concentration.*

DYNAMIC TOLERANCE

The Controls:Magic Wand palette features a dynamic Tolerance slider. Click once in an image to begin a mask or selection. Move the Tolerance slider to the right to expand the masked colors; move to the left to reduce the masked or selected color range.

We clicked the Magic Wand in the sky area and began with a Tolerance of 3 and Feather of 1. (Feather allows similar colors to be partially selected.) Changing the Tolerance to 6 and leaving the Feather set at 1 masked the entire sky. When you move the slider, it automatically updates the mask.

Our goal was to generate a color selection for the sky in this photo. We chose Select, Color Select and clicked in the image to sample the color we wanted to isolate. We adjusted the H, S and V sliders until the red mask covered only the sampled color in the preview window. Alternatively, you can use Color Mask (accessed by clicking the right triangle on the Masks section bar) to accomplish the same thing, and the mask will automatically be stored in the Masks section of the Objects palette.

To create this letter "a" with textured highlights and shadows, we began by drawing the "a" with the Scratchboard Tool variant of Pens and black color on a white background. We made a luminosity mask for the letter using Auto Mask, Using Image Luminance. We filled the Canvas with blue color (covering the letter), then we loaded the selection (Select, Load Selection), and used Effects, Surface Control, Apply Surface Texture, Using Paper and the Dry Cracks texture (from the Papers section of the Art Materials palette), and a second time Using Mask, to add the bas relief effect. To create a similar look step-by-step, turn to "Setting a Logo in Stone," in Chapter 8.

you to edit it by painting on it with a brush. For an example of Auto Mask using Current Color—the only one of these automated masking methods that produces an aliased, jagged-edged mask—turn to "Isolating Color with Auto Mask," later in this chapter.

SELECTING AND MASKING BY COLOR

Painter offers useful tools and procedures with which you can make selections and masks based on color.

Magic Wand. Painter's Magic Wand is easy to use and is a real production time-saver. The Magic Wand lets you select an area of your image based on color similarities of contiguous or noncontiguous pixels. This is especially useful for selecting a uniformly colored element in an image, without having to draw around the area with the Lasso or Pen tool. You can choose to make a transient selection or store the selection as a mask using the Magic Wand by clicking the appropriate button on the Controls: Magic Wand palette. To select a wider range of color, move the Tolerance slider to the right. To smooth the edge of the Mask or selection, check the Anti-Alias checkbox. To add soft partially transparent values and areas of similar colors to the mask, increase the Feather by moving the slider to the right.

To add areas of similar adjacent color to the selection or mask (like Select, Grow in Adobe Photoshop), Shift-click on the existing selection with the Magic Wand. To remove color from a selection, Alt/Option-click on the area. To remove a range of colors from a selection, Alt/Option-drag in the area. To add areas of similar color that are not adjacent (like Select, Similar in Photoshop), turn off the Contiguous checkbox in the Controls:Magic Wand palette, and continue adding areas of non-contiguous color by pressing the Shift key as you click on the image. To turn off the nonadjacent mode, turn on Contiguous again.

> **ADJACENT AND NON-ADJACENT**
>
> Painter's Magic Wand controls include a Contiguous checkbox in the Controls:Magic Wand palette. The selection or mask automatically updates when you turn Contiguous (adjacent) mode on or off.
>
>

Using Color Select and Color Mask. Painter offers two closely related, automated features that are useful for isolating parts of images based on color. Use Select, Color Select to generate a pixel-based selection based on the color you sample by clicking in the image. Adjust the H (Hue), S (Saturation) and V (Value) Extents sliders in the Color Select dialog box to control the range of each of these properties sampled in the image. Experiment with adjusting the Feather sliders to improve the edges of the selection. Click OK to complete the new selection, and save it as a mask (Select, Save Selection). Color Select is closely related to Color Mask; both

PHOTO: CORBIS IMAGES

To make a selection isolating the large dahlia in this photo, we used Select, Color Select, then used the Lasso to change the selection border—pressing the Ctrl/⌘ key to subtract from the selection—to exclude the smaller flower.

We set this Adobe Woodtype Ornament shape using the Text tool. We Option-dragged with the Layer Adjuster tool to make a copy of the text ornament. To convert it to shapes, we clicked the right triangle on the Objects palette's Layers section bar, and chose Convert Text to Shapes from the pop-up menu. Next, we converted the copy into an active selection (Shapes, Convert to Selection) for treating the image canvas. To add the colored texture, we chose Effects, Surface Control, Color Overlay, Using Paper, Hiding Power with Pavement texture (loaded from the Paper Textures library within the Ver 6 folder in the Painter 7 application folder).

dialog boxes function essentially the same. Color Mask is found in the pop-out menu in the Masks section. Masks generated using Color Mask are automatically saved into the Masks section. To learn more about Color Mask, turn to "Using Color Mask," later in this chapter.

Many artists begin the process of isolating complex areas of an image using Color Select or Color Mask, then finish a selection by editing it using the Lasso with the Alt/Option key to subtract from the selection and with the Shift key to add to the selection. To convert a mask generated with Color Mask to a selection for editing, choose Select, Load Selection, and choose it from the menu in the Load Selection dialog box.

CONVERTING SELECTIONS, SHAPES AND MASKS

Outline-based and pixel-based selections have entirely different origins, but there is some degree of interchangeability.

To convert a mask into an outline-based selection so you can transform the outline (scale, skew or rotate) using the Selection Adjuster tool, choose Select, Load Selection. From the Load From pop-up menu, choose the appropriate mask, click the Replace Selection button and click OK. This turns the mask into an active selection. With the marquee active, choose Select, Transform Selection.

To convert an active outline-based selection into a mask and save it in the Masks section as pixel-based information instead of outline information, choose Select, Save Selection.

To convert a shape to an active selection so can you use it to isolate an area of the image canvas, select the shape by highlighting its name in the Layers section, and choose Shapes, Convert to Selection. An added bonus, the Pen and Shape Design (Quick Curve) tools offer a Make Selection button on the Controls: Shape Design palette, allowing quick conversion of a shape you make with one of these tools.

To convert an active selection into a shape so you can edit its outline (using anchor points and control handles), or fill and stroke it (using the Shapes, Set Shape Attributes dialog box), choose Select, Convert To Shape. Painter 7 preserves the unselected areas within in selections (such as the hole in a donut shape) when converting from selections to shapes.

TRANSFORMING SELECTIONS

Painter offers great flexibility, allowing outline-based selection borders to be scaled, skewed or rotated without altering the image canvas. Selections made with the Lasso or Rectangular or Oval Selection tools, as well as selections converted from shapes, are automatically outline-based. Selections saved as masks must be converted to outline-based information before they can be scaled, skewed or rotated. To convert a selection stored in the Masks section to an outline-based selection, load the selection (Select, Load Selection), and when the selection marquee appears, choose Select, Transform Selection. (When a selection is loaded from a mask and transformed, the mask in the Masks section remains unmodified until it is replaced by another selection using the Save Selection, Replace Mask command.)

An important concept to understand when working with outline-based selections is that of *active* vs. *selected*. An *active* selection displays an animated marquee, sometimes referred to as "marching ants." As soon as you've drawn a complete boundary with a selection tool, dragged a selection into your image from the Selection Portfolio, loaded a mask as a selection or converted a shape to a selection, you will see a marquee, letting you know it's active. The image canvas within the marquee can now be painted into, filled or treated with an effect.

A *selected* selection displays eight bounding-box handles around its edges—the handles are visible only when a selection is *active* and the Selection Adjuster tool is chosen. You select selections in order to move them, or scale, skew, or rotate their outlines, or change them using commands under the Select, Modify menu to widen, contract, smooth, or border them.

The distinction between "active" and "selected" gives you great flexibility: *You can move, scale, rotate and skew a selected selection outline without affecting the pixel information within it* by applying the Selection Adjuster tool to the interior or to the bounding box handles.

Working with the Selection Adjuster tool. Since outline-based selections are based on mathematical information, they can undergo all of the following transformations, carried out with the Selection Adjuster tool, with no loss of edge quality and without moving the pixels inside the selection boundary. To *move* a selection, position the Selection Adjuster over it; when you see the four-arrowed cursor, dragging will move the selection. To *duplicate*, hold down Alt/Option (a tiny "plus" will appear next to the cursor), drag and release. To *scale*, first select a selection by clicking on it once; position the tool over one of the corner handles; when the cursor changes, drag the handle. Use the Shift key to *resize proportionally*. If you want to *resize only horizontally or vertically*, drag on the center handle of a side, top or bottom. To *rotate*, use a corner handle, adding the Ctrl/⌘ key as you position the

An active selection (left) ready to accept brushstrokes within its boundary; a selected selection (right) ready to be moved by dragging with the Selection Adjuster tool. When the Selection Adjuster is chosen, an active selection becomes selected and displays eight square handles in addition to the marquee.

Alt/Option-dragging a selected selection to make a copy

Dragging a side handle to scale horizontally

Shift-dragging one of the corner handles to scale proportionally

Using a corner handle and the Ctrl/⌘ key to rotate

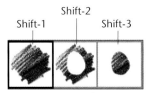
cursor before dragging. To *skew*, press Ctrl/⌘ while positioning over a center handle on the side, top or bottom, and then drag.

SAVING SELECTION OUTLINES

Use the Selection Adjuster tool to drag outline-based selections to the Selection Portfolio to store them. If you want to save shapes into this library, first convert them to selections (Shapes, Convert To Selection) and then drag them to the Selection Portfolio. If you're very organized, you might create multiple selection libraries for different jobs. To swap outlines between libraries or to set up a new, empty palette, you can use the Selection Mover, accessed by clicking the right triangle in the Selection Portfolio section bar.

Use File, Export Adobe Illustrator File to export shapes to Post-Script drawing programs. We successfully exported simple shape objects and more complex objects that included blends and compounds, opening them in Illustrator 7, 8 and 9.

SELECTIONS AT WORK

Once you've activated selections, you can choose to draw outside of them instead of inside, or use them to isolate areas of the image canvas when applying special-effects procedures found in the Effects menu.

Using the Drawing icons.

The Drawing icons are found in the bottom left corner of an active document's window. Take the name "Drawing icons" literally; they affect drawing and painting actions only, not fills or other effects. A fill or effect is always constrained to the inside of an active selection, regardless of which Drawing icon you choose. Several of the techniques in this chapter demonstrate how these icons work, and you can refer to "Selecting a Drawing Mode" in Chapter 12 of Painter's *User Guide* for a detailed explanation.

Inverting a selection. If you want to apply a fill or effect to the *outside* of your active selection, use Select, Invert. This procedure reverses the current selection. It's often useful to save a selection as a mask in the Masks section, then save the inverse of it; for instance, save an element, then save the background, also as a mask.

Stroking a selection. In Painter, you can use any brush variant *to stroke a selection marquee*. Begin by making a selection using the Oval, Rectangle, Lasso or Shape Design (Quick Curve) tool. The

To create a light-valued border for an image, make a rectangular selection, and choose Select, Modify, Border and set the width for the border. (We used 30 pixels for this 750-pixel-wide image.) With the border selection active (as shown here), choose Effects, Tonal Control, Adjust Colors. Move the Value slider to the right to lighten the values within the selection.

Multiple applications of the Smooth function (Select, Modify, Smooth) can turn a perfectly good typeface (Stone Sans, left) into a trendy, avant-garde one. Set type with the Text tool, convert the characters to shapes (choose Convert Text to Shapes from the pop-up menu on the right side of the Layers section bar), convert them to selections (Shapes, Convert To Selection), apply the Smooth operation and fill them with a color (Effects, Fill).

MASKS FROM PHOTOSHOP

When you open a file in Painter that contains a mask created in Photoshop, the area that was masked in Photoshop now seems to be exposed in Painter. Don't despair: Although the mask appears inverted, it's functionally the same as it is in Photoshop. If you need to reverse the mask, highlight its name in the Masks section of the Objects palette, click the right triangle on the Masks section bar and choose Invert Mask.

effect is more fun to observe if you choose one of Painter's grain-sensitive brushes. In the Brushes palette, choose the Large Chalk variant of Dry Media. Next, open the Papers section of the Art Materials palette and choose a texture from the default paper library. With the selection still active, use the Drawing icons (located at the extreme bottom-left of the image window) to choose whether you want your stroke inside (Draw Inside), outside (Draw Outside), or centered directly on top of the selection border (Draw Anywhere), then go to the Select menu and choose Stroke Selection.

EDITING SELECTIONS

Painter offers methods for finessing outline-based and pixel-based selections that will be familiar to Photoshop users. (To read about editing masks, see "Masks," on the facing page.)

Expanding a selection. To add to an existing selection marquee, press the Shift key and drag outside of the existing marquee with the Lasso or Rectangular or Oval Selection tool. The Add To Selection operation is also useful—it is described on page 142.

Subtracting from a selection. To remove a portion of an active selection, press the Alt/Option key and drag with the Lasso or Rectangular or Oval Selection tool. The Subtract From Selection and Intersect operations are also useful, and they are described on page 142.

The Modify menu. Four commands under the Select, Modify menu—Widen, Contract, Smooth and Border—allow you to change active outline-based selections. Widen and Contract allow you to change the size of a selection by a specified number of pixels. The Smooth command is useful for rounding corners and softening jagginess in a selection. The Border function adds a second selection marquee (based on a specified number of pixels) outside the existing marquee, selecting only the area between the two.

Feathering. Feathering a selection softens its edge. To see feathering at work, drag a selection from the Selection Portfolio into your image. Choose Select, Feather, and type 20 into the field to define the extent of the feather; click OK. Now choose Effects, Fill, select one of the options and click OK. Note the soft edges of the filled selection. The feather is always built both inward and outward from the selection boundary. Applying the Select, Feather command to an outline-based selection changes it to a pixel-based selection.

TRANSFORM FIRST. . .

If you'd like to stroke the outline of a pixel-based selection, use Select, Transform Selection to convert it to an outline-based selection before attempting to use the Select, Stroke Selection command.

The Masks section of the Objects palette. Several useful commands are found in the Masks section's pull-down menu.

Five buttons at the bottom of the Masks section offer shortcuts to important commands: From left to right, Load Selection, Save Selection, Invert Selection, Create New Mask and Delete.

INVERT MASK BUTTON

The Invert Selection button (named as of this writing, in Painter 7.0) works for inverting masks, not selections. To invert a mask, target a mask in the Masks section and click the invert button to reverse the mask.

INACTIVE, BUT USEFUL

Although the masks stored in the Masks section don't affect brushstrokes when they are dormant (not loaded as active selections with a flashing marquee), they can still be used to isolate areas of the image canvas or a specific layer, when using functions under the Effects menu such as Tonal Control, Adjust Colors and Surface Control, Apply Surface Texture, Color Overlay, Dye Concentration or Express Texture.

MASKS

You can create masks in Painter in several ways: by making a selection and saving it as a mask, by painting directly onto a new blank mask with brushes, by generating masks with procedures such as Auto Mask or Color Mask, or by using Boolean operations to calculate new masks from existing ones. For more information about Auto Mask, turn to "Isolating Color With Auto Mask" on page 153. To read about Color Mask turn to "Using Color Mask" on page 151, and for more information about calculating masks, turn to "Calculating and Operating" on page 142.

USING THE MASKS SECTION

The Masks section lists all the masks in your file by name. A Painter file can contain a maximum of 32 masks. If you'll be doing a lot of work with masks, it's a good idea to get on friendly terms with this section of the Objects palette. Here are some basics:

To view a mask as an overlay on top of the RGB image canvas, open the eye icon to the far left of the mask's name.

To hide a mask, click its eye icon shut.

To view a mask alone in black-and-white, without the RGB-Canvas, open the mask's eye icon and close the RGB-Canvas eye icon.

To view a mask as an opaque overlay, choose Mask Attributes from the pull-down menu on the Masks section bar, and move the Opacity slider to 100%. Viewing a mask as an opaque overlay can often help you see defects in the mask. Adjusting this slider changes the overlay appearance only, and does not affect the actual density of the mask.

To edit a mask, click the mask's name to select it (the mask's name will be highlighted). Open the eye icon to the far left of the mask's name. You can edit the mask by painting on it with any brush except a Water Color or Liquid Ink brush.

To apply a paper grain to a mask, highlight the mask in the Masks section and use Effects, Surface Control, Express Texture, using Paper. Experiment with the Gray Threshold and Grain sliders.

To copy mask information to another mask, select a

MASK VIEWS

To view the mask and image canvas simultaneously, in the Masks section of the Objects palette, open both the eye icon for the mask and the eye icon for the RGB-Canvas. To view the mask alone in black-and-white, toggle the RGB-Canvas eye icon closed. To hide the mask, close its eye icon.

TARGETING A MASK

In the Masks section, make sure to click on the item's *name*—not the eye icon—to target it.

To change the mask overlay to a color easier to see while making a mask for an orange Garibaldi fish, we changed the overlay color from the default red to yellow using the Mask Attributes dialog box.

We used Intersect With Selection to create the filled half-circle (above right). Begin by making a square selection with the Rectangular Selection tool and Shift key and save it by choosing Select, Save Selection, or clicking the Save Selection button at the bottom of the Masks section. View the mask as an overlay (above left) by clicking its eye icon open in the Masks section, along with the eye for the RGB-Canvas. Highlight the RGB-Canvas name again, and make a new selection partially overlapping the square with the Oval Selection tool. With the oval selection active, click the Load Selection button at the bottom of the Masks section. In the Load From pop-up menu choose the square mask, and click the Intersect With Selection button.

mask and choose Copy Mask from the pull-down menu on the Masks section bar. From the Copy Mask To pop-up menu, select a destination mask, and click OK.

To blur a mask so that loading it as a selection will produce a feathered selection, select the mask and choose Feather Mask from the pull-down menu, type a number in the field and click OK.

CALCULATING AND OPERATING

Painter offers Boolean operations, useful functions that help generate new masks that fit perfectly against existing ones. Skillful use of these techniques will save time and effort. To see these functions at work, turn to "Making Masks for Embossing," on the facing page.

To edit a mask using a selection, create a selection marquee, and choose Select, Save Selection. In the Save Selection dialog box, choose the mask you wish to edit from the Save To pop-up menu, and the operation you wish to perform.

To replace a mask with the active selection, create a selection marquee and choose Select, Save Selection. In the dialog box, from the Save To menu, choose the mask you wish to replace, then click the Replace Mask button. This choice makes the original mask permanently unavailable.

To add a mask to a selection, create a selection marquee surrounding the area you want to add to. Choose Load Selection. In the Load Selection dialog box, choose the mask you want to add to the selection and click the Add To Selection button.

To subtract a mask from a selection, make a new marquee around the area from which you want to take away. Choose Load Selection, and in the Load Selection dialog box select the mask you want to subtract from the selection and click the Subtract From Selection button.

To create a new selection from the intersection of a mask and a selection that isolates only the overlapping area, begin with a selection marquee. Choose Load Selection. In the Load Selection dialog box, choose the mask you want to use to make the intersection and click the Intersect With Selection button.

Making Masks for Embossing

Overview *Open a new file with a colored background; set a type shape; convert the shape to a selection; save the selection as a mask; use the selection to build bevel and background masks; apply special effects to create three-dimensional looks.*

The shape before converting to a selection

Using the Selection Adjuster to scale the selection

PAINTER'S EFFECTS, SURFACE CONTROL MENU contains powerful features for creating three-dimensional artwork needed for an embossed look or for interactive buttons. These features are most effective when combined with a skillful use of selections and masks. To create these tooled wood reliefs, we began with a graphic shape for the face of the graphic. Then we created a series of masks based on the original graphic—a widened face, a bevel and a background—to isolate areas for special effects application. Preparing the masks up front allowed quick previewing of a variety of effects.

1 Setting a shape and converting it to a selection. Create a new file with a light background color, or open a textured background image (we chose Beechwood from the ArtBeats *Wood and Paper* CD-ROM). Choose black (Colors section), click in the image with the Text tool and type a letter. (Using a 500-pixel-wide file, we set an ornament using the Adobe Wood Type Ornaments font.)

Before you can use the graphic character to isolate areas of the image canvas, you'll need to convert it to a shape, then to a selection. Target the Text layer in the Layers section of the Objects palette, click the right arrow on the Layers section bar to access the pull-down menu and choose Convert Text to Shapes. Now choose Shapes, Convert to Selection.

2 Moving and scaling. Choose the Selection Adjuster tool (it shares a space in the Tools palette with the Layer Adjuster). Press

3

Typing a descriptive name for the mask

4

Viewing the widened face mask along with the RGB-Canvas

5a

Loading the "widened face" mask

5b

Subtracting the "face" mask

5c

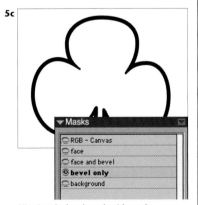

Viewing the bevel mask without the canvas

inside the active selection with the Selection Adjuster tool, and when you see the four-arrow cursor, you can safely move your selection without distorting it. To scale, drag on one of the selection handles; to scale proportionately, press Shift and drag one of the corner handles.

3 Saving and naming the selection. Saving a selection permanently stores it in the Masks section of the Objects palette as a mask. The first selection will be the top face of the bas relief, and we used it to create three masks. To save a selection, choose Select, Save Selection, or click the Save Selection button on the Masks section. When the Save Selection dialog box appears, accept the default in the pop-up menu—Save to New. Click OK. The selection is converted from outline-based to mask information. To rename the mask, double-click its name in the Masks section. We named ours "face."

QUICKER LOADING

To save a visit to the Select menu or Masks section when you'd like to load a selection—press Ctrl/⌘-Shift-E to display the Load Selection dialog box.

MODIFYING SELECTIONS

Only outline-based selections accept commands from the Modify menu such as Widen and Contract. To convert a mask-based selection to path-based information so you can modify it, choose Select, Transform Selection. For more information, turn to "Editing Selections," on page 140.

4 Widening the selection. With the "face" selection still active, choose Select, Transform Selection. You can now expand the selection to create a wider boundary around the graphic. Choose Select, Modify, Widen and set the radius by typing a number in the field (we used 10 pixels). Save this new widened selection into the Masks section, naming it "widened face."

5 Creating new masks using calculations. Next, we created a bevel mask describing the thin area between the outside widened boundary and the original face boundary. Painter offers Boolean operations, calculations in the Save Selection and Load Selection dialog boxes to make the job easier. To build a mask for the bevel, (with the selection still active) from the Load From pop-up menu choose the "widened face" mask; choose the Replace Selection radio button, and click OK. Choose Load Selection again, this time choosing "face" from the pop-up menu and under Operation, click the Subtract From Selection radio button to subtract the original face area from the widened face area, resulting in a mask for the bevel. Save and name the mask.

We also built a mask isolating the image area outside of the widened face mask. To do this, load a selection using the "widened face" mask, and then choose Select, Invert. We saved this selection as a mask, naming it "background."

6a

Using Dye Concentration in conjunction with the "face" mask

6b

Using the face mask to apply Surface Texture to create the embossed face

6c

Using the "bevel" mask to apply Surface Texture for the cut bevel effect

6 Putting the masks to work. Many operations available under the Effects menu in Painter—for instance, Tonal Control, Adjust Color; Surface Control, Apply Surface Texture; and Focus, Glass Distortion—offer a pop-up menu allowing you to apply the effect using any mask saved in the Masks section.

To **emboss** the face, creating the bas relief look in image "a" at the top of page 143, you can use the "face" mask to isolate an area of the image. Lightening the face of the graphic will enhance the illusion of relief. With no selection active (Ctrl/⌘-D deselects all) and the RGB-Canvas active in the Masks section, choose Effects, Surface Control, Dye Concentration. In the Using pop-up menu, choose the "face" mask; to lighten the area, set the Minimum slider to 80%. Click OK. Now, for the relief effect: To "pop" the graphic face out (creating a convincing 3D effect), choose Effects, Surface Control, Apply Surface Texture. In the Using menu choose "face." Set Softness to 4.3, reduce the shine to 30%, click the top left Light Direction button and click OK.

To **deboss** the face of the graphic as in image "b" at the top of page 143, with no selection active and the RGB-Canvas active in the Masks section, choose Effects, Surface Control, Dye Concentration. In the Using pop-up menu choose the "face" mask. To darken the area, set the Minimum slider to 125%. Click OK. Then choose Effects, Surface Control, Apply Surface Texture. Click the Inverted checkbox to turn it on. In the Using menu choose "face." Set Softness to 4.3, reduce the shine to 30%, choose the top left Light Direction button and click OK.

To create the **beveled** look in image "c" at the top of page 143, begin by lightening the bevel area: With no selection active and the RGB-Canvas active in the Masks section, choose Effects, Surface Control, Dye Concentration. In the Using pop-up menu, choose the "bevel" mask. To lighten the area, set the Minimum slider to 80%. To emboss the bevel, making the face and background appear to recede, choose Effects, Surface Control, Apply Surface Texture. In the Using menu, choose "bevel." Set Softness to 4.3, reduce the shine to 30%, and click the top left Light Direction button. Be sure the Inverted box is *not* checked and click OK.

To **carve the beveled area *in,*** leaving the face and background flat (image "d" at the top of page 143), begin by darkening the bevel area. With no selection active and the RGB-Canvas active in the Masks section, choose Effects, Surface Control, Dye Concentration. In the Using pop-up menu, choose the "bevel" mask. To darken the area, set the Minimum slider to 125%. To deboss the bevel, making the bevel appear to be carved into the wood, choose Effects, Surface Control, Apply Surface Texture. In the Using menu choose "bevel." Set Softness to 4.3, set the Shine at 30%, and click the top left Light Direction button. Click to turn on the Inverted feature and click OK. 🖐

Working with Bézier Paths and Selections

Overview *Use the Pen tool to create paths of straight and curved lines; convert the paths to selections; use a custom pencil to draw inside and outside of the selections.*

JOHN FRETZ

The logo sketch, including a rough grid

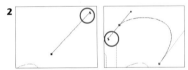

Pulling a handle from an anchor point to prepare for a curved path segment, then pressing and dragging to create the curve

Dragging on a control handle to change the path's shape

TO DESIGN A LOGO FOR THE 100-YEAR-OLD Bethany Church in Seattle, John Fretz used a custom pencil to draw inside and outside of selections to create a hard-edged, graduated look similar to his conventional colored pencil illustration style.

1 Sketching the logo. Fretz created a 4 x 4-inch pencil drawing of the logo that included a rough grid aligning the roofs of the houses. He scanned the sketch at 300 ppi and opened it in Painter to use as a template.

2 Creating a path with Bézier curves. The most efficient way to create a combination of curve and straight-line path segments is with the Pen tool. You can set up shape attributes (with no fill or stroke) to produce a skeletal line that will help you see precise lines and curves while you draw: Choose Edit, Preferences, Shapes to open the Shape Preferences dialog box. Under Drawing Options uncheck all the Fill and Stroke checkboxes. To make the anchor points and control handles easier to see and work with, check the Big Handles checkbox. Click OK. Now, choose the Pen tool and click to place anchor points for straight-line segments, and press, hold and drag to create anchor points with handles that control curve segments. When you want to close a path, place the cursor over the starting anchor point, and click when you see a small circle designating the origin point, or press the Close button in the Controls:Shape Design palette.

3 Changing the path shape. You can fine-tune a path during or after the drawing process with the Shape Selection tool. (While drawing with the Pen tool, press the Ctrl/⌘ key to temporarily change from the Pen to the Shape Selection tool.) Move the Shape Selection tool over an anchor point, a control handle, or a curve segment and drag to reposition it.

4 Changing the path to a selection. Paths must be turned into selections before you can use them to control where paint is

4a

Click on the Make Selection button to change the shape path into a selection.

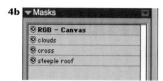

4b

Selections stored as masks in the Masks section

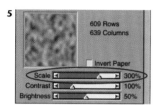

5

Scaling the Basic Paper texture

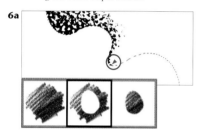

6a

Painting outside of the cloud selection using the custom black pencil

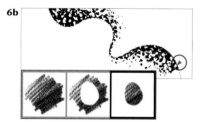

6b

Painting inside of the cloud selection

7

When the house is filled with white, the subtracted selection around the windows protects those areas, keeping them black. Fretz used his custom pencil to add black texture over the white fill.

applied on the image. You can convert a path drawn with the Pen or Shape Design (Quick Curve) tool to a selection immediately after drawing it by pressing the Make Selection button in the Controls:Shape Design palette. You can also change a path into a selection by selecting the shape in the Layers section of the Objects palette and choosing Shapes, Convert To Selection. In your image, the Bézier curves will turn into a black-and-white selection marquee. To save the selection as a mask in the Masks section for future use, choose Select, Save Selection. To name a selection, double-click on its name in the Masks sections to open the Mask Attributes dialog box. Type a new name in the field. Click OK. To return to the image canvas, click on RGB-Canvas in the Masks section.

5 Creating the pencil and surface. To re-create the graduated effect he gets with conventional pencils on rough illustration board, Fretz built a heavy, grainy pencil. To build a grainy pencil similar to the one Fretz used, choose the 2B Pencil variant of Pencils. In the General section of the Brush Controls palette, modify the variant by switching to the Cover method and Grainy Edge Flat Cover subcategory, and change the Grain setting to 10%. Increase the Size to roughly 200 pixels using the Size slider in the Controls:Brush palette. In the Spacing section of the Brush Controls palette, set the Spacing slider at 25% (so the dabs created by the larger pencil will overlap and paint continuous strokes). Now choose black in the Colors section of the Art Materials palette. In the Papers section of the Art Materials palette, Fretz chose Basic Paper because of its even texture, and scaled it to 300% using the Scale slider.

6 Drawing in and out of selections. Fretz used the Drawing Modes, three icons located in the bottom left corner of the image window, to paint inside and outside of selections. Begin by loading a selection (Select, Load Selection). To protect the area inside an active selection, click on the middle Drawing button; to protect the area outside the selection, click on the far right Drawing button. Fretz switched back and forth between these two options as he rendered a graduated, even texture using his custom pencil. (You can also use the Select, Invert command to invert an active selection.)

7 Subtracting from a selection. To fill each house with white and leave the windows black, Fretz loaded each house selection and subtracted the window selection from it: Choose Load Selection again and in the Load Selection dialog box, choose a selection and click the Subtract From Selection button to subtract it from the original selected area. Fretz filled the resulting selection with white, then he added black texture to the house with his custom pencil. He continued to add textured, even tone with the black and white pencils until he completed the logo.

Fretz saved the finished image in TIFF format, and to eliminate all grayscale information, he opened the image in Photoshop and converted it from grayscale to a 600 ppi Bitmap image.

Using Selections to Limit Paint

Overview *Make a sketch on a colored ground; draw paths, convert them to selections and store them as masks; paint and apply effects within the selections.*

RAY BLAVATT LOVES THE ENERGETIC, EXPRESSIVE line work of fashion illustrators (notably Carl Erickson and Rene Bouche) and political cartoonists (including Jim Borgman and Pat Oliphant). His background is in traditional illustration, but today most of Blavatt's work is in animation. His procedure involves drawing in Painter and then saving the illustrations for animation in Quick-Time format, importing them into Macromedia Flash and eventually exporting his work to VHS tape.

To create *Parisian,* Blavatt began by making a gestural drawing in Painter. Then he drew paths with the Pen tool directly on the sketch and converted the paths to selections so that he would have boundaries to limit paint when he painted fast. Artists familiar with drawing in a PostScript program (as Blavatt is) will like this method of drawing straight and curved line segments with the Pen, then converting the paths to selections. (To read more about different methods of making selections, turn to the beginning of this chapter.)

1 Sketching on a colored ground. Blavatt opened a new file measuring 1900 x 2100 pixels with a newsprint-colored background. He chose the Flattened Pencil variant of the Pencils, a gold color in the Colors section of the Art Materials palette and Pavement texture in the Papers section. (Load the Pavement texture as follows: choose Load library from the bottom of the resource list on the Papers section, navigate to the Ver 6 folder within the Painter 7 application folder and choose Paper Textures.) Envisioning a young woman on a fictitious street in Paris, he sketched quick, gestural strokes to lay out the drawing. He

Sketching with the Flattened Pencil variant

Adding bolder lines to the sketch

Drawing the path around a building

The Controls:Shape Design palette showing the Make Selection button

The painting with textured chalk strokes added to the sky, street and figure

Pavement texture chosen in the Papers section of the Art Materials palette

Using Dye Concentration to apply a darker tint to the selected background

changed the size of the pencil as he worked using the Size slider on the Controls:Brush palette. The Flattened Pencil incorporates the Buildup method, which allows color to be applied with transparency (overlapping strokes will darken); its Grainy Hard Buildup subcategory creates crisp-edged strokes that are affected by the current paper texture.

2 Emphasizing the line work. Next, Blavatt added darker color and textured, thick and thin lines to the drawing using the Graphic Paintbrush variant of the Brushes. (The Graphic Paintbrush reminds Blavatt of the Rough Out brush, a favorite he liked using in earlier versions of Painter, although by default the Graphic Paintbrush reveals more paper texture along the edges of the strokes, due to the Grainy Edge Flat Cover method it uses.) To lay bold strokes over your pencil sketch, choose the Graphic Paintbrush and a dark color in the Colors section. For finer line work, Blavatt sized the brush smaller (to 7.3) using the Size slider on the Controls:Brush palette.

3 Drawing paths and converting to selections. So that he could isolate areas of the drawing while painting and applying special effects, he created selections. Because his subject included straight lines (buildings) and smooth curves (the figure and streetlight, for instance), Blavatt chose the Pen from the Tools palette to draw a path around each building and the figure of the young woman. To make it easier to see the path as he was drawing it, he applied a stroke without a fill. To set up Preferences to automatically stroke paths as you draw them, without filling: Choose Edit, Preferences, Shapes and under Drawing Options, for On Draw, turn on Stroke In Current Color, turning off Fill With Current Color; for On Close, turn on Stroke In Current Color, turning off Fill With Current Color. (To draw more precise paths, some artists prefer to draw the paths without a Stroke or Fill.) Choose the Pen tool and click and drag to draw a path. (For more information about drawing paths with the Pen tool, turn to "Working with Bézier Paths and Selections," on page 146.)

When the path was complete, Blavatt converted it to a selection. (Click the Make Selection button on the Controls:Shape Design palette.) To make a soft selection edge that would help to make transparent color on the edges when he painted or filled, he feathered the selection 8 pixels (Select, Feather). Then he saved the selection as a mask so he could use it later (Select, Save Selection.) The mask will be saved in the Masks section of the Objects palette (Select, Save Selection.)

4 Adding color and texture. Painting with blues and golds, Blavatt used the Square Chalk variant of Dry Media to quickly build up color over the entire image, using a light enough touch on his stylus to reduce opacity and preserve the texture.

6a

Drawing a path for the beam of light

6b

Airbrushing within the active selection

6c

The completed beam of light

7

The Flattened Pencil variant (Pencils) and the Graphic Paintbrush (Brushes) were used to add final details to the face.

5 Enhancing the figure as the focal point. Next, he added details to the blouse and more colored texture to the figure. He chose Select, Load Selection and chose the figure's mask from the Load From menu. When the selection was active, he added highlights to the woman's blouse using the Bleach variant of Erasers. To deepen color and build shadows, he used the Darkener variant of Erasers. Then he chose a creamy pink color in the Colors section, and with Pavement texture still chosen in the Papers section, he used the Square Chalk to gently brush textured highlights over the figure's face, neck and arms. When he'd finished the figure and clothing, he reversed the selection by choosing Select, Invert so he could work on the background while protecting the figure.

To further strengthen the focal point, he added a dark burgundy "dye" to the background only, while leaving the focal point—the figure—in lighter colors. (The darkening also helped to enhance the mysterious atmosphere of the city street.) To add a "dye" to an area of your image, start by loading a selection. To re-create Blavatt's effect, make sure Pavement is the current texture in the Papers section. (When Paper is chosen in the Using menu, the luminance of the current texture chosen in the Papers section is used as the means to apply the transparent dye effect.) Then choose a deep red in the Colors section and choose Effects, Surface Control, Dye Concentration, Using Paper. Experiment with the settings. (Blavatt set a Maximum of 488% and a Minimum of 50%.) To scroll around your image in the Preview window, press in the Preview window to access the grabber hand. Click OK when you have an effect you like.

6 Airbrushing a beam of light. To balance the composition, Blavatt added a gold beam of light shining from a streetlight on the left side of the image. First he created a selection to limit the paint: Using the Pen tool from the Tools palette, he drew a path to define the beam of light; he converted the path to a selection by using the Make Selection button on the Controls:Shape Design palette. For a smooth edge, he feathered the selection to 8 pixels (Select, Feather), then he stored the selection as a mask for safekeeping (Select, Save Selection). To ensure that the color of the light matched existing color in the illustration, he used the Dropper tool to sample a gold color from the image. Next, he chose the Fine Spray variant of the Airbrushes and used firmer pressure to spray denser color near the light source, then used lighter pressure to fade the spray of color as he painted lower within the selection.

7 Final details. To complete the painting, Blavatt went back over the image and added details: With the Flattened Pencil and a dark color he touched up the woman's eyes; with the Graphic Paintbrush he added more tiny strokes of white at the top of light beam and he strengthened highlights on the woman's hair and blouse collar. At last, he used the Bleach variant of the Erasers to brighten the highlight on the roof of the background building. 🐾

Selections and Airbrush

Overview *Create a pencil sketch; create PostScript outlines in a drawing program; import outlines and sketch into Painter; add texture and gradient fills within the selections; use the Airbrush to create a metallic look.*

1a

The original pencil sketch

1b

The selected and grouped panther outlines were copied to the clipboard in Illustrator.

2a

The pasted shapes selected with the Layer Adjuster tool on the image, showing their names in the Layers section

ARTISTS USING TRADITIONAL AIRBRUSH technique cut friskets out of paper, film or plastic to protect portions of their artwork as they paint. For complex jobs this can become quite a task. That's one of the reasons why John Dismukes of Capstone Studios traded in his traditional tools for electronic ones. For this logo for Ktema, a manufacturer of promotional clothing for the entertainment industry, he started with a pencil sketch, added PostScript paths and brought both into Painter. He turned the paths into selections and painted inside and outside of the selections as he would with traditional friskets.

1 Organizing the elements. Dismukes had a scanned pencil sketch and a PostScript drawing created in Adobe Illustrator, which fit the sketch. The paths included the panther, the wing ribs and membrane, the large and small globes, and the Ktema nameplate. (If you need to import type from Illustrator into Painter, first convert the type into outlines.) Painter has the ability to recognize fill and stroke attributes and groups when PostScript art is imported. To prepare a document for importing into Painter, save a version in Adobe Illustrator 5 (or later) or EPS format.

2 Importing, positioning and scaling. Dismukes opened the original pencil sketch in Painter and began importing the paths into the document. There are two reliable ways to import PostScript outlines into a Painter file: using File, Acquire, Adobe Illustrator File (which creates a new file) or copying from the PostScript program to the clipboard and then pasting into an open file in Painter. For the second method to work, both applications have to be running at the same time. Importing the outlines as shapes into a Painter file by pasting through the clipboard is fairly fast and always reliable. To do this, select the outlines in Illustrator and copy, then switch to Painter and paste. You'll see a closed

2b

The Layer Adjuster tool changes to an arrow cursor when scaling the panther shapes to fit the template.

3

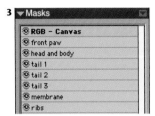

The named selections in the Masks section

4

Cloning texture into the membrane selection

5

Airbrushing highlights on the panther

6a

Applying the shadow

6b

The shadow and lens flare are shown in this detail

group of shapes appear in the Layers section of the Objects palette. Move the shape group into position on the template using the Layer Adjuster tool or the arrow keys on your keyboard. To scale shapes proportionally, choose the Layer Adjuster tool, hold down the Shift key and drag on a corner handle.

3 Converting, saving and naming. If you have a complex graphic with overlapping shapes, you may want to ungroup the shapes before converting them to selections. This will enable you to save each selection as a user mask in the Masks section (Objects palette) that can be used individually, or added to or subtracted from the other selections. To ungroup, at the bottom of the Layers section, click the Layer Commands button and from the menu choose Ungroup. To convert a shape to a selection so you can paint or fill it, select it in the Layers section and choose Shapes, Convert To Selection. The shape will disappear from the Layers section and will become an active marquee on the image canvas. Store the active selection in the Masks section as a user mask by choosing Select, Save Selection and clicking OK. To name it, double-click on its current name. Type a name for the mask in the Mask Attributes dialog box and click OK. (Click RGB-Canvas in the Masks section to see the image again if necessary.)

4 Filling selections. Dismukes created texture within the membrane selection using a Cloners brush and a modified paper texture from a second document. He filled the large globe with a maroon gradient and the small globe with a green gradient. To read more about cloning turn to "Cloning and Tracing" in Chapter 3.

5 Airbrushing. Dismukes's template showed good shadow and highlight detail. Using it as a guide, he began by laying down dark colors, gradually building forward to the white highlights. He used the Digital Airbrush variant of Airbrushes, adjusting only the Size and Min Size in the Size section of the Brush Controls palette.

6 Adding a shadow. Dismukes used a layer to create the panther's drop shadow on the maroon globe. Use the Create Drop Shadow command to do this: Load the selection by choosing Select, Load Selection. To load more than one user mask at a time as a single selection, load the first selection, then choose Select, Load Selection again and in the Load From menu, choose a second selection and Add To Selection. Continue to Load and Add to your selection until you have all of the elements active. Store this complex selection as a new user mask by choosing Select, Save Selection.

Turn the new selection into a layer by clicking on it in your image with the Layer Adjuster tool. Choose Effects, Objects, Create Drop Shadow. Use the default settings or experiment with other settings, then click OK to create the shadow.

As a final touch, Dismukes opened the image in Adobe Photoshop and applied the Lens Flare filter to the green globe. The 40 MB logo was output as a 4 x 5-inch color transparency at 762 ppi.

Working with Hand-drawn Selections

Overview *Open a scanned drawing as a template; select areas of the image using the Lasso; use selections to constrain brushstrokes, fills and effects.*

1

The original pencil sketch

2a

An active selection around the girl and hills

2b **2c**

Adding to a selected area   *Subtracting from a selected area*

3a

Paint applied within a selection

TO ISOLATE AREAS FOR PAINTING, FILLING AND LIGHTING effects in the whimsical *Ægypt*, artist Steve Campbell used the Lasso tool. He painted and applied special effects within each selection, then he unified the piece by applying effects across the entire image.

1 Sketching and scanning. Campbell started with a pencil sketch, which he scanned and opened in Painter.

2 Creating selections. To select with the Lasso tool, drag carefully around the area you want to select, ending precisely at your origin point. You may find it helpful to zoom in on your image while making detailed freehand selections. Press M to switch to the Magnifier tool, and click to zoom in, press Alt/Option and click to zoom out. You zoom in and out of your image using the Scale slider in the lower left corner of the image window.

Painter's Lasso tool lets you add to or subtract from the currently active selection. To add to the currently selected area, hold down the Shift key and drag with the Lasso to reshape an area of the border to increase the selection. To subtract from the currently selected area, hold down the Alt/Option key and drag with the Lasso tool to cut part of the active selection away.

Saving the completed selection as a user mask will store it permanently with your image in the Masks section of the Objects palette. To save a selection, choose Select, Save Selection, or click the Save Selection button on the Masks section. Campbell created a selection for each element in the drawing.

A LASSO WITH A CLUE

As a reminder of how the existing selection will be edited, a plus sign (Shift key) or minus sign (Alt/Option key) appears next to the Lasso.

Painting brushstrokes using clone color

Adding lighting and texture to the sky

Painting details on the face

Paper grain texture added to the face

Applying lighting to the tumbler's back

3 Painting inside selections. To paint within a selection, first make the selection active: Choose Select, Load Selection (or click the Load Selection button on the Masks section). Campbell loaded individual selections and used various brushes to lay in color within each selection.

To begin painting the graduated sky, Campbell made a clone of his painting file (File, Clone), and filled the clone with the Night Sky gradient loaded from the Painter 6 Gradients library. To load that gradient, insert the Painter 7 CD 2. From the bottom of the resource list on the Gradients section of the Art Materials palette, choose Load Library. Navigate to the Gradients folder on the Painter 7 CD 2 and choose Painter 6 Gradients. Now choose Effects, Fill, Gradient, with an angle of 90° in the Gradients section. Next, Campbell activated the painting file and designated the filled clone as the clone source (File, Clone Source). In the painting file, he loaded the sky selection. He chose the Captured Bristle variant of Brushes and changed it into a cloning brush (that would sample color from the graduated image while painting in the destination file), by checking the Clone Color checkbox on the Colors section of the Art Materials palette. Using the new Captured Bristle "cloner," he painted angled and curved strokes into the sky selection.

4 Adding effects to the sky. To add a graduated golden tint within the sky selection, Campbell used Effects, Surface Control, Apply Lighting (using a customized version of the Splashy Colors light), then he built up "thick paint." To give your image realistic "thick paint" highlights and shadows based on dark and light values in the brushstrokes, choose Effects, Surface Control, Apply Surface Texture, Using Image Luminance.

5 Finalizing the image. To paint the central figure's face, Campbell used the Artist Pastel Chalk variant of Dry Media (on top of Basic Paper texture) to paint soft shading within the face selection. Then he blended areas using the Just Add Water variant of Liquid.

After painting the face, he changed its appearance dramatically by applying custom colored lighting and a paper grain effect within the active selection. He used similar procedures to add rich textures and complexity to other elements in the image—including the foreground, table and tumbling figures on the horizon.

To apply a paper texture within a selection, load the selection, and choose Effects, Surface Control, Apply Surface Texture, Using Paper. If you want, you can choose a different paper texture from the Papers palette with this dialog box still open.

Finally, to further unify the image, Campbell dropped all selections (Ctrl/⌘-D), and chose Effects, Surface Control, Apply Surface Texture using Image Luminance, to apply it overall the entire image. This time he used very low settings, moving the Amount slider to approximately 20–30% and the Shine slider to 20%.

Using Color Mask

Overview *Use Color Mask and brushes to mask an area of an image; convert the mask to a selection; use Adjust Color to shift the color of the selected area.*

CTP/PHOTO: PHOTODISC

The original photo

The default Color Mask dialog box

Adjusting the sliders to isolate the leaf

CHANGING MASK COLOR

To change the mask overlay to a color that's easier to see while making a mask, display the Mask Attributes dialog box by double-clicking the mask name in the Masks section of the Objects palette and change the overlay color from the default red to a contrasting color.

COLOR MASK IS ONE OF PAINTER'S most powerful features, letting you create a mask based on a specific color in an image. In the example above, we used a combination of Color Mask and editing with brushes to create masks for individual leaves. We saved the masks in the Masks section, then used Adjust Color to change the hue and saturation of the individual leaves and the background.

1 Sampling color and adjusting the mask. Open an image and then open the Masks section in the Objects palette. Click the right triangle on the Masks section bar and choose Color Mask from the pull-down menu. When the dialog box appears, click in your image (*not* in the preview window) on the color you want to sample (the "center color" of the range of colors to be selected); the arrow will momentarily turn into a dropper as you do this. We selected a color on the tan leaf in the center of the image. To narrow the range of selected colors, drag the H (Hue) Extents slider to the left (we set ours to 10%). Press and drag to scroll the image in the Preview window so you can see how your settings are affecting selection in other parts of the image. Experiment with the S (Saturation) and V (Value) Extents sliders; we got the best results when we reduced the V Extents to 30% to isolate the leaf from darker tan colors in the background water. You may also want to adjust the three Feather sliders to create harder transitions in your mask. When you're satisfied with the preview of your mask, click OK. Painter will generate a mask based on the sampled color. The mask will automatically appear in the Masks section.

2 Cleaning up the mask. To view the mask as a red-tinted overlay on top of the image canvas, in the Masks section click the mask's name to select it, and open its eye icon. (Make sure the RGB-Canvas eye icon is also open.) To edit the mask, choose the Scratchboard Tool variant of Pens because it allows smooth painting with opaque "paint." Choose black and paint on the mask to add to your mask; paint with white to remove portions of the mask. The interior of your mask must be opaque to completely cover your subject, so unless you want some degree of transparency, use the brush to paint over any thin spots.

2a

Using the Scratchboard Tool and white paint to erase an area of the mask

2b

Using the Scratchboard Tool to erase the mask from an overlapping leaf. The mask is viewed at a reduced opacity, making both the mask and the image beneath it visible.

2c

The finished mask of the center leaf viewed at 100% opacity

2d

Replacing the original mask

3

Adjusting color within the center leaf selection

You'll need to view the mask at full opacity to identify areas where coverage is not complete. To adjust the opacity of the mask overlay, display the Mask Attributes dialog box by double-clicking the mask name in the Masks section. Move the Opacity slider to 100%. The Opacity slider has no effect on the actual density of the mask—it is for viewing only.

As a final check for your mask, turn the mask into a selection by choosing Select, Load Selection. You can use the Lasso to select any areas that you'd like to add to the selection: Press the Shift key, then use the Lasso to draw around the area you want to add. To remove an area of the selection, hold down the Option/Alt key and use the Lasso to draw around it. If you use this method, make sure you replace the original mask in the Masks section with the edited one: Choose Select, Save Selection; in the Save To menu, choose the mask name and select the Replace Mask button.

3 Colorizing with Adjust Color. To make changes to the color within a selection, begin by loading a selection (Select, Load Selection). With the selection active, choose Effects, Tonal Control, Adjust Colors, Using Uniform Color. Use this feature to change the hue, saturation or brightness in the selected area. If you prefer more radical changes, you can also paint within your selection or apply any of the commands under the Effects menu. To view your image without the mask, click the mask eye icon shut. 🖐

CLEANING UP MASKS WITH BRIGHTNESS AND CONTRAST

Here's a useful method for cleaning up masks that can save lots of time and effort. Open an image and make a mask using Color Mask, clicking in the image to sample the color you need to mask. In the dialog box, adjust the H (Hue), V (Value) and S (Saturation) Extents sliders to create the best mask you can. Then click OK. To select the mask so you can view it in black-and-white, or paint directly on it or manipulate it using commands under the Effects menu, click on the mask name in the Masks section of the Objects palette. Now, click the RGB-Canvas eye icon closed. With the mask selected, use a brush and white paint to touch up the mask. Use Effects, Tonal Control, Brightness/Contrast, to bump up the contrast and adjust the brightness to make the gray areas solid black or white. To avoid losing anti-aliasing in the mask, use moderate settings.

Adjusting settings in the Brightness/Contrast dialog box

The mask before (left) and after (right) adjusting Brightness/Contrast.

Isolating Color with Auto Mask

Overview *Use Auto Mask to generate a mask based on a selected color; load the mask as a selection; paint into the selection with various brushes.*

The black-and-white sketch

Choosing Auto Mask from the Masks section's pop-up menu

Viewing the new current color mask

WITH PAINTER'S AUTO MASK FEATURE you can isolate an area of an image by means of a mask. Once the mask has been created, you can use it to make a selection and fill the area with color or paint into it. When Susan LeVan of LeVan/Barbee Studio created *Man With Buildings,* she used brushes to paint within selections. She used Auto Mask's Current Color setting to create jaggy white "halos" around the background scratch marks, giving her piece texture, lightness and air. Repainting a printed, collaged and scanned version of the image produced the result above.

1 Establishing the composition. LeVan began a new document with a white paper color. She chose Basic Paper from the Papers section of the Art Materials palette, the Dry Ink variant of the Brushes and black color to sketch. Prior to drawing, she resized the brush smaller using the Size slider on the Controls:Brush palette.

2 Generating and viewing a mask. To create a mask for the black-and-white line drawing, LeVan used Auto Mask's Current Color option. To begin, first sample the color from your image with the Dropper tool, making that color your Current Color. (LeVan clicked the Dropper on the black line work in her sketch.) To generate the mask, open the Objects palette (Window, Show Objects), and on the Masks section bar click the left triangle to open the Masks section. Click the right triangle to access the command menu and choose Auto Mask (or press Ctrl/⌘-Shift-M), using Current Color and click OK. In your image, you'll see all

The Masks section showing the mask name

Painting within the selection with a brush

The Man 3 image   *Scan of the collage*

The image showing details painted on the face, tie, and eyes

instances of the current color masked in orange. The mask name, by default, New Mask 1, will appear in the Masks section.

Since Auto Mask using Current Color lacks the feathering capabilities of Painter's Color Mask (see "Using Color Mask," earlier in this chapter), there will be rough, aliased areas at the boundary between the selected and unselected portions of your image. LeVan likes the white "halos" that result when she uses Auto Mask for color fills because they accentuate the texture on the background.

3 Loading the mask as a selection. To work on a masked area, load an active selection from the mask: Target the mask name in the Masks section, click the Load Selection button and in Load Selection dialog box, choose the Replace Selection button. To view the RGB-Canvas and the active selection without the orange mask, click the eye icon to the left of the mask to shut the eye.

4 Painting and filling within the selection. With the selection active, LeVan changed the black line work to a textured white line by choosing Effects, Tonal Control, Negative. Then by inverting the same selection, she used it to protect the linework while she painted flat color areas on the image, as follows: Invert the selection by choosing Select, Invert. To paint within the selected area of the image canvas with a color, first choose RGB-Canvas in the Masks section to target the image canvas. Choose a color in the Colors section. Then select a brush and paint within the selected area. After painting and filling the large areas of color with the Opaque Flat and Dry Ink variants of the Brushes, LeVan inverted the selection again (to isolate the line work) and painted it green using the Square Chalk (Dry Media).

5 Printing, collaging and scanning. When LeVan had finished painting the flat color on her image, she printed the Man 3 image using a color inkjet printer, then she painted the print with acrylic paint and added other conventional media—tape and newspaper—to make a collage. When the collage was complete, she scanned it so she could rework it in Painter.

6 Adding rich color and texture. To add richness and complexity to her image, LeVan used Auto Mask, Current Color again to mask areas in the face and then painted with the Square Chalk variant. To add more texture, she painted, then repeated painting with Auto Mask several times. First she painted in pale yellow, then masked the yellow; then she painted in tan, then masked the tan; and finally she painted in pink.

LeVan painted more detail using two Brushes variants: For the tie, eye and mouth she used the Opaque Flat; the magenta splotch outside the head and the ground line were done with the Smeary Flat. Then she drew over the background with the Square Chalk (Dry Media) and an orange color. Finally, she drew the buildings with a small Scratchboard Tool variant of Pens. Then to draw the straight lines along the edges of the image, she clicked the Straight Lines button on the Controls:Brush palette and clicked from point to point. 🐾

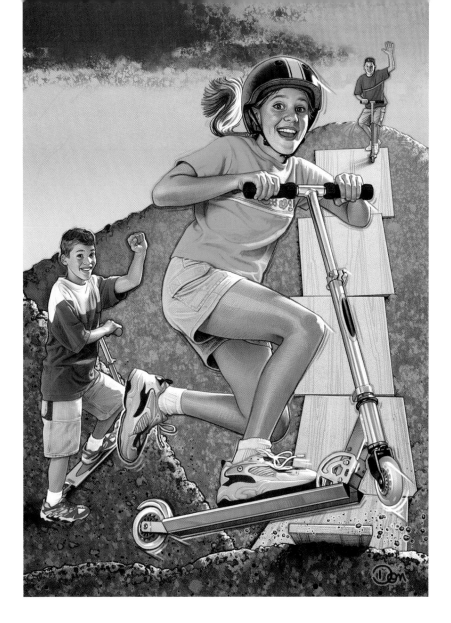

■ Before he began using Painter, **Don Stewart**, who specializes in book illustration, worked on gessoed illustration board with airbrush and colored pencil. Today he draws on the computer, using Painter's tools and brushes that match his traditional ones.

Scooter Hill (above) was commissioned by Pocket Books for the cover of the youth fiction book *Scooter Spies—The Ghost That Barked,* written by Michael Dahl. Stewart began the illustration by sketching in Painter using Pencils variants on medium-textured paper. To lay in colored washes he used Brushes variants. Then he isolated areas of his image by making

selections with the Lasso (for example, the child in the foreground) so that he could paint with Painter's Airbrushes without worrying about overspray. He used the Digital Airbrush to paint smoother areas (the skin, for instance), and to begin to build up tones and value. For more texture, he used the Fine Spray and Coarse Spray variants of Airbrushes. When the figures were modeled the way he wanted them, he added highlights and detail using the Colored Pencil variant of Pencils. To add the texture in the sky and on the mounds of dirt, he painted with contrasting colors using the Chalk variants over a rough texture.

■ **James D'Avanzo** was a young man with a lot of artistic talent and little physical mobility. He began with very basic computer graphics programs, then moved to CorelDraw, which allowed him the opportunity to create some very sophisticated images. However, it was with Painter that he blossomed as a young artist. Using Painter with the Wacom tablet and a multi-button cursor, D'Avanzo painted still lives and imaginary landscapes. The National Muscular Dystrophy association chose his image *Woods* (right) for their Christmas card for 1996.

For *Woods*, D'Avanzo chose a limited palette of deep colors to depict a haunting moonlit night. He blocked in broad areas of color using the Airbrushes and the Chalk variants of Dry Media, then he blended paint using the Grainy Water and Just Add Water variants of Liquid. To protect the shapes of clouds and moon from paint, he used the Lasso to make selections. To reverse the selected moon (so that he could paint on the sky while protecting the moon area), he chose Select, Invert. After painting the sky, he dropped the selection (Ctrl/⌘-D). To finish, he added more texture to the moon and clouds by painting a few lighter-colored brushstrokes using the Artist Pastel Chalk variant of Dry Media.

D'Avanzo created *Deep Love* (right) using saturated, complementary colors to help communicate the powerful healing of love. To create the background, he used the Lasso, then feathered and painted into the selection to create the illusion of a horizon. He used the same technique for the hand and figure. D'Avanzo worked from background to foreground, painting into the selections with a low-opacity Digital Airbrush variant of the Airbrushes.

■ When **Susan LeVan** created the works shown here, she used brushes to paint within selections. To build rough (not anti-aliased) edges on line drawings and around shapes, and to give her work more texture, she repeatedly used Auto Mask's Current Color setting and then painted back into her image.

Le Van created the illustration about relationships and making them work (above), for the *Dallas Morning News*. To begin, she drew the main elements in black with the Scratchboard Tool and Smooth Ink Pen variants of Pens. She made masks for areas of the image with Auto Mask Using Current Color and filled the selected lines with color (Effects, Fill). Then she used the Square Chalk (Dry Media) and soft colors to paint grainy strokes within each selection. Le Van painted the inscription and final details with the Dry Ink variant of Brushes and the Smooth Ink Pen.

For an illustration in the *Boston Globe* magazine's *Sunday Book Review* (left), LeVan began by drawing in Painter with a modified Dry Ink variant (Brushes). Then she masked the line work with Auto Mask Using Current Color and painted into it with the Square Chalk variant of Dry Media. For the shapes in the background, she made selections with the Rectangular Selection tool, painted into them with the Digital Airbrush variant (Airbrushes), and added more brushstrokes with the Square Chalk. To build the richly textured background, she used the Sharp Chalk variant (Dry Media) to scribble graffiti and then repeatedly masked and drew over it with more layers of color.

■ **Mike Reed** takes an approach to digital illustration that avoids the slick look sometimes seen in art created on the computer. To re-create the traditional look of pastel on rough paper, in *Artist at 50* (above) and *Polar Bears* (opposite), Reed sensitively layered textured color with the Pastel and Chalk variants of Dry Media on top of Wood Shavings paper texture (loaded from Wow! Textures on the Painter 7 Wow! CD-ROM).

For the self portrait *Artist at 50*, Reed began by making a color study with the Square Chalk variant to establish the theme and general elements in the composition. So he could limit paint while working freely, he built selections, which

he began by drawing shapes with the Pen tool. He drew shapes for the figure and clothing and also added stars, a moon, and abstract shapes in the background. He converted each shape to a selection (Shapes, Convert To Selection), feathered it (Select, Feather) and saved it as a mask in the Masks section (Select, Save Selection). Reed loaded and colored within each selection using the Square Chalk, then he brushed lightly over areas with the Square Chalk to paint highlights. He added expressive strokes to the gesturing arm to suggest movement. To finish, he added more texture to the background using the Square Chalk and blue and purple colors.

■ To begin the children's book illustration *Polar Bears* (above) for Scholastic Books, **Mike Reed** sketched the composition in soft blues, grays and purples using the Square Chalk variant of Dry Media, painting free brushstrokes on top of the Wood Shavings paper texture (from the Wow! Textures on the CD-ROM that comes with this book.) So he could paint freely in some areas while protecting other areas of his composition, he created selections using the Pen tool and then converted each shape to a selection (Shapes, Convert To Selection). Because he wanted the color areas to have soft edges, he feathered each selection (Select, Feather) with a radius of 5 pixels. Then saved it (Select, Save Selection) into the Masks section of the Objects palette so he could it later as a mask. To paint a textured gradient on the sky, he loaded a selection he'd made and brushed over the selected area with the Square Chalk using various light blue and rose colors.

To give the polar bears' bodies more dimension, he loaded selections and painted with the Artist Pastel Chalk variant of Dry Media. To add detail to the fur, he used the Sharp Chalk variant. To add the shadows under the bears, he hand-painted "gradations" with soft, grainy strokes. To finish, he painted tighter highlight and shadow details on the faces and bodies of the bears with the Sharp Chalk.

USING
LAYERS

Emerald City. *Working in source files, we painted elements for the illustration, then we painted masks for the turtle, the fishes and the paint can and brushes. We loaded selections from the masks so we could float each illustration element and use the Layer Adjuster to drag and drop it into the final composite. After dragging the items in, we used the Layer Adjuster to position them. To create a transparent look on the bottom of the paint can, we used the Digital Airbrush variant of the Airbrushes and white paint to softly erase lower areas of the can layer's visibility mask.*

LAYERS are elements that hover above Painter's image canvas, providing a great deal of flexibility in composing artwork. You can move, paint on, or apply a special effect to a layer without affecting other layers or the background canvas. So when building images you can try several possibilities by manipulating or repositioning the various elements. Then, when your layers are as you like them, you can drop them onto the canvas, blending them with the background.

In addition to *image* (or pixel-based) *layers*, Painter 7 incorporates seven other types of hovering elements: *floating objects, reference layers, shapes, dynamic layers, text layers,* and two new *media layers, Water Color and Liquid Ink.* The controls for compositing, naming, stacking, and grouping all eight kinds of elements are found in the Layers section of the Objects palette, as described in "Organizing with the Layers Section" on page 174. Each of these elements has a Composite Method that affects how it interacts (or blends) with the background and with other layers.

You can preserve layers by saving your file in RIFF format. Saving in most other formats requires *dropping* or merging, the layers.

A TIFF–TO–RIFF LIFESAVER

If you save a layered file in TIFF format (a format that doesn't support floating elements), Painter is smart enough not to automatically drop the layers in your working image. A dialog box will appear, and when you click OK, the program saves a copy of your document with layers dropped in TIFF format, but the layers stay alive in your working image. Make sure to save in RIFF format before quitting, in order to preserve the image layers, floating objects, reference layers, dynamic layers, text layers, shapes, and Water Color and Liquid Ink layers.

Recognizing items in the Layers section of the Objects palette: Image layers are designated by a stack of rectangles, a floating object by a star, a shape by a circle and triangle, a reference layer by a dotted rectangle, a dynamic layer by a plug icon, a Text layer by a capital "T," a Water Color layer by a blue water drop and a Liquid Ink layer by a black drop of ink. In the Layers section shown here, the document's Canvas is selected.

USING DRAG-AND-DROP

Here's a quick way to copy a layer or shape into a composite file from a source image. Open both images. In the source image, select the layer or shape by clicking it with the Layer Adjuster tool, then drag the item into the composite image.

For this flower illustration, the Wash Bristle and Runny Wash Camel variants of Water Color were used to paint washes on Water Color layers.

However, if you'd like to open a Painter image in Photoshop with layers intact, save the file in Photoshop format. All layers and shapes will be converted to Photoshop layers, with their names and stacking order intact. To read more about working with Photoshop, turn to Chapter 9, "Using Painter With Photoshop."

An *image layer* can pixels or transparency. When you add a new layer by clicking the Create New Layers button at the bottom of the Layers section and choosing New Layer (or by choosing New Layer from the section's pull-down menu), it's completely transparent until you paint on it. See "Working with Image Layers," below.

A *floating object* is an area of an image layer that has been isolated and lifted from the layer, to create a kind of sublayer. Each layer can have only one floating object at a time. See "Working with Floating Objects" on page 167.

Reference layers can be helpful for assembling large images from several separate source files. A reference layer is a 72 ppi screen proxy (or "stand-in") for an image layer in the current image, or for a placed image that's linked to an image file outside of the document. (See "Using Reference Layers" on page 168.)

Shapes are essentially a resolution-independent kind of layer that can be reshaped or resized without degradation. As described on page 169, shapes are outline-based elements with attributes such as stroke, fill and transparency. Shapes and their attributes are PostScript-based objects. But if you paint on a shape, adding pixel information, you have to first convert it to an image layer.

Dynamic layers are special hovering devices that allow you to make adjustments to an existing image (such as an Equalize layer or Bevel World layer), or to create entirely new effects (for instance, a Liquid Metal layer). You can create a dynamic layer by clicking the Dynamic Plugins button at the bottom of the Layers section and choosing a plug-in from the pop-up menu (see page 171).

Painter 7 features improved *Text layers (*see page 172.)

Media layers are special layers that allow startling, realistic painting effects. Read about two new types of media layers—Water Color and Liquid Ink—on page 173.

All of these hovering elements take up extra disk space and RAM. You can work around this, though. Float only what's necessary, and drop and combine layers whenever it makes sense.

LAYER OR FLOATING OBJECT?

New *image layers* can be made by selecting an area of the *Canvas* and cutting or copying. But if you select and cut or copy *from a layer other than the Canvas,* you produce a *floating object* associated with the layer you used to make it.

WORKING WITH IMAGE LAYERS

You can make an image layer by activating the Canvas layer, selecting an image area then clicking on it with the Layer Adjuster tool. This process cuts the selected area out of the canvas and floats it. Alt/Option-click to *copy* an active selection or to

To make a new layer by copying an active selection on Painter's image canvas (similar to choosing Layer, New, Layer Via Copy in Photoshop), make or load a selection in your image, hold down the Alt/Option key and choose Select, Float. (You can also choose the Layer Adjuster tool, and click or drag inside the selected area.) To *cut* from the image canvas and turn the selected area into a new layer, choose Select, Float or click or drag with the Layer Adjuster without pressing the Alt/Option key.

PHOTO: CORBIS IMAGES

If you don't hold down the Alt/Option key when you drag a selection with the Layer Adjuster, you'll leave a hole behind in the canvas if you then move the newly created layer. Occasionally this is desirable, but most of the time you'll want to use the Alt/Option!

TEXTURE ON IMAGE LAYERS

By default, image layers have a smooth surface; unlike the Canvas, they do not interact with paper chosen in the Papers section of the Art Materials palette. But you can add texture by using special effects such as the Apply Surface Texture command. To apply a paper texture to an image layer, first select the layer by clicking on its name in the Layers section of the Objects palette; then choose Effects, Surface Control, Apply Surface Texture Using Paper. Even though the preview shows differently, when you apply an effect to an image layer, the effect is applied only to areas of the layer that already contain brushstrokes, a fill or other pixel information. Adjust the settings to your liking and click OK.

duplicate an entire layer. This leaves the original pixels in place while it creates a copy. Selections to define the area to float can be made with paths drawn with the Pen tool and converted to selections, or with masks that are loaded as selections. All elements pasted into a Painter document come in as image layers, and you can also drag an image layer from the Image Portfolio section of the Objects palette into your image. Like the background layer, or Canvas, an image layer includes an 8-bit visibility mask that accompanies the 24-bit image. The visibility mask determines what parts of the pixel information on the layer are shown or hidden. You can modify the mask to blend layered images with exciting transparency effects as described on page 175.

Here's how to work with image layers once you've created or imported one:

To select a layer, click its name in the Layers section of the Objects palette. Or choose the Layer Adjuster in the Tools palette, then turn on Auto Select Layer in the Controls:Adjuster palette and click on a visible area of the layer with the Layer Adjuster tool.

To deselect a layer, click on another layer, or on the blank area below the layers' names in the Layers section. Or turn on Auto Select in the Controls:Adjuster palette and use the Layer Adjuster tool to click somewhere in the image where the current layer has no pixels.

To apply a special effect to a layer, make sure it's selected by clicking on it with the Layer Adjuster tool or by clicking its name in the Layers section. Then choose from the Effects menu. (If no layer is selected, the effect will be applied to the Canvas.) An effect can't be applied to a new transparent layer with no pixels on it.

To paint on a layer, make sure it's selected by highlighting its name in the Layers section. Choose any brush (except a Water Color or Liquid Ink variant) and paint brushstrokes onto the layer. (Water Color and Liquid Ink can paint only on appropriate media layers, which will automatically be created if you try to use these brushes on image layers.) For more information, turn to "Painting on Layers" on page 56 in Chapter 3 and to "Illustrating with Layers," on page 177 of this chapter.

To erase paint you have applied to a layer, making the area "clear" again. You can choose the Eraser variant of the Erasers (in the Brushes palette) with 100% Opacity set in the Controls:Brush palette, and paint on the layer to "erase." However, this method can yield unpredictable results—at times it may not erase completely, but may leave a white or solid-colored patch on the layer where the Eraser was used. If you get this result, choose Edit, Undo, and try "erasing" on the layer mask as described on page 167.

LAYERS AND SELECTIONS

In Painter there can be only one active selection at a time. You can use a selection to edit a portion of any *image layer, reference layer, Water Color layer* or *Liquid Ink layer* listed in the Layers section.

When creating Neural Pathway, a detail of which is shown here, David Purnell used many layers and shapes. See the complete illustration and more of Purnell's work in the gallery at the end of this chapter.

A QUICK CANVAS COPY

To quickly float a copy of the Canvas to a layer, choose Select, All, (Ctrl/⌘-A), then hold down Ctrl-Alt (Windows) or ⌘-Option (Mac) and click on the Canvas.

PHOTO: CORBIS IMAGES

To create a soft edge on this image layer, we feathered the layer's visibility mask.

To "erase" a portion of a layer by editing its mask, begin by choosing white in the Colors section of the Art Materials palette. Click on the layer in the Layers section of the Objects palette, then click on its mask in the Masks section. Click the eye icon open to view the mask in black-and-white, or click the eye icon closed to view the layer. Choose a brush (such as the Pens, Scratchboard Tool) with 100% Opacity set in the Controls:Brush palette, and paint on the mask with white to "erase." To *restore* the mask, paint with black.

To move a layer, choose the Layer Adjuster tool, turn on Auto Select Layer in the Controls:Adjuster palette, then click on the layer contents in the image window and drag. To adjust a layer's position a screen pixel at a time, click it with the Layer Adjuster and use the arrow keys on your keyboard.

To merge a layer with the canvas, select it in the Layers section and click the section's Drop button or press Ctrl/⌘-Shift-D. If you want to merge all of your layers—much like Photoshop's Flatten Image command—simply choose Drop All from the Layers section's menu. Another option is to choose File, Clone; a duplicate of the image will appear with all layers merged.

To scale, rotate, distort or flip a layer, click it with the Layer Adjuster and choose the appropriate command under Effects, Orientation.

To change the opacity of a layer, click its name in the Layers section and use the Layers section's Opacity slider.

To feather the edge of the content of a layer, select the layer in the Layers section, then switch to the Masks section and target that layer's visibility mask. Now click the right triangle on the Masks section bar and choose Feather Mask. (An image layer is the only kind of layer whose mask can be feathered.)

WORKING WITH FLOATING OBJECTS

If you'd like to reposition a portion of an image layer or edit an area on a layer, a *floating object* will be essential. A layer can have only one floating object at a time. Like its parent layer, a floating object includes its own 8-bit visibility mask. Only image layers can have a floating object.

To create a floating object that's cut out from a layer, make a selection, click on a layer's name in the Layers section of the Objects palette and choose Select, Float, or click inside the selection with the Layer Adjuster tool. The floating object will be listed below its parent layer in the Layers section, indented to show the relationship. (If you turn off visibility for the floating object by clicking its eye icon, you'll see the hole where it has been cut from the parent layer.)

PHOTO: CORBIS IMAGES

A selected reference layer, ready to have Free Transform applied, has a yellow-and-white striped bounding box with eight handles.

To make a floating object copy of information on the parent layer (without cutting out), make a selection, press the Alt/Option key, then choose Select, Float, or click with the Layer Adjuster tool. The floating object "copy" will be listed below its parent layer in the Layers section.

To recombine a floating object with its parent layer, click the Drop button in the Layers section. The floating object will also recombine with its parent layer if you do any of the following while the layer or its floating object is active (selected in the Layers section): make another selection, paint, edit the visibility mask, paste into the document or drag an item from the Image Portfolio.

USING REFERENCE LAYERS

If you work with large files and your computer slows to a crawl when you try to reposition a big image layer, consider converting the image layer to a *reference layer*. Reference layers are 72 ppi proxy images, they let you manipulate high-resolution images faster, instead of dragging huge images around your screen. Because you are working with a proxy—and not the original—you can perform multiple rotations, scaling, and skewing very quickly. When you've finished all of manipulations, convert reference layers back to image layers; all the manipulations you've made will be carried out as a single change, with much less loss of quality than if you had made them one by one on the high-resolution file.

To make a reference layer, select an image layer and choose Effects, Orientation, Free Transform. To get ready to operate on the layer, choose the Layer Adjuster.

To scale a reference layer proportionately, press the Shift key and drag on a corner handle with the Layer Adjuster tool to resize as many times as needed to get just the result you want.

To rotate a reference layer interactively, press the Ctrl/⌘ key and drag a corner handle with the Layer Adjuster.

To skew a reference layer interactively, press the Ctrl/⌘ key and drag one of the original four middle handles with the Layer Adjuster tool.

To scale, skew or rotate a reference layer numerically, choose Effects, Orientation, Set Transform, and type specifications into the fields.

To turn a reference layer back into an image (pixel-based) layer, choose Effects, Orientation, Commit Transform, or paint or apply an effect to the reference layer, clicking the Commit button when

Rick Kirkman created Postal Cat *by drawing shapes, then converting them to image layers so that he could paint on them. Turn to page 182 to read about his technique step-by-step.*

The opacity of a shape's fill can be set in the Set Shape Attributes dialog box (top), or in the corresponding Controls:Adjuster palette (bottom), which is visible when the Layer Adjuster tool is selected.

WHOLE SHAPE SELECTION

If you liked using the Whole Shape Selection tool (solid arrow) in Painter 4 to select an entire unfilled shape path, you'll be happy to know that—it's available in Painter 7. Choose the Shape Selection tool (hollow arrow) and press the Ctrl/⌘ key to use it in Whole Shape Selection mode. You can now click on a shape path to select all of its anchor points at once, making it possible to move the path to a new location, undistorted, by dragging anywhere on the shape.

prompted. If you drag a reference layer into the Image Portfolio, the stored version becomes an image layer.

WORKING WITH SHAPES

Shapes can be drawn with the Rectangular or Oval Shape tool, or the Pen or the Shape Design tool. Or they can be made from a selection (converted from a selection using the Select, Convert To Shape command) or imported from a PostScript drawing program such as Adobe Illustrator (this process is described in Chapter 4).

Before modifying a shape, you need to select it. There are three ways to select shapes: The first (using the Layer Adjuster) selects the entire shape and displays a bounding box with a black-and-yellow striped border with eight handles around its edges; this selection method allows you to duplicate, move or transform the shape. The second method (clicking with the Shape Selection tool, which is the arrowhead that shares a palette space with the Layer Adjuster) displays the Bézier path with its anchor points and handles and allows you to move the path. (If a single anchor point or area of the path is selected, by marqueeing with the Shape Selection tool, the path can be manipulated.) The third method uses the Whole Shape Selection tool (solid arrow), made available by using the Shape Selection tool with the Ctrl/⌘ key held down. It selects the entire shape, and it allows you to move it as a unit without distorting it.

To drag off a copy of a shape, you can select the shape with the Layer Adjuster tool, then press Alt/Option and drag.

To scale a shape proportionately, click it with the Layer Adjuster, hold down the Shift key and drag a corner handle.

To rotate a shape, click it with the Layer Adjuster, press the Ctrl/⌘ key and drag a corner handle.

To skew a shape interactively, click it with the Layer Adjuster, press the Ctrl/⌘ key and drag a middle handle.

To scale, distort, rotate or flip a shape, select it in the Layers section of the Objects palette and use one of the choices found under Effects, Orientation.

To duplicate a shape and transform the copy, choose Shapes, Set Duplicate Transform. Set up specifications in the Set Duplicate Transform dialog box and click OK. Now when you choose Shapes, Duplicate, the transformation will be applied to the copy.

To modify the stroke and fill attributes of a shape, select it and choose Shapes, Set Shape Attributes, or double-click on the name of a shape in the Layers section (or highlight its name and press Enter) to open the Set Shape Attributes dialog box. To change the fill or stroke of a shape to the current color that you chose while using the Shape Attributes dialog box, click once in the Stroke or Fill color field and choose a new color in the Colors section of the Art

For this restaurant logo, we drew black calligraphy letters on the canvas using the Calligraphy variant of Pens. We made a luminosity mask by choosing Auto Mask (Using Image Luminance), from the Masks section's pop-out menu, loaded the selection (Select, Load Selection, New Mask 1), then converted the selection to shapes (Select, Convert To Shape). The client planned to use the logo in a variety of ways, so we appreciated that Painter automatically created compound shapes to make the counters transparent for the letter "O," the two descending "g" shapes and the "e." Seen here are the selected filled shapes (top), and the logo applied onto Koa wood texture, from an Art Beats Wood and Paper CD-ROM (bottom). To read more about compound shapes turn to "Making a Compound," on the next page or to "Using Shapes," in Chapter 14 of The Painter 7 User Guide.

Materials palette. (This method selects the current color without displaying the color wheel. To use the wheel instead and choose a new color, simply double-click the stroke or Fill color swatch in the Set Shape Attributes dialog box.) **A word of warning:** If you paint on, or apply an effect to, a shape—rather than simply changing its stroke and fill—it will be automatically converted into an image layer when you click the Commit button. When this happens, shape attributes (such as resolution independence, and control of stroke and fill) are lost.

To convert several shapes into individual image layers, you can Shift-select multiple shapes in the Layers section and convert the shapes to image layers all at once—as long as they are stroked and filled—using Shapes, Convert To Layer.

To make a single layer from several shapes, first Shift-select the shapes, then click the Layer Commands button on the Layers section to access the pop-up menu and choose Group. With the group closed (controlled by the arrow to the left of its name in the Layers section), choose Shapes, Convert To Layer.

To duplicate, move or transform a group of shapes, you can select the group by clicking its name in the Layers section with the Layer Adjuster tool. (See "Organizing With the Layers Section" on page 174, to read more about groups.)

To move an individual shape within a group,

choose the Shape Selection tool and press the Ctrl/⌘ key to switch to the Whole Shape Selection tool. Now click on the shape with the Whole Shape Selection tool and drag the shape; or move it using the arrow keys. To move a single shape within an open group, you can also click and drag it with the Layer Adjuster tool.

Blending between shapes. To create intermediate shapes between two shapes, Shift-select

SHAPES OF A CURRENT COLOR

To automatically fill or stroke a shape with the Current Color chosen in the Colors section as you draw it, set up your Shape preferences: Choose Edit, Preferences, Shapes, check the appropriate checkboxes and click OK.

Setting up the Shape Preferences to automatically fill with the Current Color

A HIDDEN RASTERIZER

You can rasterize PostScript art from Illustrator in Painter and at the same time save a mask for selecting that area later. Choose File, Acquire, Adobe Illustrator File. Select the resulting shapes in the Layers section of the Objects palette and convert them to layers using Shapes, Convert To Layer. To flatten the image and make a selection, select each layer by choosing its name in the Layers section and use the Drop and Select command in the Layers section's pop-out menu. To store the selection for use later, choose Select, Save Selection and save it as a mask in the Masks section.

Viewing shape paths (top) and finished objects (bottom). For this filled compound outer object with blended interior object, we began by making a blend. To blend the interior blue circle with a very small white circle in its center, we selected both circles in the Layers section, then chose Shapes, Blend and specified 50 steps. To build the compound of the two outer shapes, we selected them both with the Shape Selection tool and chose Shapes, Make Compound. (Choose the Shape Selection tool and press the Ctrl/⌘ key to switch to Whole Shape Selection mode.) The Make Compound command cut a hole with the smaller eye shape, allowing only part of the outer fill to be visible.

Detail from Hot Beveled Metal. *Beginning with a text layer, we used the Bevel World dynamic layer to commit the live text to an image layer and to create a 3D effect. Then we layered two more copies of the bevel—we painted on the first copy and we created the glow using the second copy. To learn more about type effects using Bevel World, turn to Chapter 8.*

both shapes in the Layers section and choose Shapes, Blend. Make choices in the dialog box and click OK. The *Painter 7 User Guide* contains a complete explanation of the Blend dialog box.

Here's a useful application for Painter's Blend command: If you've imported an image created in Illustrator that has blends and they don't make the transition successfully into Painter, zoom in and delete the interior objects inside the blend using the Shape Selection tool and Delete key. Shift-select the two outside objects in the Layers section, then choose Shapes, Blend and specify the number of steps to regenerate the blend.

Making a compound. To cut a hole in a shape and reveal the underlying image, make a compound using two shapes: Move a small shape on top of a large one, Shift-select both of them in the Layers section, and choose Shapes, Make Compound. The top shape will cut a hole in the bottom shape to reveal the underlying image. Compounds are made automatically to create counters in letters when type is set or when type outlines are imported, and also when selections with holes are converted to shapes.

USING DYNAMIC LAYERS

Dynamic layers are special devices that allow you to create a variety of effects. To keep dynamic layers "live" (allowing changes to be made and previewed on the image without becoming permanent), the file must be saved in RIFF format. Saving in Photoshop format converts the dynamic layers to image layers, freezing the effects in their current state.

Dynamic layers, which are indicated by a plug icon in the Layers section, fall into three basic categories. The first kind is similar to an adjustment layer in Adobe Photoshop. It allows you to set up a procedure such as a brightness-and-contrast correction or a posterization of the underlying image, without permanently changing the actual image itself. Image correction tools such as Equalize, Brightness and Contrast, and Posterize and special effects layers such as Glass Distortion, Kaleidoscope and Liquid Lens

---

AUTOMATIC DROP SHADOWS

To apply a drop shadow to a single shape, select the shape in the Layers section and choose Effects, Objects, Create Drop Shadow. Enter your own specifications, or just click OK to accept Painter's defaults. When the Commit dialog box appears, asking if you'd like to commit the shape to an image layer, click Commit. Selecting a closed group of shapes and choosing Effects, Objects, Create Drop Shadow will apply an automatic drop shadow to each of the individual shapes in the group and will convert the shapes to image layers as well! To convert a group of shapes to single image layer and make an automatic drop shadow for the new layer, begin by closing the group (click the arrow to the left of the eye closed). Then select the group's name in the Layers section, click the Layer Commands button to access the menu and choose Collapse and click Commit All. Then choose, Effects, Objects, Create Drop Shadow, and apply the shadow.

Cool Water Drops. *To add a water droplet effect to this photo (simulating water drops on a camera lens), we used the Liquid Metal dynamic plug-in. First we made a clone of the image (File, Clone). Then we clicked the Dynamic Plugins button on the Layers section and chose Liquid Metal from the menu. We chose the Clone Source Map type and a high Refraction setting to make the "water" translucent with a blue reflection. Then we clicked and dragged with the Circle tool from the Liquid Metal dialog box to place the drops. A drop can be extended simply by starting to drag with the Circle tool inside the edge of an existing drop.*

Clicking the "plug" icon on the Layers section of the Objects palette will reveal the Dynamic Plugins menu.

fall into this category. To generate a layer of this type (such as a Posterize layer), click the Dynamic Plugins button at the bottom of the Layers section to access the pull-down menu and choose Posterize. Click OK to apply it. The posterization will apply to all image layers, reference layers, shapes and dynamic layers listed below the Posterize dynamic layer in the Layers section. (To read more about Painter's image-correction layers, turn to Chapter 6. For information about creating special effects with this series of dynamic layers, refer to Chapter 7.)

For a second kind of dynamic layer, you apply a special effect procedure to a selected image layer, the "source image layer," *turning it into* a dynamic layer. Because of the dynamic layer's "live" capability, you can preview changes and then return the source image layer to its original condition if you like. Three of the dynamic layers—Bevel World, Burn and Tear—require a source image layer to perform their magic. To make this kind of dynamic layer, select an area of your image with any selection tool, or select a layer in the Layers section and choose Bevel World, for instance, from the Dynamic Plugins pull-down menu in the Layers section of the Objects palette. Make adjustments to the settings and click OK. (If you start with a selection on the image Canvas, clicking Apply will automatically generate a new dynamic layer from the selection.) Read more about these dynamic layers in Chapter 7.

The third type of dynamic layer allows you to build an entirely new layer with special-effects imagery. Liquid Metal falls into this category. To read about exciting techniques using Liquid Metal, turn to Chapter 7, "Exploring Special Effects," and to "Painting with Ice" in Chapter 8.

To change a dynamic layer's options, select it by clicking on its name in the Layers section. From the pop-out menu on the Layers section bar, choose Options to open the Options dialog box for the selected layer. (You can also access the Options dialog box by double-clicking the name of the dynamic layer in the Layers section.) Make changes in the dialog box and click OK.

To convert a dynamic layer to an image layer, so you can edit the layer's mask or convert the image layer into a reference layer (to scale it using Free Transform, for instance), click the right triangle on the Layers section bar and choose Convert To Default Layer from the menu. The following actions will also convert a dynamic layer to an image layer: transforming using Effects, Orientation (to scale, rotate or skew); applying an effect from the Effects menu (such as Effects, Surface Control, Apply Surface Texture); painting on the layer; applying a dynamic layer special effect (such as applying the Tear special-effect layer to an active Burn layer); or merging a group that includes a dynamic layer.

For this text design, we began by setting small colored text on a layer. Then we made several duplicates by Option-dragging with the Layer Adjuster. We repositioned the text layers using the Layer Adjuster, and when the background was arranged, we set a large black "W" above the other layers. To achieve the inside-out color effect, we set the Composite Method for the large "W" to Reverse Out in the Layers section.

The Layers section showing the pop-out menu that includes important commands for use with Liquid Ink and Water Color layers.

When painting the illustration Maui North Shore 2, Water Color layers and their special brushes were used.

USING TEXT LAYERS

Painter 7's new Text layers combine the text shapes and Dynamic Text of previous versions. When you select the Text tool in the Tools palette and begin to set type on your image, the type is set in one block on a new layer that appears in the Layers section of the Objects palette, designated by a "T" icon. Controls for specifying text settings are located in the Text section of the Objects palette. For in-depth information about using Text layers, turn to Chapter 8, "Working with Type in Painter."

WORKING WITH MEDIA LAYERS

Painter 7 includes two brand-new media layers, Water Color and Liquid Ink. Special brushes must be used when painting on each kind of media layer. When the Canvas or an image layer is selected in the Layers section and you attempt to paint with a Water Color brush or Liquid Ink brush, a new Water Color or Liquid Ink layer is automatically generated. Chapter 3 includes in-depth information about Water Color and Liquid Ink, including "A Painter Water Color Primer" and "A Painter Liquid Ink Primer" as well as step-by-step techniques for both media.

Using Water Color layers. Painter 7 offers Water Color layers and special Water Color brushes, making it possible to add layers of wet color on separate layers. Water Color layers can be edited using selections to restrict the changes to the selected area. A portion of a Water Color layer mask can be removed by targeting the mask in the Masks section of the Objects palette, making a selection with an area-based selection tool and pressing the Backspace/Delete key. However, the visibility mask on a Water Color layer cannot be edited with brushes. If you attempt to remove a portion of the layer visibility mask using the Eraser variant of Erasers, a warning dialog box will appear. Rather than editing the visibility mask, you can restrict paint to a specific area, by making a mask and loading it as a selection (Select, Load Selection), then targeting the Water Color layer before painting. For a step-by-step technique about using selections with Water Color layers turn to "Selections and Masks for Water Color Layers" on page 185.

Using commands found under the pop-out menu on the right side of the Layers section, you can stop paint from diffusing on a Water Color layer by choosing Dry Water Color Layer, and you can wet an entire Water Color layer. Or you can add the content of the Canvas to an existing Water Color layer, or create a new Water Color layer form the Canvas content, also by choosing from the Layers section menu.

Using Liquid Ink layers. With Painter 7 it's now possible to paint with a new thick, viscous ink medium, Liquid Ink. A Liquid Ink layer is not pixel-based but resolution-independent. To paint on a Liquid Ink layer, you must use special Liquid Ink brushes found in the Brushes palette. Liquid Ink layers can be edited using

John Derry created Capitola, *a detail of which is shown here, using Liquid Ink layers. Turn to the gallery in Chapter 6 to see the complete illustration.*

For the ultimate in management using the Layers section, see how Rick Kirkman did it in "Working with Shapes and Layers," on page 182.

In the Layers section (above), for David Purnell's Molar Cross Section, *he organized some layers in groups and he locked other items so he wouldn't accidentally select them with the Layer Adjuster. Turn to page 199 to see his illustration.*

selections, but a Liquid Ink layer does not have an editable visibility mask. (A visibility mask is not listed in the Masks section when a Liquid Ink layer is selected in the Layers section.) To constrain paint to a specific area, make a selection and then target the Liquid Ink layer before painting.

ORGANIZING WITH THE LAYERS SECTION

In the Layers section, Painter assigns sequential names to layers and shapes (such as Layer 1, Layer 2 and so on) in the order they were created. Rename them by double-clicking on a name (or select the name and press the Enter key) to bring up the appropriate dialog box. Enter the name and click OK. You can hide layers or shapes by clicking to close the eye icons next to their names, so that you can more easily work with underlying items. Click the eye open to show an item again.

To lock an item (making it impossible to select it in the image window), click the lock icon to the left of its item name in the Layers section. To unlock, click to toggle the lock icon open.

Using groups. Grouping layers or shapes is an ideal way of organizing related elements in the Layers section so that they don't take up too much space. To group layers or shapes, Shift-select the elements in the Layers section, then click the Layer Commands button at the bottom of the Layers section and choose Group, or press Ctrl/⌘-G. To ungroup, click the Layer Commands button and choose Ungroup, or press Ctrl/⌘-U. If you want to apply effects (other than Scale, or Create Drop Shadow) to a group of layers or shapes, you'll need to open the group, select individual items, then apply the effect. Like individual layers, groups can be hidden or made visible by clicking the eye icon, and they can also be locked.

Using the Image Portfolio. Open the Image Portfolio section of the Objects palette by

PRESERVE TRANSPARENCY

By turning on the Preserve Transparency checkbox in the Layers section, you can confine your painting and editing to those areas of an image layer that already contain pixels. Turn Preserve Transparency off if you'd like to paint or edit outside the existing pixels—for instance, to feather the edge by applying the Effects, Focus, Soften command, which would spread pixels outside of the original area. Preserve Transparency is not available for Shapes, Liquid Ink or Water Color layers.

AUTO-SELECTING A LAYER

By choosing the Layer Adjuster tool and turning on Auto Select Layer in the Controls:Adjuster palette, you can click on the visible portion of any layer to select the layer then drag to move its contents.

READY TO COLLAPSE

If you've finished making changes to a group of layers but you still want to keep the group separate from the Canvas, consider clicking the Layer Commands button at the bottom of the Layers section and choosing Collapse. This feature merges a selected group of layers into a single layer and can be a real memory-saver.

Create an empty image portfolio by opening the Image Portfolio section in the Objects palette and choosing Image Mover from the pull-down menu, opened by clicking the triangle on the right side of the Image Portfolio section bar. Click the New button to create the empty portfolio.

LAYER MASK VISIBILITY

You can use controls in the Layer Attributes box to determine which part of a layer is masked. To see how these controls work, open the Image Portfolio and drag one of the portfolio items onto a colored background. In the Layers section, double-click on the name of the new layer you just dragged in to open its Layer Attributes box. Since the items in the Image Portfolio are layers with masks already created for them, in the Layer Attributes dialog box the Normal button should be chosen, meaning that everything in the layer outside of the mask is invisible. To reverse the effect, click the Inverted button, click OK and view the result. Clicking on the Disabled button in the Layer Attributes box will show both areas, inside and outside the mask, as if no mask existed. Keep in mind that these modes affect visibility only; any painting or effect applied to the layer will be applied to the entire layer, not just the visible areas.

clicking the left arrow on the Image Portfolio section bar. To remove layers from your image, but store them for later use or for use in another document, use the Layer Adjuster tool to drag them from the image into the Image Portfolio section. Hold down the Alt/Option key if you want to leave a copy of the layer in your document.

LAYERS AND THEIR MASKS

The visibility mask (or layer mask) that's automatically associated with the Canvas and with each image layer allows for transparent effects. You can edit layer masks using either brushes or special effect commands (such as Effects, Surface Control, Express Texture, with which you can apply a texture to a mask). To view a mask on a selected layer, select it in the Masks section and open its eye icon. For more information, see the "Layer Mask Visibility" tip on this page.

Importing a source file with its mask. Because it's faster to work with fewer layers, many artists assemble source files, then import them into a final composite file. Consider preparing a mask in a smaller source file that you plan to import into a composite (using File, Place). In the Place dialog box, check the Retain Alpha checkbox, and click OK to place the source as a reference layer in your document. To turn the reference layer into an image layer, select it in the Layers section and choose Effects, Orientation, Commit Transform. (For more information, see "Using Reference Layers" on page 168.)

ERASING AND RESTORING

In Painter you can use the Eraser variant of the Erasers to remove information on an image layer. **Caution:** Using the Eraser permanently removes the information from the layer. Editing the layer's visibility mask using white paint is much more flexible, because you can restore the image on the layer by painting the visibility mask back in. Use *white* on the mask to *erase* the layer, use *black* on the mask to *restore* the layer.

A VERSATILE MASK EXCHANGE

If you'd like to use a layer visibility mask on another layer or on the background Canvas to constrain paint or effects there, here's a way to trade masks back and forth: To copy a layer visibility mask so that it becomes a separate mask in the Masks section of the Objects palette, select the layer in the Layers section, then in the Masks section, select the layer visibility mask. Choose Copy Mask from the Masks section pull-down menu. In the Copy Mask dialog box, choose "New" to create a new mask for the image canvas based on the layer mask, or select the name of an existing mask you want to replace or modify, and click OK.

DROPPING AND SAVING A LAYER VISIBILITY MASK

To merge the visible part of an image layer so it becomes part of the image canvas but at the same time preserve its visibility mask, choose "Drop and Select" from the Layers section's pull-down menu. A selection will be made from the layer's visibility mask, and you can save it as a user mask in the Masks section, by choosing Select, Save Selection.

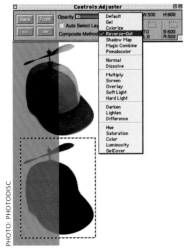

We applied two of Painter's Composite Methods to these beanies floating over a blue and white background. The top beanie uses Gel and the bottom one uses Reverse-Out.

COMPOSITE CONTROLS

Painter's composite controls can give you nifty special effects with very little effort. With a layer selected in the Layers section, choose from the Composite Method pull-down menu on the Layers section (or in the Controls:Adjuster palette when the Layer Adjuster is chosen). The scrolling list includes many of the same blending modes found in Adobe Photoshop (exceptions are Color Dodge, Color Burn and Exclusion) which are listed below the ones that are unique to Painter. "A Visual Display of the Composite Methods" below shows these controls in action.

LAYER COMPOSITE DEPTH

Painter's Composite Depth controls work only on impasto paint (see "Painting with Realistic Impasto" on page 53 and "Working with Thick Paint" on page 107 for more information about Impasto). You'll find the Composite Depth pull-down menu near the top of the Layers section of the Objects palette. The default Composite Depth method is *Add*. If you paint with an Impasto brush on a layer, *Add* raises the thick paint. *Ignore* turns off the thickness for the paint on the layer, and *Subtract* inverts the paint thickness on the layer, making brushstrokes on this layer excavated rather than raised on the surface. *Replace* changes the paint depth of Impasto on the underlying layer to the applied layer's depth wherever the layers overlap.

A VISUAL DISPLAY OF THE COMPOSITE METHODS

Painter's Composite Methods (from the Layers section of the Objects palette) change how a layer interacts with the image underneath. Here a leaf floats over a two-part background. The Default and Normal methods give the same results, as do Shadow Map and Multiply. For complete descriptions of what the modes are doing, refer to Painter's *User Guide, The Photoshop 6 Wow! Book* or Adobe Photoshop's *User Guide.*

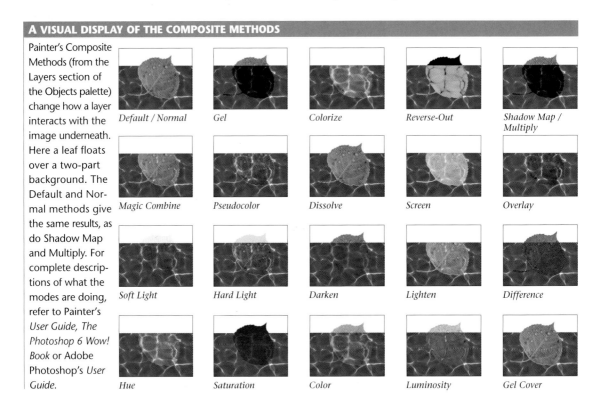

Default / Normal | *Gel* | *Colorize* | *Reverse-Out* | *Shadow Map / Multiply*

Magic Combine | *Pseudocolor* | *Dissolve* | *Screen* | *Overlay*

Soft Light | *Hard Light* | *Darken* | *Lighten* | *Difference*

Hue | *Saturation* | *Color* | *Luminosity* | *Gel Cover*

Illustrating With Layers

Overview *Begin with a blank image; or open a reference photo, clone it and make tracing paper; make new layers; paint on the layers, controlling the paint with masking if desired; and apply special effects.*

CHER THREINEN-PENDARVIS

PHOTO: CORBIS IMAGES

The optional reference photo with canvas added

The selected new layer in the Layers section of the Objects palette with Preserve Transparency turned off

Using Tracing Paper while sketching

PAINTER LAYERS BRING VERSATILITY TO THE PROGRAM, allowing you to see and preserve underlying layers and the background canvas as you paint or apply effects. See "Painting On Layers" on page 56, in Chapter 3 and "Working With Image Layers" on page 165 for more information about image layers. To create *Diving Catch*, we painted onto several layers with Painter's brushes, then added a bit of texture.

1 Opening an image, extending the canvas and cloning. You can begin with a new blank file or start by tracing a reference photo, as we did. If you'd like to begin with a blank file, without tracing a reference, skip to step 2.

Our reference photo was 883 pixels wide. In our image, the player's feet were very close to the edge of the frame, so we added 50 pixels to the right side of the image to enhance the sense of speed in the flying jump (choose Canvas, Canvas Size).

To make a clone of your reference photo, choose File, Clone. Prepare for using tracing paper by deleting the contents of the clone: Select all (Ctrl/⌘-A) and press the Delete key, leaving the original clone source image open.

2 Making a new layer. Whether you've started with a blank file or a cloned reference photo, in the Objects palette, click the left triangle on the Layers section bar to open the Layers section. To make a new empty layer, click the right triangle on the Layers section bar and from the pull-down menu choose New Layer. You'll see the new layer appear in the Layers section. To name the layer, double-click its name in the Layers section, type a descriptive name in the Layer Attributes box and click OK.

3 Sketching on the layer. (If you're tracing a reference, with your new layer still selected, turn on Tracing paper by pressing Ctrl/⌘-T.) Make sure that Preserve Transparency is unchecked in the Layers palette. We used the Sharp Pencil variant of Pencils to

4

The player selection saved as a mask. To see the mask in black-and-white, open the mask eye icon in the Masks section of the Objects palette and close the RGB-Canvas eye icon.

5

Targeting the "grass" layer in the Layers section of the Objects palette

6a

Click the right Drawing Mode to protect the area outside the selection and paint inside the selection.

6b

We painted colored brushstrokes inside the active ballplayer selection on the "player color" layer.

6c

Click the middle Drawing Mode to protect the area inside the selection and paint only outside it.

draw a sketch on the new layer. To sketch, choose a dark color in the Colors section of the Art Materials palette; choose the Sharp Pencil variant of Pencils and draw or trace to create an expressive, line drawing.

4 Making a mask. When your sketch is complete, you can make a mask (or masks) to isolate any parts. Start by making a selection, and then convert it to a mask by choosing Select, Save Selection. (You'll use the mask in steps 5 and 6.) For more information about selections and masks, turn to Chapter 4 "Selections, Shapes and Masks." To isolate the player we made a selection with the Lasso and saved it as a mask in the Masks section by choosing Select, Save Selection.

5 Arranging the layers and painting. Add more layers as you need them using the process described in step 2. We created layers for the fence, grass, shadow and ballplayer and arranged them in the Layers section with the ballplayer elements and line drawing on top. (To change the layer stacking order, drag the layer names up or down in the Layers section.)

We used the Square Chalk variant of Dry Media (adjusting the size in the Controls:Brush palette) to paint the fence, grass, shadow and ballplayer. You can use the selection you made in step 4 in conjunction with the Drawing Modes to constrain your paint, as described in step 6. Or you can carefully paint up to the edge of the subject "by hand" without using a selection as described in step 7, and then correct the edge later by editing it with an eraser.

6 Drawing inside and outside of selections on a layer. Painter allows you to use selections to constrain painting on any layer. To use the mask you made in step 4, which protects your subject while you paint around it, load a selection from the mask by choosing Select, Load Selection.

After loading the selection, you can use the Drawing Modes—three icons located in the bottom left corner of the image window—to paint inside or outside the selection. For instance, we painted inside the selection on the "player color" layer and outside it on the "fence" layer. (Keep in mind, the Drawing Modes are meant to constrain brushstrokes only; they do not work as described here to constrain effects.) To protect the area inside the active selection, click on the middle Drawing button. To protect

6d

Painting brushstrokes outside the selection on the "background fence" layer

7

Erasing along the edge of the uniform on the "grass" layer

8

Applying a paper texture to the "grass" layer

9

The line drawing layer with the Default Composite Method (left) and Gel (right)

the area outside the selection, click on the far right Drawing button. In the Layers section, click on the name of the layer you want to paint on, choose a brush and begin painting. To switch to another layer, click on its name in the Layers section, and continue to paint.

7 Hand-painting to clean up edges. If you use a selection to completely constrain all of the paint, you may create an undesirable hard edge. To preserve a fresh, hand-painted look, consider painting up to the edge without selecting, then use an eraser later to remove overlapping paint, if necessary. To use this method, begin by deselecting the selection (Select, None or Ctrl/⌘-D).

To erase some areas on our hand-painted "grass" layer that overlapped the ballplayer, we used a tiny Eraser variant (Erasers) to remove paint. To permanently remove paint from a layer, target the layer you'd like to correct by clicking on its name in the Layers section. Choose the Eraser variant of the Erasers, resize it smaller (using the Size slider on the Controls:Brush palette), and carefully remove the overlapping paint on the layer.

To erase any brushstrokes on the "background fence" layer that overlapped the ballplayer, we used the saved selection to edit it. We clicked on the "background fence" layer in the Layers section, chose Select, Load Selection to load a selection from the saved ballplayer mask and pressed the Delete key to remove all of the unwanted paint inside the selection on the "fence" layer.

8 Adding texture. By default, image layers have a smooth surface; unlike the Canvas, they do not interact with paper chosen in the Papers section of the Art Materials palette. But you can add texture using special effects such as Apply Surface Texture. When you apply an effect to an image layer, the effect is applied only to areas of the layer that already contain brushstrokes, a fill or other pixel information. To apply a paper texture to a layer, first select the layer in the Layers section, then choose Effects, Surface Control, Apply Surface Texture using Paper. To apply the texture to the "grass" layer we used a low Amount setting (about 20%), and we used Grass texture from the Wild Textures library (found in the Paper Textures folder on the Painter 7_CD2 CD-ROM).

9 Bringing out the line drawing. To enhance the loose, hand-drawn quality in our illustration by bringing out the sketch, we set the Composite Method of the "line drawing" layer to Gel. Gel is a transparent method that combines color on the layer with that on the underlying layers to create a darker color. Painter's Composite Methods are located in the Layers section under the Composite Method pull-down menu. (You can also find them in the Controls:Adjuster palette, when the Layer Adjuster is selected in the Tools palette. For a more complete description of the Composite Methods, turn to page 176 in the beginning of this chapter, or to Chapter 13 in the Painter 7 User Guide.)

Oil Painting on Layers

Overview *Make practice sketches; set up a reference layer and build a "canvas" ground; sculpt the forms of the head on a layer using tone and color; add transitional tone and detail; apply a canvas texture to the painted layer.*

1

One of the "practice" digital charcoal sketches

2a

The Layers section with the reference layer active and at a lower opacity

2b

The reference layer at low opacity (left), and the sketch on "canvas" made with the Captured Bristle variant of Brushes (right)

RON KEMPKE

YOU CAN USE PAINTER'S LAYERS, BRUSHES AND TEXTURES to create a realistic simulation of oils. Ron Kempke painted *Portrait of Cindy* using Brushes variants, working with layers on top a "canvas" ground.

1 Assembling references and making sketches. Kempke clamped a reference photo to his monitor, so he could easily refer to it when he needed to. He prefers not to clone or to do too much tracing because drawing by hand using the stylus keeps his brushstrokes freer and more expressive. Carefully studying his reference photo, Kempke drew several charcoal sketches in Painter just as a "warm up," working until he had achieved a good likeness of his subject.

2 Setting up layers and a canvas "ground." Kempke began his painting much as a portrait painter might do. But instead of projecting his painting onto a working canvas, he used a 1200 x 1400-pixel scanned photo at reduced opacity in Painter. To set up your on-screen reference, open your scanned image and open the Layers section of the Objects palette by clicking the triangle on the left side of the Layers section bar. To reduce the opacity of the photo, choose Select, All, then Select, Float. This lifts the image to a layer, leaving a white canvas underneath. By moving the Opacity slider you can fade the reference photo.

Next, Kempke used the Raw Silk texture to add the look of canvas before he started to paint. To build a canvas "ground," target the Canvas in the Layers section of the Objects palette. Apply the

3a

The shadow shapes are blocked in over the sketch.

3b

The shadow and midtone shapes are more developed in this example.

4

The image with most of the transitional tones and details added

Raw Silk paper texture to the image as follows: Open the Papers section of the Art Materials palette by clicking the left triangle on the Papers section bar and select the Raw Silk texture. Choose Effects, Surface Control, Apply Surface Texture, Using Paper. For a subtle canvas effect, reduce the Amount to approximately 20% and Shine to about 10% and leave the other settings at their defaults (Softness, 0; Picture, 100%; Reflection, 0; and light direction, 11:00).

Kempke created his painting on a layer above the reference so he could rework areas of his painting without disturbing the reference. (To add a new layer, choose New Layer from the pop-out menu on the right side of the Layers section.) He planned to apply surface texture to the brush work on the layer using the settings above to match the texture on the Canvas. When the painting was finished, the final texture application would match perfectly with the existing texture on the image canvas.

Kempke chose a neutral gray in the Colors section of the Art Materials palette and sketched using a modified version of the Captured Bristle variant of Brushes. He mapped out the proportions of the head with perpendicular lines to locate the eyes, nose, and mouth. He occasionally compared the proportions of his drawing with the reference underlay on the separate layer. He toggled the visibility of the reference layer on and off as he worked by clicking the "eye" icon to the left of the layer name. After he was satisfied with the proportions, he deleted the reference layer by targeting it in the Layers section and clicking the Delete button. (The photo clamped to his monitor was still available for reference if he needed it.)

3 Adding color and shadow. Kempke sculpted the solid form of the head with simplified shapes of the shadow colors using the Captured Bristle variant. He painted midtones, then blocked in shadow colors in flat tones for the larger masses.

Next, he added transitional tones in the areas between light and shadow. He painted these in flat tones, also, resisting the temptation to blend them with the shadow colors. These tones are among the most intense colors in the portrait.

4 Refining the portrait and adding texture. Kempke added the highlight areas in the face and hair, using broad strokes of color to loosely indicate the features. To bring the head forward by suggesting the space behind it, he added a background tone. Then he added depth and sheen to the hair and loosely suggested the teeth. In areas where he felt there was too much contrast, he added transitional tones and softened edges using a low-opacity brush. (Move the Opacity slider in the Controls:Brush palette to the left to reduce opacity.) Kempke also added brighter highlights to the eyes and nose. To complete the painting, he added "canvas" to the painted layer using the Apply Surface Texture process described in step 2.

Working with Shapes and Layers

Overview *Draw Bézier shapes in Painter; fill and name the shapes; convert the shapes to layers; paint details on the layers with brushes; edit a layer mask to achieve transparency; apply textured special effects with Color Overlay, Surface Texture and Glass Distortion.*

RICK KIRKMAN

Kirkman's scanned pencil sketch

The Shape Preferences dialog box

Dragging with the Direct Selection tool to adjust a control handle on a path

SHAPES BRING POWER AND VERSATILITY to Painter, saving many illustrators a trip to a draw program to create Bézier paths for import. With Painter's Pen tool (now similar to Illustrator's) you can completely create and edit Bézier paths, add a stroke and fill, name them, and organize them in the Layers section. After you draw shapes, you can convert them to layers and add paint and special effects. Rick Kirkman created the illustration above—one in a series of editorial illustrations for *Professional Speaker* magazine—entirely within Painter.

1 Setting up a template. Kirkman began by scanning a pencil sketch, saving it as a TIFF file and opening the scan in Painter. The file measured 2374 x 3184 pixels.

2 Creating shapes. To create your outlines, you can work either in Painter or in a PostScript drawing program. If you plan to trace a template—as Kirkman did—set up shape attributes so that you can draw with a precise skeletal line. Choose Edit, Preferences, Shapes and choose these settings: Under "On Draw," uncheck the Fill and Stroke checkboxes; under "On Close," uncheck the Stroke checkbox and check the Fill checkbox. Using the Pen tool to draw Bézier shape paths, Kirkman carefully traced his sketch. To make adjustments on the fly while drawing a path with the Pen tool

3a

Preparing to fill the selected "nose" shape with a flesh color

3b

The selected nose shape showing the flat color fill applied

4

Painting the shadow on the fish's body using the Digital Airbrush variant

5

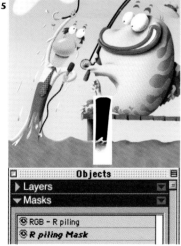

Clicking the "R piling" Mask eye open in the Masks section reveals a black-and-white representation of the mask.

(like adjusting a control handle or anchor point), press the Ctrl/⌘ key to temporarily switch to the Shape Selection tool.

3 Coloring, naming and converting. Before he started drawing each shape, Kirkman selected a color in the Colors section of the Art Materials palette close to the color he would finally use, so the shape would fill with the color when he completed the path. By double-clicking the name of each shape in the Layers section of the Objects palette, he named each shape as soon as he had created it. As he worked, he adjusted the opacity of the shapes (using the Opacity slider in the Set Shape Attributes dialog box), so he could see the layers below more clearly. After he had filled the shapes with color, Kirkman Shift-selected them in the Layers section and chose Shapes, Convert To Layer.

4 Shading individual layers. To paint on an individual layer, target it in the Layers section. To create a nice grainy look (similar to colored pencil on kid-finish illustration board), Kirkman chose Basic Paper texture in the Papers section of the Art Materials palette and added shading to the clothing using the Fine Spray variant of the Airbrushes. For a smoother look on the man's skin and eyes, he added strokes with the Digital Airbrush variant. Overlapping elements on the layers helped Kirkman create the cast shadows. For example, to paint the shadow under the fish's lips, he deselected them and selected the underlying body layer and then airbrushed the shadow directly on it.

5 Editing layer masks. Kirkman edited the visibility mask on the layer he called "R piling" to achieve a transparent look. To achieve transparency—like Kirkman's—on your layer: Target the layer in the Layers section by clicking on its name and click the left triangle on the Masks section bar to open the section. (When a layer is selected in the Layers section, the Masks section lists the layer and its visibility mask.) Now click on the layer mask's name to select the mask. Click the Eye icon open if you'd like to view a black-and-white representation of the mask, but this is not necessary to edit the mask. Next choose white in the Colors section, choose a soft Airbrush variant (such as the Digital Airbrush) and carefully paint into the mask to make the layer partially transparent. (See "Melting Text Into Water" on page 188 for a more detailed description of this technique.)

NAMING AND FILLING SHAPES

To name and add a colored fill (or stroke) to a shape, double-click on the shape's name in the Layers section. Rename the shape in the Set Shape Attributes dialog box and check the Fill (or Stroke) checkbox. With the Fill (or Stroke) color swatch active (outlined by a black and gold box), click in the Colors section of the Art Materials palette, or click a color in your Color Set to update the color in the Fill field.

PRESERVING TRANSPARENCY

To constrain your painting to within the edge of the element on a layer, turn on Preserve Transparency in the Layers section.

Kirkman targeted the "Fish body" layer in the Layers section before adding Apply Surface Texture to the fish's body.

Using Apply Surface Texture to add the 3D texture to the fish

Adding dimension to the fish's teeth by airbrushing along a selection edge

6 Adding details and texture. Kirkman added the pattern to the tie using Effects, Surface Control, Color Overlay to apply the Op texture (from Crazy Textures, in the Paper Textures folder on the Painter 7_CD2 CD-ROM). To add details to the water, he used Color Overlay to apply a colored texture using Globes from More Wild Textures (Painter 7_CD2 CD-ROM), scaling it larger using the Scale slider on the Papers section. To add more interest to the water, he added Effects, Focus, Glass Distortion using the Blobular texture from Molecular Textures (Painter 7_CD2 CD-ROM).

Using Effects, Surface Control, Apply Surface Texture, Using Paper, he added a 3D texture to the fish with Random Bubbles (Molecular Textures). He used these approximate settings: Softness, 1.0; Amount, 50%; Shine, 0; leaving other settings at their default values.

The final embellishments he added were the man's mouth, the fish's teeth and the separation of the man's pant legs. To paint these details, Kirkman drew on his many years of experience as a traditional airbrush artist using a technique very similar to traditional airbrush friskets. Using the Pen tool, he drew a shape for each element and converted each shape to a selection by choosing Shapes, Convert To Selection. To save each selection as a mask in the Masks section after he had converted it, he chose Select, Save Selection. When he wanted to use a selection as a frisket, he chose Select, Load Selection and then chose the appropriate mask from the Load From pop-up menu. When loaded, each active selection acted like a traditional airbrush frisket. For instance, to paint the fish's teeth, he selected the layer containing the teeth, loaded a selection and then airbrushed along the edges of the selection, letting the selection create the hard edge where he needed it. He let the spray from the Airbrush fade out across the selected area. This technique added more dimension and created a rounded, cushiony effect.

Adding an irregular edge. Finally, Kirkman created an irregular edge for the background. He used the Lasso to make a loose, freehand selection on the background canvas and turned it into a layer. (Drag with the Lasso and click with the Layer Adjuster). After the area was on its own layer, he reselected the canvas (click on the Canvas name in the Layers section) and deleted the unneeded background (Ctrl/⌘-A-Delete). Then he clicked on the layer and dragged it to the bottom of the layer hierarchy to serve as a background element, and he renamed it Sky. To give the sky layer a smooth edge, he feathered the layer's mask 3 pixels by selecting it in the Masks section and choosing Feather Mask from the Masks section's pull-down menu (accessed by clicking the right triangle Masks section bar). After he had feathered the edge, he added a drop shadow based on the Sky layer by choosing Effects, Objects, Create Drop Shadow. To flatten the image, he dropped all layers (choose Drop All from the Layers sections's pull-down menu). The final result can be seen in the image at the top of page 177.

Masks and Selections for Water Color Layers

Overview *Create a pencil sketch; brush in wet-into-wet washes using light colors; add transparent glazes on a new layer; make masks to constrain paint; add final details.*

CHER THREINEN-PENDARVIS / © 2001 COREL CORPORATION

1

The pencil sketch drawn using the Flattened Pencil variant of Pencils

2a

The Layers section showing an active Water Color layer and the sketch layer

2b

Painting the first washes with the Wash Bristle variant of Water Color

THE NEW WATER COLOR MEDIA LAYERS in Painter 7 make the medium wonderfully versatile. For *Fairy Tale Butterfly*, wet-into-wet techniques were used, then glazes and details were added on separate layers. Masks and selections, which work a little differently than they do with other kinds of layers, were used to limit the paint.

1 Sketching with pencil. Create a new file with a white background, by choosing File, New. In the New dialog box, we set the Width and Height at 1000 x 650 pixels and clicked OK. Before beginning your sketch, choose a natural-looking grain (for instance, Cold Press Water Color), from the Papers section of the Art Materials palette. Choose a neutral gray in the Colors section of the Art Materials palette, select the Flattened Pencil variant of Pencils from the Brushes palette and begin drawing your sketch.

2 Painting the first washes. When the sketch is finished and you choose a Water Color brush and touch the stylus to your tablet, a Water Color layer will appear in the Layers section of the Objects palette. Choose a very light color in the Colors section of the Art Materials palette and using the Wash Bristle variant of Water Color, block in large areas. When you use a light pressure on your stylus, the Wash Bristle will allow you to paint smooth, even washes with soft edges.

3 Adding deeper color on a new layer. Using several layers can give you better control over separate brush work—as it did here when we painted glazes—but you may have to sacrifice some of the effect of overall wet-into-wet. Add a new Water Color layer by choosing New Water Color Layer from the menu that pops out from the upper right corner of the Layers section. Begin this stage of your painting with medium-value colors, then gradually add darker tones to suggest volume. Keep your light source in mind as you paint. Resize the brush, or change its opacity as needed using the sliders on the Controls:Brush palette. In this stage of the painting, we added deeper purples to the wing edges, and gave

Layering richer colored washes (left) and defining the wings with deeper color (right)

4

The butterfly image with mask view turned on, showing the butterfly and leaves isolated from the background

5

Painting the background using a selection border to constrain the washes.

6a

The Layers section, showing the "Details" layer active

the veins in the wings more definition. We also added more layers for individual colors.

4 Making masks and selections. To protect the shapes of the butterfly and foreground leaves from the background paint, we made masks, similar to painting resists in conventional watercolor. The mask must then be loaded as a selection to be used with a Water Color layer. To create a mask, you can make a freehand selection using a selection tool such as the Lasso and save it as a mask in the Masks section by choosing Select, Save Selection. Or you can paint a mask as we did: Choose New Mask from the pop-out menu on the Masks section bar. Paint with the Scratchboard Tool variant of Pens and a black color so that the mask is completely opaque. For more information about masks and selections, see Chapter 4.

5 Painting the background. Add a new Water Color layer as described in step 3, this one for the background. Load the mask as a selection, by choosing Select, Load Selection and choosing your new mask in the Load From menu). Now invert the mask (Select, Invert), so that the background is selected and the subject is protected. Lay in the predominant colors using the Wash Bristle. To "bleed" more color variations and value into the shadowed areas, choose the Runny Wash Camel and make short dabbing strokes. To paint with more noticeable wet edges, try the Runny Wet Camel. We painted deeper blue and green colors on the background using the Runny Wash Camel variant.

6 Adding details. Add a new Water Color layer as described in step 3 for your detail work. Paint crisper edges to areas that need definition using a small Fine Camel brush (approximately 4–5 pixels). If the Fine Camel seems too saturated for your taste, lower its Opacity to about 20%, using the slider in the Controls:Brush palette. For more subtle edge effects, experiment with the Soft Camel and the Diffuse Camel variants, using a small size (about 6–8

6b

The details on the body and wings are nearly complete.

pixels). Make expressive strokes, varying the pressure on the stylus. To complete the study, we used the Fine Camel variant to add calligraphic details on the butterfly's body and wings. To deepen color and break up some edges, we added a few more wet-edged washes using the Runny Wash Bristle and Runny Wet variants. 🐾

RUNNING OUTSIDE

If the Force is turned up high in the Water section of Brush Controls, a very runny wash (painted with the Runny Wash Bristle, for instance) may creep outside of the edge of an active selection.

Melting Text into Water

Overview *Use the Text tool to set type over a background; convert the text to selections; float two copies of the type; use feathering, Dye Concentration and a Fill to add dimension to the type; paint on the layer masks to "melt" the bottoms of the layers.*

CHER THREINEN-PENDARVIS

Converting the Text layer to a default layer

Alt/Option-clicking with the Layer Adjuster on the selection to make a layer

The Layers section after naming the layers

Selecting the text layer mask in the Masks section of the Objects palette

YOU CAN ACHIEVE A DRAMATIC TRANSLUCENT EFFECT using Painter's brushes to paint on the visibility mask of a layer. In the image above, we used the Digital Airbrush variant (Airbrushes) on the lower part of two layers—the type and the feathered shadow behind it—to create the illusion of type melting into water. You can get a similar result using other backgrounds such as clouds, stone or wood.

1 Setting text and converting it to selections. Open an image to use as a background; our photo was 3 inches wide at 225 pixels per inch. Choose the Text tool and select a font and point size in the Controls:Text palette. Procedures such as feathering can erode a thin font, so we chose a font with thick strokes—90-point Futura Extra Bold Condensed. Open the Layers section of the Objects palette by clicking the left triangle on the Layers section bar. With the Layers section open, you'll be able to see the text layer appear when you type. Click the Text tool in the image to place the cursor and begin typing.

To achieve the result in the above image, using the text outlines to float portions of the background, it's necessary to convert the text to a default layer, then to selections. With the Layer Adjuster tool chosen and the text layer selected in the Layers section, choose Convert To Default Layer from the pop-out menu on the right of the Layers section bar. Next, reduce the layer's opacity to 0% using the Opacity slider on the Layers section; the converted text layer will disappear from your image. Choose Drop and Select from the pop-out menu on the Layers section; the type will reappear as animated marquees.

To save your selection as a mask so you can use it later, choose Select, Save Selection. Open the Masks section of the Objects palette to see the new mask (named New Mask 1).

With the marquee still active, (in preparation for making the soft shadow layer) choose Select, Feather; we used 15 pixels. Click OK. Now save this selection as a mask by choosing Select, Save Selection. This mask (named New Mask 2) will appear in the Masks section.

2 Using selections to make layers. To make the two layers needed for this technique, begin with the active feathered shadow selection (if it's no longer active, load New Mask 2 by choosing Select,

3b

Using Dye Concentration to lighten the text

3c

Filling the Shadow layer with a dark blue

3d

The Layers section showing the Composite Method for the shadow layer set to Multiply

4

Skewing the shadow to add a look of depth

5

Using the Digital Airbrush variant on the text layer (top) and the shadow layer (with the text layer hidden) to reveal the underlying image

Load Selection). Choose the Layer Adjuster tool, press the Alt/Option key and click on the active text selection to create Layer 1. (Holding the Alt/Option key makes a copy of the selected area, leaving the background intact.) Click on the Canvas name to deselect Layer 1. Now load the text selection (New Mask 1) by choosing Select, Load Selection; when it appears, Alt/Option-click on it with the Layer Adjuster tool. In the Layers section, you'll see two items named Layer, followed by a number. Double-click on the Layer 2 name (or select the name and press the Enter key) and rename it "text" in the Layer Attributes dialog box. Do the same for the Layer 1 below it, naming it "shadow."

3 Distinguishing the layers. Next, you'll make the text layer stand out from the background. In the Layers section, click once on the text layer to make it active. Now, change the color of the layer by choosing Effects, Surface Control, Dye Concentration, using Uniform Adjustment and dragging the Maximum slider to 53%. Click OK.

To create a soft, saturated shadow, in the Layers section select the shadow layer and enable Preserve Transparency. Using the Dropper (Tools palette), sample a dark color from your image and choose Effects, Fill, Using Current Color at 100% Opacity. Set the Composite Method of the layer to Multiply in the Layers section.

4 Offsetting the shadow. Give a greater illusion of depth to the type by nudging the shadow up and to the right using the arrow keys on your keyboard. To make the type appear to stand at an angle to the background, as we did, skew the shadow: With the shadow layer selected, choose Effects, Orientation, Distort. Drag the top center handle of the bounding box down and to the right, check the Better box and click OK. There's no preview of this effect, so it may take a few tries to get the look you want.

5 Painting into the layer masks. To "melt" the lower portions of the letterforms into the water, use a brush to partially erase the layer masks of both the text and shadow layers. Choose the Digital Airbrush variant of the Airbrushes. For more sensitivity, check to make sure the Opacity in the Controls:Brush palette is to set to 9%. Choose white in the Colors section of the Art Materials palette. Now select the text layer in the Layers section and select the text layer mask in the Masks section. To view the layer while editing its mask, keep the mask eye icon shut. Brush along the bottom of the letters to make the lower part of the text layer disappear. If you need to restore part of the text, switch to black paint. Painter won't restrict your restoration to the inside of the type, however, so you'll need to change to a smaller brush size. Then complete the effect by selecting the shadow layer in the Layers section and the shadow layer mask in the Masks section and brushing white along its bottom. You may find it easier to work on the shadow layer if you hide the text layer temporarily: Select it in the Layers section and click to shut its eye icon. When you're finished working on the shadow, click the text's eye icon open again.

■ "My goal from the outset was to create these works as a gift of consolation and of healing," says **Stephen Crooks**, a New York-based freelance illustrator and designer, when speaking of the series of paintings he created in memory of the tragic events of September 11, 2001. All three works depict the same view of New York City, envisioned at different times in the morning.

5:00 AM, (top), captures Manhattan in the pre-dawn hours, and symbolizes the mysterious spirit Crook finds inherent in the people who dwell there.

7:00 AM, (middle), captures the time of day when fragmented sunlight first spills over the city and symbolizes the diversity of New York.

In *10:00 AM*, (bottom), the sun rises high over New York, bathing the skyline in a heavenly glow, that symbolizes the spirit of the people of New York, undiminished by tragedy.

Crooks created the basis for the rows of buildings, the figures and water in separate source files. Then he imported the elements into a final layout file as separate layers, so they could be repositioned until he was satisfied with the composition.

With each painting, he began with the sky to establish the light source and color theme. Then he worked from background to foreground on each layer of buildings, using a favorite painting technique of diffusing and toning down the color of each receding layer. This method helped to enhance the illusion of atmosphere. To add to the atmospheric perspective, Crooks also decreased the saturation of the colors of the distant buildings using Effects, Tonal Controls, Adjust Colors.

In all three paintings, Crooks combined loose brush work with hard-edged areas using the Brushes variants from the Ver 5 library. (To load the Ver 5 brush library, choose Load Library from the Brush pop-up menu on the Brushes palette, navigate to the Painter 7 application folder and choose Ver 5.) He blocked in large areas of color using the Loaded Oils, Coarse Hairs and Big Wet Ink variants of Brushes. Then, to move color around, he used the Brushy variant of Brushes (also from the Ver 5 library).

■ **Sharon Steuer** began *Tango* by drawing two pencil studies of her cats Puma and Bear on transparent paper. Then she scanned each of them into Photoshop, where she built silhouette masks for them. With each pencil study on a separate layer, she arranged the composition, which included some resizing and rotating of the cats. Then she saved the image as a flattened TIFF for import into Painter. In Painter, she added an empty new layer between the Canvas and the cat layers. Using the

Artist Pastel Chalk variant of Dry Media and the Round Camelhair variant of Brushes on the new layer, she sketched the staircase for the cats to dance upon. Once the stairs were roughed in, she established an overall color scheme that fit with the tango theme. She added two new layers and worked black into the one, and reds into the other. With the overall colors established, she added more layers above the others for the detail work. She set the Composite Method for the new top layer to Multiply and began to paint with color. To add richer color to the overall painting and to color the sketched lines, she duplicated the layer with colored brushstrokes by Alt/Option-clicking it with the Layer Adjuster tool, then set this layer's Composite method to Gel. As Steuer worked, she added more layers and painted on them with color. She duplicated the color layers and tried out various compositing methods, including Magic Combine, Multiply and Gel. To

strengthen the line work in the right cat she selected its gray sketch layer, and moved it above some of the color layers and set its composite method to Multiply. When the painting was nearly complete, she wanted to add to its drama with lighting. So she flattened a copy of the image by choosing File, Clone and then chose Effects, Surface Control, Apply Lighting. She copied and pasted the image with lighting back into the layered file and set its composite method to Hard Light and its Opacity to 59%. Then she placed this layer below the gray line drawings so the strength of the drawings would be preserved. To finish, she added three touch-up layers, where she painted details using the custom Artist Pastel Chalk. She chose Multiply for two of the retouching layers to work with the darks, and set one to Screen to work with the lights. To entirely cover up details that were on layers below it, she set the third touch-up layer to Default.

■ **Keith MacLelland** created the mixed media illustration *Beetle Bugs* for self-promotion. He often mixes various media, such as oil paint and pastel, in Painter. He likes to create textures of his own and often applies them using grain-sensitive brushes such as the Dry Media variants.

MacLelland began by sketching in Painter using the 2B Pencil variant of Pencils on a fine-textured paper. Then he used the Scratchboard Tool variant of Pens to trace the shape of each Beetle Bug on its own layer. (To add a new layer, choose New Layer from the pop-out menu on the right of the Layers section bar.) To render

the forms of the cars, he used Brushes variants (the Smeary Round, Smeary Flat, Smeary Bristle Spray and Variable Flat), and Dry Media variants (the Oil Pastel and Square Chalk), as well as the Spray variants of Airbrushes.

For the Flower Texture used behind the cars and on the blue bug's wings, MacLelland scanned cut flowers and then opened the scan in Painter. He selected the flowers using the Lasso, then copied and pasted them into a working file. He used Effect, Orientation, Free Transform to scale the flowers to his liking, then he dropped them to the Canvas by choosing Drop All from the pull-down

menu on the Layers section. After using the Layer Adjuster to position the flowers where he wanted them, he used the Scratchboard Tool variant of Pens to draw a black dashed line connecting the flowers, while to create a western embroidery look. He selected the image by choosing Select, All and then he captured it into the Papers section of the Art Materials palette by choosing Capture Paper from the pull-down menu on the right side of the Papers section bar.

MacLelland added a new layer below the car layers and above the sky blue layer and used the Square Chalk variant of Dry Media to paint white texture. Working on the background layer, he used the Square Chalk and the Smeary variants of Brushes to paint blue and gray brushstrokes. To complete the illustration, he added detail to the shadows and highlights. He adjusted the opacity of the layer that contained the original pencil lines to retain the look of conventional pencil illustration. Finally, in the Layers section he set the Composite Method for the flower texture layer to Hard Light and lowered its opacity to 70% by adjusting the Opacity slider.

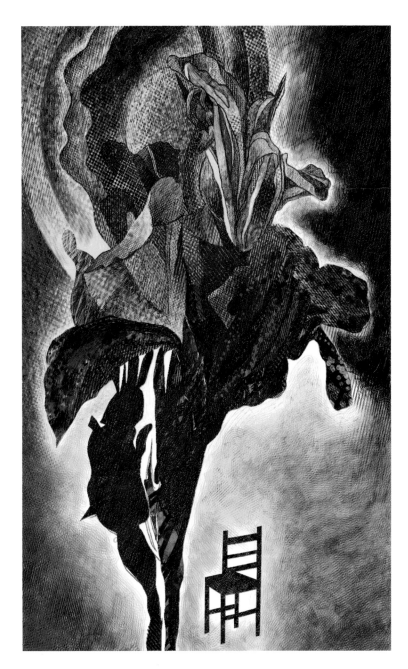

■ **Louis Ocepek** is a professor in the Department of Art at New Mexico State University. He created *Summer Reading*, a cover for *Puerto del Sol*, the semi-annual international literary journal published by the English Department at New Mexico State University. Ocepek wanted *Summer Reading* to express the perpetual dream many readers have of catching up on their reading on a perfect summer day, sitting in the shade of a big tree.

To heighten the feeling of heat, he used very warm colors in the image. To add to the magical atmosphere, he made the tree very large. He camouflaged many abstract forms in the tree to represent the imaginary worlds of the reader and writer. And he separated the chair from the tree to reinforce the idea of a lone reader, reading peacefully.

After drawing the tree, Ocepek added interest with details from photos of trees he had shot and scanned. He opened the scans and copied and pasted portions of them into his working file, where he positioned them. Then he grouped the layered pieces with the tree drawing layer by Shift-selecting them in the Layers section of the Objects palette, clicking the Layer Commands button and choosing Group from the pop-up menu. Then he merged the grouped layers into a single tree layer by clicking the Layer Commands button and choosing Collapse.

When the tree was almost complete, Ocepek built the chair. He began the chair by drawing shapes with the Pen tool. Then he Shift-selected all the Shapes, grouped them and converted them to a single layer (Shapes, Convert to Layer). After turning on Preserve Transparency in the Layers section, he filled the chair layer with a dark purple color (Effects, Fill, Current Color). Then he painted over the chair with various brushes. Ocepek kept the tree and chair on their own layers to help control their colors and textures and to preserve the distinction between the two elements in the image.

For a rich, textured look, Ocepek switched paper textures as he painted. To enhance the textured look and to make sure the textures printed clearly in offset lithography, he painted with grain-sensitive brushes—such as the Chalk variants of Dry Media. While painting, he slowly built up subtle color, adjusting the Opacity slider on the Controls:Brush palette. To create the soft, light auras around the tree and the chair, he selected each layer in the Layers section and painted it using the Bleach variant of the Erasers. To protect the completed paint on the tree while he added the auras around it, Ocepek loaded a selection he'd saved for the tree (Select, Load Selection) then edited the tree layer. Then he loaded the selection for the chair and edited its layer. To keep the paint outside each selection on the tree and chair layers, he clicked the Draw Outside (middle) Drawing Mode icon located in the bottom left of Painter's image window.

■ **John Derry** created *Piece of Cake* — an homage to the artist Wayne Theibaud—for the promotion of Painter 7, using a variety of tools including Pencils variants, colored shapes and thick Impasto. To begin, he drew a tight, black-and-white sketch using the Thick and Thin Pencil variant of Pencils. In the sketch, he established the shape of each element and the cast shadows. He drew each element on a separate layer, so he could move the elements around as he fine-tuned the composition. (To add a new layer, click the right triangle on the Layers section bar, and choose New Layer from the menu.) When he was satisfied with the composition, Derry drew a final clean, colored line sketch using a dark purple that would be used later for the shadows and the contour lines around many of the objects in the illustration. With the layered sketch active, he chose File, Clone to create a

flattened duplicate of the sketch. So that he could use Tracing Paper, he deleted the contents of the clone canvas by choosing Select, All and pressing the Backspace/Delete key. To activate Tracing Paper, he chose Canvas, Tracing Paper and carefully traced the final shapes of the elements.

Using the drawing as a guide, he drew colored shapes with the Pen tool. The vector-based shapes gave him the capability to finesse the color of individual elements by simply refilling rather than repainting. When the basic color areas were as he wanted them, he flattened the image by choosing Drop All from the menu on the right side of the Layers section bar.

Using a custom Impasto brush based on the Dry Ink variant of Brushes, Derry added the texture of thick brushstrokes to the image. (To sample color from each

area, he pressed the Alt/Option key to temporarily change from the Brush to the Dropper tool.) He painted subtle brushstrokes that followed the forms to make contours. For the cake icing, Derry used a modified Gloopy variant of Impasto to dab thick paint in-between the layers of the cake slice and around the top of the cake. Using a small Opaque Flat brush, he also painted varied color on the contour lines around the cake, candles and plate. To add more realism to the paint for the table and wall, he applied more paint in a few areas to build up thicker bristle marks. To complete the painting, Derry adjusted the lighting on the Impasto brush work so that it would have more subtle highlights and shadows. He chose Canvas, Surface Lighting and reduced the Amount and Shine settings slightly.

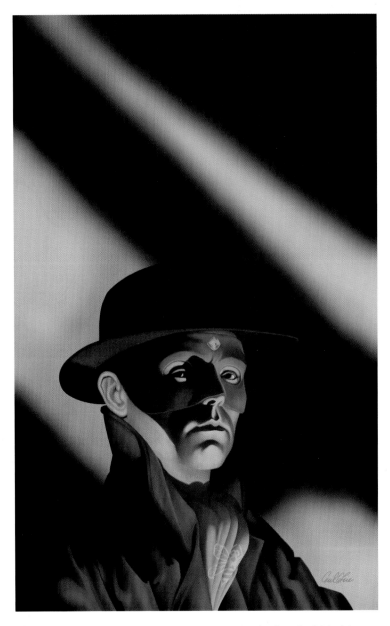

■ Bear Canyon Creative commissioned illustrator **Cecil Rice** to paint *The Green Hornet*, one in a series of illustrations for a set of audio book covers entitled *The Golden Age of Radio,* published by Dove Audio. An expert draftsman, Rice painted the portrait in Painter from start to finish using traditional painting theory. He began by gathering references from movies done in the 1930s and 1940s. Then he did three portrait sketches in Painter and presented them to his client. The chosen sketch was based on a still from an old Alan Ladd movie. For the final artwork, Rice used Canvas, Resize to enlarge the sketch to the finished size plus bleed; then he made selections and clicked with the Layer Adjuster to put each element on a layer. While painting, he blended the color in the image with Liquid variants and added more color with the Brushes and Dry Media variants. Rice continued to refine the shapes of elements, for instance, the ascot and coat, by editing the masks for those layers. When he was pleased with the figure, he painted the background using the Artist Pastel Chalk variant (Dry Media). To blend the background, he used Effects, Focus, Soften.

■ For this illustration for Glidden Paint company, art directed by Terry Pacifico of the Arras Group, artist **Nancy Stahl** painted on layers using custom brushes she built to imitate her favorite traditional brushes.

Stahl started by photographing herself in the figure's position, then assembled the photo and a sign reference into a rough composition in Painter. She used the composite image as a reference when drawing a line drawing, which she sent to her client for approval.

Using custom-made brushes she had built to imitate her favorite gouache brushes, Stahl painted the figure and the Coca-Cola sign in two separate source files. She completed most of the painting in the source files because the complex brushes performed quicker than they would in a larger composite file. To learn about her painting techniques and custom brushes, turn to "Gouache and Opaque Watermedia," on page 84.

After the figure was complete, Stahl selected it with the Lasso tool and feathered the selection a few pixels by choosing Select, Feather (so the edge of the selection would be smooth). She saved the selection as a mask in the Masks section of the Objects palette by choosing Select, Save Selection. To bring the figure into the sign file, she loaded the selection by choosing Select, Load Selection, pressed Alt/Option (to float a copy) and used the Layer Adjuster to drag and drop the copy into the sign painting file. Keeping the sign and the figure on separate layers made it easier for Stahl to add the final details.

■ For *Baseball Memories*, commissioned by The Dallas Morning News, **Chet Phillips** began by drawing with the Scratchboard Tool variant of Pens. Then he used the Pen and Lasso tools to create shapes. He converted each shape to a selection (Shapes, Convert To Selection) and saved the selection as a mask (Select, Save Selection). He floated the entire scratchboard drawing to a layer by choosing Select, All and clicking inside the active selection with the Layer Adjuster tool. Before deselecting the layer, he set the Composite Method to Gel in the Layers section of the Objects palette.

Working on the image canvas, Phillips loaded each selection (Select, Load Selection) and applied colored tints to the selected areas using Effects, Fill. To build the foreground shadows, he softly sprayed into the selections with the Digital Airbrush variant of Airbrushes, for a graduated effect.

To create the cast shadows for the older ballplayer, Phillips drew a shape with the Pen tool that was actually the taller shadow of a virile, young man. To convert the shape into a selection, he clicked the Make Selection button on the Controls:Shape Design palette and then he saved the selection as a mask in the Masks section of the Objects palette by choosing Select, Save Selection. He made a new, empty layer by clicking the Create New Layers button on the Layers section and choosing New Layer from the pop-up menu; he loaded the selection for the shadow (Select, Load Selection). Then for a soft edge, he feathered the selection several pixels (Select, Feather). Next he chose Effects, Fill and filled the selection with a custom black-to-white gradient chosen in the Gradients section of the Art Materials palette. To stretch the shadow taller, he used Effects, Orientation, Distort (with Better quality), dragged the handles to shape the shadow the way he wanted it and clicked OK. To finish the image, Phillips made a shadow for the other figure, adjusted the Opacity of the cast shadow layers in the Layers section and added more color detail with the Airbrushes.

■ **Cris Palomino** created this portrait of *Xochiquetzal,* the Mexican goddess who is the patron of artists and artisans. Years ago, Palomino had drawn Xochiquetzal on illustration board with pen, brushes and ink. She used this art as a basis for the color illustration in Painter, scanning the black-and-white portrait and opening it in Painter. To keep the color separate from the black-and-white drawing on the Canvas, she added a new layer to the file by clicking the Create New Layers button (at the bottom of the Layers section of the Objects palette) and choosing New Layer from the pop-up menu. So that she could add color to the layer that would become the background, she made sure that Preserve Transparency was turned off in the Layers section. Then she created a circular selection on the layer and filled it with a sky blue. To give the background depth, she added a purple gradient to the top of the filled circle.

Then she dropped the selection, (Select, None or Ctrl/⌘-D). Palomino added a second new layer, on which she established the portrait's predominant colors. Working on the new layer, she used the Digital Airbrush variant of Airbrushes and the Basic Crayons and several Pastel variants of Dry Media to paint Xochiquetzal in color.

After the color theme was established, she added another new layer for more richly colored highlights and shadows. Before painting on this layer, she enabled Pick Up Underlying Color in the Layers section so that she could incorporate color from the underlying color layer as she painted. She used brushes that would smear such as the Oil Pastel variant of Dry Media, the Smeary variants of Brushes and the new Tinting brushes included in Painter 7.1. These brushes would have picked up and smeared white

color from the new layer into the new paint if Pick Up Underlying Color was not enabled.

Palomino added another new layer for the finer details and brighter highlights, which she planned to paint using a modified 2B Pencil that incorporated the Soft Cover Subcategory. This Pencil would allow her to paint light color over dark. She also set the Pencil's Size and Opacity to Pressure in the Expression section of Brush Controls. Then she saved the custom Pencil by choosing Save Variant from the Variant menu on the Brushes palette. Using her new Pencil, Palomino added soft detailing to the feathers of the hummingbird, then painted finer strokes to bring out their crispness. She also used her custom Pencil to add more detail to Xochiquetzal's hair and face, most noticeably in the eyes, eyebrows and lips.

■ Medical illustrator **David Purnell** is proprietor of the New York West Medical Illustration Studio. When creating both of the illustrations on these pages for 3M Dental Products—for posting on the 3M Dental web site and for printed materials—Purnell used Painter's shapes and layers. The layers helped him to organize elements in his illustration and to keep items separate while he finished the details.

To create *Neural Pathway*, Purnell began by making a line drawing in Macromedia FreeHand and saving it in Adobe Illustrator EPS format. After client approval, he imported the vector line drawing into Painter as shapes by choosing File, Acquire, Adobe Illustrator file. He converted the individual shapes

to image layers (Shapes, Convert To Layer) and filled them with flat color fills by choosing Effects, Fill With Current Color. One-by-one, he airbrushed the layers to sculpt the anatomy in the focal area of the illustration. He left the outer areas filled with simple flat color to focus attention on the important neural pathway areas.

For the textured cross-section of bone, Purnell used a custom airbrush based on the Variable Splatter variant of Airbrushes. To build a brush that would spray narrower or wider splattery strokes depending on the pressure applied, he changed the Min Size in the Size section of the Brush Controls palette from the default 0% to 30%. To vary the size of the droplets, he also changed the Feature

size in the General section of the Brush Controls palette as he worked.

To make the bone look even more organic, he used the Distorto variant of Liquid to randomly push and pull areas of the splatter in order to vary its look. To constrain the paint within the element on the layer, he turned on Preserve Transparency in the Layers section of the Objects palette.

Purnell finished the illustration by applying effects: For instance, he targeted the jaw bone layer and applied realistic highlights and shadows based on the gray values in the spatter-airbrushed texture he had painted. He achieved this lighting with Effects, Surface Control, Apply Surface Texture Using Image Luminance, with subtle settings.

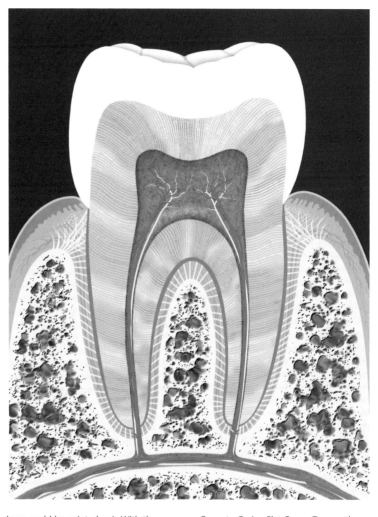

■ **David Purnell** created *Molar Cross-section* for 3M Dental Products to show the anatomy of an adult molar tooth. For a realistic look and to organize details, he decided to use "texture" layers for some of the elements which would sit on top of the flat color layers. To make masks that he could use to control the texture he duplicated each flat color layer (Alt/Option-click with the Layer Adjuster), and in the Layers section of the Objects palette he clicked the Layers menu triangle and chose Drop and Select. Then he saved the selection as a mask in the Masks section.

To create texture—for instance, the fibrous texture in the pulp chamber—he loaded the selection he had saved (Select, Load Selection), clicked the Layer Commands button and chose Group from the pop-up menu. (He turned off Preserve Transparency in the Layers section, so the

layer could be painted on). With the pulp selection active, and the pulp texture layer active, he was ready to begin applying the texture effect. When working with a selection, he used Painter's Drawing Modes to constrain brushstrokes to the inside or the outside of the loaded selection.

To achieve the cellular look of the odontoblasts on the edges of the pulp chamber, he used the paper texture Random Bubbles (from Molecular Textures loaded from the Painter 7_CD2 CD-ROM.) He varied the scaling of the texture as he worked from 100% to 30%. To apply the texture onto the layer, he used a custom grainy Airbrush that also incorporated variable Opacity and Size. So the brush would reveal grain as he painted, he changed the Subcategory in the General section of the Brush Controls palette from Soft

Cover to Grainy Flat Cover. To vary the Size and Opacity, in the Expression section of the Brush Controls palette he set Size and Opacity to be controlled by Pressure. Then he carefully airbrushed the Random Bubbles texture along the inner edge of the pulp chamber.

For the striations on the dentin layer, Purnell chose a darker ochre color than the solid ochre on the original dentin layer. He made a new "texture" layer as described, then he used a custom Airbrush (which incorporated a Rake stroke type) to draw the striations, keeping in mind the subtle S-curves that are characteristic of the anatomy.

For the textured bone, he used much the same technique as in the *Neural Pathway* piece, painting with his custom Splatter airbrush and Distorto variant, then adding Apply Surface Texture.

6

ENHANCING
PHOTOS,
MONTAGE
AND COLLAGE

Donal Jolley created Napoleon's Keepers, *shown here in this detail. See the complete photo-painting in the gallery at the end of this chapter.*

PHOTO: CORBIS IMAGES

To enhance this portrait, we began by painting a mask to isolate the dancers. To create a shallow depth of field, we used Effects, Tonal Control, Adjust Colors to desaturate the background and Effects, Focus, Soften to blur it.

ALTHOUGH PAINTER BEGAN as a painting program, the features that have been added over the years have turned it into a powerful image processor as well. Many tools are designed *just* for photographers—for instance, dynamic layers that allow you to adjust brightness and contrast, perform posterization, apply glass distortion effects and more! (For the basics of how to work with dynamic layers such as Glass Distortion, turn to page 171.) Painter 7 boasts two new color reduction features that are useful for working with photographs: woodcut and distress. (See "Creating a Woodcut from a Photo" on page 220 and "Distressing a Photo" on page 223). Painter also includes brush variants specifically designed for photographers, such as the Scratch Remover and Saturation Add brushes found in the Photo brush category in the Brushes palette. And, of course, when it comes to achieving painterly effects with photographs, Painter has no peer. If you're a photographer, a photo-illustrator or a designer who works with photos and you want to get the most out of Painter, you'll want to pay attention to the following areas of the program.

The Effects menu. Most of Painter's image-altering special effects can be found in the Effects menu. The features under the subheads Tonal Control, Surface Control and Focus are loaded with creative promise for the adventurous digital photographer.

Selections and masks. To alter only a portion of an image, you'll need to become acquainted with Painter's shapes and its selection and masking capabilities. If you're not familiar with the Pen and Lasso tools, turn to "Working with Bézier Paths and Selections" and "Working with Freehand Selections" in Chapter 4.

Painter's powerful automatic masking features—located in the Masks section of the Objects palette—give you a big jump on the tedious process of creating masks to isolate parts of your image. And a bonus: All of Painter's brushes except Water Color and Liquid

To isolate the sky from the buildings in this photo we made a Color Mask for the sky. (In the Objects palette, on the Masks section bar, click the right triangle to access the menu and choose Color Mask.) Then we used the Scratchboard Tool variant of Pens and white paint to remove from the mask any areas in the photo's foreground that had been selected with Color Mask.

Ink and the Plug-in method brushes (such as the Add Grain variant of the Photo brush) can be used to paint directly on a mask. For a detailed description of combining Painter's automatic and painterly masks, turn to "Using Color Mask," in Chapter 4.

Layers. Chapter 5 gave you an overall look at techniques using layers; this chapter focuses on using layers and masks for photo-compositing and other photo effects—for example, in "Simulating Motion," "Selective Coloring" and "Creating a Montage Using Masks and Layers," later in the chapter.

Dynamic layers. Painter offers dynamic layers that are useful for making adjustments to images. They are: Brightness and Contrast, Equalize, and Posterize. To find these tools, access the Dynamic Plug-ins pop-up menu by clicking the plug icon at the bottom of the Layers section. Several of the techniques described later in this chapter use dynamic layers. To read more about dynamic layers and how they relate to other elements in Painter, turn to the beginning of Chapter 5.

Cloning. A very powerful and versatile feature, cloning (File, Clone) lets you make multiple copies of an image, alter each copy, then recombine them in various ways while preserving access to the original. Several of the techniques described in this chapter use this or another kind of cloning method.

IMAGE-PROCESSING BASICS

With its strong focus on *creative* image manipulation, Painter has left some *production*-oriented tasks such as color-correcting CMYK images to Adobe Photoshop. But there's no need to move an image from Painter to Photoshop to perform basic image-processing tasks such as sharpening and adjusting brightness and contrast, because Painter has tools that are similar to many of Photoshop's.

Equalizing. Choosing Effects, Tonal Control, Equalize (Ctrl/⌘-E) produces a dialog box with a histogram similar to Photoshop's Levels dialog, which allows you to adjust the tonal range in an image—the difference is that in Painter the image is automatically equalized (an effect similar to clicking on the Auto button in Photoshop's Levels). Move the triangular sliders toward the ends of the histogram to decrease the effect.

Painter also features an Equalize dynamic layer that operates like Effects, Tonal Control, Equalize, but on a copy of your image so you can easily try out different tonal adjustments. To make an Equalize layer, open an image and choose Equalize from the Dynamic Plug-ins pop-up menu at the bottom of the Layers section. With Equalize selected, click the Apply button to generate the dynamic layer. When the Equalize dialog box appears, set the controls as you would for Effects, Tonal Control, Equalize. Using an Equalize dynamic layer you can preview as many changes as you like: Click the Reset button to return your image to its original condition, then apply a new correction.

Correcting the tonal range in an overexposed image using Effects, Tonal Control, Equalize. To lighten the image overall, we moved the Brightness slider to the right.

Using a feather setting of 15 pixels, we created a textured edge for this 500-pixel-wide photo. (To make a soft-edged vignette around an image, turn to page 128 in Chapter 4.)

To create a vignette with a textured edge, begin by making a selection with the Oval Selection tool. Use the Selection Adjuster tool to position and scale the selection. Next, apply a feather (Select, Feather). Save the selection (Select, Save Selection). Now for the textured edge: In the Masks section of the Objects palette, select the mask, open its eye icon and close the RGB-Canvas eye icon to view the mask in black-and-white. Select a rough paper texture in the Papers section of the Art Materials palette (such as Hot Press Water Color), and choose Effects, Surface Control, Express Texture. Adjust the sliders to confine the texture to the soft edge. Click OK. (For more information about using Express Texture, turn to "Toning with Textures" on page 218.) In the Masks section, click the mask eye icon shut and select the RGB-Canvas. Load the selection (Select, Load Selection). Next, reverse the selection (to select the area outside the oval) by choosing Select, Invert. To clear the background, press the Backspace/Delete key.

Adjusting brightness and contrast. Painter offers two ways to change image brightness and contrast. The first—Effects, Tonal Control, Brightness/Contrast—applies a correction directly to an open image or selection. But if you'd like to preview several Brightness and Contrast options, consider making a Brightness-and-Contrast dynamic layer. Click the plug icon at the bottom of the Layers section to access the Dynamic Plug-ins menu and select Brightness and Contrast. When the Brightness-and-Contrast dialog box appears, continue to adjust the settings as you preview the corrections in your image. To read more about a Brightness-and-Contrast dynamic layer, see "Making a Selective Correction" on page 210.

Stripping color from an image. There are several ways to turn a color image into a grayscale one in Painter. The quickest way is to desaturate the image using the Adjust Color dialog box. Choose Effects, Tonal Control, Adjust Colors and drag the Saturation slider all the way to the left.

Changing color. While you're using the Adjust Color dialog box, experiment with the Hue Shift slider to change the hue of all of the colors in an image (or a layer or selection). You can get greater control in altering specific colors (turning blue eyes green, for instance) by using Effects, Tonal Control, Adjust Selected Colors. Click in the image to select a color, then drag the Hue Shift, Saturation and Value sliders at the bottom of the dialog box to make the changes. Fine-tune your color choice and the softness of its edge with the various Extents and Feather sliders.

To repair a white scratch on this photo we used a two-step process, beginning with Painter's useful Scratch Remover brush (located in the Photo category, in the Brushes palette). Open a photo you'd like to repair, choose the Scratch Remover variant and for the best results, use a small brush size (we used a 1.7 pixel brush on this 350-pixel-wide image) and a low Opacity setting in the Controls:Brush palette (we used 9%). Zoom in to a magnification where you can see the scratch in detail, and carefully paint to blend the scratch into the image. This first step is usually sufficient for images with even color. But the sky in our image was graduated and required more repair. Next, we used a Soft Cloner variant of the Cloners with a small brush size and a very low Opacity, set in the Controls:Brush palette. Alt/Option-click to set the clone source to a point near the repair, then gently paint over the repaired area to bring back appropriate colors.

The scratched image (left) and the repaired image (right)

Using the Saturation Add brush from the Photo brush library to "pop" the color on the red raincoat, umbrella and reflection

We applied Micro Grain (loaded from the More Wild Textures library in the Paper Textures folder on the Painter_CD2 CD-ROM), to this photo with Effects, Surface Control, Dye Concentration Using Paper with the Maximum slider set to 200%.

To "age" this photo, we painted with the Add Grain variant of the Photo brush using Dry Cracks texture to give it a crackled texture.

The image above was sharpened to produce the result on the right using these settings: Amount, 2.15; Highlight, 90%; Shadow, 80%. A larger image can accept a higher Amount setting.

Painting saturation with brushes. To "pop" the color in a specific area, use Painter's Saturation Add brush, located in the Photo brush category in the Brushes palette. For a more subtle look, lower the Opacity to about 10%.

Adding film grain. Photoshop's Noise filter is a good way to emulate film grain. To get a similar effect in Painter, choose an even-textured Paper grain in the Papers section of the Art Materials palette, like Basic Paper (or choose Fine Grain or Synthetic Super Fine loaded from the More Paper Textures library, located in the Paper Textures folder on the Painter_CD2 CD-ROM). Then select Effects, Surface Control, Dye Concentration, Using Paper. Scale the texture in the Papers section until the grain in the Preview window of the Adjust Dye Concentration dialog box is barely visible—try 50% as a starting point. Try minor adjustments to the Maximum and Minimum sliders.

Adding grain with a brush. Painter offers an exciting pressure-sensitive brush—the Add Grain Brush—that allows you to paint grain onto your images. To begin, choose the Photo brushes icon in the Brushes palette and select the Add Grain variant. Choose a texture in the Papers section of the Art Materials palette, scale it if necessary and brush lightly onto your image. For a more subtle effect, reduce the Opacity of the brush in the Controls:Brush palette.

Creating a shallow depth of field. By softening the background of an image, you can simulate the shallow depth of field that you'd get by setting your camera at a low *f*-stop. Select the area you want to soften and feather the selection by choosing Select, Feather to avoid an artificial-looking edge. Then choose Effects, Focus, Soften.

Smearing, smudging and blurring. To smoothly smear pixels in the image, choose the Just Add Water variant of Liquid in the Brushes palette; vary Opacity in the Controls:Brush palette between 70% and 100%. To smudge the image, while bringing out the texture chosen in the Papers section of the Art Materials palette, choose the Smudge variant of Liquid. For a "wet oil" effect, try the Distorto variant of Liquid. To softly blur an area of the image, use the Blur variant of the Photo brush set to a low Opacity (about 20%).

Sharpening. Painter's Sharpen feature (Effect, Focus, Sharpen) gives you control equivalent to unsharp masking on a drum scanner. (Unsharp masking sharpens the edges of elements in an image.) Use it to give definition to a selected area of interest, or to an entire image as a final step in preparing for output. To sharpen an area in an image using a brush, choose the Sharpen variant of the Photo brush. This brush puts sharpening (very similar to the Effects, Focus, Sharpen command) on the tip of a brush.

To add a mysterious gold spotlight to this woman's portrait, we used Effects, Surface Control, Apply Lighting. We modified the Center Spot by changing the Light Color from white to gold. To make the spotlight softer, we decreased the Exposure from 1.00 to .85.

PHOTO: CORBIS IMAGES

Retouching. The Straight Cloner and Soft Cloner variants of the Cloners brush work like Photoshop's Clone Stamp tool (with the Aligned function turned on) to reproduce imagery; use the Alt/Option key as you would Photoshop's Alt/Option key to sample an area (even in another image), then reproduce that image (centered at the point of sampling) wherever you paint. The Straight Cloner variant reproduces imagery without changing it; to clone imagery with a soft edge and low opacity (like an Airbrush) use the Soft Cloner.

ADVANCED TECHNIQUES

It often takes a lot of time and trial-and-error to get cool effects in-camera or in the darkroom. Some third-party plug-in filters do an adequate job of replicating these effects, but Painter gives you more control than you can get with filters alone.

Here's a short guide for using Painter to re-create traditional photographic techniques, starting with simpler, in-camera ones and progressing to more complex darkroom procedures.

Motion blur. You can use the camera to blur a moving subject by using a slower shutter speed or jittering (shaking) your hands while you hold the camera, or you can blur the background by panning with the subject. (See "Simulating Motion" on page 208 to read about a versatile motion-blur technique that involves using an additional layer.)

To create the look of "camera jitter," just as if you had moved the camera while taking a picture, choose Effects, Focus, Camera Motion Blur. When the dialog box appears, drag in the image (not the Preview), to specify the camera's direction and distance of movement. Dragging farther in the image will create a wider blur. To move the origin of the movement along the path of motion, adjust the Bias slider.

Lens filters and special film. To re-create in-camera tinting effects achieved with special films or colored filters, use Effects, Surface Control, Color Overlay. If you want to mimic the effect of a graduated or spot lens attachment (partially colored filters), choose a gradation and fill your image (Effects, Fill) with the gradation at a reduced opacity. (You may need to add contrast to your image afterwards with Effects, Tonal Control, Equalize.)

Shooting through glass. With Painter's Glass Distortion effect or Glass Distortion dynamic layer you can superimpose glass relief effects (using a paper texture or any other image) on your photo. A small amount of this feature adds texture to an image; larger amounts can make an image unrecognizable! To apply the effect directly to your image choose Effects, Focus, Glass Distortion. To make a Glass Distortion dynamic layer for your image, click the plug icon at the bottom of the Layers section to open the pop-up menu, then choose Glass Distortion. (See Phil Howe's work with Glass Distortion in the gallery at the end of this chapter.)

To get the effect of a line conversion, a straight-line screen was applied to a photo with Effects, Surface Control, Express Texture Using Paper and the Line 40 texture from the Simple Textures library loaded from the Painter_CD2 CD-ROM.

PHOTO: PHOTODISC

For this graphic effect, we applied Painter 7's new Woodcut feature to a photo. See "Creating a Woodcut from a Photo" on page 222, for a step-by-step demonstration of a similar technique.

PHOTO: CORBIS IMAGES

PHOTO: CRAIG MCCLAIN

We posterized this Craig McClain photo using a custom Color Set of "desert" colors and the Effects, Tonal Control, Posterize Using Color Set command.

PHOTO: PHOTODISC

The original photo of a kelp frond had strong contrast, contributing good detail for this embossed image.

Lighting effects. Use Painter's Apply Lighting feature (under Effects, Surface Control) to add subtle or dramatic lighting to a scene.

Multiple exposures. Whether created in camera (by underexposing and shooting twice before advancing the film) or in the darkroom (by "sandwiching" negatives or exposing two images on a single sheet of paper), it's easy to reproduce the effect of multiple exposures by using layers or clones in Painter.

Solarization. Painter's Express Texture (Effects, Surface Control) command is a great way to re-create darkroom solarization. Read about a Painter version of a "custom" solarization on page 216.

Line screen. Instead of developing your image in the darkroom onto high-contrast "line" or "lith" paper, try getting a similar effect in Painter. Choose a lined paper texture from the Simple Textures library loaded from the Paper Textures folder on the Painter_CD2 CD-ROM. Next, choose Effects, Surface Control, Apply Screen, Using Paper to get a two- or three-color effect with rough (aliased) lines. Or try Effects, Surface Control, Express Texture, Using Paper to get a broader range of value and smoother, anti-aliased lines. Turn to "Toning with Textures," on page 218 to read about using Express Texture to apply colored, textured effects to an image. You can also apply screens using Painter 7's new Distress feature. See "Distressing a Photo" on page 223 for a step-by-step demonstration of this technique.

Posterizing an image. Painter lets you limit the number of colors in your image via posterization. To apply a posterization directly to your image choose Effects, Tonal Control, Posterize and enter the number of levels (usually 8 or fewer for best results). You can also perform a posterization using the Posterize dynamic layer. At the bottom of the Layers section, click the plug icon to open the Dynamic Plug-ins menu and select Posterize from the menu. Click Apply and enter the number of levels. Because the Posterize plug-in layer is dynamic, you can experiment and preview the effect on your image until it's the way you like it.

You can get creative posterization effects by making a Color Set (see "Capturing a Color Set" in Chapter 2) and selecting Effects, Tonal Control, Posterize Using Color Set. This is a great way to unify photos shot under a variety of conditions.

Embossing and debossing. To emboss an image, raising its light areas, choose File, Clone; then Select All and delete, leaving a blank cloned image. Now choose Effects, Surface Control, Apply Surface Texture, and choose 3D Brush Strokes from the Using pop-up menu. To raise the dark areas instead of the light, click the Invert box *or* change the Using menu choice to Original Luminance. Images with a lot of contrast give the best results, and busy images work better if less important areas are first selected and softened using Effects, Focus, Soften.

Creating a Sepia-Tone Photo

Overview *Use gradient features to tint a color or black-and-white image; adjust the image's contrast and saturation.*

The original photo

Choosing the Copper gradation

Applying the Copper gradient

Adjusting the contrast

Neutralizing the browns

CHER THREINEN-PENDARVIS / PHOTO: CORBIS IMAGES

TYPICALLY FOUND IN IMAGES CREATED at the turn of the century, sepia-tones get their reddish-brown color cast in the darkroom when the photographer immerses a developed photo in a special toner bath. You can use Painter's gradation and tonal control features to quickly turn color or grayscale images into sepia-tones.

1 Tinting the image. Open a grayscale or color photo. In the Gradients section of the Art Materials palette, select the Copper gradient from the resource list. (For a cooler brown sepia look, try the Sepia gradient, loaded from the Painter 6 Gradients library, located on the Painter_CD2 CD-ROM.) Choose Express In Image from the pull-down menu at the right end of the Gradients section bar. (Read more about gradients in Chapter 2.) Click OK in the dialog box to tint your image with shades of brown. (You can also use a similar procedure to turn a color image into shades of gray, but make sure the back and front Color rectangles in the Colors section of the Art Materials palette are black and white, respectively, and choose Two-Point in the Gradients section.)

2 Adjusting the white and black points. If you're working with an image that has poor contrast, you can adjust the white and black points by choosing Effects, Tonal Control, Equalize (Ctrl/⌘-E). When the dialog box appears, the image will be automatically adjusted so that its lightest tones are pure white and its darkest ones are pure black. The automated contrast was too dramatic for our taste, so we decreased contrast by dragging the white point slider to the right to 14.9 and the black point slider to the left to 96.0.

3 Desaturating the image. We wanted to emulate the mild tinting effect usually used for traditional sepia-tones, so we desaturated the image using Effects, Tonal Control, Adjust Colors, dragging the Saturation slider to the left to –60. Set the Hue Shift at 0% and experiment with the Saturation slider until you see the effect you want in the Preview window and click OK.

Selective Coloring

Overview *Open a color photo and copy it to a layer; desaturate the layer; paint with a brush to erase areas of the layer mask and reveal the underlying color photo.*

The original color image

Using the Adjust Colors dialog box to desaturate the floater to black-and-white

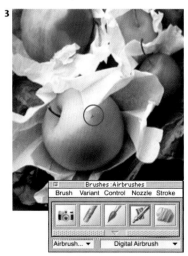

Painting on the layer's mask to reveal the color image underneath

IF YOU WANT TO FOCUS ATTENTION on a particular element in a color photo, you can turn the photo into a black-and-white image and then selectively add color back into it for emphasis. Here's a way to use Painter's layers and brushes to "paint" color on an image.

1 Copying the image. Open a color photo and choose Select, All (Ctrl/⌘-A). Press the Alt/Option key and choose Select, Float. This creates a layer with an exact copy of the original image, in register with the original.

2 Desaturating the layer. Now use the layer to make the image appear black-and-white: Choose Effects, Tonal Control, Adjust Colors, drag the Saturation slider all the way to the left, and click OK.

3 Revealing color in the underlying image. To allow parts of the color image to show through, use a brush to erase portions of the "black-and-white" layer's mask. In the Brushes palette, choose the Digital Airbrush variant of Airbrushes and choose white in the Colors section (Art Materials palette). In the Masks section of the Objects palette, select the layer mask. (To view the layer in color while editing its mask, keep the layer mask eye icon shut.) As you paint with white to erase the mask in the area you wish to colorize, the color will appear. If you want to turn a color area back to grayscale, choose black from the Colors section and paint on the area. 🖌

FINE-TUNING YOUR MASK

It's difficult to tell if you've completely covered (or erased) areas when working on a mask with a brush. To view a layer mask in black-and-white, select the layer in the Layers section, and in the Masks section, open the Mask eye icon. Choose the Digital Airbrush (Airbrushes) or the Scratchboard Tool (Pens), and paint directly on the mask to clean it up. (Black creates an opaque mask that hides the layers below; pure white creates no mask, allowing the layers below to show through; shades of gray create a semi-transparent mask.) To switch back to color view, click the layer mask eye icon shut.

Painting on the layer mask using the Digital Airbrush variant of Airbrushes

Simulating Motion

Overview *Open a color photo and copy to a layer; apply Motion Blur to the copy; paint with a brush to erase areas of the layer mask and reveal the original photo.*

CHER THREINEN-PENDARVIS / PHOTO: CORBIS IMAGES

PHOTO: CORBIS IMAGES

The original photo

Applying Motion Blur to the layer

Erasing the layer mask on the face and arm

Adjusting the opacity of the blurred layer

CREATING A SENSE OF MOVEMENT for a subject *after* the film is out of the camera is easy with Painter's layers and Motion Blur command. We blurred a layer, then erased some areas to reveal the untouched image underneath. The benefits of this method over applying effects to selections are that you can control the amount of the effect by adjusting opacity of the layers, you can simultaneously add effects other than a blur (such as lighting and texture) and you are altering a copy leaving the original intact, and this makes it easy to correct errors.

1 Copying the image. Open a color photo and choose Select, All (Ctrl/⌘-A). Using the Layer Adjuster tool, Alt/Option-click on the image. This creates a layer that's an exact copy of the original image.

2 Blurring the layer. Select the layer by clicking on its name in the Layers section of the Objects palette and choose Effects, Focus, Motion Blur. To get a dramatic blur on our 1500-pixel-wide image, we set Radius to about 80, Angle to 31° (to complement the direction the bikers were moving) and Thinness to 2%. Experiment with different Angle settings for your particular image.

3 Painting on the mask. To allow parts of the original image to show through, use a brush to erase portions of the layer's mask. In the Brushes palette, choose the Digital Airbrush (Airbrushes) and choose white in the Colors section of the Art Materials palette. Select the layers in the Layers section and in the Masks section and select the layer mask. As you paint the layer mask in the area you wish to erase, the underlying image will appear. If you want to restore an area of the blurred layer, choose black in the Colors section and paint on that area of the layer mask. To give the leading rider an illusion of more speed we erased the frontal blur, leaving long trails of motion blur behind her. We erased most of the blur on the second rider to give the illusion of slower speed.

4 Adjusting the opacity. To reduce the blur we made the layer slightly transparent by lowering the Opacity of the layer in the Layers section to 75%.

Zooming and Solarizing

Overview *Float a copy of the image, use Painter's Zoom Blur feature to zoom in on an area of the layer; paint the layer mask to accentuate the focal point; make a solarization by changing the Composite Method.*

CHER THREINEN-PENDARVIS / PHOTO: CORBIS IMAGES

1

The original photo of the volleyball players

2

The Zoom Blur dialog box after clicking in the image

3a   **3b**

The zoom-blurred layer (left) and the mask retouched to reveal the sharp underlying image of the hand and ball (right)

4

The Opacity and Composite Method settings for the solarization

WITH PAINTER'S ZOOM BLUR feature you can create zoom and pan effects that rival results you can achieve when shooting with a zoom lens. Here we used Zoom Blur to elongate the subjects, adding to the excitement and illusion of speed during a volley. Afterwards, to add more drama we changed the photo into a mysterious "night scene."

1 Copying the image. Open a color photo and choose Select, All (Ctrl/⌘-A). Choose the Layer Adjuster tool and Option-click on the image. This creates a layer with an exact copy of the original image.

2 Blurring the layer. Select the layer by clicking on its name in the Layers section of the Objects palette and choose Effects, Focus, Zoom Blur. To get a moderate blur on our 600-pixel-wide image, we set the Amount to 31%. Set the focal point of the zoom by clicking in the image (not in the Preview). To create the elongated, distorted effect of zooming in, check the Zoom In box. Click OK.

3 Painting on the mask. To enhance the focal point of the image, we erased areas of the layer mask to reveal the underlying image, for instance, the ball and hands. To allow parts of the original image to show through, use a brush to erase portions of the layer's mask. Choose white in the Colors section of the Art Materials palette and in the Brushes palette, choose the Digital Airbrush (Airbrushes). Select the layer in the Layers section of the Objects palette, switch to the Masks section and select the layer mask. As you paint the layer mask, the underlying image will appear.

4 Making a solarization. Next, we created a solarized "night scene" from the image by selecting the layer in the Layers section, choosing the Layer Adjuster tool and changing the Composite Method to Difference in the Layers section. To make the layer slightly transparent, allowing the original colored image to show through, we also lowered the Opacity of the layer to 85%.

Making a Selective Correction

Overview *Use a dynamic layer to adjust the brightness and contrast of an image; convert the dynamic layer to an image layer; make a selection; use the selection to remove a portion of the layer.*

CHER THREINEN-PENDARVIS / PHOTO: CORBIS IMAGES

1a

PHOTO: CORBIS IMAGES

The original photograph

1b

Making a Brightness and Contrast dynamic layer

1c

Increasing the Brightness by moving the lower slider to the right

HERE'S A USEFUL IMAGE-EDITING TECHNIQUE that combines a dynamic layer Brightness-and-Contrast adjustment and a selection. Using a dynamic layer has the advantage of being able to make a correction and dynamically preview the changes on the image without harming the image. To enhance the focal point of this image—shining more light onto the faces—we selectively lightened the shaded window area.

1 Editing brightness and contrast with a dynamic layer.
Open a grayscale or color photo. To make a Brightness and Contrast dynamic layer for your image, begin by clicking the left triangle on the Dynamic Layers section in the Objects palette and when the section opens, choose Brightness and Contrast from the resource list. Click the Apply button on the Dynamic Layers section to generate a dynamic layer covering your entire image. (Turn to "Using Dynamic Layers" on page 171 in Chapter 5, to read about the basics of using dynamic layers.)

When the dialog box appears, adjust the sliders and preview the correction in your image. To see more detail on the faces, we moved the Brightness (lower) slider to the right, making the image lighter. We also slightly increased the contrast by moving the Contrast slider (upper) to the right.

We only wanted the Brightness-and-Contrast adjustment to affect the shaded area within the window, so we planned to make a mask and load a selection that we could use to isolate a portion of the layer. To use a selection on a dynamic layer, the layer must first be converted to an image layer. When you've finished making adjustments, convert the dynamic layer to an image layer as follows: Click the right triangle on the Dynamic Layers section bar to open the menu and choose Commit. Next, hide the layer temporarily: In the Layers section of the Objects palette, click the layer's eye icon shut, then click on the Canvas layer's name.

2

The active selection around the window

3a

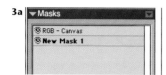

Selecting the mask to view it as a red overlay

3b

Viewing the mask as a red overlay before editing and feathering

3c

The completed mask

4b

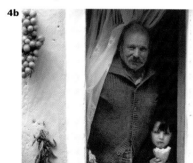

Detail from the final corrected image with more detail in the shaded areas

2 Making a selection and saving it as a mask. In our example, when we were satisfied with Brightness-and-Contrast adjustment in the window area, the blue wall was too light and flat. In preparation for using only the window area of the adjusted layer, we made a selection of the window area on the image canvas and saved it as a mask. In the Tools palette, choose the Pen tool or Lasso and make a selection. (We drew a shape with the Pen tool and converted it to a selection using Shapes, Convert to Selection.) When you've completed the selection, choose Select, Save Selection to save it into the Masks section of the Objects palette.

3 Editing and feathering the mask. To get a clear view of the mask as we edited and feathered it, we worked back and forth between viewing it as a red overlay (on the image) and as a black-and-white mask. We used the Digital Airbrush variant of the Airbrushes and white paint to spray soft edges along the top of the window and added a 3-pixel feather to the entire mask to give it a soft transparent edge. If your mask needs editing, select the mask name in the Masks section. To view your mask as a red overlay, click both the mask eye icon and the RGB-Canvas eye icon open. To view the mask in black-and-white, click the RGB-Canvas eye icon closed. With the mask active you can give it a soft edge by applying feathering as follows: Click the right triangle on the Masks section bar to open the menu and choose Feather Mask. Type a feather width in the field and click OK. Now shut the mask eye icon and click on the RGB-Canvas in the Masks section to prepare for the next step.

4 Using the selection to edit the layer. In our example, we used the selection to remove the area on the Brightness-and-Contrast layer outside the window. Now that your mask is complete, load the selection from the mask, as follows: In the Layers section, click on the Brightness-and-Contrast layer name to select it, and also open its eye icon to display the layer. Choose Select, Load Selection and choose the mask that you saved (New Mask 1) to isolate the area on the layer. To reverse the selection (so that the area outside of the window is selected) and to remove the unwanted portion of the layer, choose Select, Invert and press the Backspace/Delete key. 🖌

USING SELECTIONS WITH LAYERS

You can have several masks saved in the Masks section of the Objects palette and choose any one of them to load as a selection to then isolate paint or effects on any image layer. Choose Select, Load Selection and pick the selection you need from the menu. In the Layers section of the Objects palette, click on the name of the layer with which you want to work.

Hand-Tinting a Photo

Overview *Retouch a black-and-white photo; color the image using Tinting brushes and several layers set to Gel Composite Method.*

CHER THREINEN-PENDARVIS

Using Equalize to adjust the tonal range of the black-and-white photo

Repairing scratches with the Soft Cover variant of Cloners

The new layer in the Layers section, with Composite Method set to Gel

HAND-TINTING IS A GREAT WAY to give an old-fashioned look to a black-and-white print. It also gives the sensitive artist plenty of opportunity to add depth to an image using hues, tints and shades. For this example, *Rell with Bird's Nest Fern,* we hand-colored a portrait of Hawaiian friend Rell Sunn using Painter 7.1's new Tinting brushes, applying transparent color to layers above the image, so we would not disturb the existing photo. If you do not have Painter 7.1 installed, you can download the update from the Corel web site (ftp://ftpcache.corel.com/pub/Painter/7).

1 Equalizing the image. To preserve shadow detail during tinting, choose a light image without solid shadows, or correct the tonal range after scanning as described below. Because we no longer had the 35mm slide, we scanned an 8 x 10-inch print at 100%, 150 pixels per inch. The print was slightly overexposed, so we darkened it, taking care to preserve detail in the shadows. If your image needs tonal correction, select Effects, Tonal Control, Equalize (Ctrl/⌘-E). Your image will be automatically adjusted when the dialog box appears. For a more subtle result, experiment with spreading the triangular sliders on the histogram; or move them closer together for more contrast. Use the Brightness slider to make the gray tones brighter or darker overall.

2 Retouching scratches. To touch up scratches, use the Magnifier tool to enlarge the area that needs retouching. Using the Brush tool, choose the Soft Cloner variant of Cloners in the Brushes palette. Establish a clone source by Alt/Option-clicking on your image near the area that needs touch-up, then begin painting. A crosshair cursor shows the origin of your sampling. If necessary, re-establish a clone source as you work by Alt/Option-clicking again.

3 Making a new layer and coloring the background. Create a new layer by clicking the right triangle on the Layers section

3b

Coloring the "background" layer with the Basic Round variant of the Tinting brush

4a

Flat, transparent washes on the "clothing" and "skin and hair" layers

4b

The Layers section showing the "clothing" layer selected

5b

Bringing out highlights on the shirt using the Soft Eraser variant of Tinting

bar and choosing New Layer from the pop-up menu. So the paint will appear transparent, in the Layers section, set the layer's Composite Method to Gel. Also, disable Preserve Transparency (so you can add pixels to the layer) and turn off Pick Up Underlying Color, so the Tinting brushes will not pick up gray from the Canvas as you paint. Choose a color in the Colors section and the Basic Round variant of the Tinting brush from the Brushes palette. Begin to brush color onto your image. If the color looks too strong, reduce the opacity of the Basic Round variant using the Opacity slider in the Controls:Brush palette. For grainier brushstrokes, try the Soft Grainy Round variant.

4 Coloring elements on separate layers. It's often helpful to color areas of the image (such as the skin, clothing and background) on separate layers to make it easy to edit a specific element. Add more layers as needed by choosing New Layer from the menu on the right side of the Layers section bar. Remember to set each new layer to Gel Composite Method before you start to paint. We added new layers for each of these elements: the skin and hair, clothing, and the foreground plants.

5 Emphasizing the area of interest. After you've painted color washes, look at the overall balance and color density of your image. Add more or brighter color to the areas that you want to emphasize and apply less saturated colors to make other areas appear to recede. For detail work, reduce the size of the Basic Round variant using the Size slider on the Controls:Brush palette. To remove color from oversaturated areas or to clean up edges, use the Soft Eraser variant of Tinting, adjusting its Opacity setting in the Controls:Brush palette as you work. The Blender and Softener variants are useful for making color or value transitions smoother.

We used the Blender variant to smooth the brush work in the face and shirt, by softly brushing over the areas using a low-opacity version of the brush.

Saving the image. If your coloring extends for more than one work session, save your image in RIFF format to preserve the layers set to Gel Composite Method. If you'd like import your image

5b

We used the Blender variant to smooth areas in the face and shirt.

into Adobe Photoshop, you'll want to flatten a copy of the image first, because Gel method is not available in Photoshop and the color on your tinted layers may change if you open the layered file in Photoshop. Choose File, Clone to quickly make a flattened copy, then save the image as a TIFF file.

Blending a Photo

Overview *Open a photo and clone it; use the Just Add Water variant of Liquid to smear pixels in the image; restore a portion of the original with the Soft Cloner variant of Cloners.*

Hathaway's original photo of the dogs

Choosing the Just Add Water variant of the Liquid brush

Making loose strokes with the Just Add Water variant at 40% opacity

Partially restoring the dog's face using a low-opacity Soft Cloner variant of Cloners

TO CREATE THE EXPRESSIONISTIC *DOGS OF THE SURF*, Andrew Hathaway used Painter's Just Add Water brush to paint directly onto a clone of one of his photographs, transforming it into an intense, emotionally charged abstract painting. He gave the piece a touch of realism with a Cloners brush, using it to restore a hint of the original photo to the clone.

1 Choosing a subject and making a clone. Open your photo in Painter, then choose File, Clone to make a copy of your image to alter. Hathaway chose one of his own photos—an image of two dogs running toward him on the beach—then cloned it.

2 Blending with a Water brush. Hathaway used the Just Add Water variant of Liquid; since it uses the Soft Cover submethod and doesn't show paper texture, it's the smoothest of the blending brushes. For a more subtle smearing effect, you may want to reduce the Opacity in the Controls:Brush palette. To make more expressive strokes, with the brush size changing as you vary pressure on the stylus, in the Size section of the Brush Controls palette, move the Min Size slider to about 15%. Now, make some strokes on your clone. Hathaway painted energetic, angled, smeary strokes on the clone to emphasize the focal point and perspective in the foreground; then he smeared the background into more abstract shapes. He modified his brush as he worked, varying Size between 10 and 30 pixels, and lowering the Opacity to 30–40%.

3 Partially restoring from the original. As a last step, Hathaway used the Soft Cloner variant of the Cloners brush with a very low opacity (5%) to subtly restore the foreground dog's face. Try this on your clone. Use the Soft Cloner brush to bring the original back into the blurred areas of your image. Experiment with the Opacity slider in the Controls:Brush palette until you find a setting that suits your drawing style and pressure. 🖌

Cloning a Portrait

Overview *Retouch a photo and soften background detail; clone the image with brushes; paint details by hand; add texture.*

1a

The original photograph

1b

Using darker colors to paint over the busy flowers in the background

2

Adding hand-painted details to the hair

3

Adding relief to the brushwork with Apply Surface Texture Using Image Luminance

LAUREL BECKER

PAINTERLY CLONING IS A GREAT WAY to add natural atmosphere to photos. To create *Flower Girl,* Laurel Becker began by retouching a photo. Then she enhanced a clone of the photo by painting expressive brushstrokes and adding texture. When cloning, after blocking in the image, add hand-painted details, highlights and shadows.

1 Scanning, adjusting and retouching. Becker scanned an 8 x 10-inch photo at 100% and 150 ppi. Then she bumped up the image contrast using Effects, Tonal Control, Brightness /Contrast. To focus attention on the girl, she selected the background and "played down" the busy foliage details. If your background is busy, consider making a selection and using Effects, Focus, Soften to blur details or paint over areas with darker colored brushstrokes, as Becker did. (For information about making selections, turn to Chapter 4.)

2 Cloning and painting. Next, Becker cloned the photo (File, Clone). For this portrait, she chose Basic Paper in the Papers section of the Art Materials palette and the Captured Bristle variant of Brushes. Before beginning to paint, she checked the Clone Color box in the Colors section (Art Materials), to sample color from the original image. Then she painted over the entire clone. As she worked, she sized the brush using the Size slider on the Controls:Brush palette. She used a larger brush while painting loose strokes behind the girl and a tiny brush to paint the details on the face, dress and hair. She turned off Clone Color, then painted brighter highlights on the cheeks, nose, eyes, chin and lips, her brush following the contours of the forms.

3 Adding texture. After she was finished painting, Becker added relief and texture to her brushwork using two applications of Effects, Surface Control, Apply Surface Texture: The first, Using Image Luminance, Amount 20% and Shine 0%; the second, Using Paper, Amount 20% and Shine 0%. She left other settings at their defaults. 🖌

Making a Custom Solarization

Overview *Use Express Texture on positive and negative clones of an image; merge the images by filling with a Clone Source.*

The original image after equalizing (left), and the negative clone

Creating black-and-white positive (left) and negative versions of the clones using Express Texture

Merging the positive and negative images

Adjusting the image's brightness and contrast

IN THE DARKROOM, SOLARIZATION OCCURS when a negative is exposed to a flash of light during the development process, partially reversing the photo's tonal range. To achieve this effect digitally, we tested other image-processing programs and filters, and found that we got the most control and detail using Painter's Express Texture feature. This technique gives you a lot of control over the image's value contrast and it frequently creates a glowing edge-line effect where contrasting elements meet.

1 Making positive and negative clones. Open an image with good value contrast, then choose Effects, Tonal Control, Equalize (Ctrl/⌘-E) to increase its tonal range. Choose File, Clone twice. Make one of the clones into a color negative by selecting Effects, Tonal Control, Negative.

2 Making black-and-white separations. Use Painter's Express Texture feature to convert both clones to black-and-white: Choose Effects, Surface Control, Express Texture, and select Image Luminance from the pop-up menu. Experiment with the sliders and click OK. Repeat the process for the second clone. We set Gray Threshold to 72%, Grain to 72% and Contrast to 160%. These settings helped emphasize the gradient effect in the sky.

3 Merging the two exposures. Choose File, Clone Source and choose the positive clone. Now fill the negative image with a percentage of the positive (the "flash of light"): With the negative window active, choose Effects, Fill, Clone Source. Set the Opacity slider between 40% and 60%.

4 Pumping up the tonal range. To achieve a broader tonal range while maintaining a silvery solarized look, we selected Effects, Tonal Control, Brightness/Contrast. We increased the contrast (the top slider) and decreased the brightness. 🦋

Solarizing Color

Overview *Use Correct Colors, Color Correction to make positive and negative tones; enhance the solarization by compositing a desaturated layer.*

EARLY DARKROOM SOLARIZATIONS were black-and-white, but today they include color as well. Classic color solarizations have solid areas of color and glowing gradations with elements often separated by edge-line effects. To achieve the effect of a color solarization digitally, we used Painter's Color Correction, Freehand Curve function.

1 Choosing an image. For the best results, open an image with good value contrast and color.

2 Solarizing the image. Choose Tonal Control, Correct Colors. When the Color Correction dialog box appears, from the pull-down menu choose Freehand. As you'll notice in the Color Correction dialog box, the standard curve is a diagonal line from lower left to upper right. Making an inverted "V" shaped curve will create both positive and negative tones in an image. Press the Shift key and click in the center, then in the lower right corner to snap the line into an inverted "V." If you have trouble making the "V" shape, click the Reset button and begin again. To achieve a broader tonal range in the solarization, we selected Effects, Tonal Control, Brightness/Contrast and subtly increased the contrast (top slider).

3 Enhancing the solarization. We wanted to achieve more dramatic tone and color in our image, so we copied the solarized image to a layer that we could use to intensify the effect. Open the Layers section of the Objects palette by clicking the left arrow on the section bar. Choose Select, All (Ctrl/⌘-A), press the Alt/Option key then choose Select, Float.

Now, to make the image on the layer gray, while preserving its tonality, choose Effects, Tonal Control, Adjust Colors and move the Saturation slider all the way to the left. (Leave the Hue and Value sliders at 0.) To give the solarization richer colors and tones, we composited the gray layer with the colored image on the Canvas using the Luminosity Composite Method in the Layers section. For different color effects, experiment with other Composite Methods such as Pseudocolor and Darken. 🖌

The color photograph from Corbis Images

Setting the curve for the solarization in the Color Correction dialog box

The color image on the Canvas (left) and the desaturated layer (right)

Toning with Textures

Overview *Use Painter's Express Texture feature to make two line conversions of a color image; colorize the two images and merge them into a single file.*

CHER THREINEN-PENDARVIS / PHOTO: PHOTODISC

1

The original photo

2

Scaling down the Angle Weave texture

3

Express Texture settings for Light Exposure

CONVERTING CONTINUOUS-TONE PHOTOGRAPHS into custom line art effects—like mezzotints, etch tones and straight-line screens—can be accomplished either in the darkroom or with a graphic-arts camera using a screen made of film printed with a textured pattern. There are digital plug-in filters that give similar results, although they often eliminate much of the original's fine detail. By using Painter's Express Texture feature on two separate, textured exposures and then "sandwiching" them, you can retain more highlight and shadow detail during the conversion process than through any other digital means.

1 Selecting an image and cloning. Open a file with good tonal balance and contrast. Make two clones of this file—by choosing File, Clone twice. Save and name one clone "Light Exposure," and the other "Dark Exposure."

2 Choosing a texture. Select a paper texture that resembles the screen effect you wish to achieve. To get a random line effect, we chose Angle Weave loaded from the Wild Textures library (located in the Paper Textures folder, on the Painter_CD2 CD-ROM); to preserve detail in our 738-pixel-wide image, we scaled the texture to 50%.

3 Making a light exposure. To create a light, "overexposed" image that brings out shadow detail, click on the Light Exposure clone to make it active. Choose Effects, Surface Control, Express Texture, Using Paper. Drag all three sliders to the left and experiment to see which settings bring out the most shadow detail: We got the best results in our image by setting Gray Threshold to 64%, Grain to 64% and Contrast to 200%.

4 Making a dark exposure. Next, create an "underexposed" image—dark, with texture visible in the midtones and highlights. Select the Dark Exposure clone and again choose Effects, Surface Control, Express Texture. Drag all three sliders farther to the right,

Express Texture settings for Dark Exposure

Applying a brown-to-white gradation to Dark Exposure (left) and a brown-to-tan gradation to Light Exposure

Filling Dark Exposure with Light Exposure

near their original (default) settings of 110%, 80%, 300%. We got good results by setting Gray Threshold to 112%, Grain to 88% and Contrast to 300%.

5 Coloring the clones. Tinting the two clones before merging them gives richer tonal depth to the final image, than coloring it after merging the images. Start by selecting the Two-Point gradation in the Gradients section of the Art Materials palette and choose colors for the front and back Color rectangles in the Colors section. Next, choose Express in Image from the Gradient section's menu, and click OK. We applied a brown-to-white gradation to Dark Exposure, and a brown-to-tan gradation to Light Exposure.

6 Combining the images. Painter offers many ways to blend images; we got the best results on our example by filling with a Clone Source. Begin by making Light Exposure the Clone Source by choosing File, Clone Source, Light Exposure. Now fill Dark Exposure with Light Exposure: With the Dark Exposure window active, select Effects, Fill. Click the Clone Source button and experiment with a 40–60% Opacity setting (we chose 50%). Click OK.

As a final step to increase the color and tonal range, we selected Effects, Tonal Control, Equalize (Ctrl/⌘-E). The effect was too strong, so we selected Edit, Fade at a 50% setting. 🐚

TRADITIONAL LINE CONVERSION EFFECTS

Here's our best guess at the Painter textures required to emulate the look of a few traditional line conversions, using Express Texture on a single 553-pixel-wide color image. Use these examples as inspiration for your own experimentation. To give your image a greater tonal range before using Express Texture, you may want to use Effects, Tonal Control, Equalize.

Mezzotint: *Fine Grain (More Paper Textures library, from the Painter_CD2 CD-ROM), scaled to 50%*

Dry brush: *Wheat String (More Wild Textures library, from the Painter_CD2 CD-ROM), scaled to 65%*

Halftone: *Halftone 1 (More Paper Textures library, from the Painter_CD2 CD-ROM), scaled to 40%*

PHOTO: PHOTODISC

Creating a Woodcut from a Photo

Overview *Open a photo and clean up the background; copy the Canvas to make a new layer; create a color woodcut plate on the Canvas; create a black woodcut plate on the new layer; retouch the black plate; add clouds and texture.*

JOHN DERRY

WITH PAINTER'S NEW WOODCUT FILTER you can start with a photo and achieve a look similar to a conventional wood block print. You can simply use the color arrived at by the Woodcut filter defaults, or you can enjoy complete control over choosing the colors.

The traditional wood block printing process involves simplification of detail in the lines and color areas. Inspired by Japanese wood block prints from the 1800s, John Derry created *Pagoda*, which is based on one of his own digital photos. Painter's Woodcut filter helped him to reduce the number of colors in the image and to fine-tune the colors for the final artwork.

1 Choosing a photo. Open a photo with good contrast and color. A bold image with a strong focal point will work best for this effect.

2 Cleaning up the sky. To focus more attention on the pagoda, Derry simplified the sky by selecting it and applying a blue fill. Choose the Magic Wand in the Tools palette and click in the sky. Adjust the Tolerance in the Controls:Magic Wand palette until most of the sky is selected; at this point, edges are most important,

The original digital photo of the pagoda

Setting the Tolerance for the Magic Wand in the Controls:Magic Wand palette

2b

The Image viewed with the mask eye icon open (left), and the active selection with the blue fill applied (right)

3

The visibility of Layer 1 is turned off and the Canvas is selected.

4a

Increasing the Color Edge to make simpler, smoother shapes (left) and brightening the gold color (right)

4b

The color woodcut plate

since you can clean up any small internal "debris" by painting on the mask later. Save the selection as a mask in the Masks section of the Objects palette by choosing Select, Save Selection. In the Masks section, open the eye icon to the left of the mask's name. Choose *black* in the Colors section of the Art Materials palette and paint on the mask where you need to *add* more mask; use *white* to *remove* areas of the mask (for instance, to remove debris). To use the mask to isolate the sky, choose Select, Load Selection. (See Chapter 4 to read more about working with masks and selections.) Next, fill the selection with blue by choosing Select, Fill, with Current Color.

3 Setting up layers. The Woodcut process is easier to control when the color elements are on a separate layer from the black elements. Derry started his layering by making a duplicate of the original image. To put a duplicate of the image canvas onto a layer, choose Select, All (Ctrl/⌘-A), press the Alt/Option key and choose Select, Float. In the Layers section of the Objects palette, turn the new layer's visibility off by toggling shut the eye icon to the left of its name.

4 Cutting the color "wood block." In the Layers section, click the canvas name to activate it for the colors. To access the Woodcut dialog box, choose Effects, Surface Control, Woodcut. When the dialog box appears, disable the Output Black checkbox. The options for Black Output will now be grayed out. In the lower portion of the window, accept the default number of colors (16), and smooth out the edges of the color blocks by adjusting the Color Edge slider to the right. (Derry set it at approximately 11.46.)

When the edges were as he liked them, he fine-tuned a few of the colors. For instance, he chose a tan color swatch (at the bottom of the dialog box) and made the color brighter. Click on a color square to select it; a red outline will appear around it. Now that it's selected, you can choose a new color in the Colors section of the Art Materials palette and the swatch will change to the new color. To sample a color directly from the image Preview window, press the Ctrl/⌘ key and click on the Preview. To change the color, choose a new color in the Colors section.

To see other areas of your image in the Preview window, drag with the grabber hand cursor to move around the image

WOODCUT PREVIEWS

It's possible to view two previews in the Woodcut dialog box: the working woodcut image and the original image. By default the woodcut image is visible. To see the original image, drag the Grabber hand in the Preview window. When you release, the preview of the woodcut will be visible again.

The Woodcut dialog box with the standard preview showing a color woodcut image (left) and dragging with the Grabber hand to reveal the original image (right).

5a

Setting the Composite Method for Layer 1 to Multiply

5b

To achieve more detailed black edges, the Black Edge slider was adjusted to the left.

6a

The black plate (shown with the Canvas hidden) with black in the sky (left), and with the sky retouched (right)

6b

The in-progress woodcut with both color and black plates in place

preview. When you're satisfied with the colors, click OK to accept.

5 Cutting the black plate.

To begin making the black plate, target Layer 1 by clicking on its name in the Layers section and open its eye icon. At the top of the Layers section, set its Composite Method to Multiply so the white that will be generated on the layer by the Woodcut effect will disappear. Now, choose Effects, Surface Control, Woodcut and turn on Output Black and turn off Color Output in the dialog box. For more detailed edges, adjust the Black Edge slider to the left. (Derry set it to approximately 25.75.)

6 Cleaning up the black plate. The settings that worked well for the detail in the pagoda left too much black in the sky. Using the Scratchboard variant of Pens and white paint, Derry removed the black by painting white over the sky. He chose the Scratchboard Tool because it paints with a crisp edge. An Eraser variant would have produced a softer edge.

7 Adding clouds and texture. Next, Derry painted simple cloud shapes on a new layer using a large Scratchboard Tool and white paint. (To add a new layer, click the right triangle on the Layers section bar and choose New Layer from the pull-down menu.) Increase the size of the Scratchboard tool using the Size slider in the Controls: Brush palette (Derry adjusted his to about 25.4). Paint loose brushstrokes that complement your composition. Then Derry dragged the layer below the black plate layer in the Layers section so the black would appear to be "printed" on top.

For added realism, Derry completed the woodcut by adding a subtle paper texture to the colored layer. To add texture, click on the colored layer in the Layers section. Select Basic Paper in the Papers section of the Art Materials palette, then choose Effects, Surface Control, Dye Concentration, Using Paper. In the dialog box, try moving the Maximum slider to the right until a subtle paper texture effect is visible. Adjust the settings to your taste and click OK. 🐾

7

The clouds and texture have been added

Distressing a Photo

Overview *Open a photo; copy the image to a new layer; use Distress to make it black-and-white and texturize it; combine the layer and the canvas using a transparent Composite Method.*

CHER THREINEN-PENDARVIS

CHER THREINEN-PENDARVIS

1a

The original photo

1b

Scaling the Crosshatch paper texture

2

Applying the Distress effect

3

The image showing the layer set to Screen Composite Method before reducing Opacity.

BY DEFAULT, THE NEW DISTRESS FILTER IN PAINTER 7 adds texture and changes a color image to black-and-white. In this example, we used custom settings to apply the filter to a layer, then set its Composite Method to Screen, so the effect would combine with the colored photo beneath it.

1 Choosing a photo and a texture. Open a photo with good contrast and color. A bold image with a strong focal point will respond best to this technique. Choose a high-contrast texture that will complement your photo. We chose Crosshatch in the Papers section of the Art Materials palette. To achieve a finer texture in the final image we scaled the texture down to 42%.

2 Making a layer and applying the effect. The Distress process is easier to control when the filter is applied to a copy of the image on a layer, and then the filtered and original versions are combined. To put a duplicate of the image onto a layer in the Layers section of the Objects palette, choose Select all (Ctrl/⌘-A), then press the Alt/Option key and choose Select, Float.

With the layer active, access the Distress dialog box by choosing Effects, Surface Control, Distress. Experiment with the settings in the dialog box, to suit your taste. We increased the Edge Size to 20.30 to bring out the highlights; lowered the Edge Amount to 36% to darken the shadows; reduced Smoothing to 1.00 so the filter would not "round" the edges and reduced Threshold to 43% to lighten the image subtly. When you've achieved a texture with the amount of white you want, click OK.

3 Blending the treated layer with the original photo. In the Layers section, drop out the black areas of the layer to reveal the photo underneath, change the Composite method to Screen. For a more subtle effect, we also lowered to opacity of the layer to 75% using the slider in the Controls:Adjuster palette. 🖌

Creating a Montage Using Masks and Layers

Overview *Create masks for the component photos in Photoshop or Painter; copy them into a single document; use a brush to edit the layer masks when compositing them; paint on the final image.*

JOHN DISMUKES / CAPSTONE STUDIOS

1

The original photos

2

The cut-and-pasted comp ready to be scanned and used as a template

WHEN CONTINENTAL CABLEVISION asked John Dismukes of Capstone Studios to illustrate a direct-mail piece, he and his team turned to Painter. He combined photographs and splashy color with loose airbrush and chalk brushstrokes to illustrate the theme "Can Summer in California Get Any Better?"

1 Gathering illustration elements. Begin by collecting all of the individual elements that you'll need for your illustration. Dismukes and his associates photographed separate images of clouds, a pair of sunglasses, ocean foam, palm trees, and a television on the sand. The photo negatives were scanned in Kodak Photo CD format.

2 Making a template from laser prints. Dismukes' team created a traditional comp by printing the individual elements, then photocopying them at different scales and assembling them using scissors and adhesive. They turned the completed comp into a template by scanning it at 72 ppi, opening it in Painter and sizing it to the final image size of 4 x 5 inches at 762 ppi, using Canvas, Resize. The template would act as a guide for Dismukes to accurately scale and position the various elements. If you choose to include this step, don't be concerned about the "bitmapping" that occurs when scanning the comp at a low resolution; when the composition is finished, the template will be completely covered by the source images.

3 Masking unwanted portions of the source images. Working in Photoshop, Dismukes used the Pen tool to cut masks for the sunglasses, ocean foam, palm trees and television on the

3

Three of Dismukes' Photoshop masks

4a

The glasses source file with active selection, ready to copy and paste or drag and drop into the background image

4b

Bringing the layers into the composite file

5

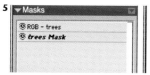

Selecting the layer mask in the Masks section of the Objects palette

6a

Using the Digital Airbrush variant to erase the portion of the cloud layers's mask that covers the TV

beach. He converted each path to a selection, saved the selection as an Alpha Channel, then saved each image as an RGB TIFF file, including the alpha channel. You can accomplish the same result in Painter. Open one of your source photos and use the Pen or Shape Design tool (Tools palette) to draw a shape around the desired portion of the image. When you're done, choose Shapes, Convert To Selection; then to save the selection as a mask, choose Select, Save Selection. View the selection as a mask by opening its eye icon in the Masks section of the Objects palette. You should see your image covered by a red overlay—the default color for the mask. To view only the mask in black-and-white, click the RGB-Canvas eye icon shut in the Masks section.

4 Compiling the source files. When you've finished masking the images, bring them into a single document. Open the template if you have one, or the photo that will become your background image. Choose the Layer Adjuster tool and in the Objects palette, click the left triangle on the Layers section bar to open the Layers section. Then open each of the source images and choose Select, Load Selection and Alt/Option-click on each selection to make a layer. Loading the selection and making a layer prepares Painter to export the item from the source image with its mask.

There are three ways to import source images into a composite file: Copying and pasting through the clipboard, performing a drag-and-drop, or using the File, Place command to bring the source image in as a reference layer. To paste using the clipboard, select the layer in the source image with the Layer Adjuster tool, choose Edit, Copy, then make the background image active and choose Edit, Paste. If your component images are approximately the right size, the easiest way is probably to drag-and-drop: Select the layer in the source image with the Layer Adjuster. Now use the Layer Adjuster to drag the masked item to the background image.

If you're working with large files, positioning and scaling can be accomplished much more quickly using reference layers. To import an image as a reference layer with a mask, save the source file in RIFF format (to preserve its mask), then choose File, Place, navigate to the source image and choose Open. In the Place dialog

6b
Compositing the clouds inside the glasses

6c
Revealing the cloud layer around the tree

7
Using Adjust Colors to increase saturation in the image

8

Adding squiggles and lens glare (top) and smudges and blurs

box check the Retain Alpha checkbox and click in the image to place the layer. (For more information about reference layers, see "Using Reference Layers" on page 168 in Chapter 5.)

5 Putting the masks to work. To view the mask on a layer, select the layer in the Layers section, and in the Masks section open the layer mask's eye icon. To switch back to Color View, shut the layer mask's eye icon.

6 Positioning the layer and painting on its mask. First scale, rotate and position one layer on top of another and make sure that the top layer is selected in the Layers section. Now, fit the top element inside the element below it by using a brush to erase a portion of the top layer's mask, as follows: Begin by selecting the layer name in the Layers section, then click on the layer mask's name in the Masks section. Choose the Digital Airbrush variant of Airbrushes and choose white in the Colors section of the Art Materials palette. Begin painting around the edge of the top layer to erase part of its mask, making it appear "inside" of the layer beneath it. Paint with black to restore the mask.

When you've completed all compositing, turn off visibility for the template layer in your file by selecting its name in the Layers section and shutting its eye icon. Then make a copy of your image with the layers merged with the background by choosing File, Clone. This step gives you a lot of flexibility—you have an "original" with layers intact, and a "working image" (the clone) on which you can paint and make other adjustments.

7 Shifting colors. To make the image "pop" a bit more, Dismukes increased the color saturation. Choose Effects, Tonal Control, Adjust Colors, and experiment with the Hue Shift, Saturation and Value sliders to modify the colors in your image.

8 Painting on the photo montage. To transform the television into a lively caricature in vivid color, Dismukes first used the Digital Airbrush variant to add details such as glare on the glasses. He switched to the Impressionist variant of the Artists brush to paint on the sand and water, and then painted spontaneous, textured squiggles around the TV and on the sand and water with the Artist Pastel Chalk variant of Dry Media using the Big Canvas paper (loaded from the More Paper Textures library, in the Paper Textures folder, on the Painter_CD2 CD-ROM). As a final touch, Dismukes switched to the Grainy Water variant of Liquid. To smear while revealing texture, he changed the subcategory to Grainy Hard Cover in the General section of the Brush Controls palette and added the smudges and blurs on the sand and television.

Finishing the job. Using the same style, technique, tools and colors, Dismukes created similar illustrations on a smaller scale that were used throughout the brochure, as well as a border around the edge of the piece. 🖌

■ For *Capitola Encaustic*, a photo-illustration created with Liquid Ink, **John Derry** began by shooting a photograph of the colorful buildings in the town of Capitola, California with his Sony digital camera. He envisioned an image with bold colors and simple shapes. So before he began to paint on the photo, he reduced the number of colors by posterizing it using the Effects, Tonal Control, Posterize command, choosing eight Levels. Next, he put a copy of the Canvas on a layer by choosing Select, All, pressing the Alt/Option key and choosing Select, Float. He chose the Sparse Camel variant of the Liquid Ink brush, and reduced its size slightly in the Controls:Brush palette. In the Layers section of the Objects palette, he enabled the Pick Up Underlying Color box so that when he painted new brushstrokes, color from the underlying layer would blend with the current color he was using. Derry sampled color from the photo using the Dropper tool as he worked.

(To temporarily switch from the Brush tool to the Dropper, press the Alt/Option key.) He painted over the image using the Sparse Flat variant, changing the size of the brush as he worked. To achieve the look of thick paint, he double-clicked the Liquid Ink layer name in the Layers section and slightly increased the Amount setting. Derry wanted to build up the look of thick paint with overlapping strokes, so he created another new Liquid Ink layer (by clicking the right triangle on the right side of the Layers section bar and choosing New Liquid Ink Layer). For a crosshatched, overlaid look, he built up Liquid Ink brushstrokes on the new layer, on top of the existing strokes on the layer below. (For more information about Liquid Ink, see "A Painter Liquid Ink Primer" on page 110 and "Encaustic Painting with Liquid Ink" on page 115.) To bring more detail from the photo back into the illustration, he placed another copy of the posterized photo on top of the Liquid Ink layer and reduced its opacity to 50% in the Layers section.

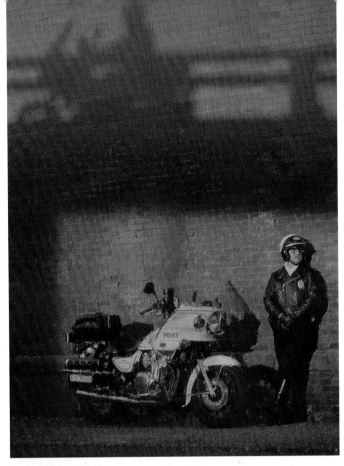

■ **Philip Howe** was commissioned by Harry Hansen to create *Police,* a photo collage painting to promote positive aspects of law enforcement. The final piece—printed on canvas and enhanced with oil paints—is part of a traveling show of police art touring the United States. To build the image, Howe began with two source photos: a horizontal photo of a brick wall with a cast shadow of a motorcycle rider, and a vertical photo of a policeman standing against a brick wall. Beginning in Photoshop, Howe copied the rider image and pasted it into a copy of the vertical wall image as a layer. He worked back and forth between Photoshop and Painter as he retouched the brick areas above the standing figure's head to match the bricks of the top image. When the retouching was complete, Howe began the process of building relief on the background wall image in Painter. He applied Effects, Focus, Glass Distortion Using Image Luminance and the Refraction Map Type, using strong settings. Next, he opened the original vertical brick wall image and again applied Effects, Focus, Glass Distortion, Using Image Luminance and the Refraction Map type, this time using subtle settings. Finally, he selected the composite file and defined the subtly distorted image as the clone source (File, Clone Source.) Using an Airbrush Cloner variant, he cloned the subtle distortion onto areas of the image canvas to softly smooth out areas of the relief.

When Microsoft commissioned **Philip Howe** to illustrate their *Encarta CD-ROM Interactive Encyclopedia* packaging, he created a photo montage that included a transparent glass effect. Howe began by building two source files of the same size: the first a montage that incorporated an illustrated background, a time line and several photos; and a second image, a retouched cloud photo. To begin the crystal effect, he opened both the cloud image and the montage and made the montage the clone source (File, Clone Source). Working in the cloud image, he applied Effects, Focus, Glass Distortion, Using Original Luminance and the Refraction Map type to create the crystal. (The crystal effect appeared only where there were dark-and-light values in the montage clone source.) To combine both images, he cloned the montage into the crystal image, taking great care to preserve the crystal effect around the edges of the image. To further define the head against the clouds, he used white paint and an Airbrushes variant to paint a glow around the inside edge of the back of the head. Finally, to increase the glass effect, Howe used Effects, Surface Control, Dye Concentration, Using Original Luminance, keeping the montage as the clone source.

■ For *Switches*, a collage made of several photos, **Aleksander Jensko** began by shooting his own photographs with a Nikon Coolpix digital camera. The rich textures in his collage were created by combining the layers when the collage was complete and then adding brush work painted with Painter 7's new Water Color brushes and the Coarse Spray variant of Airbrushes. To begin, Jensko opened all of the source photos: a black-and-white photo of a window curtain, an image of switches, a blurry photo of a woman, an image of a wooden crate with stenciled lettering and a photo with pronounced grain. He opened a new file, then copied and pasted each source image into the composite. Jensko used the Layer Adjuster tool to position the elements to his taste. To make areas of certain elements transparent (the Switches and the woman layers, for

instance), he modified the layer visibility masks by painting on them with the Digital Airbrush variant of Airbrushes to hide portions of the layers. He created the edge effect on a new layer and set the layer's Composite Method to Overlay to make it translucent. For additional transparency effects, he used transparent Composite Methods and reduced opacity on some of the layers. When the composite was as he liked it, he dropped all of the layers to the Canvas by Shift-Selecting them and choosing Drop All from the pull-down menu on the right side of the Layers section bar. He created the grainy texture behind the woman by spraying dark color using the Coarse Spray variant of Airbrushes. To complete the image, he added watercolor brush work. To put the collage on a Water Color layer, he targeted the Canvas and chose Lift Canvas To Water Color Layer from the menu on the right

side of the Layers section bar. Once the image was on a Water Color layer, he could use various Water Color brushes, including the Dry Bristle and Wash Camel to paint subtle brushstrokes and soft washes.

■ "Although the program is called Painter," says renowned photographer **Pedro Meyer**, "it's important not to exclude photography from its repertoire, given that the program can also be used effectively in that medium."

Both of the images on this page (taken with a Nikon D1 digital camera) reflect Meyer's observations in the year 2000, when he made many flights to and from Los Angeles and Mexico City. After mak-

ing the montages, he adjusted their coloring, making each one look as much as possible like a real, single photo.

Meyer's photographic eye captures a moment at sunrise, in *Firstbird at Century City*. Intrigued by the scale of the buildings in the photo, he added the bird to it to distort scale and proportions.

Apocalypse LAX is a photo montage, that Meyer created to communicate the accelerated pace of modern life. "When we

play with the proportions of photographic images, we add to the confusion about what is and what could be. Before digital photography it was very hard to make credible images which had these traits. It was quite complicated and time-consuming. These days, almost all it takes is the imagination to use the tools in ways which are more about the ideas than in showing off the virtues of the tools themselves," says Meyer.

■ "My intent was to create a message of hope," says **John Derry** about *Imagine*, a collage which he created soon after the tragic events of September 11, 2001. When in New York City the previous July, Derry had shot many photos using his Sony DSC-F505V digital still camera. *Imagine* incorporates three of these photos, an image of clouds (shot while in flight), a photo of the World Trade Center towers and a photo of the Strawberry Fields memorial to John Lennon in New York City's Central park. The memorial symbolizes the death of one man, and the towers the death of many; both are powerful symbols of dark days in American history. Through it all, the Imagine mosaic shines as a sunlike symbol, radiat-

ing hope. Derry opened the three source files, and cut a "drop out" mask for the towers. Using the Pen tool from the Tools palette, he quickly drew a path around the towers. He converted the path to a selection by clicking the Make Selection button on the Controls:Shape Design palette, then he saved the selection in the Masks section of the Objects palette by choosing Select, Save Selection. Derry saved the three source images and placed them into a new composite file by choosing File, Place. This command allowed him to bring each element into the collage file, with a mask (enable Retain Alpha). The names of the files also appeared as layer names in the Layers section of the Objects palette. Derry

rotated the image of the towers to accommodate the Imagine mosaic using Effects, Orientation, Free Transform, holding down the Ctrl/⌘-key and dragging a corner handle. Once the elements were in position, he used the Digital Airbrush variant of Airbrushes to hide portions of the Imagine and cloud layers. He clicked on a layer, then on its visibility mask in the Masks section, then he used white paint to make soft transparencies in areas of the two layers. To enhance the "sun" effect, he added a new, empty layer, on which he airbrushed soft, white strokes radiating out from the edges of the Imagine mosaic tiles. To finish, he set the layer's Composite Method to Overlay in the Layers section.

■ **Ellie Dickson** began each of these photo illustrations by scanning a black-and-white photo in RGB-mode. In Photoshop, she made loose freehand selections with the Lasso and filled the selections with tints of color (using Color mode). Dickson opened the tinted image in Painter and applied strokes with a low-opacity Artist Pastel Chalk variant of Dry Media, using the Soft Cover subcategory for a smooth look. She softened the Pastel strokes using the Just Add Water variant of Liquid and intensified the image's watery look with the Distorto variant of Liquid. Finally, to emphasize details in the images, she modified the 2B Pencil variant of Pencils, changing its method to Cover in the General section of the Brush Controls palette, so she could paint light over dark.

Dickson created *Sprawlers* (top), beginning with a treasured family photo. For this image, she used warm, saturated color and painted loosely over the image with modified Dry Media and Pencils variants.

For *Warren* (bottom), Dickson's client requested a portrait print with a painterly look. She began by scanning the aged and torn photo: She opened the scan in Photoshop, retouched it using the Rubber Stamp tool and applied color tints. In Painter, she painted over the image using a custom Artist Pastel Chalk. Facial details were important, so Dickson completed the faces of the subjects using a very small custom 2B Pencil variant. The final piece was output to an Iris 3047 ink jet printer as a 24 x 36-inch print on soft rag paper.

■ For *Colin and Alex,* **Michael Campbell** began by taking the original photograph of his father and his son while they walked together in the New Forest in Hampshire, England. He used a 35 mm Nikon camera with a zoom lens and Fuji 400 ISO negative film. When he decided several years later that he wanted to make an 11 x 14-inch print, he no longer had the negative. So he scanned the 4 x 6-inch print and opened it in Photoshop, where he adjusted levels to get a full range of tones to include black. He darkened the image and added contrast. This can also be accomplished in Painter using the Effects, Tonal Control, Equalize command. (Ctrl-⌘-E) Campbell wanted the picture to look more like a hand-tinted black-and-white photograph rather than a straight color print. He used Image, Adjust, Hue/Saturation to reduce the saturation to get the look of a tinted black-and-white print

with a dreamlike quality. (To reduce the saturation of your image using Painter, choose Effects, Tonal Control, Adjust Colors and move the Saturation slider to the left.) When the tonal adjustments were as he liked them, he saved the image as a TIFF file.

Campbell opened the image in Painter and added a new layer by clicking the right triangle on the Layers section bar and choosing New Layer setting its composite method to Darken. Using a light, warm gray color and the Fine Spray variant of Airbrushes, he darkened areas of sky in the top of the image. He dropped the layer by choosing Drop from the menu on the right side of the Layers section bar. Then he added another new layer, and set its Composite Method to Screen. Using the Coarse Spray variant of Airbrushes and white paint, he airbrushed

light mist into the background of the image. He reduced the effect slightly by setting the opacity of the layer to 80% in the Layers section. Again, Campbell flattened the image, and he added a third new layer, which he set to Default Composite Method. This time, he used the Pepper Spray variant of Airbrushes and black paint to spray the grain over the image. He lowered the opacity of this layer in the Layers section to reduce the blackness of the grain. When the grain was complete, he flattened the image again, and opened it in Photoshop where he adjusted the tonal values for the final time. Campbell printed his image using an Epson 2000P printer on a heavy-weight archival Matte paper.

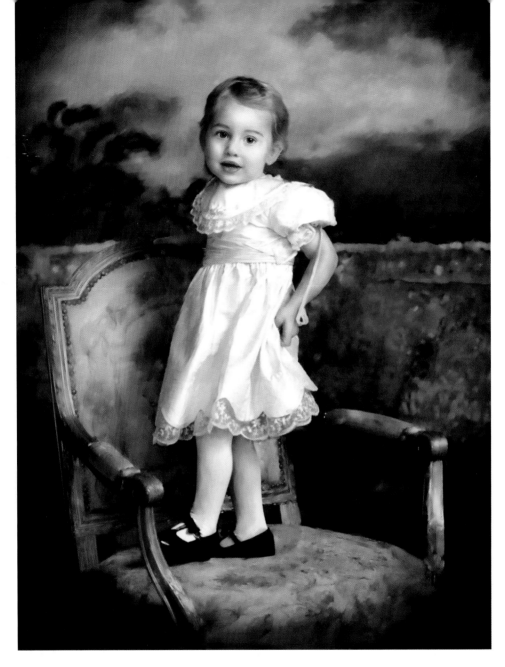

■ An internationally acclaimed studio portraitist, **Phillip Stewart Charris** has created elegant and timeless likenesses of celebrities, individuals and families for over three decades. Known for his life-size portraits, which are printed, and then mounted on canvas, Charris has drawn inspiration from artists such as John Singer Sargent, Raphael and Rembrandt. The portrait *Pretty Little Girl* was photographed in his studio in Southern California. Then a transparency was scanned, saved as an RGB TIFF file and opened in Painter. To protect the figure while he worked on the background, Charris made a mask. Then, using expressive brushwork, he painted over the image background with the Sable Chisel Tip Water variant of Brushes (loaded from the Ver 5 Brushes library in the Painter 7 application folder). To smooth some areas, he painted finer strokes with a low-opacity Just Add Water variant of Liquid. He used the brushes not to apply color, but to blend and smear pixels in the image in a painterly way. For the figure and clothing, Charris used smaller versions of the same two brushes. When brushing over the face and hair, he carefully painted with a small brush to preserve the important details. "The photographer must seek out the personality of the sitter, which lies beneath a veil that subtly alters the surface of the face. Piercing that veil to reveal the subject's character is something that, after the posing is taken care of, can only be done for a fraction of a second," says Charris.

■ *Napoleon's Keepers* began as a photographic idea for a poster about the famous cannon, but **Donal Jolley** wanted to create an image with more of a painterly feeling. He took the original photograph on the top of Kennesaw Mountain, Georgia in the fall after the leaves had fallen. The sky in the photo was a bright blue and the lighting was from a direct afternoon sun. The strong contrasts caused by the intense sunlight allowed him to see the forms in the photograph clearly. Jolley made a mask for the blue color in the sky using the Color Mask command and saved it into the Masks section of the Objects palette. (For information about Color Mask, turn to "Using Color Mask" on page 155.) He loaded the sky selection (Select, Load Selection) and he pressed the Backspace/Delete key to remove the original sky.

Then, working in a source file, he created a new sky; he pasted in several photos of clouds he had taken. After positioning them, he removed unwanted areas on the layers by editing the masks on the layers with white paint. (For more information, turn to "Layers and Their Masks" on page 175.) Then he merged the layers and added more color to the clouds by painting over them with low-opacity Dry Media and Brushes variants. For a more painterly look, he blended areas of the clouds with the Just Add Water variant of the Liquid brush. Working in the final composite file, Jolley pasted in the finished sky as a new layer in the Layers section of the Objects palette. Then he selected the Canvas in the Layers section and made it into a layer by clicking it with the Layer Adjuster tool. He painted over the image using several brushes,

such as the Round Camelhair and Smeary Round variants of Brushes. Jolley repainted the cannon with brass color, so it would look newer. Also, he painted over the landscape, eliminating many of the trees and replacing them with hand-painted trees. For the smoke, he began by adding a new layer, then airbrushing using a low opacity Variable Spatter variant of the Airbrushes. For more a realistic smoke-like effect, he smeared it with the Just Add Water variant of Liquid. To complete the hazy look on the smoke, he set the layer's Composite Method to Magic Combine and reduced its Opacity to about 50% in the Layers section. Once the basic composition was complete, he painted over the entire image with brushes to brighten color and add more contrast and texture. To finish, he added a few more details to the people.

EXPLORING
SPECIAL
EFFECTS

An innovative artist, Laurence Gartel combines digital photography with painting and special effects, as shown in this detail of Coney Island Baby. *He used Liquid Metal layers, Apply Surface Texture and transparent Composite Methods to add depth and excitement to the piece. To view the complete painting, turn to page 267 in the gallery.*

PAINTER'S SPECIAL EFFECTS ARE SO NUMEROUS and complex that an entire book could be written about them alone. Because they're so powerful, there's much less need for third-party filters than with Photoshop or other image processors. But with that power comes complexity; some of these effects have evolved into "programs within the program." This chapter focuses on five of Painter's most frequently used "mini-programs"—Apply Surface Texture, Apply Lighting, Patterns, Glass Distortion and Mosaics. It also covers several special-effects dynamic layers—including Bevel World, Burn, Tear and Liquid Metal—and a handful of other exciting effects.

ADDING EFFECTS WITH SURFACE TEXTURE

One of the most frequent "haunts" of Painter artists is the Effects, Surface Control, Apply Surface Texture dialog box. You'll find it used in a number of places throughout this book. The Apply Surface Texture dialog box contains intricate, powerful controls, allowing you to apply paper textures to images, build realistic highlights and shadows for masked elements, and more. First, the Softness slider (located under the Using pop-up menu) lets you create soft transitions, such as smoothing the edge of a mask or softening a texture application. Adding Softness can also increase the 3D effect produced when you apply Surface Texture Using Mask (when working with an image that contains a mask). And with the Reflection slider (bottom Material slider), you can create a reflection in your artwork based on another image or the current pattern.

Another very important Surface Texture control is the preview sphere, located below the image Preview. Think of the sphere displayed as a dome supporting lights above your image. Although the preview sphere seems to show a spotlight effect, any lights you set are applied evenly across the surface of your image.

Creating textured, dimensional brushstrokes with Apply Surface Texture Using Image Luminance

Creating the illusion of type under water (top), with Apply Surface Texture using Original Luminance and a reflection map. We applied the reflection using a clone source image of a cloudy sky (tinted red to match the color in the type by using Effects, Tonal Control, Adjust Colors).

Experiment with adding more lights by clicking on the sphere. Adjust an individual light by selecting it and changing its color, and adjusting its Brightness and Conc (concentration). Use the Exposure slider to control ambient light in the environment.

You can get some interesting effects by changing your color choices for the lights. For instance, if the area to be lit contains a lot of blue, you can add more color complexity by lighting with its complement, an orange-hued light.

Applying a reflection map. Reflections can add interest to shiny type and to other surfaces like glass or metal objects in your illustrations. The Reflection slider allows you to apply an image that you designate as a clone source to your illustration as a reflection. Open an image and make a selection or mask for the area where you'll apply the reflection. You can use a pattern as a source for a reflection map or you can open an image the same size as your working file (the current Pattern is applied automatically if you don't choose another image as clone source). (Turn to "Making an Environment Map" and "Applying a Environment Map," later in this chapter to read about how Michelle Lill builds custommade reflection maps and applies them to her images. And for more inspiration, check out Michelle Lill's E-Maps folder on the *Painter 7 Wow! CD-ROM*, and the Pattern libraries in the Patterns folder on the Painter_CD2 CD-ROM.)

Creating 3D effects. You can use Apply Surface Texture to enhance the surface of your image and give dimension to your brushstrokes. Image Luminance, in the Using pop-up menu, adds depth to brushstrokes by making the light areas appear to recede or "deboss" slightly. If you want to bring the light areas forward, check the Invert box. Experiment with the sliders to get the effect you desire. You can get a stronger 3D effect by clicking to add a second light (a bounce or a fill light) to the preview sphere with a lower Brightness or a higher Concentration (Conc) setting.

REFLECTING ANOTHER IMAGE

To use a separate image as a reflection map, bend it using Effects, Surface Control, Quick Warp to achieve a spherical or rippled look. (Quick Warp is applied to the entire image, not just to selections or to a single layer.) Open the reflection image and designate it as the clone source (File, Clone Source). Then (in the original image, not the map image) choose Effects, Surface Control, Apply Surface Texture Using Original Luminance to apply the effect to an entire image. To see the reflection, move the Reflection slider to the right, or distort the reflection effect by moving the Softness slider to the right. Experiment with the other settings.

In Still Life, *Chelsea Sammel created drama in her image using Effects, Surface Control, Apply Lighting. Then she painted over some areas with Brushes variants. She finished the image with an application of Apply Surface Texture Using Paper and a rough paper texture.*

When you use Surface Texture together with Apply Lighting, you'll get more dramatic results if you choose similar lighting directions for both commands.

SOFT LIGHTING TRANSITIONS

If you're using Apply Lighting on a selection, you'll get a softer transition between lighted and unlighted areas if you use Select, Feather (with a high Feather setting) on your selections before you apply the light.

MOVING LIGHTS

To access the Lighting Mover in Painter, so you can copy lights from the Painter Settings file into a new custom library, press Ctrl/⌘-Shift-L. To load the new library, click the Library button in the Apply Lighting dialog box.

Combining Surface Texture with other effects. Apply Surface Texture works especially well when combined with other Painter tools. "Creating an Impressionist Look," on page 245 uses a Glass Distortion dynamic layer and Surface Texture to add paint-like texture to a photo; John Derry used a combination of Glass Distortion and Surface Texture to give the illusion of refracted water in "Creating a Tidepool," on page 256; "Draping a Weave," on page 258, uses a powerful Glass Distortion displacement in combination with Surface Texture to achieve the look of draped fabric. And Steve Campbell used Surface Texture and Apply Lighting together to add gradations to textured areas while creating the illustration "Art in Wartime" on page 266 in the gallery.

ADDING DIMENSION WITH LIGHTING

Painter's *User Guide* gives a good description of how to adjust the controls under Effects, Surface Control, Apply Lighting. Here are some tips and practical uses for the tool.

Applying Lighting to unify an image. Like most of the Surface Control effects, applying lighting across a composite image can help to unify the piece. (If the lighting effect is too dramatic, try using Edit, Fade immediately afterwards to reduce it.)

Preventing hot spots. You can avoid "burnout" of lit areas by increasing the Elevation of the light, reducing the light's Exposure or Brightness, or giving the light a pastel or gray color.

Lighting within selections or layers. Add instant dimension to a selection or a layer by applying lighting within it.

Creating subtle gradient effects. To achieve colored gradient effects in an image, some artists prefer lighting with colored lights instead of filling with a gradient; they prefer the Apply Lighting command's smooth luminosity shifts over the more "mechanical" result usually achieved when using gradations.

Painting back into lit areas. For artists who want to achieve a more painterly effect, the Apply Lighting command can look a bit artificial. In creating Still Life (left), Chelsea Sammel used Apply Lighting and then she broke up the lit area with brushstrokes, sampling color from the image as she worked.

Creating softly lit backgrounds. On a white background, start with the Splashy Colors light effect. Increase the Brightness and Elevation and reduce the Distance on both colored lights until they form very soft-edged tinted circles on the background. Click in the Preview to add another light or two and change their colors. Move the lights around until the color, value and composition are working. Save and name your settings and click OK to apply the effect. Repeat this process two or three times, returning each time to your saved effect and making minor adjustments in light color, light position and other settings.

Painter's F-X brush variants are capable of creating many subtle or dramatic effects such as fire, glows and shattering, to name a few.

For Caterpillar, *Matt Dineen used the Furry Brush variant of the F-X brush to paint the caterpillar's colorful hair. See the gallery at the end of this chapter for other examples.*

Grunion Run *is an illustration for a calendar designed and illustrated by Kathleen Blavatt. She used several special effects brushes to paint the image. Beginning with a black-and-white pen drawing, she modeled the hills using the Pixel Dust variant of Pens (loaded from the Ver 5 Brushes library in the Painter 7 application folder). She added sparkling texture to the sky using the Fairy Dust variant of the F-X brush. Blavatt painted the water with the Piano Keys variant of the F-X brush. She added textured brushstrokes to the sun's head using the Grain Emboss variant of Impasto.*

EXPLORING PATTERNS

On the Patterns section bar in the Art Materials palette, there are commands that let you make seamless wrap-around pattern tiles. (To access the menu, click the right triangle on the Patterns section bar.) Once a pattern has been defined and is in the Patterns section, it becomes the default Clone Source when no other clone source is designated. You can apply a pattern to an existing image, selection or layer with Cloning brushes, with the Paint Bucket tool (by choosing Fill With: Clone Source in the Controls: Paint Bucket palette), with any of the special effects features that use a clone source (such as Original Luminance or 3D Brushstrokes), or by choosing to fill with a pattern or clone source (Ctrl/⌘-F). (The Fill dialog box shows a Pattern button if no clone source image is designated; if a clone source *is* available, a Clone Source button appears.) Use the pattern feature to create screen design backgrounds, textile design, wallpaper—anywhere you need repeating images. (For step-by-step techniques, see "Creating a Pattern" and "Applying a Pattern" later in this chapter.)

CANCELING A CLONE SOURCE

To turn off a clone source so you can fill an image with the current pattern (if the clone source is another image), close the clone source image. If you've cloned from one place to another in the *same* image, click on a pattern in the Patterns section of the Art Materials palette to clear the clone source.

Capturing a Pattern. To make and store a pattern image in the Patterns section, select an area of your document with the Rectangular Selection tool (or press Ctrl/⌘-A to select the entire image) and on the Patterns section bar, click the right triangle and choose Capture Pattern. To offset your pattern use the Horizontal and Vertical Shift options and the Bias slider to control the amount of the offset. Experiment with these settings to get nonaligned patterns—for example, to create a brick wall look, wallpaper or fabric.

Using Pattern wrap-around. Painter creates a wrap-around for the pattern tile you create. Here's a great way to see it work. Select a pattern in the Patterns section. From the pop-up menu on the right side of the Patterns section bar, choose Check Out Pattern; a pattern tile image will appear. Choose the Image Hose icon in the Brushes palette. Select an Image Hose nozzle from the Art Materials palette's Nozzles section. Begin spraying across your image and beyond its edge. Notice how the hose images "wrap around" the edges of the pattern tile (so that when the pattern is captured and an area is filled with these pattern tiles, the edges will match seamlessly).

Making a Fractal Pattern. Choosing Make Fractal Pattern from the Patterns section bar menu automatically creates a pattern as a new file when you click OK in the make Fractal Pattern dialog box. If you have a lot of memory allotted to Painter, you'll be able to create large tiles; if not, the larger size options will be grayed out.

The evolution of a fractal pattern. The original pattern was made by choosing Make Fractal Pattern from the Patterns section menu (top left), then a hard edge was added with Effects, Surface Control, Express Texture Using Image Luminance (top right). We loaded the Earthen gradient from the Painter 6 Gradients library in the Gradients folder on the Painter_CD2 CD-ROM, and applied it via Express in Image (chosen by clicking the right triangle on the Gradients section bar (lower left). To change the color, we adjusted the Bias to 46% in the Express in Image dialog box (lower right).

Some of the textures you can create with Make Fractal Pattern make very cool paper textures: Select the area of the fractal pattern that you want for your texture (or choose Select, All) and on the Papers section bar, click the right triangle and choose Capture Paper.

Enhancing fractal patterns. You can add any special effect to fractal (or regular) patterns and they still remain patterns. Here are two creative applications of fractal patterns.

To create a hard-edged fractal pattern with wild color, make a Fractal Pattern, setting Power to –150%, Feature Size to 75% (for a relatively coarse pattern), and Softness to 0. Click OK. Select Effects, Surface Control, Express Texture Using Image Luminance. Adjust the Gray Threshold and Grain sliders to about 80%, and set the Contrast slider at 200% for a contrasty effect. Click OK. Now color the pattern by choosing the Spectrum gradation from the Gradients section of the Art Materials palette and clicking the right triangle of the Gradients section bar and choosing Express in Image. Experiment with shifting the distribution of color in the image by dragging the Bias slider. Choose Select, All and capture the pattern.

To make an abstract topographical map image with color and relief, create a new pattern using Fractal Pattern's default settings: Power, –150%; Feature Size, 100%; Softness, 0%; Angle, 0°; Thinness, 100%; and Channel, Height as Luminance, click OK. Give the image a "topographical" look by choosing Effects, Surface Control, Apply Surface Texture, Using Image Luminance (Amount, 200%; Picture, 100%; and Shine, 0% and Reflection, 0%). Tint the image with Express in Image and the Earthen gradation, loaded from the Painter 6 Gradients library, in the Gradients folder on the Painter_CD2 CD-ROM. Now, add a little relief by applying a second pass of Apply Surface Texture, Using Image

After creating this topographic map using Make Fractal Pattern, we added clouds for more atmosphere by copying our original Fractal pattern file and pasting it into the map image as a layer. We changed the Composite Method in the Layers section of the Objects palette to Screen to apply only the light parts of the clouds to the topographic map image. Then we adjusted the Opacity slider for the clouds layer to 90%.

CREATING REPEATING TEXTURES WITH MAKE PAPER

Using the Make Paper dialog box, accessed by clicking the right triangle on the Papers section bar (Art Materials palette), you can make seamless repeating textures to apply to your images. For the image below, Corinne Okada created her own repeating texture that resembled a grid of pixels to represent the digital output process. She created the grid of beveled squares with Make Paper using the Square Pattern, then chose her new paper from the list on the papers section and applied the texture to the central portion of her image using Effects, Surface Control, Color Overlay.

Left: Detail from a package design created by Corinne Okada for The Digital Pond. Above: Okada's settings for the grid of beveled squares.

To change the hue of an image, use Effects, Tonal Control, Adjust Colors, then drag the Hue Shift slider. Use Uniform Color to shift the hue of the entire image, or use Image Luminance to change color properties only in the lighter (but not white) areas.

Highpass (under Effects, Esoterica) acts like a color filter. It looks for smooth transitions in dark areas (as in a sky or shadowed background) and replaces them with abrupt edges or halo effects. Keep the Radius slider to the left for a more pronounced halo effect. To further enhance Highpass, try using Effects, Tonal Control, Equalize.

PHOTO: CHER THREINEN-PENDARVIS

The initial, unaltered photograph

Adjust Colors, Uniform Color: Hue Shift, –44%; Value, 25%

Adjust Colors, Image Luminance: Hue Shift, 20%; Value, 25%

Highpass: Amount, 26.05

SHOOTING THROUGH GLASS

Conventional diffuser screens attach to the camera lens, breaking up or softening the image as it refracts through the screen. Painter's Glass Distortion layer works the same way but with more variety. To make a Glass Distortion layer for your image, select Glass Distortion from the Dynamic Plug-ins menu at the bottom of the Layers section on the Objects palette. Choose Paper for the Using menu and experiment with refracting your image through different textures chosen in the Papers section. On this photo, we used Diagonal 1 from the More Paper Textures library (in the Paper Textures folder on the Painter_CD2 CD-ROM).

Luminance (Amount, 100%; Picture, 100%; and Shine, 0%). To add a swirl to your "map" choose Effects, Surface Control, Quick Warp and click the Swirl button. Experiment with different Angle Factor settings in the dialog box.

CREATING EFFECTS WITH GLASS DISTORTION

Try using another image as a "refractor" for your main image. With Painter's Glass Distortion features you can superimpose glass bas relief effects (using a paper texture or another image). You can apply the procedure directly to your image by choosing Effects, Focus, Glass Distortion. Or you can use a Glass Distortion layer, which lets you preview the effects on a copy of your image without changing the original image; however, the Effects, Focus, Glass Distortion command features a dialog box with more controls. (To learn more about using Effects, Glass Distortion turn to "Diving into Distortion" and "Draping a Weave" later in this chapter. To read about using a Glass Distortion layer, turn to "Creating an Impressionist Look.")

WORKING WITH MOSAICS

Tile mosaics became a popular medium at about 200–300 BC in the Roman Empire, Greece, Africa and Asia; floors and walls of many buildings were decorated with mosaics made of small pieces of glass, stones or shells. They were most often built to celebrate a historic event or for religious purposes.

Inspiration for mosaics. You can build mosaics using Painter's Mosaic brush and dialog box in any of three ways: by drawing them from scratch, by basing them on a line drawing that you've

To create Pencil and Brush, *artist John Derry built a mosaic in Painter beginning with white grout.*

A colored pen-and-ink sketch was used as reference for this mosaic. Top: The cloned sketch (with Tracing Paper turned on) shows the mosaic in progress with recently applied tiles. Bottom: The same stage with Tracing Paper turned off. Click Tracing Paper on and off without closing the Make Mosaic dialog box by using the checkbox.

The default grout color is white, shown here (left) in the Select Grout Color dialog box, which uses the Apple color picker. Dragging the Lightness slider to the left darkens the color of the grout.

scanned, or by creating a clone-based mosaic using an existing piece of art or a photo. Keep in mind that because of the nature of the Mosaic tool, your decorative design or photo reference should have a strong compositional focal point. If you want to use a photo that has a busy background, consider simplifying it first by desaturating or blurring. (For tips on neutralizing busy backgrounds, see the beginning of Chapter 6.)

Laying down tiles. Here's a way to try out Painter's Mosaics. Open a new blank file, or a reference on which to base your mosaic. Visualize the forms in your design before you begin laying down the tiles, and rotate your page by dragging with the Rotate Page tool (nested with the Grabber tool in the Tools palette) to accommodate your drawing style so you'll be able to make smooth, controlled strokes to describe the forms.

Choose Canvas, Make Mosaic to open the Make Mosaic dialog box. Opening the dialog box will turn the background of the currently active image white, the default grout color. To change the grout color in the Select Grout Color dialog box, click in the Grout box, and choose a new color. Then choose a contrasting color in the Colors section of the Art Materials palette to paint some tiles. Switch colors again and continue to make tiles. Once you have tiles in place, you can sample color from an existing tile by pressing the Alt/Option key as you click on it. You can undo an action without closing the Mosaic dialog box by pressing Ctrl/⌘-Z. To erase a tile, press the Ctrl-Shift/⌘-Control keys and stroke with the Mosaic brush over the tile. While working on a mosaic, save it in RIFF format to preserve the resolution-independent nature of the mosaic. (Because mosaic tiles are mathematically described, a mosaic can be resized without loss of quality.) For an in-depth explanation of Painter's mosaic-building tools check out Chapter 11 of the *Painter 7 User Guide*. And to read about using a photo-reference for a mosaic, turn to "Building a Clone-Based Mosaic," on page 254.

SPECIAL EFFECTS USING DYNAMIC LAYERS

Painter features seven kinds dynamic layers (plug-ins) that allow you to create exciting special effects quickly. They are Glass Distortion, Kaleidoscope, Liquid Lens, Burn, Tear, Bevel World and Liquid Metal. In the paragraphs below, we focus on special-effects applications for several of these plug-ins. (To read more about working with plug-in layers turn to the introduction of Chapter 5; see Chapter 6 to see how dynamic layers apply to image correction and photography. Turn to "Creating an Impressionist Look" later in this chapter to read about using the Glass Distortion dynamic layer in combination with Apply Surface Texture. And the *Painter 7 User Guide* contains good descriptions of each of these dynamic layers.)

Painting with metal and water. Painter's versatile Liquid Metal dynamic layer allows you to paint with bas relief and give it

Hiroshi Yoshii painted Bird *with Painter's Liquid Metal. He used colored environment maps and multiple Liquid Metal layers to sculpt the bird's outline and body.*

Athos Boncompagni used the Liquid Metal Brush tool to draw trees and falling stars for this wrapping paper design.

©CDM-F-LLI MAGRO (ITALY)

We used the Kaleidoscope plug-in to make a seamless tile from a Corbis Images photo. To read a step-by-step description of the technique, turn to "Making a Seamless Tile" in Chapter 11, "Using Painter For Web Graphics."

the look of chrome, steel, ice, water and other materials. The Liquid Metal layer works in an existing file to make a layer on which you create the metal. To make a dynamic layer, open an image, click the Dynamic Plug-ins icon at the bottom of the Layers section of the Objects palette and choose Liquid Metal from the menu. To paint with chrome, select the Brush in the Liquid Metal dialog box and choose Chrome 1 or Chrome 2 from the Map menu. Drag in the image with the Brush. For thin lines, try a Size of 8.0 and a Volume of 25%. For thick lines, increase Size to 50 and set Volume over 100%.

If you'd like to paint with bubbles or water drops that reflect your image, begin by making a clone of the image (File, Clone). On the clone, make a Liquid Metal layer. From the Map menu choose Clone Source, choose the Circle or Brush and drag to paint on the layer. For fairly flat drops use an Amount of 0.5 to 1.5. For the look of 3D water drops on a camera lens, move the Amount slider to between 3.0 and 4.0. For bubbles use an Amount of 5.0.

You can color the objects on a Liquid Metal layer based on a clone source (as above) or on the current pattern. Begin by making a Liquid Metal layer. In the Liquid Metal dialog box, choose Clone Source from the Map menu. Select a pattern in the Patterns section of the Art Materials palette or open an image and define it as the clone source (File, Clone Source). Now use the Circle or Brush tool to apply metal to the layer.

Tearing, burning and beveling. The Tear, Burn and Bevel World layers require a selected "source image layer" to perform their effects. To **Tear** or **Burn** an image's edges, begin by opening a file. You can select a layer in the image and apply the plug-in to it or you can reduce the image canvas to accommodate the torn or burned edge to come: Choose Effects, Orientation, Scale—we scaled our image at 80%. The Scale command will automatically create a "source layer." With the layer still selected, click the Dynamic Plug-ins icon at the bottom of the Layers section and choose the Tear or Burn plug-in from the menu. To change the color of the torn (or burned) edge, click in the Color box and choose a new color. **Bevel World** allows you to create complex bevels quickly. You can apply a bevel to a "source layer" in an image or make a unique beveled frame for an image. Open an image you'd like to frame, choose Select, All, and choose Bevel World from the Dynamic Plug-ins menu on the Layers section. Choose your settings and click OK. To read more about Bevel World, turn to "Creating Beveled Chrome," in Chapter 8 on page 282.

To design this striking beveled button Michelle Lill captured a custom-made environment map as a pattern, and applied it to the button graphic using the Reflection slider in the Bevel World dialog box. To learn more about reflection maps, turn to "Making an Environment Map" and "Applying an Environment Map," later in this chapter.

Diving into Distortion

Overview *Use Glass Distortion to displace an image using a clone source; then combine a dramatic distortion with a subtle one to create a water-stained effect.*

The original photograph

The water image displacement map

Settings for the subtle distortion

The Extreme clone (left), and the Subtle clone (right)

Cloning in a dramatic water drop

PAINTER'S GLASS DISTORTION can move pixels in an image based on the luminosity of another image. We used it here to simulate water drops on a camera lens.

1 Choosing images and making clones. Choose an image for a displacement map (the water drops in this case) that has good contrast; both crisp and soft-focus images can give good results. Because you'll be applying the displacement map image to the original image as a clone source, you'll need to size the map image to the same pixel dimensions as the image you want to distort. (Our images were 883 x 589 pixels.) Make two clones of the image you want to distort by choosing File, Clone, twice. Save the clones, naming them Extreme and Subtle, then size and position them on your screen so that you can see both of them.

2 Applying the distortion. Open the displacement map image. Now, click on the Extreme clone, and designate the displacement image as the clone source (File, Clone Source). With the Extreme clone active, choose Effects, Focus, Glass Distortion, Using Original Luminance, and choose the Refraction Map model. (Refraction works well for glass effects; it creates an effect similar to an optical lens bending light.) Our settings were Softness, 2.3 (to smooth the distortion); Amount, 1.35; Variance, 6.00. We left Direction at 0, because it has no effect when using a Refraction map, and clicked OK. Click on the Subtle clone, and apply Glass Distortion with subtler settings. (Our settings were Softness 15.0; Amount, 0.07; and Variance, 1.00.) We wanted the diving board to curve, while preserving smoothness in the image.

3 Restoring from the Extreme clone. We added several dramatic water drops from the Extreme clone to enhance the composition of the Subtle image. Click on the Subtle clone to make it active and choose the Extreme clone as clone source. Use the Soft Cloner variant of the Cloners brush to clone dramatic effects from the Extreme clone into your Subtle image. 🐾

Creating an Impressionist Look

Overview *Combine Glass Distortion and Surface Texture special effects to transform a photo into a painting, creating brushstrokes and building up paint.*

CHER THREINEN-PENDARVIS / PHOTO: CORBIS IMAGES

The original photograph

Applying Glass Distortion to the photo

Adding highlights and shadows to the distorted image with Surface Texture

BY COMBINING TWO POWERFUL EFFECTS, Glass Distortion and Apply Surface Texture, you can create an Impressionist look with textured highlights and shadows—turning a photo into a painting. This effect can be applied to an entire image, a selection or a layer, giving you much more flexibility than you would have in the darkroom working with diffuser screens and masks.

1 Choosing an image and making a selection. Choose an image with a strong focal point and good highlights and shadows. You can achieve good results with either crisp or soft-focus images. In preparation for generating a Glass Distortion plug-in dynamic layer for the image in the next step, choose Select, All.

2 Initiating strokes. Choose a coarse paper texture—woven textures with a broad tonal range help to emulate the look of paint on canvas. We chose Raw Silk from the default Painter Textures library, and scaled it down to 88% to complement our 883-pixel-wide image. To diffuse or break up the image into paint-like strokes on paper, apply the Glass Distortion dynamic layer: In the Dynamic Layers section of the Objects palette, click the plug icon at the bottom of the palette and choose Glass Distortion from the pop-up menu. In the Using menu select Paper. Choose subtle settings—our settings were Amount, 0.71; Variance, 2.06; and Softness, 0. Click OK to apply your settings.

3 Adding texture and shadows. To add realistic relief to complete the painted effect choose Effects, Surface Control, Apply Surface Texture. (If the Commit dialog box appears asking you if you'd like to convert the dynamic layer to an image layer, choose Commit.) In the Using menu choose Paper. Use subtle-to-moderate Surface Texture settings to avoid a harsh look and to preserve the original image. We used Amount, 90%; Picture, 100%; Shine, 10%; Softness, 0 and Reflection, 0; (to raise the highlights, we turned on Inverted). Choose a light direction that complements the light in your photograph, and click OK. 🖌

Creating a Seamless Pattern

Overview *Set up and capture a basic pattern layout; check this pattern out of the library; add more elements, shifting the pattern as needed; capture the final pattern; save it in a pattern library.*

ARENA REED

Reed's basic pattern layout image with peach fill and spiral "doodle"

2a

Setting up the Vertical Shift in the Capture Pattern dialog box

2b

Choosing Check Out Pattern from the Patterns section bar on the Art Materials palette

PAINTER'S AMAZING PATTERN-GENERATION tools make it easy to build even a complex pattern tile. You can capture a very basic layout for your tile into a Pattern library and then "check it out" of the library to add complex elements. The new elements will automatically wrap from one edge of the pattern to the opposite edge as you paint, to make a pattern that tiles seamlessly! *Shifted Flowers* is a pattern created by Arena Reed. See "Applying Patterns" on page 248 to see how Reed used this and other patterns.

1 Setting up your pattern layout. To start the pattern files, choose File, New, and in the New dialog box, set up a small image. Reed's image was 240 x 400 pixels. In the Colors section of the Art Materials palette, choose the basic background color you want for your tile, then choose Effects, Fill, Fill With Current Color to fill the new image Canvas. To create the base color for her pattern tile, Reed filled the image with a light peach color.

On your color-filled background, quickly sketch a "stand-in" for your pattern element. This will give you a repeating element to look at as you set up any vertical and horizontal offsets you want for your pattern. Reed painted a spiral "doodle" as her placeholder.

2 Capturing the pattern. With your basic pattern layout (solid-color background and stand-in pattern element) complete, capture the layout as a pattern tile: From the pop-up menu on the Art Materials palette's Patterns section bar, choose Capture Pattern. In the Capture Pattern dialog box, set up any Horizontal or Vertical Shift that you want for

> **USE THE CANVAS**
>
> When creating seamless tiles, plan to create your pattern elements on the Canvas, because the Capture Pattern command only works well on the Canvas.

3a

Pressing Shift-Spacebar and dragging in the image to shift the pattern

3b

The painted background with the first branch (left) and the completed branches, leaves and flowers (right)

3c

The nearly completed seamless pattern with most of the flower buds and details in place

4

Saving the completed pattern using the Capture Pattern dialog box

5

Dragging and dropping new patterns into the newly created "my patterns" library

your pattern, and watch how your stand-in element repeats as you experiment with the Bias slider. Reed chose a Vertical Shift and set the Bias slider to 40%. Name your pattern and click OK to accept. The working pattern will be saved to the current Patterns library.

3 Embellishing the tile. To access Painter's automatic seamless tiling feature for developing the pattern tile, make sure that your new pattern is selected in the Patterns library and choose Check Out Pattern from the pop-out menu on the right side of the Patterns section bar. A new Painter window will open with the pattern tile in it.

By working in this "checked-out" pattern window, you'll be able to embellish your tile without having to do a lot of retouching at the edges. Notice that you can shift the pattern tile and view the repeating element: If you press the Spacebar and Shift keys, the cursor will change to a hand, and you can drag in the image window to shift the pattern so you can see the offset that you built into it in step 2.

Now you can paint to embellish your basic layout, turning it into your final pattern tile. Reed used the Smeary Round variant of Brushes to paint a deep pink color over the background. Because of Painter's seamless wrap-around feature for checked-out patterns, her brushstrokes automatically wrapped around, and there were no obvious tile edges as the pattern repeated.

As you paint, shift the pattern continually (with the Shift key and Spacebar) to check the design and make sure it's balanced. Reed shifted the pattern as she used the Variable Colored Pencil variant of Pencils to draw the branches and their flowers, and to add the details.

4 Capturing the final pattern. When your pattern is complete, add the final tile image to the Patterns library: Choose Capture Pattern from the pop-out menu on the Patterns section bar. In the Capture Pattern dialog box, leave the Shift and Bias settings as they are, give the pattern a new name (Reed named hers "Shifted Flowers") and click OK.

5 Saving your patterns in a library. Continue to make more patterns if you like, following the instructions in steps 1 through 4. Then store your new pattern(s) in a library for safekeeping: Click the right triangle on the Patterns section bar to open the pop-out menu and choose Pattern Mover. When the dialog box appears, the currently loaded pattern library, with the pattern(s) you created, will appear on the left of the mover. To create a new library, click the New button, then name and save the new empty pattern library. To copy an item from the current pattern library, click on the pattern thumbnail and drag and drop it into the new library. If you leave all of your custom patterns in the default Painter Patterns library, the library can become very large, taking up a lot of disk space. So after you've copied your new patterns to the new library, it's a good idea to delete the original(s) from the default library: For each one, click on the pattern swatch and then click the Delete button. 🐾

Applying Patterns

Overview *Make selections and fill them with patterns; add stitching on a new layer; give the stitching highlights and shadows; add clouds that have stitching and Surface Texture.*

ARENA REED

The Mixed Spirals pattern is chosen in Reed's pattern library.

Reducing the opacity to 60% for a translucent fill

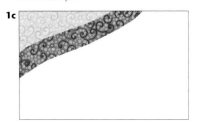

Here the Mixed Spirals and Spirals in Blue patterns have been applied to the sky.

YOU CAN APPLY A PATTERN TO AN EXISTING IMAGE, selection or layer with Cloning brushes, with the Paint Bucket tool (by choosing Fill With: Clone Source in the Controls: Paint Bucket palette), with any of the special effects features that use a clone source (such as Original Luminance or 3D Brushstrokes), or by choosing Effects, Fill, Fill With Pattern (Ctrl/⌘-F).

Arena Reed built the colorful landscape image above, *Dreams in Distant Lands*, by filling selections with several illustrated patterns she created, then drawing stitching with pattern pens.

1 Setting up a new image, selecting and filling. Create a new image by choosing File, New. (Reed's image was 1200 x 1500 pixels.) For practice in using a pattern library, you can follow along with the process Reed used for the image above. Or you can create your own patterns store them in a pattern library, then use them to create an image. (See "Creating a Seamless Pattern" on page 246 for more information.)

Reed's pattern library is located on the Painter 7 Wow! CD-ROM, in the Arena Reed's Patterns folder. Begin by copying the library from the Painter 7 Wow! CD-ROM to your Painter 7 application folder. Then, from the bottom of the Patterns list on the Patterns section on the Art Materials palette, choose Load Library. Navigate to the Painter application folder, select Patterns_arenaReed and click the Open button.

1d

The quilt with basic fills completed

2

Reed created the stitching using the Pattern Chalk and custom patterns.

3

Apply Surface Texture was used to add highlights and shadows to the stitches.

4

The completed clouds with "embossed" stitching

For each area you want to fill with, make a selection (with the Lasso, for instance), then click in the Patterns section to choose a pattern from the library and choose Effects, Fill, Fill With Pattern. As you fill, you can vary the scale of the pattern using the Scale slider on the Patterns section. Reed made selections and filled them to create a landscape design, varying the scale and the opacity of her fills. The top of the sky was filled with her Mixed Spirals pattern at a reduced opacity of about 60% so the pattern would appear lighter in the sky than it would be in the foreground, where she planned to apply it at 100% opacity.

2 Making stitching on a new layer. Next, Reed created stitching on a separate layer using custom patterns that were applied with the Pattern Chalk variant of the Pattern Pens. To try out the Pattern Chalk, make a new layer on your image by choosing New Layer from the menu on the right side of the Objects palette's Layers section bar. Click with the Magnifier tool to zoom in on your image. Choose a color in the Colors section of the Art Materials palette and choose the Pattern Chalk variant of Pattern Pens in the Brushes palette. For wiggly-line style stitching, choose the stitching_luminance3 pattern in the Patterns section, and paint stitching along the edges of the filled areas. For smaller stitches, reduce the size of the Pattern Chalk using the Size slider in the Controls:Brush palette. Try out the other stitching patterns in Reed's library.

3 Adding highlights and shadows to the stitches. To make the stitching look more three-dimensional, apply subtle highlights and shadows to the stitching layer. Choose Effects, Surface Control, Apply Surface Texture and in the dialog box, set Using to the stitching layer's mask and use these approximate settings: Amount, 15%; Shine, 0; Softness, 2; and leave the other settings at their defaults.

4 Making clouds. Reed created a new layer for each cloud so they could be arranged and scaled independently. Add a new layer, draw a cloud shape with the Lasso tool and fill the selection with the Overlapping Circles pattern. After filling, adjust their color: Choose Effects, Tonal Control, Adjust Colors and in the dialog box, increase the Value and change the Hue to create contrast with the background. Use the Layer Adjuster tool to reposition the cloud layers. To scale them, choose Effects, Orientation, Free Transform, then choose Effects, Orientation, Commit Transform to accept. Choose one of the stitching patterns and stitch the edges of the clouds. After the clouds are as you like them, you can group them in order to make it easier to add dimension to the stitches. Shift-select their names in the Layers section and Group them (Ctrl/⌘-G). Then Collapse them by clicking the Layer Commands button on the bottom of the Layers section palette and choosing Collapse from the menu. Now, add highlights and shadows to the clouds by choosing Effects, Surface Control, Apply Surface Texture, using the same settings as in step 4. ✍

Making an Environment Map

Overview *Choose a file and resize it; make a selection; use Quick Warp to bend the image into an environment; capture it as a pattern.*

MICHELLE LILL

YOU CAN USE PAINTER'S QUICK WARP FEATURE to bend any image into a useful environment map, an image that shows an environment as if it were seen through a fish-eye lens or reflected in a shiny metal sphere. Multimedia designer Michelle Lill creates her own environment maps—like the one above on the left, and uses the maps to enhance images by applying them as she did in the image on the right.

1. Opening an image and making a selection. Open the image that you want to use as the basis for your reflection map. To conserve disk space and optimize performance, Lill recommends that a reflection map image be a square that is 256 pixels or less. Using the Rectangle Selection tool, make a 256 pixel square selection (holding down the Shift key as you drag to constrain the selection to a square), as you check the Width in the Controls:Selection palette. If you need to move or scale the selection, use the Selection Adjuster tool. (Turn to "Transforming Selections" in Chapter 4 for more about manipulating selections.) Copy the selected area (Edit, Copy), and paste it into a new file by choosing Edit, Paste Into New Image.

1a

Michelle Lill's original photo

1b

Making a square selection on the image

2 Bending the image. To get the "fisheye lens" effect that adds realism to the map (since most surfaces that reflect their environment are not flat), Lill chose Effects, Surface, Control, Quick Warp and selected the Sphere option. She used the default settings of Power 2.0 and Angle Factor 2.0. The effect was applied to the entire canvas.

2

Applying the Quick Warp Sphere option

3 Saving the image as a pattern. To save the map into the current Pattern library, capture it as a pattern: With the environment map image open, select all, click the right triangle on the Patterns section bar and choose Capture Pattern from the menu. Name the map when prompted and click OK. The environment map is now a permanent member of the library. Now you can use the map to enhance special effects—as Lill did in her water illustration above. To read a step-by-step description of how Lill used a custom environment map to enhance an image, turn to "Applying an Environment Map," on the next page.

3

Naming the water map in the Capture Pattern dialog box

Applying an Environment Map

Overview *Open a file and set type shapes; convert the shapes into a layer; add an environment map, dimension and a soft drop shadow to the type; add a border to the image.*

MICHELLE LILL

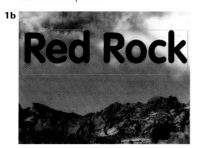

1a Choosing a font and size in the Controls:Text palette

1b The text set on a layer over the image

1c The selected Text layer in the Layers section of the Objects palette

2 Choosing Lill's custom-made environment map in the Patterns section

TO CREATE THE TITLE DESIGN *RED ROCK*, multimedia designer Michelle Lill used a custom-made environment map in combination with one of Painter's most powerful and versatile tools, Apply Surface Texture.

1 Opening an image and setting the type. For this example, Lill began by setting 60-point VAG Rounded Bold text on top of a photo. Begin by opening a background image (Lill's image was 889 pixels wide). Select the Text tool and choose a font in the Controls:Text palette. For the best results, choose a bold font with a broad stroke and rounded corners. Position the cursor in your image and type the text.

When you're finished setting the text, select the Layer Adjuster tool and drag to reposition the text layer to your taste. (To read more about using Painter's text features see Chapter 8, "Working with Type in Painter.")

2 Selecting the reflection map. Open the Patterns section of the Art Materials palette and choose the Exterior Reflection Map pattern from the list. Lill used her own pattern, made from the same Red Rock photo she used for the background. (To read about how to make your own environment map, check out Michelle Lill's method in "Making an Environment Map," on page 246.

3 Adding reflection and dimension to the type. To achieve a strong reflection in the type and a realistic 3D look, Lill used two applications of Apply Surface Texture. Begin by selecting the text layer with the Layer Adjuster tool, then choose Effects, Surface Control, Apply Surface Texture. Before the Apply Surface

3a

Committing the text to an image layer

3b

Michele Lill's Red Rock environment map

3c

Settings for the second Surface Texture application showing dimension on the type

4a

Setting up an automatic drop shadow

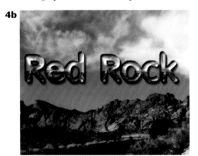

4b

The Red Rock image with the drop shadow applied to the text layer

Texture dialog box appears, a Commit dialog box will appear. It's necessary to convert the text layer to an image layer before you can apply an effect. Click OK in the Commit dialog box. To reflect the environment map onto your type, use these settings: In the Using menu choose the text mask to restrict the reflection to the type. Move the Reflection slider to 100% (so the environment map shows up) and move the Softness slider to the right (to scale the reflection map). Adjust the other settings to suit your image. The Surface Texture dialog box is interactive, so you can scale your pattern while viewing the reflection map in the Preview window. When the reflection looks good, click OK in the Apply Surface Texture dialog box. Lill's Apply Surface Texture settings for the first application are as follows: Softness 40.0; Amount 200%; Picture 100%; Shine 40%; and Reflection 100%.

Now add a realistic 3D look to the text by choosing Apply Surface Texture a second time. This time, check the Inverted box (to add a second light source); decrease the Reflection slider to 0% by moving it all the way to the left; and decrease the Softness to about 10. Lill's second Surface Texture application settings are as follows: Softness 10.0, Amount 100%, Picture 100%, Shine 40% and Reflection 0%. Click OK. The image with Apply Surface Texture can be seen at the beginning of this story.

4 Adding a shadow and a soft black border. Next, Lill added a black drop shadow to her text, adding to the 3D look and giving her image more contrast. To generate the shadow, she chose Effects, Objects, Create Drop Shadow. In the dialog box, she specified settings for the X and Y coordinates to fit her image, and she increased the Opacity of the shadow to 80%, left the other settings at their defaults, and she checked the Collapse To One Layer box to combine the text and shadow.

Then, to finish the image with a more graphic look that would complement the shadow, Lill added a softly feathered black border to her image. To create her border effect, begin by choosing Select, All. Then from the Select menu choose Select, Modify, Contract. In the Contract Selection dialog box, type in 12 pixels. Now choose Select, Feather and set the feather to 24 pixels. Finally, Lill filled the selected, feathered edge with black. Begin by choosing black in the Colors section of the Art Materials palette. Choose the Paint Bucket, in the Controls:Paint Bucket palette make these choices: From the What To Fill menu choose Image, and from the Fill With menu choose Current Color. Click inside the active selection with the Paint Bucket tool. 🐾

Building a Terrain Map

Overview Create a terrain map from elevation data; make a custom gradient; color the map; use Apply Surface Texture to give it realistic dimension.

Olympic National Park

1

The grayscale image representing elevation

2a

Building a custom gradient for the map

2b

The map with the custom gradient applied using Express in Image

3

Gordon's settings in Apply Surface Texture, used to produce the terrain map

TO CREATE THIS REALISTIC MAP of Mount Olympus, Washington, Steven Gordon built a color terrain background from real data. As principal cartographer and owner of Cartagram, Gordon produces custom maps for electronic and print publication, specializing in tourism maps with relief renderings of the terrain.

1 Making a grayscale-to-height image. To begin the map, Gordon downloaded a digital elevation model (DEM) file from the USGS (www.usgs.gov). He processed it using a shareware DEM reader he found by searching for the keyword "DEM" in an Internet search engine. The resulting PICT image contained grayscale values mapped to elevation values, which Gordon could then use in building the image.

2 Coloring the image. Gordon opened the grayscale PICT file in Painter and built a custom gradient to color the map. To make your own gradation, open the Colors and the Gradients sections of the Art Materials palette; in the Gradients section choose the Two-Point gradation. Now open the Edit Gradient dialog box by clicking the right triangle on the Gradients section bar and choosing Edit Gradient. Using the dialog box, you can create a new gradation with color control points representing elevation zones (as Gordon did). Add control points to the center of the gradient by clicking in the Gradient bar. Click each control point and then click in the Colors section to choose a color for that point. Gordon's gradation progressed from dark blue-green valleys to white mountain crests. When the gradient looks good, click OK and then save it by choosing Save Gradient from the Gradients section's menu. Apply the gradient to your image by choosing Express in Image from the Gradients section's menu.

3 Building Terrain. To add realistic relief to your map, choose Effects, Surface Control, Apply Surface Texture, Using Image Luminance. Click the Inverted box to make the light areas in the map "pop-up." To blur undesirable detail, move the Softness slider to the right. Adjust the Amount to build dimension and shadow. Gordon decreased the Amount to 85% to keep the shadows from being too dark and prominent. He used the default 11:00 light direction setting and left the Shine at the default 40%. ⓦ

Building a Clone-Based Mosaic

Overview *Choose a photo reference and retouch it if needed; make a clone of the retouched photo; use the Make Mosaic dialog box to design and lay down colored tiles in the clone.*

S. SWAMINATHAN

1

The original photograph

2a

Increasing the contrast in the source image

2b

Detail of the retouched source image

MOSAICS HAVE BEEN USED AS A NARRATIVE and decorative art form since Hellenistic and Roman times. Because of its graphic nature, the mosaic is a medium that can be used to express strong emotion. S. Swaminathan created the digital mosaic *Soul of Homelessness*, based on his photograph of a homeless man. His vision was to create an abstracted mosaic portrait of the man that would portray the dignity he projected.

1 Selecting a source image. Choose a photo with a strong focal point and meaningful content, so the mosaic technique does not overpower the image. The photo should also have a broad tonal range and good color detail to help build value and color complexity into the tiles. Swaminathan began with a 675 x 920-pixel photo.

2 Retouching and cloning. To separate the subject from the background, Swaminathan used a modified Digital Airbrush variant of Airbrushes to simplify the background of the photo, adding soft blue and white strokes. He also increased the contrast in the image using Effects, Tonal Control, Brightness/Contrast.

When he was satisfied with the retouching, he cloned the image. Choose File, Clone to make a clone of your source image. In preparation for laying down colored tiles in the clone based on the color of the clone source image, enable the Clone Color checkbox in the Colors section of the Art Materials palette.

3a

Designing a horizontal tile to use on the face

3b

Using Tracing Paper to view the clone source while positioning tiles on the clone

4a

Erasing a course of tiles in the hair

4b

Adding new irregular tiles in the hair

3 Laying tiles. With the clone active, open the Make Mosaic dialog box (Canvas, Make Mosaic), and enable the Use Tracing Paper box so you can see the source image while laying down the tiles. To change the Grout from the default from white to black, click the Grout square and in the Select Grout Color dialog box and move the Lightness slider all the way to the left. To design a custom tile, begin by setting Dimensions for the tile; choose a Width, Length and Grout size. Make a stroke on your image to test the settings. Press Ctrl/⌘-Z to Undo a test stroke without closing the Make Mosaic dialog box. Experiment with the settings until you get just the look you want.

Swaminathan began with the face, which would become the focal point of the mosaic portrait. As he worked, he varied the size of the tiles, using larger tiles for the broader areas of the face (the forehead and cheeks), and smaller tiles to render detailed areas (the shadowed right side of the man's nose, eyes and eyebrows).

Generally, he worked from the center out, beginning with the face and hair and then rendering the shirt, shoes and background. To depict the long hair (and to contrast with the more uniform shapes of tiles on the subject's jacket) he designed narrow, irregularly shaped tiles. To vary the tile shapes and grout (as Swaminathan did), choose Randomness from the Settings pop-up menu to access the sliders. Begin by moving the Cut slider to the right to increase Randomness in the shape of the tile ends. To vary the spacing between tiles, move the Grout slider to the right. Experiment with each of the sliders individually until you arrive at the look you want.

SAMPLE WITH A CLICK

To sample color from an existing tile in your mosaic (with Clone Color turned off in the Colors section of the Art Materials palette), press the Alt/Option key and click on a tile. You won't see the Mosaic brush's crosshair cursor change to the Dropper when you're working with the open Make Mosaic dialog box, but you *will* be able to sample the color.

CORRECTION SHORTCUT

To remove tiles without clicking the Remove Tiles icon, press the Ctrl-Shift/⌘-Shift keys and drag the Mosaic brush over the tiles that you want to remove.

4 Completing the image. To refine the tile design, Swaminathan sampled color from existing tiles and applied the color to new tiles. (Before sampling color from a tile, turn off Clone Color in the Colors section then press the Alt/Option key and click on a tile). To erase tiles, click the Remove Tiles icon and drag the cursor over the tiles that you want to remove. Click back on the Apply Tiles icon and drag to add new tiles.

Adding highlights and shadows. Finally, Swaminathan used Apply Surface Texture to add realistic highlights and shadows like those you would see on the slightly uneven surface of handmade tiles. Choose Effects, Surface Control, Apply Surface Texture Using Image Luminance. Try these subtle settings: Softness, 0; Amount, 20; Picture 100; Shine, 25; and Reflection, 0. Click OK.

Creating a Tidepool

***Overview** Create a sandy background; spray plants onto the ocean floor using the Image Hose; light the scene; combine special effects to "ripple the water."*

Wheat Stalks texture applied to the blank image (left), then Super Softened

Applying Surface Texture with Original Luminance to the sand-colored clone

The Pressure Plant nozzle file with images from small to large size

The Expression section with Size and Rank 1 set to Pressure

JOHN DERRY

THE ILLUSION OF LIGHT REFRACTING through water is essential to creating a realistic underwater scene. In *Tidepool*, after using a variety of Image Hose nozzles to paint undersea plant life, John Derry engineered the look of rippling water by applying Lighting, Glass Distortion and Surface Texture to the image.

1 Creating a soft sandy bottom. To begin as Derry did, open a new 1200-pixel-wide image with a white background. Select black in the Colors section of the Art Materials palette, choose Wheat Stalks paper texture in the Papers section of the Art Materials palette (loaded from the Textures 1 library located in the Paper Textures folder on the Painter_CD2 CD-ROM). Scale it to 400% using the Size slider. Apply the black texture to your file with Effects, Surface Control, Color Overlay, Using Paper and Hiding Power at 100% Opacity. Derry liked the Wheat Stalks texture but felt it needed softening to look like rippled sand. Soften the background by choosing Effects, Focus, Super Soften; enter 12 when the dialog box appears. Click OK.

2 Giving the rippled sand color and texture. To make the background look like sand, you can combine a sand-colored file with the gray rippled image. First, clone the gray image (File, Clone), choose a sand color and fill the clone with color (Ctrl/⌘-F, Current Color, 100% Opacity). Next, combine the sand-colored clone with the gray image. Go to Effects, Surface Control, Apply Surface Texture and choose Original Luminance. For a subtle effect use these settings: Amount, 25; Picture, 90; Shine, 30. Set the Light Direction at 11 o'clock, Brightness at 1.19, increase Concentration (Conc) to 5.00 (to decrease the spread of the light) and Exposure at 1.41.

3 Loading a nozzle and spraying images. Most of the Image Hose nozzles that Derry used in this piece can be found in the Tidepool Nozzles library on the *Painter 7 Wow!* CD-ROM, in the John Derry's Nozzles folder. To choose an Image Hose nozzle from the current library in the Nozzles section of the Art Materials palette, open the Nozzles section and click on a nozzle. To paint with a

3c

Using short spiral strokes to Spray plants and pebbles onto the sandy ocean floor

4

Creating a soft, diffused custom light

5a

Applying Glass Distortion to initiate the ripple effect

5b

Adding Surface Texture to complete the illusion of rippling water

nozzle, select the Image Hose icon in the Brushes palette and begin painting. To make a nozzle spray in a specific way, change the hose variant in the Brushes palette or use the controls in the Expression section of the Brush Controls palette.

Load the Tidepool library from the *Painter 7 Wow!* CD-ROM by choosing Load Library from the bottom of the nozzle list on the Nozzles section. For the undersea image, choose the Pressure Plants nozzle, select the Image Hose icon and paint with short, spiral strokes in your image. Derry added strokes to the piece using a number of nozzles: Shadowed Coral, Pastel Coral, Shiny Coral, Pointed Plant, Nasturtium, Pressure Plants and Pebbles. See Chapter 9 in the *Painter 7 User Guide* to learn how to create your own Image Hose nozzle.

INDIVIDUAL NOZZLE FILES

To load an individual nozzle that isn't part of a library, press Ctrl/⌘-L while the Image Hose is chosen (or choose Load Nozzle from the menu accessed by clicking the right triangle on the Nozzles section bar), open a folder containing nozzle files and open a nozzle. Once you've loaded a nozzle, you can choose to add it to the current library (Add to Library), or view it (Check Out Nozzle) from the menu on the Nozzles section bar.

4 Applying Lighting. To create a diffused lighting effect with soft pockets of light and dark areas, Derry modified an existing light, copied it four times, then modified the individual lights. To create a look similar to the one he achieved, choose Effects, Surface Control, Apply Lighting, Slide Lighting. Reduce the Brightness, Distance and Spread settings, then click on two new locations in the Preview window to create two more lights with settings identical to the original. To reposition a light, drag on the large circle, and to aim the light in a new direction, drag on the small circle. Make further modifications to one of the three lights, then click in the Preview window two more times to create two more lights with those new settings, making a total of five lights. To create a softer effect on the whole scene, drag the Exposure slider to the left and the Ambient slider to the right. Store your custom light in the library by clicking the Save button, then click OK to apply the lighting to the image.

5 Creating a water ripple effect. Derry used a powerful but subtle combination of Glass Distortion and Apply Surface Texture to create a realistic water ripple effect. To ripple your image, in the Papers section choose the Seismic texture loaded from the Wild Textures library (in the Paper Textures folder on the Painter_CD2 CD-ROM) and scale it to 400%. Now select Effects, Focus, Glass Distortion using Paper and accept the default settings of Amount, 0 and Variance, 1.00, with the Refraction Map type. To add a subtle bump to the transparent water ripple, choose Effects, Surface Control, Apply Surface Texture using Paper: Amount, 22%; Picture, 100%; and Shine, 0%. Click the 11 o'clock Light Direction button to set a general light direction. 🖌️

Draping a Weave

Overview *Paint a grayscale file that will be your source image; fill a clone of that file with a weave; use a combination of Glass Distortion and Surface Texture to wrap the weave around the source image.*

CHER THREINEN-PENDARVIS

The grayscale form file with strong values

The Art Materials Palette Preferences dialog box showing the Weaves checkbox enabled

YOU CAN USE PAINTER'S WEAVES, located in the Weaves section of the Art Materials palette, to fill any selection or document, using either the Fill command or the Paint Bucket tool. Weaves can be used in fashion design and they make good backgrounds for scenes, but their flat look can be a drawback. To create the appearance of fabric—to hang behind a still life, for instance—we added dimension to a weave by "draping" it over a painted form using a powerful Glass Distortion displacement effect along with Apply Surface Texture.

DISPLAY THE WEAVES SECTION

If the Weaves section isn't visible in the Art Materials palette, choose Edit, Preferences, Palettes and from the pop-up menu choose Art Materials. In the Art Materials Palette Preferences dialog box enable the Weaves checkbox.

1 Making the form file. Think of the form file as a kind of mold—or fashion designer's dress form—over which you'll drape your fabric. Create a grayscale form file that has strong value contrast and smooth dark-to-light transitions. As a reference for our 500-pixel-square form file, we draped fabric over a chair and sketched it in Painter, then cleaned up the sketch with the Digital Airbrush variant of Airbrushes. Since any hard edges in the form file would make a noticeable break in the weave's pattern, we softened the image with Effects, Focus, Super Soften. We used a 7-pixel Super Soften setting on our file.

Choosing a weave in the Weaves section

Filling the clone with the weave

Applying Glass Distortion to the weave

Adding highlights and shadows to the distorted image using Surface Texture

If you don't want to paint the form file, here's a fast, but less "organic" way to create it. Open the Make Paper dialog box by clicking the right triangle on the Papers section of the Art Materials palette. Choose Line from the pop-up menu, use a high spacing setting and to make vertical lines, set Angle at 90°. In the Save As field, type a name for the new paper. Choose it in the Papers section and choose black in the Colors section. Then select Effects, Surface Control, Color Overlay, Using Paper and Hiding Power at 100% Opacity. Use Super Soften as described above.

2 Making a clone and filling it with a weave. Choose File, Clone to make a duplicate of the form file with identical dimensions. Now choose a weave from the Weaves section of the Art Materials palette. When the Weaves section is visible, choose a weave in the Weaves section, and fill the clone with your weave (Ctrl/⌘-F, Weave, 100%). We used the Baird 4 weave from the Scottish Tartans library (loaded from the Weaves folder on the Painter_CD2 CD-ROM).

3 Initiating the distortion. Here's where the movement begins. Choose Effects, Focus, Glass Distortion, Using Original Luminance. Now let Painter know the direction that you want the fabric to go when it overlies the form file. When a clone image is displaced by Glass Distortion using Original Luminance, the distance each pixel moves is based on the luminance of each pixel in the source file. We chose Vector Displacement to move pixels in a specific direction, and used the Amount slider to get a moderate "ripple" effect in the Preview (we chose 1.54), leaving Variance at 1.00. To establish the direction (and make the light areas move up and to the right, dark areas move down and to the left—based on the form file), we moved the Direction slider to 80°. We added a Softness of 15.2 to smooth any rough edges that might be caused by the distortion of the weave. Experiment with your settings; the Softness, Amount and Direction may change based on the size of your file.

4 Adding highlights and shadows. Using Apply Surface Texture adds to the illusion of folded fabric by contributing highlights and shadows based on the form file. Choose Effects, Surface Control, Apply Surface Texture, Using Original Luminance. Experiment with your settings—paying special attention to how the lighting controls affect the look—and click OK. We set Softness to 20.3 (to smooth the image and slightly increase the depth of the folds), Amount to 151%, Picture to 100% (to make the image lighter while maintaining weaving detail), and Shine to 0%, then chose the 9 o'clock Light Direction button.

■ **Chelsea Sammel** created *Wonderful Hands* using Painter's Water Color, Felt Pens, Dry Media and F-X variants, which were applied over the Hand Made paper texture (loaded from the ver 6 paper library in the Painter 7 application folder). Sammel created the illustration using three layers. First, she sketched the composition using a variety of Water Color brushes on a Water Color layer. When the sketch was complete, she converted the Water Color layer to a standard layer by choosing Convert To Default Layer from the menu on the right side of the Objects palette's Layers section

bar. Then she added more color to areas behind the hands using a custom Conté variant that was based on the Artist Pastel Chalk variant of Dry Media. To blend the new brushstrokes with the dried water-color, she used the Grainy Water variant of Liquid. Next, she added a new empty layer to her image by clicking the right triangle on the Objects palette's Layers section bar and choosing New Layer from the menu. On the new layer, she painted more brightly colored brushwork around the hearts and hands using the Felt Marker variant of Felt Pens. To add more color and

effects, she made another new layer and painted strokes using F-X variants: She used the Glow variant to brighten the dark areas around the hands and hearts, and to break up edges she used the Confusion variant. To add an embossed texture around the hands, she brushed lightly with the Add Grain variant of the Photo brush. To add more paper texture to the layer with the watercolor and Conté brushstrokes, she chose Effects, Surface Control, Apply Surface Texture, Using Paper. As a final touch, Sammel painted a few brushstrokes with a small Spatter Water variant of Water Color.

■ **Hiroshi Yoshii** is known for his fantastic characters and animals and his unique illustration style. Yoshii created *Party* using Painter's Dry Media and Liquid variants, which were applied over the Ribbed Pastel paper texture (loaded from the ver 6 paper library in the Painter 7 application folder). When working with the Dry Media variants in Painter 7.1, Yoshii prefers to disable the Directional Grain checkbox in the Papers section of the Art Materials palette, because he can achieve more control over the grain while modeling the forms of his characters. He began by drawing a tight black-and-white sketch of his composition using the Sharp Chalk variant of Dry Media. Then he used the Sharp Chalk and Large Chalk variants of Dry Media to color the drawing. Yoshii carefully built up layers of chalky strokes so that the paper texture would be preserved. To softly blend areas, he used the Just Add Water variant of Liquid. He also added details and redefined edges using a tiny Sharp Chalk. Finally, to further enhance the grainy effect, he chose Effects, Surface Control, Apply Surface Texture Using Paper, with subtle settings.

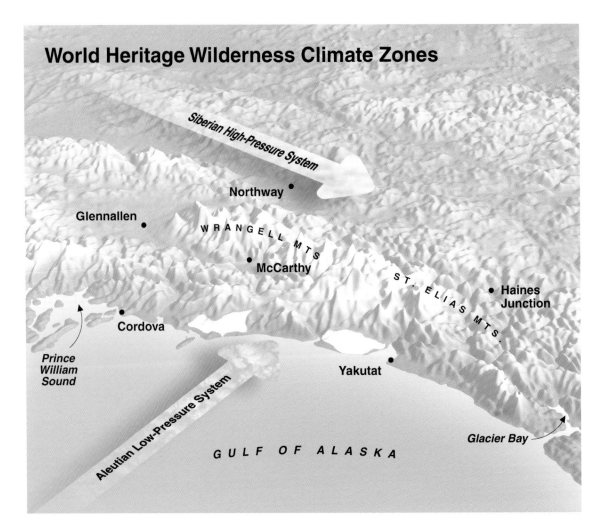

World Heritage Wilderness Climate Zones

Siberian High-Pressure System

Northway

Glennallen

WRANGELL MTS

McCarthy

ST. ELIAS MTS.

Haines Junction

Cordova

Prince William Sound

Yakutat

Aleutian Low-Pressure System

Glacier Bay

GULF OF ALASKA

■ Alaska Geographic commissioned **Steven Gordon** to create this weather map of south-central Alaska for their publication *World Heritage Wilderness*. Using the process described on page 253, Gordon created a grayscale PICT of the terrain and colored it with Painter's Express in Image command from the Gradients section of the Art Materials palette. In Bryce, Gordon used a copy of the original grayscale terrain PICT to create the perspective landscape. He imported the color PICT he had made in Painter and wrapped the landscape with it. Back in Painter, Gordon imported the landscape and created a coastline vignette with the masking tools. To begin the three-dimensional arrows, Gordon drew shapes in FreeHand, and saved the file as a PICT. He used Bryce to help visualize the three-dimensional arrows, as follows: He opened the file in Bryce, where the arrows became 3D objects and part of an overall scene.

When he had positioned the arrows the way he wanted them and the scene's view and lighting were set, he saved the scene as a Photoshop file, and then opened it in Painter. Gordon wanted to use the Bryce file as a guide for tracing, so he cloned it (File, Clone), deleted the contents of the clone (Ctrl/⌘-A and Backspace/Delete), and turned on Tracing Paper (Ctrl/⌘-T). Then he used Painter's Pen tool to trace the two arrow shapes and he used the shapes to make selections (Shapes, Convert To Selection). For the clouds in the arrows, he dragged and dropped an image of clouds (taken with a digital camera on a warm spring morning) into the composite file. He used the arrow selections to capture the imagery from the cloud layer by activating the layer, loading the selection (Select, Load Selection), and Alt/Option clicking with the Layer Adjuster tool to copy the selected area of the clouds image to a

new floating object. To make the floating object into a standard layer, he dragged it above the layer it was copied from in Layers section. To differentiate the two kinds of cloud masses represented by the arrows, he used the Effects, Tonal Control, Adjust Color feature to make the moisture-laden Aleutian Low grayer, and the drier Siberian High bluer. To complete the illusion of depth, Gordon added drop shadows to the arrows using Painter's Effects, Objects, Create Drop Shadow command. Next, he used the Digital Airbrush variant of Airbrushes to spray the two white glacier fields with light blue color. To finish, he flattened the layers in his file by choosing Drop All from the Layers command menu (accessed by clicking the right arrow on the Layers section bar). Gordon saved the Painter image as a TIFF file and placed it in FreeHand, where he added the rivers, the type and the leader arrows.

■ **Chet Phillips** created *Haiku* for *Service Workstation Expert* magazine. He expressively drew a black-and-white illustration with the Scratchboard Tool variant of Pens, much as he would use an ink pen on paper. Then he cut the black-and-white drawing to a separate layer by choosing Select, All, then Select, Float. Next, he composited the layer using the Gel Composite Method, chosen from the Composite Method menu in the Layers section of the Objects palette. He selected the Canvas in the Layers section and used the Airbrushes and Dry Media variants in varying sizes to color the background. He added light blue airbrush strokes to the right edge of the computer monitor to simulate a glow and painted the dark blue sky and the lake area with the Artist Pastel Chalk variant of Dry

Media. When the coloring was complete, Phillips merged the layers by clicking on the black-and-white drawing layer name in the Layers section and choosing Drop from the pop-out menu on the right side of the Layers bar on the Objects palette. For the look of an antique woodcut print, Phillips applied subtle paper textures to the image using special effects. He sampled a dark brown color from his image using the Dropper tool and chose Effects, Surface Control, Color Overlay, Using Paper and the Hiding Power option, with a very low opacity setting. He then applied several additional applications of Color Overlay with different textures using the dark brown. The built up Color Overlay applications simulated the texture that a wood block print receives when it rubs against the grain of the wood.

■ *Creative Journey,* conceived by **Brian Moose,** is a narrative illustration that incorporates many of Painter's special effects. The narrative begins on the left of the image with a pencil sketch of a night sky and the moon over a sea of creativity. Then it evolves through many areas of Painter—pastel, pen-and ink, airbrush, oil, and impasto, and mosaic tiles—and finally culminates with a stained-glass effect and the "creative destination." Moose used a broad range of Painter's brushes and special effects to realize his concept: He used Painter's Airbrushes when painting the auroras in the starry sky. Using a soft-edged Pattern Pen to paint with the

current pattern in the Patterns section of the Art Materials palette, he painted the snake-like patterns next to the can boat and the string patterns in the water. Moose used the Fire and Glow variants of the F-X brush to paint highlights and glows around the tips of the brushes. For the liquid flowing out of the can, he drew a filled shape with the Pen tool. (The options for filling a shape as you draw are accessible by choosing Edit, Preferences.) He converted the shape to a layer (Shapes, Convert To Layer). To give the liquid some dimension, he manipulated the layer's mask, as follows: He clicked on the mask's name (Shape 1 Mask) in the

Masks section of the Objects palette and opened its eye icon. Using the Digital Air-brush variant of Airbrushes, he painted soft white and black strokes to represent high and low areas. He closed the eye icon and deselected the mask by clicking on the Layer's name (RGB-Shape 1) in the Masks section, and with the layer still selected in the Layers section, he added relief to the liquid flowing from the can. He used the mask information to determine how the texture was applied. Moose chose Effects, Surface Control, Apply Surface Texture, choosing Shape 1 Mask from the Using pop-up menu.

■ **Jeremy Sutton**'s colorful image *Love Getaway* began with an original photo shot by Celeste Dobbins of CelestePhotoArt.com. Sutton opened the photograph in Painter and saved a copy of the image, which he cropped to suit his design. He cloned the cropped image by choosing File, Clone. To give the image its bright color, he clicked the right triangle on the Art Materials palette's Gradients section bar and chose Express sin Image. With the Express in Image dialog box open, he experimented by choosing gradients in the

Gradients section of the Art Materials palette and adjusting the Bias slider. He finally settled on a brightly colored spectrum gradient and clicked OK to accept. At this point Sutton saved the colored image. Next, he made a selection to isolate the wedding couple and motorcycle from the background in the colored image and saved the selection as a mask in the Masks section of the Objects palette (Select, Save Selection) so he could use it later. To create the texture on the background, he floated a copy of the back-

ground to a Water Color Layer by choosing Lift Canvas To Water Color Layer from the menu on the right side of the Objects palette's Layers section bar. Once the background was on a Water Color layer, he loaded the selection of the couple (Select, Load Selection) and pressed the Delete key to delete the couple, leaving the background. Sutton painted with several Water Color brushes, creating textures. Then he dropped the layer to the image canvas by choosing Drop from the menu on the right side of the Layers section bar. Next, he cloned the image with the watercolor brushwork, naming the new clone and giving it a unique name. Then he reset the clone source to the version of the image he had colored with the Gradient, by choosing File, Clone Source and choosing the colored image from the menu. Next, he chose Select, Load Selection to activate a selection of the couple and motorcycle. Using the Cloners brushes, he cloned the wedding couple and motorcycle back into the final image.

■ *Art in Wartime* by **Steve Campbell**
began as a low-resolution sketch of a sax
player drawn during a trade show demo.
"Once I decided to work up the original
image at higher resolution, I knew I was
going to add a rain of bombs falling as
my hero plays his sax," says Campbell,
Before adding the bombs and other elements, he used the Studio Artist program
to render the image at the higher resolution of 300 pixels per inch and also to
create a rough, complex textures at the
new size. When the processing was complete, Campbell opened the new image
in Painter and isolated the figure and
background elements, by making selections using the Lasso tool and floating
the elements to layers. (Alt/Option-click

on an active selection with the Layer
Adjuster tool to cut it to a layer.)
Campbell painted the rainbow using
Brushes variants. With a custom Image
Hose he painted the flora at the sax
player's feet. Using the File, Place command, he added the 3D bombs that were
created in Ray Dream Studio, placing
them as several layers. The city in the
background was drawn with Painter's
Shape tools and its layers were given par-
tial transparency (as were some of the
bombs layers), by adjusting their Opacity
in the Layers section. Campbell painted
and sketched using several Brushes variants and smudged using the Just Add
Water variant of Liquid on the figure.
Then he adjusted the Composite Method

for some of the layers. He used the Digital Airbrush variant of Airbrushes to paint
smoky clouds. When he was finished
working on the layers, he combined the
sky, bombs and city layers into one layer
by choosing Group from the Layer Commands pop-up menu at the bottom of
the Layers section, then choosing Collapse from the same menu. Next, he created a copy of the same layer, by choosing Select, All, then Alt/Option-clicking it
with the Layer Adjuster tool. He used
Effects, Surface Control, Apply Lighting
on this layer, and then adjusted the
strength of the lighting effect on the
image by reducing the Opacity of the
"lighted" layer.

■ To create the surreal photo-collage *Coney Island Baby*, **Laurence Gartel** began by scanning each of the source photos into Photoshop, where he made selections to isolate the subjects from their backgrounds. He opened a large new blank file, copied each component image and pasted it onto its own layer in the composite. Next he opened the layered image in Painter and used the Layer Adjuster tool to position elements until the composition seemed balanced. To build a flashy surreal look, Gartel added several Liquid Metal layers by clicking the Dynamic Plugins button at the bottom of the Layers section and choosing Liquid Metal from the menu. He used the Brush tool in the Liquid Metal dialog box to paint chrome brushstrokes of different

thicknesses on the woman's face, neck and hair and to outline the ice cream cone. To reposition droplets of the chrome, he used the Liquid Metal Selection tool (arrow). He applied Standard Metal and Chrome using the pop-up Map menu in the dialog box. For some of the layers, he increased the Refraction setting to create the look of clear glass. The "live" nature of the Liquid Metal dynamic layers allowed Gartel to finesse the Liquid Metal on each layer until he was satisfied with the effect. When these elements were complete, he converted the dynamic layers into image layers by choosing Convert To Default Layer from the menu accessed by clicking the right triangle on the Layers section bar. To create the granular texture in the lower right

of the image, Gartel made a new layer by choosing New Layer from the same menu, and painted the area with dark gray. With a rough texture chosen in the Papers section of the Art Materials palette, he increased its size using the Scale slider. Then he chose Effects, Surface Control, Apply Surface Texture, Using Paper, with strong settings to apply the texture with highlights, shadows and shine. To complete the image, Gartel changed the Opacity and Composite Method in the Layers section of the Objects palette for a few of the layers (for instance, the purple Liquid Metal droplets in the middle area of the work). (To see more of Gartel's work, turn to the gallery in Chapter 12.)

■ *Musica* (above) and *Obsesión* (right) were created by **Eduardo Diaz**, also known as **Kaffa**. To paint *Musica*, Diaz began by using the Opaque Bristle Spray and Variable Flat variants of Brushes to block in the shapes of the instruments. To blend new color with existing color, he used the Smeary Bristle Spray variant. For crisper lines and edges, he switched to the Calligraphy variant of Pens. Finally, to add three-dimensional highlights and shadows to the paint, he chose Effects, Surface Control, Apply Surface Texture, Using Image Luminance, with moderate settings.

For *Obsesión* Diaz began by blocking in areas of color using the Digital Airbrush variant of Airbrushes. Then, with the Rocky texture chosen in the Papers section of the Art Materials palette, he added textured brushstrokes by brushing lightly with the Gritty Charcoal variant of Dry Media. To draw the hair, eyebrows and lines around the eyes and mouth he used the Scratchboard Tool variant of Pens. For the look of thick, textured paint, he used Effects, Surface Control, Apply Surface Texture, Using Image Luminance with subtle settings. Then he used Apply Surface Texture again, this time Using Paper, with even subtler settings. To further enhance the textured effect on the floating eyes, he made a selection of the eyes with the Lasso tool, then pressed the Alt/Option key and chose Select, Float to put a copy on a new layer. Then he used Apply Surface Texture, Using Image Luminance on the layer.

■ *Trattoria* is an image from **Michela Del Degan's** *Storia 2000* series. Del Degan began the illustration by adding a new empty layer to her image by clicking the triangle on the right side of the Layers section bar (Objects palette). On the new layer, she created a black-and-white sketch using the 2B Pencil variant of Pencils over Basic Paper texture. When the sketch was complete, she colored the image using several layers, often painting an object on its own layer. First, she laid in brown colors over the background using the Chalk variants of Dry Media. For the clock, she began by making oval selections, then filled them with blue and white using the Paint Bucket from the Tools palette, setting the fill color in the Controls:Paint Bucket palette. Using the Sharp Chalk variant of Dry Media, she

redefined the outlines on the clock and drew wood grain and shadows. To add the glassy sheen to the clock face, she used the Digital Airbrush variant of Airbrushes and light gray paint. Next Del Degan colored the plants and other elements with the Smooth Ink Pen variant of Pens, adding highlights with the Digital Airbrush and refining the elements with the Sharp Chalk variant. To add 3D texture to the hat, she selected it with the Magic Wand and chose Effects, Surface Control, Apply Surface Texture Using Paper. Then she drew over it using the Sharp Chalk. She added a new layer, and drew the pasta-eating character using the Smooth Ink Pen and Digital Airbrush, as before. For his hair, she added another new layer, and painted the curls with the Opaque Bristle Spray variant of Brushes.

She smoothed over areas on the face using the Round Camelhair variant of Brushes. The dish of spaghetti and the bread were also drawn with the Smooth Ink Pen. For the embossed effect on the bread, she used the Add Grain variant of the Photo brush over a fine, even-textured paper. Finally, she touched up the outlines of many objects in the illustration with 2B Pencil variant of Pencils. To create the Trattoria sign, she used the same brushes as before using white and red paint. For the highlights on the sign she used Effects, Surface Control, Apply Lighting and the Plain Light choice. Finally, she added a highlight on the character's face using the Dodge variant of the Photo brush. She also used the Dodge variant to paint diagonal strokes across the window to create the illusion of window glass.

8

WORKING WITH TYPE IN PAINTER

Diablo Publishing commissioned Susan LeVan to illustrate an article in Sutter Health *magazine about head injuries. LeVan used Painter's Text layers to build elements for her illustration.*

PAINTER IS A POWERFUL TOOL FOR DESIGNING creative display type and for special effects. With Painter you can set type and put an image inside it; add texture to type; rotate type, stretch it and paint on it; fill and stroke type for a neon look; add type with special effects to your illustration (for a book cover design, for example); and create three-dimensional chrome type for a logo. You can set text on a path, fill the type with a color, add a shadow and much more. This typography primer will help you get the most out Painter's type tools.

A TYPOGRAPHY PRIMER

Painter is not recommended for setting large amounts of text—it's a good idea to leave this task to your favorite page layout program, such as QuarkXPress or PageMaker. Instead, we'll focus on type as a design element using display type, because this is where Painter's tools shine. Display type is generally set in sizes 14-point or larger; it's usually used for feature headlines in magazines, for book covers, for posters and billboards and for Web page headers, to name a few applications.

Fonts and font families. A *font* is a complete set of characters in one size and one typeface. The characters usually include uppercase and lowercase letters, numbers, punctuation and special characters. A *font family* is all of the sizes and style variations of a typeface (for instance, roman and italic styles in light, medium and bold weights).

Serif and sans serif. One way typefaces differ from one another is in the presence or absence of *serifs,* the small cross-strokes on the ends of the strokes that make up the letters. Serif faces were the first typefaces designed for printing. The serifs help our eyes to recognize the shape of a letter sooner and to track horizontally

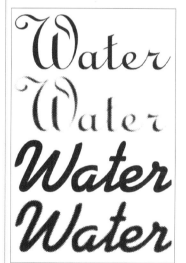

The letter "E," showing the City font family, which includes upper-and lowercase City Light and City Light Italic, City Medium and City Medium Italic and City Bold and City Bold Italic

Serif fonts have small cross-strokes at the ends of the strokes. The letter "G" is shown here in a serif font, Goudy, (left) and a sans serif font, Stone Sans Semibold (right).

The letter "T," demonstrating examples of several type classes. From left to right, top row: Black Letter, Fette Fraktur; Roman, Century Old Style; Slab Serif, City Bold; Bottom row: Script, Reporter Two; Sans Serif, Stone Sans; and Novelty, Arnold Boecklin.

from one letter to the next across a page, which makes these faces typically easier to read than sans serif faces.

The term *sans serif* refers to type without serifs. Usually sans serif fonts have a consistent stroke weight. Because of this quality, they can be ideal for display type because they look good in larger sizes and are good candidates for graphic treatments such as beveling and edge texture application. A sans serif font with very broad strokes has plenty of weight to work with when you apply special effects!

Classes of fonts. Fonts can be further grouped into several classes: Black Letter, Roman, Slab Serif, Sans Serif, Script and Decorative. *Black Letter* type resembles the style of hand-lettering that was popular during the time of Gutenberg's first printing press in 1436; Fette Fraktur is an example. These faces are usually used for an old-fashioned, formal look. Many typefaces fall into the *Roman* classification, including Old Style (for instance, Caslon and Century Old Style), Transitionals (Times Roman), and Modern (Palatino). The Old Style fonts have angled serifs, while the modern Roman faces have straight vertical or horizontal serifs. *Slab Serifs* are also known as Egyptians, and they are characterized by even stroke weights and square serifs (examples are City Bold and Stymie). *Sans Serif*, mentioned earlier, is also considered a classification of type. Examples are Helvetica, Franklin Gothic, Futura and Stone Sans.

Designs for *Script* type were originally inspired by penmanship. Script fonts with dramatic thick-and thin strokes (such as Linoscript) are often not good candidates for special effects because many techniques

We set type using two script fonts, Linoscript (top) and Monoline Script. Our example shows the original typeset word above the type with textured edges. As you can see, the Monoline type kept its integrity of design through the special-effects application because of its thick, even stroke weight, while the thick-and-thin Linoscript did not.

271

Each typeface has its own aesthetic and emotional feel, as shown in this example. With Painter's text you can easily set type in different faces and colors. Shown here, from left to right are Fenice Ultra, Brush Script, Vag Rounded Black and City Medium. In this example, each letter was set on a separate layer so the different fonts could be applied.

John Dismukes employed Painter's airbrushes, selections and layers to hand-letter The 1800 Grand Margarita *logo, shown here in this detail. To view the entire image and more of Dismukes's exceptional work, turn to page 292 in the gallery.*

For the storyboard for The Crossing Guard, *shown here in this detail, Geoff Hull used Painter. To see more of Hull's innovative typography work, turn to the gallery at the end of Chapter 10.*

involve blurring of the edges or beveling, which can destroy the thin strokes. If you'd like to try special effects and still preserve the script typeface, find a font with thick strokes, such as Kaufmann Bold, Monoline Script or Reporter Two. For an example of a logo created using Kaufmann Bold type, then treated with effects that include Apply Surface Texture, turn to "Setting a Logo in Stone," on page 286.

Finally, the *Novelty* category is diverse and graphic. These faces are often used to communicate emotion in special projects like poster designs (Arnold Boecklin and Stencil are examples).

Legibility. Have you ever driven past two billboards and noticed that one was easy to read as you drove by, and the other was not? The easier-to-read one was more *legible* than the other. When it's easy to recognize the words so you can absorb their meaning quickly, the type is legible. Legibility was important when you drove by the billboard, or when you were able to efficiently scan the headlines on the front page of a newspaper this morning.

When you set type in Painter, choose fonts carefully if you intend to manipulate them with special effects. Are you using the typeface simply as an element in a collage, where the letters are employed for graphic purposes only and content is not as important? Or do you plan to set an important, legible headline and enhance it with beveling? If the latter is the case, make sure to choose a font with strong enough strokes to withstand the bevel effects, such as a bold sans serif face. Turn to "Creating Beveled Chrome" on page 282 for a step-by-step example of a three-dimensional chrome effect applied to sans serif type with Painter's Bevel World plug-in.

DESIGNING WITH PAINTER'S TYPE TOOLS

Each type element that you design has its own purpose: a Web page header, a food advertisement in a magazine, a billboard, the headline for a feature story in a magazine or a signage design. Know your client and research the style aesthetics needed for the design. This knowledge will help you choose the tools to use for the project.

Painter's Text is editable, which means you can easily change the size, color, font or content of the text, until you decide to convert the text layer into an image layer so you can paint on it or add special effects, or convert it to shapes so you can edit the outlines or do hand-kerning of the individual letters. Painter can display TrueType or Adobe Type 1

TWO COMBINED INTO ONE

With Painter 7, the functionality of dynamic text and type shapes from earlier versions have been combined into one solution for text. If you like to use type shapes, it's easy to convert a text layer to shapes by choosing Convert Text to Shapes from the menu on the right side of the Layers section bar on the Objects palette.

This Frutiger Black text was set using the Text tool from the Tools palette. It shows the bounding box around the selected type and the insertion point crosshair.

When the Text tool is clicked in the image window, a new Text layer represented by a "T" icon is generated in the Layers section.

The Text section of the Objects palette contains controls for specifying the appearance of the type including setting the Composite Method for the layer, adding a shadow and putting type on a curve.

fonts if the printer font is installed. Painter can't display bitmap fonts because it needs the printer font's outline information to render the text. Each text layer can display a single font.

Setting text in your image. Begin by opening the Objects palette (Window, Show Objects) and click the left arrow on the Text section bar to open the section. Click the cursor anywhere on the image and enter your text. The type will be displayed on a special new Text layer in your image.

Using controls in the Text section, you can specify a font and the size, leading, tracking, and alignment. You can also add a shadow and apply a curve style to the baseline of the type. Any changes that you make will be applied to the entire text layer.

To specify the size, adjust the Point Size slider or click on the number to the right of the slider and enter a numerical value. Adjust the Tracking slider to globally change the spacing between the letters.

To specify the alignment of the text, click the Align Left, Align Center or Align Right icon.

If you'd like to set more than one line of text, press the Return key (without moving the cursor), and Painter will begin a new line of type. To remove the last letter you typed, leave the cursor where it is and press the Backspace/Delete key. To adjust the spacing between multiple baselines of the Text, adjust the Leading slider, or enter a numerical value.

Applying a new color. The current color chosen in the Colors section of the Art Materials palette will automatically be applied to the text as you set it. If you'd like to change the color of the text, make sure that "Text" is chosen in the Settings For menu in the Text section. Choose a new color in the Colors section and the text will update to display the new color.

Adding a shadow. When you'd like to add a shadow to your type, click the Outside Shadow or Inside Shadow icon in the Text

Choosing 200-point Frutiger Black in the Controls:Text palette

This type was set along a path using the Curve Perpendicular style.

section. By default, a black shadow will be applied and in the Settings For menu, Shadow will automatically be chosen. To adjust the opacity or the softness of a shadow, use the Opacity and Blur sliders. To blur the shadow more on one edge than on the opposite edge, enable the Directional Blur checkbox and adjust the Angle slider. For a colored shadow, choose a new color in the Colors section.

Setting type on a curve. The Text controls in Painter 7 include the capability to create a Bézier path for the type baseline right in Text section. To begin, enter your type on the image. To place the type on a curve, click on a non-straight Curve Style icon: The first icon is Curve Straight, which will not create a curve. The other three icons will generate a curved baseline and allow you to edit the baseline using Bézier curves: the Curve Ribbon style specifies that the vertical strokes of the type will be straight up, and Curve Perpendicular places each character perpendicular to the curve, without distorting the letters. The fourth option, Curve Stretch, distorts the shape of individual letters to fit the space created by the bend of a curve. Use the Centering slider at the bottom of the Text section to move the type along the baseline curve. See "Setting Text on a Curve" on page 278 for a step-by-step description of the process.

Converting Text to Shapes. After you set type with Painter's Text tool, you can convert each letter that you set to an individual vector object on its own layer by choosing Convert Text to Shapes from the menu on right side of the Layers section bar. Shapes have certain advantages over

The Curve Ribbon style chosen in the Text section of the Objects palette allowed us to rotate this text set in the Bauer Bodoni Italic font around a path. We set text and clicked the Curve Ribbon button to place the text on the curve. Then we used the Add Point tool to add an anchor point near the center of the path and used the Shape Selection tool to manipulate the path.

SELECTING A WORD

To select an entire word on a text layer so you can edit it, begin by clicking on the Text layer's name in the Layers section, then double-click on the word with Text tool to select it.

Double-clicking with the Text tool

MOVING A SHADOW

After adding a shadow to type, if you'd like to move the shadow, click on the shadow with the Layer Adjuster tool and drag in the image.

We dragged the shadow slightly down and to the right.

SLANTING OR ROTATING TYPE

In Painter 7 you can skew or rotate type easily. After you've completed setting the type, choose the Layer Adjuster tool in the Tools palette. To rotate it, press the Ctrl/⌘ key and drag on a corner handle. To slant the type, press the Ctrl/⌘ key and drag on the top or bottom handle.

This Futura Extra Bold type was slanted by pressing the Ctrl/⌘ key and dragging the bottom handle to the left.

We created this clear, embossed look by setting text in the Machine Bold font, converting it to an image layer, then using Apply Surface Texture and Composite methods.

PHOTO: CORBIS IMAGES

type: They have editable Bézier curve outlines and unique transparency capabilities. You can stroke and fill them, then change fill and stroke. As with type, you can rotate them without loss of quality. Because each letter is a separate element, it's easy to do custom kerning of the individual letterforms, which isn't possible with text.

Convert text to shapes when setting small amounts of type, when you want to pay special attention to spacing between individual letters, or when you want to edit the outline shape of the letters. Also, shapes are useful when you want to make a quick selection or mask from type (Shapes, Convert To Selection)—for instance, when you want to put an image inside of the type. (For more information about shapes, turn to "Working With Shapes," in the beginning of Chapter 5.)

When to convert text to pixels. If you'd like to paint on type, add special effects such as Apply Surface Texture or manipulate a layer visibility mask on the type layer to erode the edges of the type, you'll need to convert the text layer to an image layer. To convert a text layer to an image layer, choose Convert To Default layer from the menu on the right side of the Objects palette's Layers section bar. If you attempt to paint on a text layer without converting it, a Commit dialog box will appear, asking if you would like to convert the text layer to an image layer. Click Commit to convert it.

To create this painted text, we began by setting type in the Sand font and converted it into an image layer by choosing Convert To Default layer from the menu on the right side of the Layers section bar. The Opaque Round variant of Brushes vas used to add colored brushstrokes.

To make the type break up into sharp ice shards, we set type on a Text layer using Futura Extra Bold, then painted on the type with the Shattered variant of the F-X brush, clicking the Commit button when the warning dialog box appeared.

PHOTO: CORBIS IMAGES

AN ORGANIZATIONAL GROUP

When you convert text to shapes, Painter sets each character's shape on a separate layer and automatically groups the text on the layer into one group. The group makes it possible to move individual characters or to move the type as a unit. And a bonus: the group will be named after the text it was derived from. For more information about working with shapes, turn to the beginning of Chapter 5.

GO FOR CONSISTENT-LOOKING LETTER SPACING

Kerning is the process of removing or adding space between pairs of letters so that the spacing is *visually* consistent. To kern type visually, train your eye to see the negative spaces *between* the letters. After adjusting the spacing, the spacing should appear balanced. To hand-kern individual letters in Painter, you must convert the text layer to shapes by choosing Convert Text to Shapes from the menu on the right side of the Layers section bar on the Objects palette. Using the Layer Adjuster tool select each shape in the Layers section of the Objects palette and move it using the arrow keys on your keyboard.

This text was set in Meta Bold. The original text had "uneven" letterspacing (top), so it was converted to individual shapes and kerned to tighten the spacing and to make it more consistent (bottom).

Putting Type Over a Photo

Overview *Set headline type, scale and position it; draw a rectangular shape and use it to lighten an area of your image to make the body copy on top of it more readable; adjust the opacity of the type.*

The settings in the top of the Text section of the Objects palette

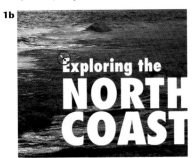

Scaling the text proportionally by Shift-dragging on a corner handle

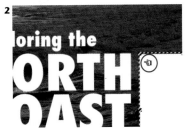

Positioning the text box using the Layer Adjuster tool

The lower portion of the Text section of the Objects palette showing the reduced opacity of the type

PAINTER OFFERS MANY TECHNIQUES to make text and other objects stand out against a background. Here's one of our favorite methods, applied to a comp for a magazine layout.

1 Preparing the type. Open your photo, select the Text tool and open the Text section of the Objects palette by clicking on the left triangle on the Text section bar. In the Text section, choose a typeface from the Font pop-up menu (we chose Futura Condensed Extra Bold). Choose a size using the Point Size slider. To fill the type with white as you set it, select white in the Colors section of the Art Materials palette. Then click in your image and type your headline. To adjust the spacing between the letters, use the Tracking slider. When you're finished, you can use the Layer Adjuster to move the text. To scale the text interactively, make sure the text layer is selected in the Layers section, position the Layer Adjuster tool over a corner of a text layer and when the arrow cursor appears, press the Shift key (to scale proportionally) and drag.

2 Adding the text bar. We wanted a text box we could reposition to try out different layout options, so we drew a white-filled rectangle with the Rectangular Shape tool. After drawing your rectangular shape, use the Layer Adjuster tool to move or resize it.

3 Adjusting the opacity.
Finally, get the "screened-back" look by selecting the shape in the Layers section of the Objects palette and adjusting the Opacity slider in the Layers section. We set ours to 70%. We also selected each text layer in the Layers section and adjusted their opacity using the Opacity slider in the Text section of the Objects palette. 🐾

SEE-THROUGH LAYERS

You can use the keyboard to change the opacity of an image layer or a shape. Select the layer in the Layers section of the Objects palette, choose the Layer Adjuster tool and press 1 for 10% opacity, 2 for 20%, and so on. Lowering a layer's opacity temporarily can help you position it over a background template.

Putting an Image Inside of Type

Overview *Open an image; choose a font and set type; select an area of the background based on the outlines of the type; clear the background, leaving the type filled with the image.*

1a

The type set on the image

1b

Moving the Tracking slider to the left to tighten the spacing between the letters

2

Moving the text layer with the Layer Adjuster tool

3

The selection marquee is visible on the image after Drop and Select has been chosen.

YOU CAN PUT AN IMAGE INSIDE OF TYPE quickly in Painter 7. Here's an easy method, applied to a comp for a travel poster.

1 Choosing an image and picking a font. Open an image with a focal point that will fit into the letterforms you plan to set. Choose File, Save As, to save a copy of the image under a new name to preserve the original image. The type will be set in the current color chosen in the Colors section Art Materials palette, so choose a color that will stand-out against the image. (The color will disappear later, in step 3.) Pick a font with very thick strokes (we chose Futura Extra Bold), so there will be plenty of area to display the image. Choose the Text tool in the Tools palette and open the Text section of the Objects palette by clicking the left triangle on the Text section bar. In the Text section, choose a font and size; then set your type. If you'd like to adjust the spacing between the letters (as we did), use the Tracking slider in the Text section.

2 Positioning the type. So you can see the image information through the letters, lower the opacity of the type using the Opacity slider in the Text section. Choose the Layer Adjuster tool in the Tools palette and experiment with placement by dragging the type on the image until a recognizable portion of the image is visible through the reduced opacity type. Because the type is still "live text" you can adjust the size, tracking or other parameters at any time.

3 Capturing the image inside the type. Now that the type is where you'd like it, convert the text layer to an image layer: Click the right triangle on the Layers section bar and choose Convert To Default Layer from the pop-out menu. Now adjust the Opacity in the Layers section to 0%. The layer visibility has disappeared, but you can still use the edges of the pixels on the layer to make a selection based on your text: Click the right triangle on the Layers section bar and choose Drop and Select from the pop-out menu. To reverse the selection so the background is selected, choose Select, Invert. Finally, delete the background by choosing (Backspace/Delete). 🎨

TYPE LAYER OPACITY CONTROL

Opacity of a type layer does not change when you have the Layer Adjuster chosen and you use the Opacity slider in the Controls: Adjuster palette. So you will have to change the opacity in the Text section of the Objects palette.

Setting Text on a Curve

Overview *Set the text; choose a Curve Style; use the Shape Selection tool to finesse the length and shape of the path; adjust the text on the path.*

We set type using the Sand font and used the Tracking slider to tighten letterspacing.

Choosing the Curve Stretch style

Using the Shape Selection tool to pull an end point, and lengthen the curve

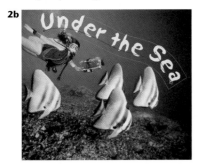

With two more points added, the curve is taking shape.

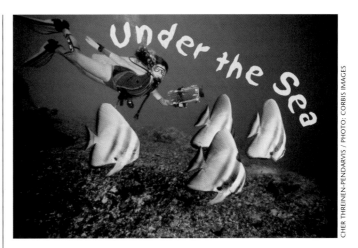

IT'S A SNAP TO SET TEXT ON A CURVE in Painter. The Text controls in Painter 7 allow you to create a Bézier path for the type baseline right in the image window. Here's a quick method, applied to a comp for an advertising layout.

1 Setting the type and applying it to a curve. For this technique you can begin with a new blank image, or start with a photo, as we did. Choose the Text tool in the Tools palette and open the Text section of the Objects palette by clicking the left triangle on the Text section bar. In the Text section of the Objects palette, choose a font and size and set your type. We chose the typeface Sand, because its organic shape and playful feel would work well with the Curve Stretch curve style we planned to use.

Click on the Curve Stretch button in the Text section and you'll see the text curving around the baseline of a newly generated path in your image. The Curve Stretch curve style distorts the letters to fit the spaces in the curve. The slight distortion added to the ripply underwater effect. To reposition the text layer on the image, use the Layer Adjuster tool.

2 Adjusting the path. To change the shape of the path, choose the Shape Selection tool in the Tools palette (it's the hollow arrow that's nested under the Layer Adjuster), select the text layer in the Layers section of the Objects palette and click on an end point. Pull on the end point to lengthen the path. To change the shape of the curve, drag a control handle in the direction that you want the curve to go. As you manipulate the path, aim for gentle curves so the type will flow smoothly.

To add more anchor points (for instance, to make a gentle wavy line, like we did), choose the Add Point tool in the Tools palette and click the baseline curve. To remove a point, choose the Delete Point tool in the Tools palette and click the anchor point. Use the control handles on each anchor point to finesse the curve. To adjust the position of the text on the path, use the Centering slider in the Text section. We set Centering at 2%.

A Spattery Graffiti Glow

Overview *Use the Text tool to set text over a background; convert the text to an image layer, then to selections; stroke the selections using the Draw Outside mode, to spatter the background outside the type.*

WITH THE HELP OF PAINTER'S TEXT LAYERS, selections and Draw modes you can stroke around the edges of type with an Airbrush to create this fast, fun title solution.

1 Choosing an image and setting type. Open an image to use as a background; our photo was 864 x 612 pixels. Choose the Text tool in the Tools palette, then select a font and size in the Controls: Text palette. (We chose 200-point Berthold City Bold Italic.) Click in the image and begin typing. If the Layers section of the Objects palette is open, you'll see a text layer appear when you begin typing. To adjust the spacing between the letters, open the Text section of the Objects palette and adjust the Tracking slider.

The text set in City Bold Italic

2 Converting the text to selections. To achieve the result at the top of this page, it's necessary to convert the text to an image layer, then to selections. Select the text layer in the Layers section, click the right triangle on the Layers section bar and choose Convert To Default Layer from the menu. Now reduce the opacity of the layer to 0% using the Opacity slider in the Layers section and choose Drop and Select from the menu on the right side of the Layers section bar. The layer will disappear from the list in the Layers section and will reappear as animated marquees. To prepare the selection for stroking, choose Select, Transform Selection.

The selection marquee created from the layer

Choosing the Pixel Spray variant of the Airbrushes

3 Stroking outside of the selection. With the help of Painter's nifty Draw icons in the bottom left of the image window, we used a brush to stroke around the edge of the selection. The Draw icons allow you to use a selection just as you would a traditional airbrush frisket, to paint inside or outside of the selection. From the pop-up in the bottom left corner of the image window, choose the Draw Outside (center) icon. In the Brushes palette choose the Pixel Spray variant of the Airbrushes. (We increased the size of the brush to 60 pixels, using the Size slider on the Controls:Brush palette.) Choose white in the Colors section of the Art Materials palette, then choose Select, Stroke Selection and watch as Painter gives your type a fine grained, spattery glow. Try stroking your selection with other Airbrushes such as the Coarse Spray or the Variable Spatter variant. 🖌

Selecting the Draw Outside mode and stroking outside the active selection

Stroked and Glowing

***Overview** Create a dark, textured background; use the Text tool to set text; convert the text to shapes; apply a fill and stroke; make two copies of the shapes and convert each to a layer; feather the layer masks; fill each of the two glow layers with a color to create soft glows.*

CHER THREINEN-PENDARVIS

1a

Choosing Track Lighting in the Apply Lighting dialog box

1b

Adding Surface Texture to the background

2

The grouped cherry-red type shapes on the completed background

PAINTER IS THE IDEAL TOOL FOR CREATING quick design solutions. When building these color comprehensives for a new restaurant's signage, we created a variety of solutions using Painter's text and shapes wit strokes and glows. Here are two of them.

1 Making the background. Open a new file (ours was 883 x 675 pixels) and fill the image canvas with a dark color (but not black) in the Colors section of the Art Materials palette and then choosing Effects, Fill, Fill With Current Color. (Neon glows best at night!)

We added atmosphere to the background—simulating track lighting on a stucco wall—by applying two effects that Painter is famous for: Apply Lighting and Surface Texture. First we turned on the lights by choosing Effects, Surface Control, Apply Lighting. We chose Track Lighting, accepted the default settings for the light and clicked OK. To suggest the stucco wall behind the lights, we selected Basic Paper in the Papers section of the Art Materials palette prior to adding the 3D texture effect. To apply the 3D texture we chose Effects, Surface Control, Apply Surface Texture, Using Paper. We turned Shine down to 0 (for a matte look) and left the other settings at their defaults.

2 Setting the text and converting it to shapes. For these solutions we set and converted the text to shapes, because in step 4 the shapes would make it easier to add a stroke to the type. Our objective was to create a variety of neon looks for our client.

To suggest the look of a neon tube, we chose a bold typeface with thick, even strokes and smooth curves (170-point Vag Rounded Bold), that would work well with the stroking we planned to add. Choose the Text tool in the Tools palette and open the Text section of the Objects palette and select a font. Choose a bright, neon-like color in the Colors section of the Art Materials palette. Open the Layers section of the Objects palette (so you can see the text layer appear as you type). To set your text, click in the image and begin typing. To globally adjust the spacing between the letters of the text, use the Tracking slider in the Text section.

To convert the text layer to shapes, select it in the Layers section and choose Convert Text to Shapes from the pop-out menu on the right side of the Layers section bar. Painter will convert the text layer to letterform shapes and group them. If you'd like to "hand-kern" the letters, in the Layers section, open the eye icon to the left of the group

3a

Applying a stroke to the type shapes

3b

The type shapes with gold stroke applied

4

Choosing Feather Mask on the Masks section of the Objects palette to add a feather to the layer mask for the glow

of shapes. Click on a letter's name in the Layers section and use the arrow keys on your keyboard to adjust the space between the letters.

3 Stroking the type. Our concept was a sign made out of solid, brightly colored material, backlit with a neon glow. With shapes, you can add a colored stroke to enhance your design. Click on the shape group in the Layer section to select it, choose Shapes, Set Shape Attributes and click the Stroke checkbox to apply a stroke. Change the stroke's color by clicking the Stroke's color swatch and then by clicking on a new color in the Colors section. (We chose a golden orange.) We increased the stroke width to 6.0 using the Width slider and clicked OK. To rename the shape group, double-click on its name in the Layers section and when the Layer Attributes dialog box appears, name it "Stroked/Filled Type."

4 Adding colored glows. To give the title a multicolor glow, we made two copies of the shape group (for each copy, Alt/Option-click on the shapes in the image with the Layer Adjuster) and converted each duplicate to a single layer (choose Shapes, Convert To Layer). Rename the first layer "Yellow Glow." Drag the "Yellow Glow" layer below the "stroked/filled" layer in the Layers section so you'll be able to see the glow effect when it's applied. Rename the second layer "Red Glow." Position it below "Yellow Glow" in the Layers section. For soft glowing edges, we feathered both layer masks. To feather the "Yellow Glow," click on its mask in the Masks section (Objects palette), click the right triangle on the section bar and choose Feather Mask using a feather of 20 pixels. To select the Layer again, click back on RGB-Yellow Glow in the Masks section. Next, in the Layers section, turn on Preserve Transparency and fill the "Yellow Glow" layer with a gold color that complements the stroke and fill (Effects, Fill with Current Color). To make the Red Glow, select it in the Layers section and repeat the process above, but this time use a feather of 50 pixels in the Feather Mask dialog box. The final image with the fill, stroke and glows can be see at the top of the facing page.

A variation. With Painter's shapes it's easy to change the inside of the letters to transparent for the look of neon tubes, rather than a cut-out sign. With the group of shapes selected in the Layers section, choose Shapes, Set Shape Attributes and uncheck the Fill box. The transparent neon variation is shown below. 🐾

The multicolored glow shows through the type shapes when the Fill attribute is turned off.

Creating Beveled Chrome

Overview *Open a file and apply lighting to build a background; set text; convert the text to shapes and then to a layer; bevel the forms and apply a reflection; add a shadow.*

1a

Creating a new soft diagonal spotlight based on the Slide Lighting light

1b

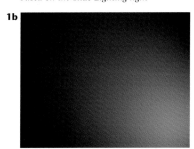

The softly lit background, ready for the type

2

The selected type shapes and the background with lighting

PAINTER'S BEVEL WORLD DYNAMIC LAYER allows you to try an endless variety of custom bevels on a selected layer quickly, without time-consuming masks and channels. To create this three-dimensional chrome title, we applied effects that included custom lighting, a rounded bevel with a reflection map and a shadow.

1 Creating a background with custom lighting. Begin by creating a new file with a deep blue-green background (our file was 800 x 500 pixel file). To add depth to the background we applied soft diagonal lighting that would complement the bright, shiny chrome to come. To open the Lighting dialog box, choose Effects, Surface Control, Apply Lighting. When the dialog box appears, click on the Slide Lighting choice. In the Lighting Preview, drag the large end of the light up a little higher in the Preview. Turn the light around by dragging its small end to point in the opposite direction—to the lower right of the image canvas. Now increase the Brightness of your light: We moved the Brightness slider to 1.30 and adjusted the Distance to 1.14 to increase how far the light shone across the image canvas. We adjusted the Elevation to 35° to decrease the distance between the light and the image canvas and decreased the Spread to 27° to narrow the beam of light, thus adding to the soft spot effect. To save your new light, click the Save button and name it when the Save Lighting dialog box appears.

2 Setting the type and converting it to shapes. Now that the backdrop is finished, you're ready to create the type. Choose a contrasting color in the Colors section of the Art Materials palette to automatically fill the text with color as you type. The contrasting color will make it easier for you to see your type as you adjust the space between individual letters. Select the Text tool. Open the Text section of the Objects palette, choose a font and size in the Text section and set the type. We set 120-point type using Vag Rounded Bold. (If you don't have the typeface we used, choose a bold font with broad strokes to accommodate the beveling effect to come.) So you can adjust the spacing of individual letters, convert the text to shapes by choosing Convert Text to Shapes from the pop-out menu on the right side of the Layers section bar on the Objects palette. Painter

3a

The rough bevel generated by the Bevel World layer default settings

3b

Our settings in the Bevel World dialog box

4

We used "emap 27" from the "emaps 2" library on the Painter_CD2 CD-ROM.

5

The Drop Shadow dialog box with settings for casting the shadow down and to the right of the chrome type

will convert the text layer to letterform shapes and group them. If you'd like to "hand-kern" the letters, in the Layers section, open the eye icon to the left of the group of shapes. Click on a letter's name in the Layers section and use the arrow keys on your keyboard to adjust the space between the letters. Make sure to leave room between the letters to allow for the bevel to be extended outside of each letter.

3 Beveling the type. In preparation for using the Bevel World dynamic layer, merge the shapes group to a single image layer by selecting the group in the Layers section and choosing Shapes, Convert To Layer. With the layer still selected, click the Plugins button at the bottom of the Layers section on the Objects palette and choose Bevel World from the pull-down menu. To build a 3D effect with a smooth rounded shape that would show off the reflection map we planned to add, we used these settings: Bevel Width slider to 15% (for narrower sides and a broader top); Outside Portion, 14% (for a small bevel outside the original pixels on the layer); Rim Slope, 26° (for a rounder top); Cliff Portion, 50% (the vertical distance between the base and rim); Cliff Height, 29% (to reduce the height of the sides); Cliff Slope, 45° (the angle for the middle of the bevel); Base Slope, 45° (leaving the angle of the outermost portion at its default); Smoothing, 52% (to add roundness to the base, cliff and rim of the bevel and to make any ridges smoother). Ignore the outside color, because it will disappear when the reflection is applied. Leave the dialog box open.

4 Achieving the chrome effect. The secret to achieving this chrome effect is choosing a bright shiny environment map in the Patterns section of the Art Materials palette, then going back to the Reflections slider in the lower part of the Bevel World dialog box. We chose an environment map that included shiny metal reflections and bright red colors. To apply the reflection map that we used, you'll need to load the "emap 2" library. To load this library, choose Load Library from the resource list on the Patterns section and navigate to the "emap 2" library on the Painter_CD2 CD-ROM. Select "emaps 2" and click Open. Back in the Patterns section, choose "emap 27" from the resource list menu. Now move the Reflection slider in the Bevel World dialog box to the far right (we used 99%). Your type will magically change to bright shiny chrome! Click OK to close the Bevel World dialog box.

5 Adding a shadow. To increase the depth of our image, we added a drop shadow using Painter's automatic drop shadow feature. To build your shadow, select the beveled layer and chose Effects, Objects, Create Drop Shadow. In the dialog box, we set X-Offset to 7 pixels, Y-Offset to 10 pixels and increased the Opacity to 80%. For a softer shadow, we set Radius to 15.0 pixels, and we left the Angle (114.6°, which would cast the shadow down and to the lower right of the object) and Thinness (45%) at their defaults. (A low Thinness setting creates a streaked look similar to a motion blur.) 🐾

Painting with Ice

Overview *Set Text to use as a template for "hand-lettering;" paint icy script on a Liquid Metal plug-in layer; composite a copy of the layer to enhance the design.*

CHER THREINEN-PENDARVIS

PHOTO: CORBIS IMAGES

The original photograph

The Text section of the Objects palette with settings for our title

The image with the Text set and in position

YOU CAN CREATE TEXT EFFECTS QUICKLY with dynamic layers. To begin this cover comp for an online travel agency catalog, we set type using a Dynamic Text layer. Using this text as a template, we "hand-painted" new 3D letters onto a Liquid Metal dynamic layer using a tablet and stylus. Then we applied special settings to give the liquid letters a clear, frozen look.

1 Choosing an image. We began by selecting a photo that measured 768 x 512 pixels. Although the final art used online would be smaller, we preferred to work at a larger size so we could zoom in and finesse the details then reduce the size later. We chose a photo with a Mediterranean theme and refreshing colors that would complement the "ice" or "glass" title.

2 Setting Dynamic Text. To make it easier for you to see the type over the image, choose a contrasting color in the Colors section of the Art Materials palette to automatically fill the text with color as you type. Select the Text tool in the Tools palette. Open the Text section of the Objects palette, choose a font and size and set the type directly on the image. (We set our text using the Reporter Two font). To adjust the spacing between the letters, use the Tracking slider in the Text section. To interactively resize the type, use the Size slider in the Text section. To use the Layer Adjuster tool to resize the type: Position it over a corner of the text, when the arrow cursor appears, drag on the text. Drag the text with the Layer Adjuster to reposition it in your image. When you've finished making adjustments to your text, click OK.

3 Drawing with crystal-clear ice. Using the text as a template, we drew new letters using a Liquid Metal plug-in layer. Set up your Liquid Metal layer as follows: Open the Layers section of the Objects palette, click the Dynamic Plugins button at the bottom of the Layers section and choose Liquid Metal. Painter will generate an empty, transparent Liquid Metal dynamic layer, and

3a

The settings in the Liquid Metal dialog box for the icy look

3b

Beginning to hand-letter the Liquid Metal type using the dynamic text as a template

3c

The underlying template layer is visible through the "ice."

3d

The icy type with text layer removed

4

Detail of the icy type showing the underlying layer's Composite Method set to Darken

the Liquid Metal dialog box will appear. With the title as an underlay, we used a stylus to trace the text with the Liquid Metal brush tool. To begin, move the Refraction slider all the way to the right (so you can paint with crystal-clear ice.) Choose the Brush tool in the Liquid Metal dialog box and carefully paint your title.

Adjust the Amount, Smooth, Size and Volume settings to your liking. To select all of the Liquid Metal so that you can apply new settings, choose the Liquid Metal Selector (arrow) and drag a marquee around what you've painted. Our settings were Amount, 5.0; Smooth, 90; Size, 16.0; Volume, 97; Spacing, .331; Map, Standard Metal, with Surface Tension checked. We reduced the Refraction setting to 90%, because it helped the type stand out from the photo.

After completing your letters, click OK to close the Liquid Metal dialog box. Then delete the Text layer you used as a template: Select its name in the Layers section of the Objects palette and click the Delete (Trash can) button.

A Liquid Metal dynamic layer is *live*, which means you can continue to finesse the dialog box settings. To keep a layer dynamic, do not "commit" the layer (change it into an image layer), and make sure to save the file in RIFF format. For more information about dynamic layers, turn to Chapter 5, "Using Layers and Shapes."

4 Compositing a second layer. As you can see in your image, Painter's Liquid Metal dynamic layer "refracts" an underlying image. To give the ice more texture and make it look shinier, we set up another layer between our ice layer and the image beneath. To begin, make a copy of the Liquid Metal layer (Alt/Option-click with the Layer Adjuster tool). To enhance the copy of the Liquid Metal layer using tonal effects, choose Effects, Tonal Control, Brightness/Contrast and slightly increase the contrast. When the Commit dialog box appears, asking if you'd like to convert the dynamic layer to an image layer, click Commit. To add more texture and bring out the highlights in the icy type, we changed the underlying layer's Composite Method in the Layers section to Darken. 🖌

So many options! When you have the underlying layer in place, experiment with changing the Composite Method in the Layers section to different settings. We experimented with Gel (left), and Pseudocolor (right). Control the effect with the layer's Opacity slider.

Setting a Logo in Stone

Overview *Open a background image; enhance its texture; set text for the logo; convert it to shapes; convert the shapes to a selection; make a border; copy the selection area to a layer; use Apply Surface Texture to create a three-dimensional look.*

1a

The background image from ArtBeats

1b

Applying texture to the background image based on luminosity in the image

2a

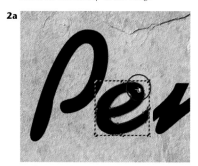

Tightening the space between the letters

YOU CAN CREATE THE ILLUSION of a logo carved out of sandstone with Painter's Apply Surface Texture. By selecting part of a background image, you can also use Apply Surface Texture to emboss type, logos and other graphics, while preserving the image texture and striations, as in the image above. For this surfboard designer's classic style, we used a "retro" script typeface (Kaufmann Bold) and Painter's type shapes to build the logo. Kaufmann's even stroke weight and its clean, flowing lines help to make the logo easy to read from a distance. (If your logo was created in a Post-Script program such as Adobe Illustrator turn to Chapter 4 for information about importing vector artwork.)

1 Preparing the background. Open an image to use as a background. We chose Sandstone from the ArtBeats Marble and Granite 2 collection, then we resized the image to 883-pixels-wide. (The point size of the type chosen in step 2 and the Surface Texture settings in step 7 reflect the size of the file we used.) To give the sandstone a realistic texture based on its light-to-dark values, we chose Effects, Surface Control, Apply Surface Texture Using Image Luminance. We used a subtle Amount setting of 22%; for a matte effect, we reduced Shine to 0, leaving the other Material settings at their defaults. Under Light Controls, we chose the top left Light Direction button (to complement the natural lighting in the image), increased Brightness to 1.23, and left the other settings at their defaults.

2 Setting the logo type and converting to shapes. Next, open the Layers section of the Objects palette so that you can see the type shapes appear in the list as you type. Open the Text section of the Objects palette. Click in the image with the Text tool, choose a font and size in the Text section and begin typing. (We chose 80-point Kaufmann Bold.)

The overall letter spacing looked good, but we wanted to move the capital "P" closer to the other letters, so we converted the text to shapes. Fine-tune the spacing of individual letters, as follows: click the right triangle on the Layers section bar and choose Convert Text to Shapes. The text layer will be converted into a group

2b

The selected, grouped type shapes for the logo in final position

3a

The shapes converted to a selection

3b

Viewing the mask as a red overlay

4a

Loading a selection from the type (New Mask 1) and adding it to the border selection

5

The Layer Adjuster tool positioned over the selected area, ready to copy

composed of individual letter shapes. Open the group by clicking the triangle to the left of the group name, select a letter you want to move by clicking on its name in the Layers section then use the arrow keys on the keyboard to nudge the letter into position. When the kerning is complete, click the triangle to shut the eye icon and thus close the group. To scale the entire group proportionately, press Shift and drag one of the corner handles. To move the group, drag with the Layer Adjuster tool.

3 Converting the type to a selection and storing it as a mask. Before you can use the type shapes to apply effects to the image, you'll need to convert them to a selection. Using the Layer Adjuster tool, select the type shape group in the Layers section and choose Shapes, Convert To Selection. The shape group will disappear and the selection (a black-and-white animated marquee) will appear. To store the selection as a mask, choose Select, Save Selection. The mask will be listed in the Masks section of the Objects palette as New Mask 1. So you have a guide when you make the oval section for the border in the following step, view the mask as a red overlay on your image by opening its eye icon in the Masks section of the Objects palette.

4 Adding a border selection to the type. Next, we made an oval selection for the border. Choose the Oval Selection tool (it shares a space in the Tools palette with the Rectangular Selection tool) and drag to make an oval, set up where you want the inside of the border to be. To reposition or scale your selection, choose the Selection Adjuster. (It shares a space with the Layer Adjuster.) For more information about working with selections, turn to "Transforming Selections," and "Editing Selections" in the introduction to Chapter 4.

To give the selection a border, choose Select, Modify, Border and specify a width (we used 18 pixels). A second marquee (the border), will be added outside the current selection marquee to form a border selection. Now combine the border selection with the type: Load the type selection by choosing Select, Load Selection, choose New Mask 1 from the Load From menu, and under Operation choose Add To Selection. Clicking OK will then build a new selection based on the type and the border. Save this new selection as a mask by choosing Select, Save Selection. For more variations on using masks to emboss a graphic, turn to Chapter 4, "Making Masks for Embossing" on page 143.

5 Making two layers. We made two layers in preparation for the Surface Texture applications that are to follow in step 6. To copy the contents of the selection and make two layers, position the Layer Adjuster tool inside the marquee and Alt/Option-click two times. (After the first click the marquee will disappear, but the second click will still work to make a second layer.) In the Layers section, to name the top layer, double-click on its name to access the Layer Attributes dialog box. Name the layer "Logo 1" and click OK. Click on the layer below it in the Layers section and name this second layer "Logo 2."

6a

Surface Texture settings for Logo 1 layer

6b

Surface Texture applied to Logo 1 layer

6c

Surface Texture applied to Logo 2 layer, with the layer offset slightly

7

Applying Surface Texture to the TM symbol

6 Giving the logo dimension. We wanted a realistic 3D look in which the letters and logo would be raised above the sandstone surface. To get a strong enough shadow without burning out the highlights on the logo, we applied Surface Texture to both logo layers. We used subtle settings on the top layer for the bevel itself and stronger settings on the bottom layer for the shadow, which we would offset for emphasis. To begin, select the "Logo 1" layer by clicking on its name in the Layers section and choose Effects, Surface Control, Apply Surface Texture. When the dialog box appears, choose the "Logo 1" mask from the Using menu. Use subtle Amount and Softness settings (we used Amount, 46%; and Softness, 3.3). Adding Softness will allow you to raise the height of the emboss, but too much softness can make an image blurry. We turned Shine down to 0 (for a matte finish on the sandstone), clicked the top left light button and left the other settings at their defaults.

To produce a wider shadow in our image, we used a stronger Amount setting—138%—when we applied surface texture to the "Logo 2" layer, leaving the other settings alone. Then we used the arrow keys on the keyboard to offset "Logo 2" under "Logo 1" so we would see just a small portion of the shadow, moving the "Logo 2" layer 1 pixel to the right and 2 pixels down. The Surface Texture settings and the number of pixels you'll move the lower layer to offset the shadow will depend on the size of your file.

7 Adding the symbol. For the TM symbol, we set 14-point Stone Sans Bold type. We converted the TM text to shapes, then to a selection (as in step 3), and Alt/Option-clicked to make a layer. Since the TM was set in small type it required Surface Texture settings with less Softness. Our settings were: Softness 1.0; Amount, 100%; Shine, 0, and we left the other settings at their defaults. 🐾

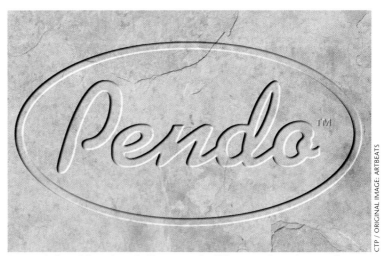

For a variation of the embossed effect, we used a different sandstone image and checked the Invert box in the Apply Surface Texture dialog box to change the direction of the lighting.

■ **Susan LeVan** used several layers when she created *Going Global* for her agents Bruck and Moss: She began by drawing the figures on separate layers with the Smooth Ink Pen variant of Pens and the Square Chalk and Oil Pastel variants of Dry Media, and added their drop shadows using Painter's Effects, Objects, Create Drop Shadow command. For the background behind the figures, LeVan used two patterns that she had made in separate source files. To build the "text" pattern, she used Futura, Bubble Dot and a few other fonts to set letters and symbols using the Text tool and sized them using the Size slider in the Text section of the Objects palette. She positioned them with the Layer Adjuster tool. When the text elements were complete, she dropped the text layers to the Canvas by choosing Drop All from the menu on the right side of the Layers section bar. Then she captured the text design as a pattern in the Patterns section of the Art Materials palette by choosing Capture

Pattern from the pop-out menu on the right side of the Patterns section bar. (See "Creating a Pattern" and "Applying Patterns" in Chapter 7.) Now working in the final image, she added new layers and filled each one with the type or globe pattern by selecting one of the custom patterns in the Patterns section and choosing Effects, Fill, Fill With Pattern. To make the white areas of the layers transparent, she set the Composite Method to Gel in the Layers section. LeVan wanted to add more color and texture interest to the background, so she adjusted the size of each pattern using the Scale slider in the Patterns section and filled two more new layers with them. She selected white areas on the new layers and deleted them. Next, she colored one of the layers gold and the other green by turning on Preserve Transparency in the Layers sections and filling the layers with new color. Finally, she set their Composite Method to Colorize and adjusted the Opacity of each layer.

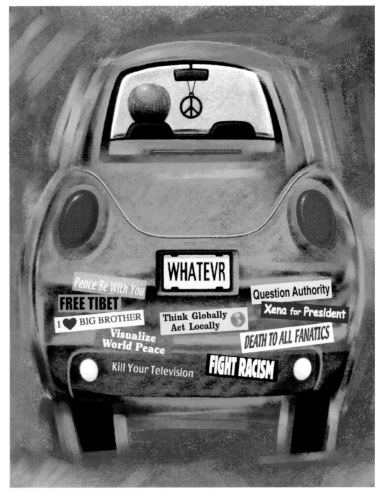

■ "I can't emphasize enough that traditional drawing and rendering skills are indispensable in my approach to digital imaging," says **Mike Reed,** who built this illustration for the cover of *The Utne Reader* magazine. The concept for the cover—how aging baby-boomers' attitudes towards activism have changed—was decided by the art director and editorial staff of the magazine. To begin the image, Reed opened a new file, the exact size of the magazine cover. To import a scan of the art director's page layout, so he could see the type exactly as it would appear in the final printed piece, he chose File, Place. Then he set the Composite Method to Gel in the Layers section of the Objects palette, so he could see through the layout layer. Again using File, Place, he imported a scanned photo of a VW bug and resized it using Effects, Orientation, Free Transform. In the Layers section, he moved the type layer to the top so he could use it as a guide while he

worked. Reed selected the VW bug layer in the Layers section. To simplify and stylize the car, he drew loose brushstrokes over it with the Square Chalk variant of Dry Media. When the VW bug was roughed in, he began adding the bumper stickers to the image. Reed created the bumper stickers using slogans supplied to him by the magazine editorial staff. Leaving the main illustration open, he created a new document that measured 1 x 3 inches at 300 pixels-per-inch. Using the Text tool from the Tools palette, he set type for several bumper stickers on individual Text layers, then he adjusted the size and spacing using the controls in the Text section of the Objects palette. When he was happy with each sticker, he converted each text layer to an image layer by choosing Convert To Default Layer from the pop-out menu on the right side of the Layers section bar. Then to complete each bumper sticker, he used the Rectangular Selection tool to make a selection around the type on the

layer. To fill the background outside the type with a color, he used the Paint Bucket. At this point, he wanted to change the color of the type as well. So, using the Paint Bucket, he filled each letter of the type with another color. Because Reed didn't want the flat colors of the bumper stickers to contrast with the texture of the final illustration, he added texture to each one with Effects, Surface Control, Dye Concentration, Using Paper. He selected each sticker with the Rectangular Selection tool, and then used the Layer Adjuster tool to drag and drop it into the main illustration file, where he positioned it. He repeated this process until all the bumper stickers and the license plate were positioned in the file. With all of the elements in place, Reed added freehand detail to the rest of the image. He slowly built up textures using the Sharp Chalk, Artist Pastel Chalk, Square Chalk and Oil Pastel variants of Dry Media over the Woodshavings texture, loaded from the Painter 7 Wow! CD-ROM.

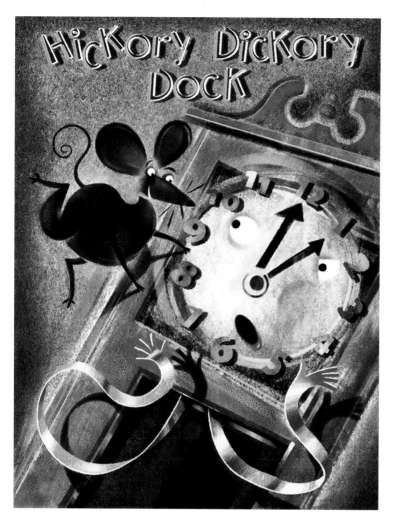

■ *Hickory Dickory* was created by **Mike Reed** as a promotion for his agent, HK Portfolio. To develop the illustration, Reed painted with the Dry Media variants on several layers and used the Text tool to set the type for the title and clock numerals. He sketched the composition in saturated colors using the Square Chalk variant of Dry Media on Wood Shavings paper texture (from the Wow! Textures on the CD-ROM that comes with this book). So he could paint freely in some areas while protecting other areas of his composition, he made soft-edged selections by feathering each selection (Select, Feather), then saving it (Select, Save Selection) so he could use the selection later as a mask. He created new layers for the background, the clock's body, the hands and the mouse. Working on each layer, he painted loose brushstrokes using the Square Chalk and varying colors. To refine areas, he used the Oil Pastel and Artist Pastel Chalk

variants of Dry Media. For the title and numerals, Reed set type in the Block font. He set the title on one text layer and the numerals on individual text layers so he could rotate them easily as follows: He chose the Layer Adjuster in the Tools palette, positioned the tool over a corner of a number, then pressed the Ctrl/⌘ key to make the cursor change into a circular rotation symbol, and then dragged to rotate the element. When the numerals were in place, Reed grouped all of the numeral layers and collapsed them into one layer, then he converted the layer to pixels by choosing Convert to Default Layer from the menu on the Layers section bar. He softened the edge of the layer's mask by selecting it in the Masks section and choosing Feather Mask from the menu on the Masks section bar. With the mask still active, he applied texture by choosing used Effects, Surface Control, Express Texture Using Paper and the Wood Shavings texture. He adjusted

the sliders until the edges of the numbers showed the rough texture. He applied the same effects to the edges of the title. Then he enabled Preserve Transparency in the Layers section and painted over the numbers and title with the Square Chalk using various colors. For the shadow on the title, he duplicated the title layer by Alt/Option-clicking on it using the Layer Adjuster. Then he dragged the copy below the title in the Layers section. Using a darker color, he painted this shadow layer using the Square Chalk. Then he feathered the mask of this shadow layer as he'd done before, this time using a 10-pixel feather. He created the shadow for the letters and the hands of the clock in much the same way. When the shadow layers were complete, he set their Composite Method to Gel in the Layers section. Finally, using the Oil Pastel and Sharp Chalk, he added a few reddish details to the mouse and brighter highlights to the clock's hands.

■ **John Dismukes** of Capstone Studios is well known for his creative logo design and hand-drawn typography. He used similar processes to design and airbrush the three images on these pages. Dismukes begins each design by drawing many sketches, and when the direction is established, he draws a tight visualization of the typography on paper. The approved pencil sketch is then scanned and used as a template in FreeHand to create PostScript outlines. He imports the outlines into Photoshop and builds elements on layers. Then he opens the file with layers in Painter for the airbrushing. In Painter, some of the layers are duplicated and used to make selections (via Drop and Select from the Layers section bar menu), and they are then saved as masks. (Alternately, outlines can be imported directly into Painter as shapes via File, Acquire, Adobe Illustrator file and then converted

to layers.) Dismukes uses selections to limit paint as he airbrushes using the Digital Airbrush variant of Airbrushes. For a step-by-step description of a similar technique using Painter, turn to "Selections and Airbrush," on page 151.

The *Grand Marnier Metallic Cactus* illustration (top) was commissioned by Alcone Marketing Group and art-directed by Liliana Marchica. Dismukes began with a tight sketch, but he wanted a rough look for this logo, so he did not import outlines. He painted masks for the type, then converted them to selections he could use to limit the paint. Using the Digital Airbrush, Dismukes airbrushed the lettering. To add texture to the leaf, he cloned texture onto a layer from another file: He opened a texture file with the same dimensions as the logo file, defined it as the clone source by choosing File, Clone

Source and used a Cloning brush variant to softly brush the texture onto the layer.

For the packaging of an action game, art director (Mark Rein) and client (Epic Games, Inc.) wanted a logo with a progressive, "Gothic Tech" style. After scanning his tight sketch, Dismukes began *Unreal* (above), by importing the sketch and outlines into a new file. For an underpainting, he filled the type with brown. Using the imported outlines, he made masks for the letter faces and bevels. With selections loaded from the masks to constrain the spray, he carefully airbrushed the shadows and highlights, working from dark to light. To intensify the bronze color, he duplicated the finished layer and set its Composite method to Multiply, with 30% Opacity.

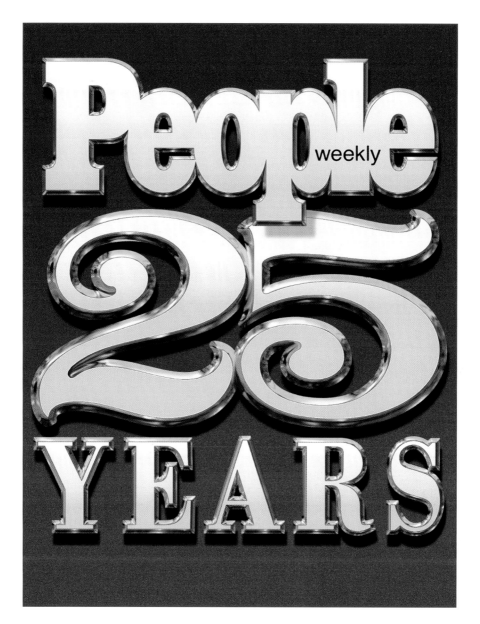

■ For *People's 25th Anniversary logo*, a cover illustration for Time Warner's *People Weekly magazine*, **John Dismukes** and **Jo-Anne Redwood** worked closely with their team at Capstone Studios and the art directors from *People* magazine, Phil Simone and Hilli Pitzer. Making hundreds of sketches, Dismukes and Redwood designed the type to complement the existing *People* magazine logo, make a strong statement, and be legible from a distance. After the design was approved, Dismukes took the time he needed to perfect the letterspacing, and then carefully rendered the realistic reflections. Like a traditional airbrush artist using friskets, Dismukes built a mask for the front face of the type and another for the bevels. After making a new layer, he filled the letters with light gray. Then he loaded the bevel selection and used the Digital Airbrush variant of Airbrushes to paint detailed reflections, highlights and shadows. Finally, he loaded a selection from the face mask again, and with a tiny airbrush, he painted the fine strokes that set off the flat front of the letters from their beveled sides. He finished by adding a drop shadow and background. "For high-quality work, you have to bring artistry to the computer," says Dismukes.

USING
PAINTER
WITH
PHOTOSHOP

When creating Quarry, *Marc Brown used Illustrator, Photoshop and Painter. To see more of his work, turn to page 308.*

IT'S EASY TO MOVE FILES back and forth between Painter 7 and Photoshop. And what does Painter have to offer the Photoshop user? Fantastic natural-media brushes that give your images warmth, a multitude of textures and fabulous special effects! In addition to the work showcased in this chapter, several of the other artists whose work appears in this book have used both Painter and Photoshop in the development of their images. If you're an avid Photoshop user and would like to see more examples of how others have combined the use of the two programs, check out the work of these artists for inspiration: Jeff Burke, Ellie Dickson, John Dismukes, Larry Gartel and Donal Jolley. The index in the back of the book lists page references for each of their names.

PAINTER TO PHOTOSHOP

Here are some pointers for importing Painter 7 files into Photoshop:

- To preserve image layers when moving an image from Painter 7 into Photoshop, save a file in Photoshop format. Photoshop will open the file and translate the layers with their names and the layer hierarchy intact. (Photoshop rasterizes any dynamic layers such as Text, Liquid Metal, and Water Color, as well Shape layers.)

- If a Painter file contains layers that extend beyond Painter's live image area, and that document is opened in Photoshop 4 and later versions, the areas outside of the live area are retained. (Photoshop 3 clipped the layer information outside the live area.)

- Painter offers most of the Photoshop Blending modes; some exceptions are Color Dodge, Color Burn and Exclusion. And Painter has seven additional Compositing Methods of its own. Photoshop converts Magic Combine to Lighten mode, Gel to Darken mode, Colorize to Color mode, and Shadow Map to Multiply. When Photoshop encounters a Painter-native Composite Method it can't convert (such as

John Dismukes used FreeHand, Photoshop and Painter when building the Risk Game Board, *a detail of which is shown here, for the Parker Bros./Hasbro Games Group. See the entire image on page 305.*

DYNAMIC LAYERS

When a Painter file that includes a Dynamic Layer such as Liquid Metal is opened in Photoshop, the layer is preserved but the dynamic capabilities are lost. To retain the dynamic properties for further editing in Painter, save a copy of your file with live dynamic layers in RIFF format.

A PATH TO PHOTOSHOP

You can store path information with a selection in Painter for import to Photoshop, and it will appear in the Photoshop Paths palette. When you make a selection with Painter's Lasso or Rectangular or Oval Selection tool or set text and convert it to shapes then to a selection in Painter (by choosing Convert Text to Shapes from the pop-out menu on the Layers section bar and then choosing Shapes, Convert to Selection from the Masks menu), path information is automatically stored in the file. If you save a selection as a mask in the Masks section you can build path information back into the file: Choose Select, Load Selection to create a selection based on the mask, then convert this mask-based selection to outline information using Select, Transform Selection. (Painter's Transform Selection command adds vector information to the selection border.) Then if you save the Painter file in Photoshop format, these kinds of outlines will appear in Photoshop's Paths palette.

Pseudocolor or Reverse-out), it converts that layer to Normal.

- To preserve the selections in Painter's Mask List in the Objects palette and use them in Photoshop as channels, save a Painter file in Photoshop format. When you open the file in Photoshop, the named masks will automatically appear in the Channels palette.

PHOTOSHOP TO PAINTER

Here are some pointers for importing Photoshop files into Painter 7:

- If you prefer to begin your file in Photoshop, and the file contains layers, Painter can open Photoshop format files saved in RGB, CMYK and Grayscale modes.

- Although Painter 7 will open CMYK files in both Photoshop and TIFF formats, keeping files in RGB color mode when porting files from Photoshop to Painter will make the best color translation, because RGB is Painter's native color model.

- If you save your Photoshop image (version 4 or later) with layers in Photoshop format, Painter 7 will open it and translate the layers with their names intact. If you are using Photoshop 3, save the file in Photoshop 3 format.

- Photoshop type layers will be rasterized by Painter. However, shape layers, layer clipping paths and clipping groups will not translate.

- Photoshop layer masks do not translate consistently into Painter.

- A Photoshop document made up of transparent layers only—that is, without a Background layer—will open in Painter as layers over a white-filled background in the Canvas layer.

- Painter can recognize most of Photoshop's Blending modes when compositing the layers (some exceptions are Color Dodge, Color Burn and Exclusion). Painter converts blending modes that it doesn't recognize to the Default Compositing method.

- Layer sets created in Photoshop will not be recognized by Painter, but the layers within them will translate.

- A layer with a live layer style will disappear when the file is opened in Painter. You can try this work-around: Converting a "styled" layer to a series of rasterized layers (Layer, Layer Style, Create Layers) before attempting to open it in Painter. But this often doesn't work either, since the conversion often involves a clipping path group, and clipping groups don't translate to Painter.

- Photoshop Alpha Channel masks are recognized by Painter 7. The channels will appear in Painter's Masks section. To view a mask in black-and-white, select the Canvas, and in the Masks section, click the mask eye icon open and shut the RGB-Canvas eye icon.

- Photoshop layer masks will also convert to layer masks in Painter. (They will be listed in the Masks section rather than in the Layers palette, as they are in Photoshop.) To view a layer mask, select the layer in the Layers section and click the layer mask eye icon open in the Masks section to view the layer visibility mask.

Compositing, Painting and Effects

Overview *Scan a drawing and a sheet of paper and composite the scans; add color and texture with brushes; add a colored lighting effect; open the image in Photoshop and convert it to CMYK.*

JOHN FRETZ

1a

The sheet of speckled Oatmeal paper

1b

The pencil-and-charcoal drawing on paper

2

Compositing the scans of the Oatmeal paper and the sketch

JOHN FRETZ COMBINED TRADITIONAL DRAWING materials and digital ones in Photoshop and Painter to build the composite illustration *AM Exercise* for an American Lung Association calendar.

1 Drawing and scanning. As a basis for his illustration, Fretz drew a black-and-white study using pencil and charcoal on a rough newsprint paper. Then he used a flatbed scanner to scan the drawing and a sheet of Oatmeal paper into Photoshop using RGB mode.

2 Compositing the scans. Fretz built the image in Photoshop because he was more familiar with Photoshop's compositing procedures. (His compositing process, which follows, can be accomplished almost identically in Painter.) Fretz copied the drawing and pasted it as a new layer on top of the Oatmeal paper background. To make the white background of the drawing transparent, he applied Multiply blending mode to the drawing layer using the menu on the Layers palette.

For the soft, irregular edge on the background layer, Fretz first used the Lasso to draw a selection around the perimeter of the image. He reversed the selection by choosing Select, Inverse and feathered it 30 pixels (Select, Feather), then he filled the border area with 100% white. He saved the file in Photoshop format to preserve the layers for import into Painter.

3 Modifying brushes. At this point, Fretz opened the composite drawing in Painter where he planned to add color and texture. Before beginning to paint, he made two custom Soft Charcoal brushes. The first, for adding soft values, used the Soft Cover subcategory; the second, for subtly darkening color, used the Grainy Soft Buildup subcategory and a low opacity. To make Fretz's

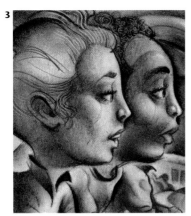

3

Building up color on the faces using the custom Soft Charcoal brushes

4

Creating a colored glow in the sky using Apply Lighting

5

Painting details on the foreground

"darkener," in the Brushes palette, choose the Soft Charcoal variant of Dry Media. In the General section of the Brush Controls palette, change the method to Buildup and the subcategory to Grainy Soft Buildup. A lower opacity will give you more control when building up color, so in the Controls:Brush palette, change the Opacity to about 15%. Save your new variant by choosing Save Variant from the Brushes palette's Variant menu. Name it and click OK.

Adding color and texture in Painter. Fretz chose Basic Paper texture in the Papers section of the Art Materials palette. To enlarge the texture to complement the grain of the Oatmeal paper background, he used the Scale slider on the Papers section. He brushed color onto his drawing using two grain-sensitive brushes, the Large Chalk and Square Chalk variants of Dry Media and used his custom Charcoals to deepen color saturation in some areas. Choose a Chalk brush and begin painting color onto your image background; switch to the custom Soft Charcoal variant using Grainy Soft Buildup to darken color. To change the brush size and the opacity while you work, use the Size and Opacity sliders in the Controls:Brush palette.

4 Emphasizing the sky with lighting. For a warm glow in the sky that faded across the people's faces, Fretz applied a colored lighting effect within a soft-edged selection. Begin by choosing the Lasso tool and making a loose freehand selection. Now give the selection a soft edge by applying a feather: Choose Select, Feather, type in a feather width, and click OK. Now apply the lighting effect to make the sky glow as Fretz did: Choose Effects, Surface Control, Apply Lighting. In the Lighting dialog box, choose the Center Spot light. To give the light a colored tint, click on the Light Color box to open the Select Light Color dialog box. Then choose a color by clicking on it in the color picker. (If the circle is black, move the slider to the right.) Click OK. To move the spotlight to a new location in the Preview window, drag the large end of the light indicator. To save the custom light, click the Save button and name the light when prompted, then click OK to apply the light to your image, and deselect (Ctrl/⌘-D).

5 Painting final details. To make the layer and image canvas into one surface on which he could paint details, Fretz merged all the layers. (In the Objects palette, click the right arrow on the Layers section bar to open the menu and choose Drop All.) Then he chose the Scratchboard Rake variant of Pens, and modified it by reducing the number of bristles. To build a similar brush, open the Rake section of the Brush Controls palette. Reduce the number of Bristles to 5. Fretz added finishing strokes in various colors to several places in the foreground, the grass, and highlights on the cars. He also used a smaller brush and more subtle colors to add textured strokes to areas of the background.

Fretz saved a copy of the image as a TIFF file. He opened the file in Photoshop and converted it to CMYK for use in the calendar.

Expressive Painting and Layering

Overview *Make a drawing and scan it; using three versions of the file, add color and blend, and add surface texture; composite the file and add details.*

PHILIP HOWE

Howe's pencil sketch

The silhouette mask made in Photoshop

The drawing with reddish-brown tint

FOR THIS ADVERTISING ILLUSTRATION for Wacom Graphics tablets, Philip Howe created a fantasy portrait of a boy befriended by a wild creature. Howe prefers Painter's brushes and effects for achieving the realistic look of oil paints, but he chooses to make his masks and to do the compositing in Photoshop because he is more familiar with Photoshop's selections and masking procedures. He built this image in three layers: a soft sepia underpainting with no texture added, a sepia underpainting with surface texture and a painted layer with heavy surface texture.

1 Drawing developmental sketches. After Howe made several pencil sketches, the designer (Paul Nelson), the client (Wacom), and Howe settled on the concept. Howe refined the approved pencil sketch and scanned it. When creating an illustration for print, he prefers working at the final file size needed, because he has more control over the textural effects he wants to achieve in the final print separation without the softening that can occur through interpolation if the image is scaled. His scan measured about 5600 x 4600 pixels.

2 Making a silhouette mask. Howe compares his technique to that of an airbrush artist who saves all of his early masks. Using Photoshop's Magic Wand, Howe made a selection for the white background in the sketch and saved it as a mask in the Channels palette. He cleaned up the silhouette mask using Photoshop's Paintbrush and Eraser tools.

3 Adding color to build an underpainting. For the sepia underpainting, Howe colored the sketch, as follows: He began by loading the silhouette mask as a selection, then chose a reddish-brown color as the Foreground Color, chose Layer, New, Layer via Copy (to copy the selected area to a new layer), turned on

Howe's blending with the Liquid brush

The creature's head showing airbrushed color, blending and surface texture

The completed creature with the boy on his back, airbrushed and blended

The right arm showing airbrushed sky, and completed composited layers

Preserve Transparency (to constrain the fill he was about to apply to the existing pixels) and chose Edit, Fill Using Foreground Color in Normal mode at 100% Opacity. He set the Blending mode for this layer to Multiply.

To tint the lines in the sketch with sepia, Howe worked on the Background layer. He loaded the silhouette mask again and colored the boy and creature by choosing Edit, Fill, using Color mode, which tinted the gray lines but preserved the white areas. Next, Howe merged the layers to produce a single Background layer with an all-over sepia tint, but still showing the line work.

4 Achieving the effect of oil paint. Howe opened the image in Painter and saved it twice under two file names. He wanted an effect similar to oil paint on canvas. Working on one of the two files, he added more color with the Digital Airbrush variant of Airbrushes. He used modified Liquid variants to build up brushstrokes and to blend the creature's hair. For most of the blending and pulling of paint, Howe used a custom Liquid brush based on the Grainy Water variant: In the General section of the Brush Controls palette, he changed the Method from Cover to Drip, then changed the Subcategory to Grainy Drip. While painting, he used a light touch with the stylus to pull the paint expressively. He painted subtle directional strokes, creating a soft oil-like effect over the image.

5 Adding more texture. To emphasize the directional brushwork, Howe used Effects, Surface Control, Apply Surface Texture, Using Image Luminance, with strong settings. He saved the file to use later.

Next he worked on the other Painter file he had saved. To emboss the hair and hard edges in the drawing, he chose Effects, Surface Control, Apply Surface Texture, Using Image Luminance with subtle settings. As before, he saved the image for use later.

6 Compositing the painted layers and adding details. Back in Photoshop, Howe combined the two files he had saved in Painter with the Photoshop file. With each of the files open in Photoshop, he used the Move tool to drag and drop the lighter-textured files into the painted file with the heavier texture. In Photoshop's Layers palette, he set all of the blending mode to Normal. Next he combined the images, preserving just the right amount of texture. A way to do this in Photoshop without permanently changing the component images is to add a layer mask to each layer and paint it with an Airbrush and black paint to hide parts of the layer. (The process of compositing and hiding portions of the layers by editing the layer visibility masks can be accomplished in Painter 7 in a similar way.) Howe then airbrushed a loose background landscape, setting the foreground figures out from it and adding a sense of depth.

When he was satisfied with the overall look, he saved the layered file before he made a flattened copy for output. That way he knew he could go back and add texture or softness if he liked, further manipulating the layer masks in the original unflattened file. 🖌

Collage Using Cloning and Layers

Overview *Scan photos into Photoshop and retouch; use Painter's brushes and textures to build a background image and add textured brushwork to source files; build the composite image in Photoshop; add blending and airbrushed highlights in Painter.*

ART DIRECTION AND IMAGES: BURKE / TRIOLO PRODUCTIONS / DESIGN: BOB MARRIOTT, MARRIOTT & ASSAY
CLIENT: ACAPULCO RESTAURANTS

Burke's custom Ringlets texture was used for the background.

1b

The test file with tonal variations

WHEN JEFF BURKE AND LORRAINE TRIOLO—owners of Burke/Triolo Productions—were commissioned to create new menus for Acapulco Restaurants, they turned to Photoshop for image compositing and to Painter for a textured, painted look. The final composed menu pages are filled with unique, stylized graphics that reflect the texture and style of Old Mexico and suggest the qualities of handmade food and old-world service.

Burke began by exploring techniques in Painter, settling on a rough-edged, textural look with lively brushstrokes, which he presented to the client and the designer. After approval, he built the interior menu pages using several elements: a background paper texture image, textured food images and border graphics. The source files were all composed into a single image file in Photoshop and then opened again in Painter, where more texture and brushwork were added. Later, in QuarkXPress, the type and the dingbat illustrations were placed on top of the composed image as EPS files. The folded menu was composed of several panels, each built using the same process. The steps that follow use panel 3 as an example. Turn to pages 303 and 304 in the gallery to see a beverage menu panel and the front cover of this menu.

1 Building a textured background. The partners realized that a textured feel would contribute to the old-world atmosphere they wanted to achieve. To accomplish this, Burke created a new

2

The retouched food photograph

3a

Using the Chalk Cloner brush to paint a rough edge around the elements

3b

Refining the texture around the edge of the plate and beverage

3c

The food photograph with brushwork nearly complete

document in Painter that matched the page size of the menu, measuring 9 x 14.5 inches at 300 pixels per inch. He created a custom paper texture in Painter, called Ringlets. (To read about making a custom paper texture turn to "Applying Scanned Paper Textures" in Chapter 3, on page 96.) Then, using a warm-colored Oil Pastel variant of Dry Media, he brushed the texture over the surface of the page, using light pressure on the stylus. He saved this master texture image for use on each panel of the menu.

Burke converted the light, delicate paper texture to CMYK and created a test file with tonal variations. He sent the test file to his service bureau for a Fuji ColorArt film proof, and when the proof came back, the partners chose the darkest, yellowest variation.

2 Scanning and retouching the images. The team at Burke/ Triolo scanned the food images on a Scanview ScanMate 5000 drum scanner, then converted them to RGB. Burke used Photoshop's Rubber Stamp tool to lightly retouch scanning imperfections and to improve details, such as stray rice grains, sauce smears on the plates and dark areas in the food. To whiten most of the background, he made a loose selection completely outside of the elements and reversed it by choosing Select, Inverse. Then he pressed the Delete key.

3 Texturizing the source images. Burke opened each food image in Painter and created a clone by choosing File, Clone. He chose Big Grain Rough paper texture in the Papers section of the Art Materials palette (loaded from the Painter 6 Textures library on the Painter_CD2 CD-ROM). Using the Chalk Cloner variant of Cloners, with brush sizes varying between 20 and 100 pixels, he gently painted over the image in the clone file along the edges of the plates, the base of the glasses and the stone surface material, in varying densities. This produced a painterly quality in the images reminiscent of painting by hand. By constantly varying the size of the brush and by using a light touch on the stylus, he changed the amount of chalk texture applied. His goal was to add texture to the original without obscuring it completely. As specialists in food styling and photography, Burke and Triolo know that it's important to avoid obscuring the food products in an image.

To add subtly colored brushwork to the edges of the elements, Burke used an Oil Pastel variant of Dry Media. He sampled the color from the image (using the Alt/Option/⌘ key) and then painted diagonal strokes. He likes using the Oil Pastel when applying dark colors over a light background or light over dark, because the brush smears color slightly, making the strokes appear to bleed. He carefully applied the treatment consistently over the photo.

Wherever the image became too obscured with brushwork, Burke uses the Soft Cloner variant of Cloners to gently bring back detail from the original, after designating the original retouched

The named layers in the composite file, shown here in the Layers palette in Photoshop (above) and the Layers section of the Objects palette in Painter (below)

Burke painted with the Just Add Water variant to blend the border elements into the page.

A detail of the final image with airbrush highlights added

photo as the Clone source by choosing File, Clone Source. After completing each individual food image, he saved it for later.

4 Compositing the menu elements. Because the layout also included border graphics created in Adobe Illustrator, these elements were rasterized (converted from CMYK PostScript elements to bitmapped RGB graphics) so they could be blended into the final page composition. To do this, the designer's QuarkXPress document was modified to remove all of the elements except certain borders (and some headline type, which was retained for position, but later removed). Burke saved the page individually as a separate EPS file from QuarkXPress.

Burke built each panel of the menu as a single image file in Photoshop. However, the elements could have been combined in Painter in almost exactly the same way. He opened the master paper-textured background and the treated food image in Photoshop and dragged and dropped the food image file on top of the background into the position specified in the designer's layout. To blend the images softly into the paper background, he added a layer mask to the food element layer.

Finally, Burke opened the QuarkXPress EPS file and dragged and dropped it into position. To create the illusion of plates and other objects overlapping the graphic elements, he added layer masks for the graphic elements where they appeared to go "behind" the food objects. He also removed the headline type at this point. Because he wanted to use Painter to add brushwork that would blend elements that were currently on separate layers, he merged the layers in the file. Then he saved the file as an RGB TIFF.

5 Adding final details in Painter. Burke opened the file in Painter and prepared to add texture and brushstrokes throughout the image. For editing flexibility he began by creating a clone of the image by choosing File, Clone. To enhance and blend the graphic borders into the image, he used the Oil Pastel variant of Dry Media (sized to about 30 pixels), and roughly filled in the hollow borders with a warm-white color. Then, to gently blur the colored border graphics into the background paper, he used the Just Add Water variant of Liquid. Again, if he overdid the effect, he switched to the Soft Cloner brush (with the original image designated as the Clone Source) and restored detail and clarity.

6 Airbrushing highlights. To complete the menu panel, Burke wanted to embellish the bright highlights on the plate, glass and food. For optimal flexibility, he added a new layer for the highlights by clicking the New button on the Layers section (making sure that Preserve Transparency was turned off in the Layers section). Using the Digital Airbrush variant of Airbrushes and a bright, warm-white color, he softly painted strong, yet natural brushstrokes to "blow out" the highlights.

■ **Burke/Triolo Productions** is famous for its unique food photography. The team at Burke/Triolo created the illustration above for the *Tequila beverage panel* of the new menu for Acapulco Restaurants. For continuity, they used the same textures and brushwork style throughout all of the menu panels. These techniques are described more fully in "Collage Using Cloning and Layers" on page 300. For the panel above, Burke/Triolo wanted a composition with a flat perspective, so they chose not to shoot all of the bottles in one photo, but to shoot three photos of the bottles, with a shallow depth of field, then composite the images.

Lorraine Triolo began by building the still-life arrangements. The team lit the arrangements with dramatic backlighting that would reflect on and shine though the bottles. They photographed the elements and then drum-scanned the photos. Before the Painter treatment and final imaging was done by **Jeff Burke**, a collage was built by **Lew Robertson**, a photographer and digital artist working with Burke/Triolo. Robertson built a composite image of the bottles and table top in Photoshop that incorporated several layers. When the collage was complete, Burke opened a copy of the file, flattened the layers, and saved it as a TIFF file for import into Painter, where he planned to add textured brushwork and highlights. In Painter, he made a clone of the image (File, Clone) so that he could add brush work to the clone and use the original as a clone source if needed to add back some of the original detail. To make the foreground in the clone white, he made a loose freehand selection of the area with the Lasso tool, gave it a soft feather by choosing Select, Feather and pressed the Delete/Backspace key. He chose the Big Grain Rough texture (loaded from the Painter 6 Textures library on the Painter_CD2 CD-ROM) and used the Chalk Cloner variant of Cloners to roughen up some of the edges of the foreground bottles and glass. To add light color to the foreground, he used the Oil Pastel variant of Dry Media to paint light-colored, diagonal brushstrokes. For the dramatic highlight glows on the glassware, Burke used the Digital Airbrush variant of Airbrushes and very light color, enhancing the mood of the image while controlling the strokes so that the brand names on the labels remained readable. The final painted file was saved as a TIFF and laid out with other elements in QuarkXPress. (See page 302 for more about how the panels were completed.)

■ When partners **Jeff Burke** and **Lorraine Triolo** were commissioned to create the new *Acapulco Restaurants menu cover,* several people played important roles: Photography and imaging, Jeffrey Burke; food and prop styling, Lorraine Triolo; art direction, Jeff Burke and Bob Marriott; Design Firm, Marriott & Assay; and Client, Acapulco Restaurants.

To begin the menu cover, Burke built a composite that included several images of food and live models, shot in the studio against a white cove background. To add to the atmosphere, he incorporated a sky image from a recent Caribbean vacation, as well as an outdoor fountain photographed with a point-and-shoot digital camera. He made masks for several of the images in Photoshop using the Lasso and Pen tools and dragged and dropped elements into a composite file. After several preliminary compositions and the client sign-off on a final arrangement, he flattened the file and saved it in TIFF format. (Burke could have brought the file into Painter with layers, but he wanted a flat document with all of the elements merged together so that he could use Painter's brushes to paint over the entire image, completely integrating the elements.)

Burke opened the file in Painter and used much the same process as described in "Collage Using Cloning and Layers" on page 300. He cloned the file and used the Big Grain Rough texture (loaded from the Painter 6 Textures library on the Painter_CD2 CD-ROM) and a pressure-sensitive tablet and stylus. He smudged the edges of some of the elements and added colored brushwork to some areas using the Oil Pastel variant of Dry Media. By selectively blending areas in the image with the Just Add Water brush, and leaving other edges in focus, Burke created a dynamic feeling of movement in the illustration. For instance, in the server's skirt and blouse, the leading and trailing edges are blurred with soft diagonal brushwork, but the sash and ruffle are sharper. To lead the eye to the food tray, Burke airbrushed a glow under the tray and along the sleeve of the blouse. Because the food was the focal point of the composition, Burke avoided adding brushwork here. To balance the design, he left the faces of the mariachis in clearer focus than most of the other elements. It was easy to restore the focus where it was needed by designating the original file as the clone source (File, Clone Source) and using the Soft Cloner.

Finally, Burke airbrushed highlight hints on the image on a separate layer (for editing flexibility), using the Digital Airbrush to "blow out" the highlights, while keeping the look natural.

■ **John Dismukes** and **Jo-Anne Redwood,** principals of Capstone Studios, began the *Risk Game Board* for the Parker Bros./Hasbro Games Group, by creating many pencil sketches on paper. After settling on the look they wanted, they presented a tight visualization to the art director of the project, Steve Krupsky. After approval, the pencil sketch was scanned and used as a template in Macromedia FreeHand to create Post-Script outlines, which were saved in EPS format. Because he was more familiar with layers in Photoshop when he built the map, Dismukes imported the outlines into Photoshop, where he made layers for the water, each land region, the legend and the border. (Alternately, the outlines could have been brought directly into Painter as shapes via File, Acquire, Adobe Illustrator File and converted to layers. For a step-by-step description of a similar

technique using Painter, turn to "Selections and Airbrush" on page 151.) To give each element a basic color, he turned on Preserve Transparency in the Layers palette and filled the areas with mid-tone colors. (He planned to add highlights and shadows in Painter with the Digital Airbrush later.) He saved the file in Photoshop format, so it could be opened in Painter with its layers and masks intact. Dismukes loves the responsiveness of Painter's Airbrushes and their performance with a pressure-sensitive tablet and stylus. When he opened the file in Painter, he turned on Preserve Transparency in the Layers section of the Objects palette and, using the Digital Airbrush variant of Airbrushes, he hand-painted the edge of each individual layer to create a "retro-style" bevel. For each bevel, he first sampled color from the

region using the Dropper tool, and then painted the bevels using light and dark variations of the color. As he worked, he changed the size and opacity of the Digital Airbrush, paying careful attention to detail and spending the time needed to hand-paint realistic highlights and shadows along the edges. He also used the Digital Airbrush to give the chrome studs in the map's border realistic dimension. For the luminous texture on the water, Dismukes selected a rough custom paper texture in the Papers section of the Art Materials palette, then chose Effects, Focus, Glass Distortion, Using Paper, with Refraction. To strengthen the focal point of the composition, he applied a custom lighting effect to the water layer, by choosing Effects, Surface Control, Apply Lighting. (To see more work from Capstone Studios, turn to pages 292–293.)

■ Graphic designer and artist **Donal Jolley** created *Winter Morning* and *Clay Chapel*, two of twelve images for the *Turning Point 2002 Calendar*. To begin the calendar, Jolley worked with his client David Jeremiah to select reference photos. Beginning in Photoshop, Jolley opened the reference photos for *Winter Morning* (shot by Robert Hayes) and *Clay Chapel* (taken by Jolley). He removed unwanted elements from the foreground, trees and skies by cloning using the Rubber Stamp tool. To achieve the mood he wanted in each image, he intensified the yellows and oranges in *Winter Morning* and the foreground greens in *Clay Chapel* using Photoshop's Hue and Saturation controls. So that he would be able to isolate areas of the images (for instance, the

snow, sky and water in *Winter Morning* and the truck and church in *Clay Chapel*), he made selections and saved them as alpha channels. Then he saved the image with its alpha channels in Photoshop format, so he could work on it in Painter. Jolley planned to use Painter's brushes for textured brushwork that would add painterly movement to the images and break up the smooth photographic look. Using several layers and paying careful attention to the volume of the forms, he painted with the Artist Pastel Chalk and Square Chalk variants of Dry Media (with a rough paper texture chosen in the Papers section of the Art Materials palette). When he wanted to constrain paint to a particular area of a layer (such as the

sky), he loaded a selection based on the alpha channel he had saved for that area by choosing Select, Load Selection and choosing it in the Load From menu. Then he painted within the area. When he wanted to sample color from the layers below, he enabled Pick Up Underlying Color in the Layers section. To blend and pull color while adding texture in the sky, he used the Grainy Water variant of Liquid. To achieve a "salt" effect on the water reflections in *Winter Morning*, he used the Fairy Dust variant of the F-X brush. Then he added final colored details to the snow, church and water with a small Artist Pastel Chalk.

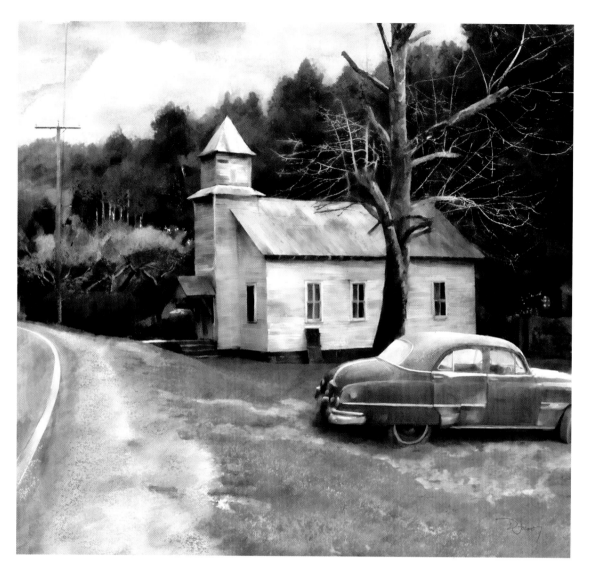

For *Clay Chapel*, **Donal Jolley** used Water Color brushes in addition to the Dry Media and Liquid variants. Jolley appreciates the flexibility of painting on layers. When he wants to make changes to an area he often paints the changes on a new layer, so he can control the strength of the effect using the Opacity slider in the Layers section. After establishing the overall brushwork using the Square Chalk and Artist Pastel Chalk variants and blending with the Grainy Water variant, he painted transparent watercolor glazes onto the old car to enhance the look of the rusty metal. He also added light watercolor washes on top of the pastel brushwork on the midground trees, then

painted texture on the foreground grass and road using the Splatter Water variant of Water Color. When the brushwork on *Winter Morning* and *Clay Chapel* was complete, Jolley added more texture as follows: First he saved a copy of each image using a different name and flattened the layers in the copies by choosing Drop All from the menu on the right side of the Layers section bar. Next, he made two duplicates of each image by selecting all (Ctrl/⌘-A) and Alt/Option-clicking with the Layer Adjuster. On the top layer, he used Effects, Surface Control, Apply Surface Texture, Using Paper, also with subtle settings to add paper grain. On the next layer, he used Effects, Surface

Control, Apply Surface Texture, Using Image Luminance, with subtle settings, to "emboss" the brushstrokes. Then he adjusted the Opacity of both layers to his liking, using the slider on the Layers section. He saved a duplicate of each of the final layered Photoshop format files in TIFF format, which flattened the images. Because Jolley was more familiar with color correction and conversion in Photoshop, he opened both final TIFF files in that program, made color adjustments and then converted the images to CMYK for printing in the calendar.

■ Designer/illustrator **Marc Brown** was commissioned by Angie Lee, art director at Grindstone Graphics, to create *Museum Store* (above). He created *Iron Casters* (right) for Amanda Wilson, art director at The Evans Group Advertising. Brown employed similar techniques to create both illustrations. He started with a loose pencil drawing, then scanned the drawing and placed it into Adobe Illustrator as a template. In Illustrator he drew the elements on individual layers and filled them with flat color. To rasterize the image, he copied each Illustrator layer and pasted it into Photoshop as a layer. (This process can also be accomplished in Painter by drawing shapes and filling them with color, or by importing Illustrator art into Painter. See Chapters 4 and 5 for more information about using and importing shapes.) At this point, Brown opened the layered file in Painter. He used Airbrushes variants and the Chalk variants of Dry Media to add colored details to the faces and clothing, blending color with Liquid variants. After he had completed the composite, he merged the layers by choosing Drop All from the Layers section bar's menu on the Objects palette. To finish, he broke up some of the smooth edges by painting them with the Just Add Water variant of Liquid.

■ **Rhoda Grossman** was commissioned by *Emergency Medical Services* magazine to create this painterly collage illustration for an article titled "Create the Carnage and We Will Come," which discussed the tendency for rescue workers to plunge into dangerous situations without sufficient regard for their own safety. Grossman's image depicts an over enthusiastic rescue worker armed only with an oxygen tank and a hard hat (emblazoned with the "Star of Life" logo for emergency services). The menacing eye and smoking gun represent a variety of dangers that might be awaiting the rescue worker behind the door.

To begin the collage, Grossman opened source files for the menacing eye, the hand with gun, the oxygen tank, the hand with palm facing out, the helmet and various facial parts she could use to

assemble the head of the worker. She copied elements from the source files and pasted them into a composite file, where she arranged them using the Painter's Layer Adjuster tool. When she had the elements where she wanted them, she chose File, Clone to quickly make a flattened copy. The Clone command dropped all layers in the clone, but the original was left with its layers intact. She saved the new flattened image under a unique name so that she would not overwrite the original layered file. Next, she used the Grainy Water variant of Liquid (over Basic Paper texture) to smear and blend the hard edges of the items into each other and into the background. She avoided smooth transitions, wanting her brushwork to show. She enhanced the smoke from the gun using the Distorto variant of Liquid. When she was happy

with this stage, she saved the image as a TIFF file, then opened it in Photoshop.

Working in Photoshop, she applied the Find Edges filter (Filter, Stylize, Find Edges), and then faded the effect to 35% (Edit, Fade). This reduced the saturation, lightened the image and enhanced the brushstrokes. She saved this stage of the file again using TIFF format and under a unique name.

Next, Grossman opened both the filtered image and the painted, flat image in Painter. She wanted to add more emphasis to the brushstrokes, so she created a new clone of the painted image (File, Clone), and with this clone active, she chose Effects, Surface Control, Apply Surface Texture, Using Image Luminance. Then she used the Soft Cloner variant of Cloners both to bring back the previous painted stage wherever the texture was too strong, and to add elements from the filtered image. She made each of the two files in turn the Clone Source by choosing File, Clone Source and choosing from the menu of file names . Finally, she saved the image as a TIFF file, then opened it in Photoshop again, where she converted it to CMYK for placement in the magazine's page layout.

■ *Thai Rocks* (above), and *Happy Hula* (right), by **Jack Davis,** were created with much the same style and brushwork as Davis's traditional oils on canvas, which incorporate brilliant colors painted onto a black "ground."

Davis began *Thai Rocks* by taking photos on location. For *Happy Hula,* he began with an original photo taken by Susan Merritt. He scanned the photos into Photoshop, then copied and pasted bits and pieces of the photos into a reference file and increased the saturation of the images. When the composition looked right, he flattened the file and saved it in Photoshop format. Then he opened it in Painter and cloned it (File, Clone). Davis deleted the contents of the clone and filled the background with black. Next, he turned on Tracing Paper (Canvas, Tracing Paper) and chose the Big Wet Luscious variant of Brushes, loaded from the New Paint Tools library (located on the Painter_CD2 CD-ROM). To rough in blocks of color based on color in the reference collage, he checked the Clone Color box on the Colors section of the Art Materials palette. After he had laid in the basic composition, he turned off Tracing Paper and the Clone Color option and completed the painting. For the figure and foreground details in *Happy Hula*, Davis also used a small Dry Brush, also from the New Paint Tools library, with Clone Color turned on in the Colors section. As a last step, he added realistic highlights and shadows to the brushstrokes—building the look of thick paint—using Effects, Surface Control, Apply Surface Texture, Using Image Luminance with subtle settings.

■ The most recent works of artist **Pamela Wells,** which focus on feminine archetypes, are sold in commercial and fine-art markets. For *Winter/Spring,* Wells was inspired to create a visual metaphor for the transitional time between seasons. She began the image by shooting photos of a model to use as reference for her composition. Later she would paint two characters from these photos, changing facial features so the characters looked different. Wells scanned the photos into Photoshop and made a rough collage in that program to use as a reference while working in Painter. She merged the layers and saved the file in TIFF format. Wells opened this reference file in Painter and made a clone by choosing File, Clone. In preparation for using Tracing Paper, she

deleted the contents of the clone by pressing Ctrl/⌘-A and then the Backspace/Delete key. Then she turned on Tracing Paper by pressing Ctrl/⌘-T and used a pressure-sensitive tablet and stylus to draw a detailed black-and-white line sketch with the 2B Pencil variant of the Pencils. Because she wanted to begin the coloring by filling areas with flat color, she made sure to create solid lines to enclose the areas she wanted to fill. She could then apply color fills to the figures and clothing, for example, using the Paint Bucket from the Tools palette. To model the forms of the figures and their clothing, she carefully painted over the filled areas. Wells used the Soft Charcoal variant of Dry Media to apply layers of

color using a light pressure on the stylus. To blend areas, she laid subtly different colors over existing ones. For instance, to render the skin, she brushed the areas with a light tan color, then covered them with a darker orange and finally a peachy red. To add texture to the fabric and brighter colors to the flowers, she used more contrasting values and a tiny Soft Charcoal variant. When she had finished painting the illustration, Wells saved it as a TIFF file and opened the image in Photoshop, where she applied a few minor color and brightness adjustments. To read about how Wells made a fine-art print of her image, turn to the beginning of Chapter 12, "Printing and Archival Concerns."

MULTIMEDIA AND FILM WITH PAINTER

Film artist Dewey Reid created this pre-production comprehensive for the Nike All Conditions Gear *TV commercial using scanned images and Painter's brushes, effects and Scripts; he worked back and forth between Painter and Adobe Premiere, using Premiere for timing and transitions.*

WHETHER YOU'RE AN ANIMATOR, film artist, designer, or 3D artist, Painter's multimedia capabilities offer you dozens of practical techniques. Multimedia artists appreciate the creative freedom offered by Painter's brushes, textures and effects. If you're producing an animation or making a movie, many of the techniques and effects shown in this book can be applied to frames in a Frame Stack, Painter's native animation format, or to an imported movie clip. Although it isn't a full-featured animation or film-compositing program, Painter is good for making comps so you can preview motion. And Painter gives 3D artists a wide variety of choices for creating natural, organic textures to be used for texture mapping. In addition, the ability to record painting scripts lets you make tutorials to show others how your painting was built and even lets you batch-process a series of images.

WORKING WITH SCRIPTS

Painter's versatile Script feature lets you record your work, then play the process back, either in Painter or as a QuickTime or AVI (video for Windows) movie. But if you use this feature a lot, you'll soon discover its limitations—for example, its inability to record some Painter operations can produce a different effect during playback.

There are two basic kinds of scripts—Painter's automatically recorded Current Script and scripts that are recorded by enabling the Record feature. Both kinds of scripts are visible in the Scripts section of the Objects palette when you install Painter: The white icon represents the Current Script and the icons with pictures represent scripts that were manually recorded by artists while they worked, to demonstrate various

The Scripts section of the Objects palette with a custom script chosen in the top row and the Current Script shown as a white icon (at lower right)

A CURRENT SCRIPT PREFERENCE

You can tell Painter how long to save current scripts by specifying the number of days in the Preferences, General dialog box. (The default is one day.) A word of caution: Saving several days of scripts can use a lot of hard disk space!

A Current Script showing the instructions for an application of Surface Texture. The white icon in the top row of the Scripts section represents the Current Script.

You can use these buttons on the front of the Scripts section to begin recording a single script (center red button) and to stop recording when you're finished (left square button).

Athos Boncompagni saved a series of scripts when creating La Luna e le Stelle, and played them back at higher resolution to build a larger image. Turn to page 331 to read more about the image in the gallery. For more information about using scripts in this way, see the tip "Increasing File Resolution With Scripts," on page 314.

kinds of images that can be created using Painter. If you record your own scripts they will also appear in the Scripts section.

Understanding the Current Script. The Current Script starts when you launch Painter and closes when you quit the application. While you work, Painter transparently records your actions automatically, saving them as the Current Script in the Painter Script Data file in the Painter application folder. If you have launched and quit Painter several times during a 24 hour day, you'll notice several white icons in the Scripts drawer, with the dates and times for each work session listed in the pull-down resource list menu on the Scripts section, for instance "2/22/02 8:07 AM."

Playing back a complete Current Script in which you created and saved more than one image can cause problems. For instance, if you opened a file, added brushstrokes and saved it, playing back the Current Script may result in Painter finding the first file, redrawing your strokes over the image and then resaving over the file. A more practical way to use an automatically recorded script is to open it and copy a specific series of commands from it (a lighting and texture effect, for instance), to paste into a new script, which can then be played back on other images.

Using a portion of a current script. To use a portion of a current script, copy specific commands from it and paste them into a new script, begin by opening the Scripts section of the Objects palette. Click the right triangle on the Scripts section bar and from the menu select Open Script. In the dialog box that opens, choose Current Script from the Painter Script Data file list and click Open. The Current Script cannot be edited, but to use only a specific set of instructions from it, you *can* copy them to the clipboard and paste the instructions into a new script. Then you'll be able to use your new script to re-create just that series of actions. To do this, open the Current Script, Shift-select the instructions that you want to use (you may want to start at the bottom of the list, where the most recent instructions are found), choose Copy from the Scripts menu, choose Close Script and then choose New Script from the menu. Type a name for your new script in the Script Name dialog box, and click OK. Then choose Paste from the Scripts menu, and choose Close Script. To play your new script, choose Playback Script from the menu then select the new script by name from the pop-out list in the Scripts section and click the Playback button.

Recording a planned script. To record a series of deliberate actions into a script (instead of copying and pasting from the automatically recorded script), click the right triangle on the Scripts section bar to open the menu and choose Record Script to begin recording, or click the Record button (the red dot) on the Scripts section. When you've finished working on your image choose Stop Recording Script (or click the square Stop button). When you click OK, the dialog box will close and Painter will prompt you to name

To add lighting and a paper texture to this Mediacom video clip, we played a special effects script (using Effects, Surface Control, Apply Lighting and Apply Surface Texture) on each of the frames

your script. The new named script will appear in the pop-out list in the Scripts section, available for later playback. To play the new script, select it from the list and click the Play (forward arrow) button.

Recording and saving a series of scripts. If you want to record the development of a complex painting (so you can use the script to demonstrate how you created the painting) but you don't want to finish the painting in one sitting, you can record a series of work scripts to be played back. First note the dimensions of your file by choosing Canvas, Resize, then click OK to close the dialog box. Click the right triangle on the Scripts section bar, choose Record Script. Include a number in the name of your script (such as "01") to help you remember the playback order. Then begin your painting. When you want to take a break, stop recording (Scripts section bar, Stop Recording Script). When you're ready to continue, choose Record Script again and resume working on your image. Record and save as many scripts as you need, giving them the same basic name but numbering them so you can keep track of the order. To play them back, open a new file of the same dimensions as the original, then choose Playback Script from the menu on the Scripts section bar. Choose the "01" script, and when it's done playing, choose the next script: It will play back on top of the image created by the first script. Continue playing back scripts in order until the image is completed. (You can also record a script so that it can be played back on a canvas of a different size; see the tip below.)

QUICKTIME CAN'T CONVERT

Many of the prerecorded scripts that ship with Painter contain Painter commands that QuickTime cannot convert, and consequently these scripts can't be turned into QuickTime movies. It's not possible to use the Record Frames on Playback function with scripts that contain commands such as File, New, or File, Clone (an Illegal Command error message will appear).

INCREASING FILE RESOLUTION WITH SCRIPTS

You can use Painter's Scripts function to record your work at low resolution, then play it back at a higher resolution. This technique gives you a much crisper result than simply resizing the original image to a new resolution. Here's how to do it: Start by opening the Scripts section of the Objects palette. Click the right triangle on the Scripts section bar to open the menu and choose Script Options. In the Script Options dialog box check the Record Initial State box, then click OK. Open a new file (File, New) and choose Select, All (Ctrl/⌘-A). From the Scripts section menu, choose Record Script (or press the round red button on the Scripts section) to begin recording. Then begin painting. When you're finished, from the menu on the Scripts section bar, choose Stop Recording Script (or click the square black button on the Scripts section). Open a new document two to four times as large as the original (this technique loses its effectiveness if your new file is much bigger than this), Again press Ctr/⌘-A, to

Choosing Script Options from the pull-down menu on the Scripts section of the Objects palette

select the entire Canvas. Then choose Playback Script from the menu, or click the black triangle button (to the left of the red button) on the Scripts section. Painter will replay the script in the larger image, automatically scaling brushes and papers to perfectly fit the new size. A word of caution—scripts can be quirky: Your higher-resolution image may not match the lower-resolution one if you use imported photos, complex selections, shapes or the Image Hose, for instance.

The Frame Stack palette for Donal Jolley's animation Rattlesnake *showing the movement in frames 13–14.*

When you're turning a script into a frame stack by checking the Record Frames on Playback box (accessed by clicking the right triangle on the Scripts section bar and choosing Script Options), a long script may result in a huge frame stack. There is currently no way to preview the number of frames that will be created when you enter an interval number in the dialog box, so you need to make sure you have plenty of hard disk space available.

To record the painting process of Mill Valley *(360 x 504 pixels, painted with Pastel and Water brushes), we made a movie using Save Frames on Playback and an interval of 10. The resulting movie was 100.6 MB with 142 frames.*

Automating a series of operations. Recording a series of actions can save you a lot of time when you need to apply the same effect to several images. Test a combination of operations (such as a series of choices from the Effects menu) until you get something you like. Choose Record Script from the menu on the Scripts section bar (accessed by the right triangle), and repeat the series of choices that produces the effect you want. After you've stopped recording and have saved your script, you can apply the operations to a selection, a layer or a still image by selecting your script in the Scripts section and clicking the forward arrow button on the front of the section).

You can also apply your script to a Frame Stack. Turn to "Automating Movie Effects" later in this chapter for a detailed explanation of this technique.

Saving a script as a movie. This is a great option if you'd like to "play back" a painting for someone who does not have Painter. QuickTime movies can be played on Macintosh and PC/Windows computers with a freeware QuickTime projector such as Movie Player (included on the Wow! CD-ROM that accompanies this book). First you'll record your work as a script, then you'll play it back on a new file, and then you'll save it as a QuickTime/AVI movie.

Begin by clicking the right triangle on the Scripts section bar and choosing Script Options. In the Script Options dialog box, turn on Record Initial State (otherwise Painter will play back the first few commands or brushstrokes of your script using whatever colors, brushes and textures are active, instead of the ones you actually used during the recording of the script). Check Save Frames on Playback. You can leave the time interval Painter uses to grab frames from your script at 10, the default, but you may want to experiment with lower settings instead, to get a smoother playback result.

Next, open a new file of the dimensions you want for your eventual movie file. Click the right triangle on the Scripts section bar, choose Record Script from the menu, and make your drawing. When you've finished, from the same menu, choose Stop Recording Script; name your script and click OK to save it. Now Painter will

To save a script as a movie, check Save Frames on Playback in the Script Options dialog box (chosen by clicking the right triangle on the Scripts section bar and choosing Script Options). Painter will grab a part of your script as a frame at the interval (tenths of a second) that you set. A lower setting in the interval box (such as 1 or 2) results in smoother playback than the default setting of 10, but file sizes for lower settings are larger because more frames are created. For instance, a short script with an interval setting of 1 resulted in a 4.2 MB Frame Stack; the same script recorded with an interval of 10 produced a 1.4 MB file.

A storyboard frame from the MGM *movie* Stargate. *Peter Mitchell Rubin used Painter to build digital storyboard illustrations for the movie, saving them as numbered PICT files and animating them with Adobe Premiere.*

To change the continents from brown to green in this Cascom video clip, we recorded a script while performing the Color Mask procedure and Color Overlay tinting process on one frame, then stopped recording and saved our script. After undoing the effects applied to the first frame, we chose Movie, Apply Script to Movie and took a break while Painter completed the masking and tinting process on all 243 frames. Above: The Frame Stack palette shows frame 141 with the operations applied, and frame 142 as yet untouched.

convert the script to a movie. First, watch your recorded script played back as a Painter Frame Stack by opening a new file (same dimensions) and choosing Playback Script from the menu, choosing your script from the list and clicking the Playback button. Painter will prompt you to enter a name for your new movie file. Name it, click Save and then specify the number of layers of Onion Skin and color depth by clicking on the appropriate buttons. (For most uses, select 2 layers of Onion Skin and 24-bit color with 8-bit alpha.) Click OK, and your script will unfold as a Frame Stack. When it's finished playing, save it in QuickTime/AVI movie format by choosing Save As, Save Movie as QuickTime. The QuickTime/AVI file will be smaller than a Frame Stack (if you use a Compressor choice in the Compression Settings dialog box) and will play back more smoothly. (Because most compression degrades quality, compress only once—when you've completed the project. Film artist Dewey Reid suggests using Animation or None as the Compressor setting.) To read more about preserving image quality when working with movies, turn to "Importing and Exporting," on page 318.

Making movies using multiple scripts. You can save a series of successive scripts, then play back the scripts as frame stacks and save them as QuickTime movies without compression to preserve quality. Then you can open the movies in a program such as Adobe Premiere, Adobe After Effects or Avid Video Shop and composite the movies into a single movie.

ANIMATING WITH FRAME STACKS

If you open a QuickTime or AVI movie in Painter, it will be converted to a Frame Stack, Painter's native movie format. Frame Stacks are based on the way conventional animators work: Each frame is analogous to an individual transparent acetate cel. You can navigate to any frame within a stack and paint on it or apply effects to it with any of Painter's tools (see "Animating an Illustration" on page 321).

Artists accustomed to specialized animation and video programs such as Adobe After Effects and Adobe Premiere will notice the limitations of the Frame Stack feature (there are no precise timing or compositing controls, for instance). If you use one of

A frame from an animation based on a video clip. We began by using Painter's Water Color brushes to illustrate the frames, which created a Water Color layer. Because a Water Color layer sits on top of the entire Frame Stack, we copied the layer to the clipboard, then dropped it to the Canvas when we had finished painting the frame. We advanced to the next frame and pasted in the copied watercolor and added new brushstrokes, repeating this copying, dropping, pasting and painting process until the frames were complete. As a final touch, we applied an effects script (with Apply Surface Texture Using Paper) to complete the piece.

these programs, you will probably want to work out timing and compositing in the specialized program, then import your document into Painter to give it an effects treatment.

When you open a QuickTime or AVI video clip in Painter or start a brand-new movie, you'll specify the number of frames and color bit depth to be used in the Frame Stack. You will be asked to name and save your movie. At this point the stack is saved to your hard disk. A Frame Stack will usually take up many more megabytes on your hard disk than it did as a movie (depending on the kind of movie compression used), so have plenty of space available. Each time you advance a frame in the stack, Painter automatically saves any changes you have made to the movie. When you choose Save As, Painter will ask you to name the movie again. This is not a redundant Save command, but an opportunity to convert the file to another format: Save Current Frame as Image, Save Movie as QuickTime or AVI format, or Save Movie as Numbered Files (to create a sequence of frames to composite in another program such as Adobe Premiere).

USING A VIDEO CLIP REFERENCE

Painter's cloning function allows you to link two movies—a video clip and a blank movie of the same pixel dimensions—and use the video as a reference on which to base an animation. Open a video clip that you want to use as a reference (File, Open), then make a blank movie (File, New Movie) of the same pixel dimensions as your video clip. (The second movie doesn't need to have the same number of frames). Under File, Clone Source, select the video clip. In the blank movie frame, turn on Tracing Paper (Ctrl/⌘-T). Using the clone source as a guide, choose a brush and paint on the frame. To use the Frame Stacks palette to advance one frame in the original, click the appropriate icon (circled in the palette shown below), or press Page Up on your keyboard. Do the same to advance the clone one frame. Use Movie, Go to Frame to move to a specific frame in either clone or original. You can also apply special effects such as Effects, Surface Control, Apply Surface Texture and Color Overlay, or Effects, Focus, Glass Distortion (all using Original Luminance), to your new movie using the clone source.

We opened a video clip (shown here in the Frame Stack palette) and a new Frame Stack, both using two layers of Onion Skin to show the position of the diver in both frames. Click on the circled button to advance one frame in the Frame Stacks palette.

Frames 1 and 2 of the Diver video clip (top row), and corresponding frames in the animation (bottom row), painted with the Sharp Chalk variant. Tracing paper is active on the bottom right image.

Creating animated comps. Painter provides a good way to visualize a rough animation. An animatic (a comp of an animation, consisting of keyframe illustrations with movement applied) can be comprised of images drawn in Painter, scanned elements, or numbered PICT files created in Painter, Photoshop or even object-oriented programs that can export PICT files (such as Illustrator). (See "Making an Animated Comp" on page 325, featuring Dewey Reid's illustrations in a demonstration of an animatic technique.) You can also alter individual frames in a movie with Painter's effects or brushes. For a demonstration of frame-by-frame painting, see "Animating an Illustration" on page 321.

Rotoscoping movies. There are numerous ways to rotoscope (paint or apply special effects to movie frames) in Painter. Many of the techniques in this book can be used for rotoscoping—brushwork, masking, tonal adjustment or filters or Effects, Surface Control, Apply Lighting and Apply Surface Texture, or Effects, Focus, Glass Distortion, for example.

Basing an animation on a movie. You can use Painter's Tracing Paper to trace images from a source movie to a clone to create an animation. This feature lets you shoot video and use it as a reference on which to base a path of motion. This process is described in the tip "Using a Video Clip Reference" on page 317.

IMPORTING AND EXPORTING

With a little planning and understanding of file formats, still and animated files can easily be imported into Painter and exported out of Painter to other programs.

Preserving image quality. Because compression can degrade the quality of image files, when you obtain source files to bring into Painter, choose uncompressed animation and video clips. And because quality deteriorates each time you compress (the degree of degradation depends on the compression choice), save your working files without compression until your project is complete. If you plan to composite Painter movies in another application, such as Adobe Premiere, After Effects or Avid Video Shop, save them without compression. For an in-depth explanation of compressors for QuickTime or for AVI, see Chapter 20 in the *Painter 7 User Guide*.

Importing multimedia files into Painter. Painter can accept QuickTime and AVI movies from any source, as well as still image PICT files and numbered PICT files exported from PostScript drawing programs, Photoshop and Premiere. To number your PICT files so that they're read in the correct order by Painter, you must use the same number of digits for all the files, and you must number them sequentially, such as "File 000," "File 001," "File 002" and so on. With all files in a single folder, choose File, Open

Jon Lee of Fox Television used Painter's brushes and effects to progressively modify the logo for the comedy Martin, *creating numbered PICT files for an animated sequence. The modified files were animated on a Quantel HAL.*

Highly saturated colors can smear when output to video. Choose Effects, Tonal Control, Video Legal Colors to make the colors in your file compatible with NTSC or PAL video color. In the Preview, press and release the grabber to toggle between the RGB and Video Legal Colors previews; click OK to convert the colors in your file.

and check the Open Numbered Files option. Select the first numbered file in your sequence and, when prompted, select the last file. Painter will assemble the files into a Frame Stack.

You can create a mask in a Painter movie and use it in your Frame Stack, or export it within a QuickTime movie to another program such as Premiere or After Effects. To make a movie with a mask, choose one of the options with a mask in the New Frame Stack dialog box. (You can also make a Frame Stack from a sequence of numbered PICT files in which each file includes its own mask.) To export the movie from Painter as a QuickTime movie and include the mask, choose Save As and select the QuickTime movie option. When the Compression Settings dialog box appears, in the Compressor section, choose Animation or None from the top pop-up menu to make the mask option available, then choose Millions of Colors+ in the lower pop-up menu. Click OK.

Exporting Painter images to multimedia applications. Since multimedia work is created to be viewed on monitors and the standard monitor resolution is 72 ppi, set up your Frame Stacks and still image files using that resolution. Most files used in multimedia have a 4 x 3 aspect ratio: 160 x 120, 240 x 180, 320 x 240 or 640 x 480 pixels. Television also has a 4 x 3 aspect ratio, but for digital television the pixels are slightly taller than they are wide. Artists and designers who create animation for broadcast usually prepare their files at "D-1 size," 720 x 486 pixels. Digital television uses a ".9" pixel (90 percent the width of standard square pixels). The narrower pixel causes circles and other objects to be stretched vertically. To create a file for D-1 maintaining the height-to-width ratio (to preserve circles), begin with a 720 x 540-pixel image. When the image is complete, scale it non-proportionally to 720 x 486. This will "crush" the image slightly as it appears on your computer screen, but when it's transferred to digital television it will be in the correct proportions.

QuickTime movie files can be exported from Painter and opened in multimedia programs such as Premiere, After Effects and Macromedia Director. If you're using one of these programs to create an 8-bit color production, you'll save processing time if you start with an 8-bit Frame Stack in Painter: Choose the 8-bit Color System Palette option in the New Frame Stack dialog box (after choosing File, New and naming your movie). If you don't set up your file as 8-bit in Painter, you should consider using Photoshop or Equilibrium Debabelizer—both offer excellent color-conversion control.

We used a modified photo to create this repeating pattern. To generate seamless, tiled textures for 3D, use any of the commands in the menu of the Patterns section of the Art Materials palette. Turn to "Exploring Patterns" on page 239 in the beginning of Chapter 7 and to "Creating a Pattern" on page 246, for more about working with patterns.

Many experienced artists prefer to export their Painter images as PICT files rather than as movies because they can easily remove frames from the sequence if they choose. To export Painter still images to applications such as Premiere and After Effects, or to other platforms, save them as single PICT images or as a series of numbered PICT files. You can include a single mask in a Painter PICT file that can be used in compositing in Premiere or After Effects. See "Animating a Logo," on page 327, for a demonstration of exporting Painter images to another platform.

You can also import Painter-created QuickTime movies and still PICT images into Macromedia Director. A QuickTime movie comes in as a single linked Cast Member in the Cast Window, which means it will be stored outside the Director file, keeping file size manageable. 🖌

CREATING TEXTURE MAPS FOR 3D RENDERING

A *texture map*—a flat image applied to the surface of a 3D object—can greatly enhance the realism of rendering in 3D programs such as Bryce, Strata Studio Pro, Ray Dream Studio or Infini-D. Many kinds of images can be used for mapping—scanned photographs, logo artwork or painted textures, for example. 3D artists especially like Painter's ability to imitate colorful, natural textures (such as painted wood grain or foliage). There are several kinds of texture maps: A *color texture map* is an image that's used to apply color to a 3D rendering of an object. Other types of mapping affect other qualities of the surface; for instance, a *bump map* (a two-dimensional representation of an uneven surface), a

transparency map (used to define areas of an image that are transparent, such as glass panes in a window) and a *reflectance map* (used to define matte and shiny areas on an object's surface). If you're developing more than one of these texture maps to the same 3D object, you can keep them in register by using Save As or making clones of the same "master" Painter image to keep file dimensions the same. Remember to save your surface maps in PICT format so the 3D program will be able to recognize them.

These floating globes were rendered by John Odam in Strata Studio Pro. He created a texture map in Painter using the Wriggle texture from the More Wild Textures library (in the Paper Textures folder on the Painter_CD2 CD-ROM) and applied the texture to the objects as follows: color map (A), bump map (B), reflectance map (C) and transparency map (D). The Studio Pro document size was 416 x 416 pixels; the texture map size was 256 x 256 pixels.

Animating an Illustration

Overview *Create an illustration; open a new movie document; paste the drawing into the movie into each frame as a layer; copy an area you want to animate; position it and drop it as a layer into a precise position; advance to a new frame and repeat the pasting, moving and copying process; use brushes to paint on individual frames.*

DONAL JOLLEY

1a

Jolley's finished Painter illustration

1b

Making a selection of the tail and rattle

1c

The Layers section showing the Tail layer selected

CREATING AN ANIMATION—whether you use Painter or draw on traditional acetate cels—is labor-intensive because of the sheer number of frames required to get smooth motion. But working digitally does have advantages. You can save a lot of time by copying and pasting a single illustration onto multiple frames. Corrections to digital art are easier to make than with conventional methods; and, thanks to the Frame Stacks player, you can see results immediately.

To begin *Rattle Envy*, Donal Jolley painted and animated a comical snake with Painter's brushes. Once the basic animation was complete, Jolley composited some extra layers at a reduced opacity to add the feeling of movement, further enhancing the effect with painted speed blurs.

1 Planning the animation and illustrating. Create an illustration in Painter, choosing a file size no more than a few inches square at 72 ppi (Jolley's illustration was 3 x 3 inches at 72 ppi.) Use Painter's brushes to paint just the essential image; you'll be adding the details to each individual frame later. To keep the animation process simple, choose a subject that you won't need to redraw in every frame, such as a character winking an eye. Jolley sketched a whimsical rattlesnake, and then copied the tail area, eyebrows and tongue elements to separate layers so that he could transform them later to create motion in the animation.

After sketching the snake using the Scratchboard Tool variant of Pens, Jolley added color and modeled forms using the Digital Airbrush variant of Airbrushes and the Square Chalk variant of Dry Media. Then he added more linework and shadows using the Colored Pencils variant of Pencils and blended color with the Grainy Water variant of Liquid.

He carefully selected each of the areas he planned to animate—three elements in the illustration—the tail area, the eyebrows, and the tongue—and pasted copies of them on separate layers as described below. In addition, he created a layer with a copy of the of only the stationery parts of the snake's body without the tail, eyebrows and tongue, so when he rocked the tail back and forth or moved the parts, the area underneath it would be white.

When you've finished your illustration, make a selection around an area that you want to animate (Jolley used the Lasso tool), press Alt/Option and choose Select, Float to place a copy of

Beginning a new Frame Stack, 3 x 3 inches, 72 ppi, with 33 frames

Pasting the base illustration into the movie

Clicking the Rewind button to return to frame 1

Frame 3 with Tracing Paper/Onion Skin (three layers) turned on

The red marker shows that Frame 4 is active.

it on a new layer. Repeat for any other parts that you want to animate. Also prepare a layer that includes everything that will *not* be animated. Now, click on the non-animated layer's name in the Layers section and choose Select, All, and copy it to the clipboard (Ctrl/⌘-Shift-C). It's now ready to be pasted into a movie. Leave the original illustration file open so you can copy elements from it into your movie.

2 Starting a new Frame Stack. To open a new movie file, choose File, New. Choose a small size so Painter will play the movie quickly; then click the Movie Picture Type, and enter enough frames to give you a smooth animation. Jolley created a 3 x 3-inch movie at 72 ppi (that matched the dimensions and resolution of his illustration), with 33 frames to start, though he added more frames as he needed them using Movie, Add Frames, so that his finished animation was 38 frames. Click OK; name and save your movie, and in the New Frame Stack dialog box, choose Jolley's options: three layers of Onion Skin (so you can see three frames back into the stack) and full 24-bit color with an 8-bit mask.

3 Pasting the illustration into the frame stack. Paste the non-animated part of your illustration from the clipboard into the movie file—it will come in as a layer—then use the Layer Adjuster tool to move it into position. Copy it in its new position, then drop it to the Canvas by choosing Drop from the menu on the right side of the Layers section bar on the Objects palette (or press Ctrl/⌘-Shift-D). Because a layer sits on top of the entire frame stack, make sure that you've dropped it before you begin the next step. To advance the frame stack one frame, click the step forward icon on the Frame Stack palette (or press the Page Up key on your keyboard). Paste the copied base illustration into a new frame in the same position (press Ctrl/⌘-Shift-V) and drop, repeating the paste and drop sequence for each frame of the movie.

4 Creating movement by offsetting layers. Then, to return to the first frame in the stack, click the Rewind button. Back in your original illustration file, choose the Layer Adjuster tool and select the layer for a part that you want to animate by clicking on

4d

The frame stack palette, showing movement in frames 30–32

5

Frame 29 shows a copy of the tail layer pasted in, rotated and at 58% opacity

6a

Frame 32 showing the Gritty Charcoal smudges and a low-opacity layer

6b

Frame 30 showing a speed blur painted with the Grainy Water variant

its layer name in the Layers section, and choose Ctrl/⌘-C to copy it. Now activate your frame stack file and choose Ctrl/⌘-Shift-V to paste it into exact position.

So that he would have an unmanipulated copy that he could use later, Jolley made a copy of the pasted tail area layer by Alt/Option-clicking on it with the Layer Adjuster tool. Then he hid the copy by shutting the eye icon to the left of its name in the Layers section.

With the original tail section layer selected, he chose Effects, Orientation, Free Transform and used the feature to rotate the tail. When you choose Free Transform, an eight-handled bounding box will appear. Now choose the Layer Adjuster tool, press the Ctrl/⌘ key and position the tool over a corner handle. Drag to rotate the layer to a position that you like. So you can bring the layer in its new position into the next frame, store a copy of the layer in the clipboard by pressing Ctrl/⌘-C. Then press Ctrl/⌘-Shift-D to drop the layer onto the current frame, and go to the next frame by pressing Page Up on your keyboard. Paste the copied illustration again, and use the Layer Adjuster tool to reposition the element in the frame; then drop it.

As you work, look at the Frame Stacks palette to check your progress. You can view previous frames "ghosted" in your main image—much like an animator's light box—by choosing Canvas, Tracing Paper (Ctrl/⌘-T). The number of previous frames displayed is determined by the number of Onion Skin layers you chose when you opened the movie. To change the number of layers, close the file, reopen it, and choose a new number of layers. Use Ctrl/⌘-T to turn the Onion Skin view on and off as you work. Click the Play button to play the animation, and take note of the areas that need to be smoother.

5 Making the animation smoother. After playing the animation, Jolley wanted to make the transition between some of the frames smoother and slower. So he used the tail area layer copy that he had hidden in the Layers section (in step 4) as a basis to add several more low-opacity layers to a few of the frames. Then he replayed the animation again to check its smoothness. To blur a few of the edges, he used the Just Add Water variant of Liquid on some of the frames.

6 Adding more motion with brushstrokes. Now that he liked the way the animation played, Jolley added to the feeling of motion by painting more noticeable brushstrokes on the tail area. Using the Gritty Charcoal variant of Dry Media, he painted darker smudges on the tail—altering it slightly in each frame. He also added speed blurs by smearing the edges of the snake's tail and the rattle using the Grainy Water variant of Liquid. When the frame stack was completed, Jolley saved it as a Quicktime movie. (Turn to "Importing and Exporting" on page 318.)

Automating Movie Effects

Overview Open a video clip; test a series of effects on a single frame; undo the effects; repeat the effects while recording a script; apply the script to the entire clip.

CTP / VIDEO: MEDIACOM

1

Frame 1 of the original video clip

2

The Apply Surface Texture and Apply Lighting settings chosen for the movie

3

Choosing Movie, Set Grain Position to create a "live" texture on the movie

4a

The Stop button (left) and the Record button (center)

4b

Detail of effects on Frames 35 and 50

WITH PAINTER'S SCRIPTS FEATURE, you can automate any series of recorded effects and apply them to each frame of an entire movie.

1 Starting with a video clip. Tests will be processed faster if you begin with a small video clip like the one we used—320 x 240 pixels with 67 frames. When you open a video clip (a QuickTime or AVI movie), Painter converts it to a Frame Stack. (When you save the Stack, give it a new name so the original clip isn't replaced.)

2 Testing a series of effects on a frame. Before you test a sequence of effects on a single frame, set up multiple Undos so you can return the clip to its original state: Choose Edit, Preferences, Undo, and enter a number that exceeds the number of effects you plan to use. Choose a rough paper texture (we chose Really Thick Paint from the Painted Effects 2 library on the Painter 7 Wow! CD-ROM) and apply it to Frame 1 in your movie with Effects, Surface Control, Apply Surface Texture, Using Paper (we settled on Amount 22%, Picture 90% and Shine 12%). Next, we added a look of cloud-filtered sunlight by choosing Effects, Surface Control, Apply Lighting. We customized the Slide Lighting, named it "sunlight," and saved it. (See Chapter 7 for more about lighting techniques.) When you've finished testing, undo the effects you applied to Frame 1. (Painter will remember the last settings you used in the dialog boxes.)

HI-RES MOVIE EFFECTS

If you want to apply effects to a broadcast-quality (640 x 480 pixels) video, use an editing program (such as Premiere) to create a low-resolution version on which to test a combination of effects. Because it takes a higher setting to get a result in a larger file, you may want to adjust the settings before treating the larger file.

3 Moving paper grain in the movie. To add subtle interest to your movie, you can change paper grain position on a frame-by-frame basis by choosing Movie, Set Grain Position. We chose the Grain Moves Linearly button and a 2-pixel horizontal movement.

4 Recording and playing back the session on the movie. Begin recording the effects by clicking the Record button in the Scripts section of the Objects palette; then repeat your sequence of effects. When you're finished, click the Stop button. Give your script a descriptive name, and undo your effects again. To apply your script to the movie, choose Movie, Apply Script to Movie. When the dialog box appears, find your new Script in the list, click the Playback button, and watch as Painter applies the recorded series of effects to each frame. 🐾

Making an Animated Comp

Overview *Set up a layered illustration file; record the movement of a layer using scripts; play the script back into a movie.*

DEWEY REID

Reid's original street scene illustration

Painting the mask on the background

The topmost layer (with the Canvas hidden) showing the dropped-out area that will reveal the background scene underneath

The Dino character showing the painted mask (left), and with the background dropped out

TO VISUALIZE MOTION in the early stages of creating an animation, Dewey Reid often makes an animated comp (a conceptual illustration with a moving element). Adding motion is a great way to help a client visualize a concept, and it's more exciting than viewing a series of still images. Reid's storyboard, above, shows frames from a movie created by recording a script of a moving layer.

Using scripts and the Record Frames on Playback feature, you can record a layer's movement. When you play the script back, Painter will generate a Frame Stack with the appropriate number of frames, saving you the tedious work of pasting in and moving the character in each frame. After you've made your Frame Stack, convert it into a QuickTime movie (or AVI/VFW on the PC) for easier and faster playback using a freeware utility like Movie Player.

1 Beginning with an illustration. Begin with an image at the size you want your final movie to be. Reid started with a 300 x 173-pixel street scene illustration from his archives.

2 Setting up a layered file. Like conventional animation where characters are drawn on layers of acetate, this animation technique works best when all elements in the image are on separate layers. You may want to create masks for the various elements in separate documents, then copy and paste them into your main image. (For more about layers and masking, turn to Chapter 5.)

Reid envisioned three "layers" for this comp: a background image (the street scene) in the bottom layer, a copy of the street scene with a painted mask in the top layer, and a dinosaur positioned between the two street scenes that would move from left to right across the "opening" created by the mask. Reid made a duplicate layer from the Canvas by selecting all and Alt/Option-clicking on the image with the Layer Adjuster tool. To make it easier to see the top layer as you work, hide the Canvas layer by clicking its eye icon shut in the Layers section of the Objects palette. Select the top layer. To remove an area of the layer's mask, choose a brush that will apply opaque color (such as the Scratchboard Tool variant of Pens) and choose white in the Colors section of the Art Materials palette. In the Masks section of the Objects palette, target the layer mask and then paint with white

2d

The Dino layer, selected in the Layers section and in starting position, ready to be moved by the arrow keys

3a

Setting up the Script Options to Save Frames on Playback

3b

Saving and naming the script

4

The Dino script selected in the Scripts section of the Objects palette

5

Choosing the QuickTime button in the Save Movie dialog box

to erase. When you've finished, select the RGB-Layer in the Masks section. To see the background layer again, click open the eye icon for the Canvas in the Layers section. You'll see a complete background image, since the lower layer shows through the hole in the top layer.

In a separate file, Reid painted a mask to isolate Dino the dinosaur from the background and turned the mask into a selection by choosing Select, Load Selection. He copied Dino to the clipboard and pasted him into the street scene RIFF file. (An easy way to add a character is to drag an item from the Image Portfolio section of the Objects palette into your image—like the apple, the orange or the butterfly, for example.) In the Layers section, Reid dragged Dino down to a position between the two street scene layers. Using the Layer Adjuster and the arrow keys, Reid positioned the dinosaur so that only the red nose was visible behind the left front building, establishing Dino's starting position in the animation.

3 Recording the script. Click the right triangle on the Scripts section bar in the Objects palette to open the menu and choose Script Options; uncheck Record Initial State, check Save Frames on Playback and enter a number for Every ¹⁄₁₀ths of a Second (Reid chose 5), and click OK. Select the layer that will be moving by clicking on its name in the Layers section (for Reid, the Dino Layer). Choose Record Script from the menu on the Scripts section bar (or click the round red button on the front of the Scripts section). Then hold down an arrow key to move the layer smoothly in the RIFF file. When you have completed the path of motion, choose Stop Recording Script from the Scripts section menu (or click the Square button) and name the script. Return the character to its starting position by pressing Ctrl/⌘-Z.

4 Playing back the script into the movie. Click the right triangle on the Scripts section bar to open the menu, choose Playback Script, choose your script from the list in the Apply Script to Movie dialog box and click Playback. When prompted, name your movie a different name than the RIFF file. Click the Save button and Painter will convert your RIFF image to a movie (leaving the original RIFF intact) and will add the movie frames needed. As the movie is generated, you will see the frames accumulating in the Frame Stack palette. When Painter finishes generating the Frame Stack, turn off visibility for the layers that are above the Canvas by clicking their eye icons in the Layers section. (If you don't hide the layers, you won't be able to see your movie, which is recorded on the Canvas.) Finally, press the Play button on the Frame Stacks palette to play your movie!

5 Converting the Frame Stack to QuickTime or AVI. To play the movie without having Painter loaded, convert the Frame Stack to QuickTime or AVI format: Choose File, Save As, and when the dialog box appears, choose Save Movie as QT/AVI. Give your movie a new name (such as "Dino movie.qtime"), click Save and in the Compression Settings dialog box, select a choice from the top pop-up menu (Reid recommends Animation or None).

Animating a Logo

Overview *Make a clone of existing artwork and modify it with Painter's brushes and effects; save it, make another clone, and alter the new clone; continue to progressively make and alter clones, restoring the image when needed by pasting a copy of the original logo from the clipboard.*

1

Starting with the existing Martin logo

2a

Lee began manipulating the logo by selecting and scaling a portion of the cloned image (left). Then he selected and inverted a portion of the next clone in the sequence (right).

"IMPROVISATIONAL, FRESH, SPONTANEOUS, and very flexible!" says Jon Lee, Director of Art and Design for Fox Television, when describing his artistic experience with Painter. For the Fox TV program *Martin,* Lee built an animated title sequence like a painting, saving frames at different stages of development. He created a wild, hand-done, organic look to express the comedic street sensibility of the TV show.

Lee created a series of 35 keyframes in Painter (keyframes are the frames that establish essential positions in an animated sequence), eight of which are shown above. When he finished, he moved them from his Macintosh to a lightning-fast Quantel HAL system, where he added dissolves to blend one frame into the next. (Dissolves can also be achieved on the Macintosh desktop in Adobe After Effects or Adobe Premiere.)

1 Beginning with existing art. Lee began by opening the existing Martin logo in Painter. He copied and pasted it into a new file measuring 720 x 486 pixels (the aspect ratio of the Quantel HAL) with a black background, then merged the layers by clicking right triangle on the Objects palette's Layers section

2b

Adding colored boxes to Frame 05 with the Rectangular Selection tool and the Fill command

2c

Using a variety of Liquid brushes to pull paint onto the background in Frame 07

2d

A motion blur effect applied in 14 (left), and then cloned and filtered in Frame 15

3a

Adding hand lettering and colored brush strokes to a clone of Frame 15 in Frame 16

3b

Restoring readability with a layer in Frame 17

bar, and choosing Drop from the menu.

Choose an image that you want to manipulate in your animated sequence and open it in Painter. Save your file in PICT format, naming it "01." In order for a numbered sequence of files to automatically play in numerical order, the files must be named using the same number of digits, such as 01, 02 . . . 10, 11 and so on.

2 Manipulating progressive clones. After planning how many keyframes you'll need and how the artwork will progress through the frames, begin your manipulation. Clone the first document (File, Clone) and use Painter's tools and special effects on your clone. If you don't like the result of a brushstroke or applied effect, undo it and try something else. When you're satisfied with the result, save the file, name it "02," and make another clone from it. The new clone will become the next canvas for your experimentation. Working quickly and intuitively, Lee treated the logo with a wide variety of brushes, filters and effects from the Effects, Surface Control menu, saving progressive versions in a numbered sequence.

3 Restoring the logo. After a few progressively altered clones, your image may become unrecognizable. To restore the original to some degree, go to your original file, select all and copy, then paste it into your current clone. Adjust the Opacity using the slider in the Layers section and Drop the layer. Lee used this technique to periodically restore the readability of the type, working the original logo back into the progressive image.

Outputting the Painter files. When Lee was finished with the series of PICT frames, he used Electric Image Projector (a subprogram within Electric Image) to automatically shuttle the files over to the Quantel HAL platform for compositing and output to Beta videotape for broadcast. The workstation is set up with the Quantel HAL and Mac systems side-by-side; they're connected with an Intelligent Resources card that helps convert the digital imagery from one platform to another. Part of the translation process involved converting RGB color to the NTSC video color system for television.

On the HAL, Lee "stretched" the 35 original frames to 90 frames; the HAL added the appropriate number of frames to achieve the dissolves between each pair of keyframes, keeping the animation even and smooth. To create a 10-second title sequence at 30 frames per second, Lee needed 300 frames total. He made a loop of the 90-frame sequence and let it cycle until it filled the necessary frame count. 🐾

■ **Marc Brown** created the splash screen for *The Adventures of Pinocchio Activity Center CD-ROM,* which was based on the 1996 movie *Pinocchio.* Brown began the illustration in Adobe Illustrator. To rasterize it, he pasted each Illustrator layer onto a layer in Photoshop and saved the file in Photoshop format. He opened the file in Painter and used Painter's brushes to render details on each layer, working from the background to the foreground. He laid in color details in the bluish-gray trees in the background using the Round Camelhair variant of Brushes. To blend color, he used the Just Add Water variant of Liquid. To build the shafts of light, he activated a selection (Select, Load Selection) and feathered it (Select, Feather). Then he filled the selection with yellow (Effects, Fill using a 30% Opacity). To paint the midground and foreground, the yellow forest floor, the green bushes and the red trees, he used the Round Camelhair brush. For Pinocchio, Brown referred to reference photos from the movie while painting using the same two brushes.

■ **Lawrence Kaplan** of Hot Tech Multimedia turned to Painter's special effects to "make a painting come to life" in a music video. Working with the New York artist **Crash**, Kaplan co-directed the four-and-a-half minute animated music video *What She Wants* for Warner Bros. Reprise Records. For a series of frames early in the video, he created a "morphing" animation using Painter's Liquid Metal. He began by opening a new movie with one frame and made a Liquid Metal dynamic layer. Using the Brush in the Liquid Metal dialog box (and the Standard Metal Map type), he painted a quantity of Liquid Metal into the first frame and clicked OK to close the dialog box. He copied the Liquid Metal layer to the clipboard, then dropped the layer (Ctrl/⌘-Shift-D) into the first frame. Kaplan added a new frame, pasted the Liquid Metal layer into the new frame and pressed the Enter key to open the Liquid Metal dialog box again. Using the Arrow tool, he selected areas of the metal and deleted them, then added more metal and clicked OK. Kaplan repeated the process of adding frames and editing the layer to complete the series of frames, morphing the dancing figure into a heart that changes into two figures and fades away into the bottom of the frame, then saved the file.

When creating the images on these two pages, **Athos Boncompagni** used scripts saved during several work sessions to record the development of the images so that he could play them back, one on top of the other, to demonstrate how the images were created. (For more information about how to use a series of scripts, turn to "Recording and Saving a Series of Scripts" on page 314.) He also used Painter's ability to playback the images at a higher resolution. (See the tip "Increasing File Resolution with Scripts" on page 314.)

Testalibro is a proposal for a book cover. Boncompagni started with a blank 6 x 9-inch canvas. In the Script Options dialog box, accessed by clicking the right triangle on the Scripts section bar on the Objects palette, he disabled Record Initial State. (This would enable him to have Painter redraw the image using a different size Pen and color, later.) Next, so he could play the script back at a different resolution later (as described on the opposite page), he chose Select, All (Ctrl/ ⌘-A); this would store the file dimensions as part of the script information. Then he clicked the Record button. He drew the line drawing and added cross-hatching with the Scratchboard Tool variant and black ink, then clicked the Stop Recording button on the Scripts section. Next, he reduced the size and opacity of the Scratchboard Tool (using the sliders in the Controls:Brush palette), chose a brown color in the Colors section of the Art Materials palette, then played the pen-and-ink script back on his image using brown ink to paint finer brown lines over the black. To add more color to the illustration, he began recording a new script, chose Select, All and used Water Color brushes to add transparent washes. The he clicked the Stop button on the Scripts section and saved the script. To add more color to the illustration, he began recording a new script, chose Select, All and used Water Color brushes to add transparent washes. He stopped recording and saved this script also.

■ When creating *La Luna e le Stelle*, **Athos Boncompagni** used scripts saved during several work sessions to record the development of the image, as described on the opposite page, but with one difference. He wanted to use the scripts to increase the size of the 5½ x 7-inch image for better results when printing it at an 11 x 14-inch size. So that he would be able to playback the process at the larger size using the same brushes and colors, Boncompagni enabled Record Initial State in the Script Options dialog box. He opened a new file by choosing File, New and chose Select, All (Ctrl/⌘-A). Then from the Scripts section menu, he chose Record Script to begin recording. He created his image in stages, and when he was finished with a work session, he chose Stop Recording Script from the menu on the Scripts section bar. To re-create his image at the higher resolution, he opened a new 11 x 14-inch file, pressed Ctr/⌘-A to Select, All, then chose Playback Script from the menu. He played the scripts back in the order he had saved them, on top of one another and watched as Painter rebuilt his image. (For more information about how to use a series of scripts, turn to "Recording and Saving a Series of Scripts" on page 314.)

■ **Dewey Reid** of Reid Creative, illustrated the 30-second animation *Yuri the Yak* for Sesame Street, a production of Children's Television Workshop. In the story segment, Yuri travels the countryside eating yellow yams and yogurt, and teaching the letter "Y." Reid stresses the importance of preproduction planning in animation. He created the *Yuri the Yak* animation with a total of only 35 drawings (it could have taken hundreds). His background in conventional animation helped him determine which drawings to make, and which to generate by tweening in an animation program, saving time and a lot of work. Reid used Painter to create individual parts of the Yak, such as the head, body and arms. He opened the illustrations in Photoshop and created a mask for each image, then saved the illustrations as PICT files in a numbered sequence. (He prefers using PICT files rather than QuickTime movies, since PICT files allow higher quality. Also, a sequence of PICT files allows for more flexibility— it's easier to remove a frame or two, if necessary.) He imported the masked files into Adobe After Effects, created animation cycles for each of the Yak parts, then joined animation cycles together. A virtuoso with effects, Reid completed his artistic vision by adding subtle lighting and texture. He opened the animation in Painter as a Frame Stack. After recording a script of Effects, Surface Control, Apply Lighting and Apply Surface Texture, he chose Movie, Apply Script to Movie to add the effects to the frames.

■ *Snuffy 1 and 2* are two compositional layout illustrations by **Cindy Reid** of Reid Creative for a proposed Sesame Street production of Children's Television Workshop. The animation was conceived to accompany the children's song "I Wish I Were Small." In frame 1, Snuffy (who is normally mammoth-size) becomes small enough to fit into a bird's nest; in frame 2, small enough to fit in a buttercup. To create both frames Reid shot photos of a bird's nest, a bee, the sky and clouds, foliage and buttercup flowers for "scrap." She scanned the photos into Photoshop and pasted the images onto layers to build two composite files. When the elements were in place, she opened the layered composite file in Painter, where she added painterly brushwork to each layer using the Grainy Water variant of Liquid. She added details using a small Sharp Chalk variant (Dry Media). When the brushwork was complete, she flattened the image by choosing Drop All from the Objects palette's Layer section bar menu.

■ Creative director and film artist **Dewey Reid,** working with Colossal Pictures, engineered the preproduction for the *Nike All Conditions Gear* TV commercial. To begin the preproduction visualization, Reid scanned a variety of images. Then he used Painter to create keyframes to establish the essential positions in the animated sequence. He imported the Nike logo (by copying it from Illustrator and pasting it into the Painter file as shapes while both applications were running), converted the logo shapes to selections (Shapes, Convert To Selection) and applied a feather to the selections. He embossed the artwork in stages, with Effects, Surface Control, Apply Surface Texture (Using Mask), creating the illusion that the logo pushes up through the scanned images. Reid saved the keyframes as numbered PICT files,

then used Adobe Premiere to create transitions (such as Cross Dissolves) between the keyframes. He manipulated a few of the masks in Adobe After Effects. Back in Painter, Reid painted clouds of dust with the Digital Airbrush variant of Airbrushes and used Effects, Surface Control, Image Warp to subtly change the shape of the clouds. He imported the dust image into Premiere and moved the dust across one series of frames. After working out the timing in Premiere, Reid used Painter to add special effects to the entire movie to increase the 3D look. A whiz with scripts, he opened the movie as a Frame Stack and treated it with an effects script that included Effects, Surface Control, Apply Lighting and Apply Surface Texture, Using Image Luminance.

■ **Jean-Luc Touillon's** passion for drawing shows in *Film*, a series of sensitive sketches which he animated using Painter's frame stack feature. (Six of the 25 drawings in his animation are shown here.) Touillon began in Painter by creating a colored, textured background that looked like an aged plaster wall. First he laid down earth-tone colored paint using Brushes and Dry Media variants. Then he added 3D texture with Effects, Surface Control, Apply Surface Texture Using Image Luminance. When the background was complete, he saved the file. To create each drawing, he opened a copy of the background file and drew a study with a Pens variant (using a live model for reference), then saved each file in PICT format under a unique numbered name —01, 02, 03 and so on. When the drawings were complete, he chose File, Open and created a frame stack from the drawings that included 25 frames. (See page "Importing and Exporting" on page 318 for information about building a frame stack from PICT files.) Touillon added finishing touches to the frames using the Pens variant, and when he was satisfied with the frame stack, he saved it as a QuickTime movie.

■ **Jean-Luc Touillon** also known as "**Jasiu**" created the illustrations for *l' histoire digitale évolutive d'une ville imaginaire,* an interactive mystery story on CD-ROM, while working with the team at LA F@KTORY in Paris. Touillon built the frames for the story entirely within Painter. QuickTime VR was used to produce the panoramic environment.

With QuickTime VR, the viewer can manipulate the camera by zooming in and out and scrolling 360° to the left and right as they tour the imaginary city. To begin, Touillon created a new frame stack and painted on the individual frames using the Artist Pastel and Basic Crayon variants of Dry Media. To blend the paint, he used the Grainy Water variant of

Liquid, creating a dream-like atmosphere. When the images were complete, he saved them as a series of PICT files. Touillon later assembled the frames using Metropolis and Macromedia Director software. For information about using QuickTime VR, see http://www.apple.com/quicktime/qtvr and http://www.iqtvr.org

■ An innovative storyboard artist, **Peter Mitchell Rubin** used a variety of Painter's brushes and compositing controls to create the storyboards for the MGM movie *Stargate.* The Giza, Egypt, sequence is shown here. Rubin outputs his illustrations from Painter as numbered PICT files, then animates them in Adobe Premiere. Rubin's love of drawing shows in his storyboards. He works very quickly, in gray, at 72 ppi. His document size depends on the amount of detail needed, but is usually under 600 pixels wide. The aspect ratio depends upon how the film will be shot. Rubin organizes the thousands of drawings that he creates for a film in folders according to scene. He sets up QuicKeys macros to automate actions wherever possible, automating the processing of all the files in a folder. When Rubin adds other elements to an image, he pastes the element, drops it, then paints into it to merge it seamlessly into the composition. He also uses Painter's Cloners brushes. For example, he created the texture in Frame 15 (left column, third frame down from top) by photographing the actual set sculpture used in the movie, scanning it and cloning the scan into his drawing.

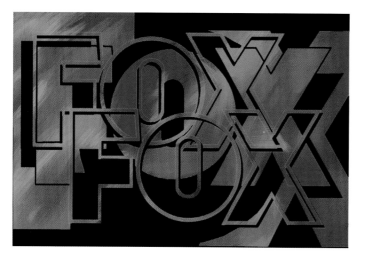

■ As both a broadcast designer for Fox Television and a freelance graphic designer, **Geoff Hull** employs a spontaneous, progressive approach when designing with type.

Hull began the *Fox Logo Pattern* with a black background. He imported a file with both solid and outline versions of the Fox logo (using File, Acquire, Adobe Illustrator file—which creates a new file). He copied the shapes from the new file and pasted them into the larger background file, then converted the two logo shape groups into two layers. Working quickly and intuitively, he painted on the logo layers with Brushes variants and saturated color. To build a layered look, Hull made additional copies of the layers and added more brushstrokes. In busier areas, he erased portions of layers by painting the layer masks with white paint.

To create the animated title sequence for the TV show *Wild Oats*, Hull envisioned a hand-done, calligraphic look. He began the image with a white background and set type in Painter using the font Earthquake, a typeface from the T26 foundry. After setting black text, he made a clone (File, Clone) and erased its contents. He chose Canvas, Tracing Paper and expressively traced the letterforms. For the frames of the animation Hull made a series of progressive clones, switching clone sources (File, Clone Source) among the original and several later versions of the title sequence.

Hull created *The Crossing Guard* storyboard for a Miramax Films movie title and trailer. He began with a black background and set individual letterform shapes in Painter using Mason from the Emigré font library. After converting the shapes to layers, he filled them with color and erased portions of the letters by painting the layer masks with white paint. He also used Effects, Orientation, Scale on the layers to vary the size of the elements.

■ Commissioned by Diadem Productions, a producer of multimedia Bible study software, **Ted Larson** created these images as part of a slide show for an educational CD-ROM about the books of Daniel and Zechariah.

Larson used similar techniques to create all three of the illustrations on these pages. He began by sketching in Painter to establish a composition. Then he built a gray-toned composite image that included an environment rendered in Bryce 3D (for instance, the cave wall in *Daniel in the Lion's Den* and the river water in *Vision on the Tigris*), his own photos of cliff rocks and foliage, and stock photos of lions (from a Corel stock-photo CD-ROM). The Messiah, the angel figures, and Daniel seated in the shadows (in the Lion's Den image) were developed from scans of photos Larson took of models in simple-robed costumes. He created the hair and beards with theatrical wigs and crepe hair. He built the angels' wings from two eagle photos from a Corel CD-ROM. When he was satisfied with the composition, he merged the layers and used various brushes in Painter to color the images. In all three images, Larson gave the angels' hands a metallic look by applying a custom bronze gradient using the Express in Image command (located in the menu on the Gradients section bar). To intensify the colors in the image he used Effects, Tonal Control, Adjust Color.

For *Daniel in the Firey Furnace*, Larson began by assembling a black-and-white composite image. He made an empty new layer for the coloring, and to make the layer like a transparent color overlay on top of the gray image, he set the Composite Method of the layer to Color. Then, using warm colors to convey the heat, he loosely painted color in the firey areas using low-opacity Airbrushes variants. He brightened areas of the flames with the Fire and Glow variants of the F-X brush.

Larson wanted to convey a warm Rembrandt-like look in *Daniel in the Lion's Den*, so he chose deep monochromatic earth colors with a touch of gold ochre, making the angel the main source of light. Larson brushed subtle sepia color over the image using Water Color brushes. He also used the Splatter Water variant of Water Color at low opacity settings. For touch-up, he added a new layer and painted with a small Digital Airbrush variant of Airbrushes. After the sepia coloring was developed, Larson used Painter's Glow and Fire variants to build special lighting effects around the angel and on the cave wall.

■ To create *The Vision upon the Tigris,* **Ted Larson** began the composition by drawing a color sketch in Painter. He used the Sharp Chalk and Charcoal variants of Dry Media to rough out the position of the three figures and to establish an angle for the river. Next, in Bryce 3D, Larson rendered a river water image, and placed it in a scene with a perspective grid. He used the grid to help scale the figures and palm trees along the river. He made silhouette masks for the trees and grass banks and scaled the images to fit his composition. For the figure elements, Larson photographed friends dressed in costume, scanned the photos and opened them in Photoshop, where he applied the Solarize filter. He saved the angel files and opened them in Painter. After he had pasted the wings into each angel source file, he made silhouette masks for the wings, so he could select and distort them to match the perspective of the figures, using the Distort command. Larson painted the evening stars, rippled water reflections and light rays in Painter using Airbrushes and F-X brushes. Then he tinted the finished black-and-white composition with a custom gradient (choosing Express in Image from the Gradients section bar's menu in the Art Materials palette). To add more color to the figures and clothing, Larson painted transparent washes using Water Color brushes. For more color and texture in some areas, he used the Variable Splatter and Digital Airbrush variants of Airbrushes with low opacity settings.

Using
Painter for
Web
Graphics

Ben Barbante created Efolio, *an illustration for his Web site's index page. To see the entire image, turn to page 353 in the gallery.*

WHAT DOES PAINTER OFFER AN ARTIST who designs graphics for the World Wide Web? In addition to its powerful natural media brushes, compositing tools, mosaics and other effects, Painter can help you prepare images for Web pages. For example, you can set type for titles with the Text tool, use shapes to draw polygons, convert the shapes to layers and define the polygons as clickable regions for use on your Web page. Use the Image Slicer to segment an image into smaller parts so the viewer can see pieces of the image as they load, then export some of the slices with JavaScript rollovers. You can open source video in Painter as a frame stack and grab stills to use as graphics or as references for your Web illustrations, or export the frame stack directly from Painter as a GIF animation. (If you need help with the painting techniques or compositing methods referred to in this chapter, you can find more information in Chapters 3, 4 and 5. Turn to Chapter 10 for information on scripts and frame stack animations. And see Appendix E for recommended books relating to Web design.)

CREATING GRAPHICS FOR THE WEB

Painter has tools that make it easy to adapt graphics for the Web. For instance, you can save in GIF and JPEG (the two most popular image formats used on the Web). And you can tell Painter to do some of the coding to help you set up image maps or linked graphics. Here are some tips for creating Web graphics in Painter.

First, there are two basic uses for images on a Web page. One is an in-line graphic or "static" image embedded in a page without a link to another location—for example, an embedded background graphic. The second use for graphics is as "hot spots," or "buttons." A hot spot is a clickable region on your artwork that will allow the user to hyperlink (or travel) to another location on the Web, either within the same Web site or at another site. There are two general types of hot

ON-SCREEN TYPE AND COLOR

Type on-screen can be difficult to read in small sizes, so it's important that it be as clear as possible. For both type and drawings, flat color with crisp edges often works best. Anti-aliasing and gradations don't compress well—they can become blotchy.

Susan LeVan created images for "Off" and "On" button states, for the Nichole Shoes Web site. To see the entire set of buttons, turn to page 356 in the gallery.

turn to page 356 in the gallery.

spots. The simpler one is a *button* that links to one location (URL, or Uniform Resource Locator) such as www.peachpit.com. The second is an *image map*—an image that has been divided into regions, each of which lets you link to a different URL.

Making an image map. You can choose any kind of graphic as an image map: title type, a photograph or an illustration you've painted. Define an image map by selecting all or part of an image (by dragging around it with a selection tool and copying it to make a layer). Then double-click on the new layer's name in the Layers section of the Objects palette to access the Layer Attributes dialog box. Use the checkbox to make it a WWW Map Clickable Region. In the Save As GIF Options and JPEG Encoding Quality dialog boxes, you can choose to export a client-side image map (directions for the image map are included in the HTML for the page) or server-side image map (directions for the map are stored on the server) by telling Painter to create an image map definition file with dimensions for the hot spots. Client-side image maps are more efficient to use when designing for newer browsers, but if you want your image map to work with older browsers as well, consider including both client-side and server-side directions in the HTML for the image map. For more information, see "Building an Image Map for a Web Page" on page 349.

Using Web-friendly file formats. The JPEG and transparent GIF formats that Painter supports are two of the most popular file formats used in Web page design. Transparent GIF files make use of the mask you've saved with the file, allowing a graphic to be placed on the page with an irregular edge or with holes cut into it to reveal the background underneath. You can make a transparent GIF by choosing File, Save As, GIF, and then using the Output Transparency checkbox In the Save As GIF Options dialog box. Click the Preview Data button to preview the transparency. We suggest using GIF format to save simple line art and flat-color graphics without gradations and soft edges. Save photos and painted artwork in 24-bit JPEG format.

Building small files that load fast. Web-savvy designers recommend making graphics files small, between 20 and 30K, because most Web visitors will not wait for images that take a long time to load. Typical modem speed is 56,600 bps and graphics of 20–30K will download within 1–3 seconds. To make GIF images small, use Painter's Save As GIF Options dialog box to compress the number of colors from millions to 256 (8-bit) or fewer. Save as GIF in the exact pixel dimensions needed for the page design. When you use JPEG format to preserve the 24-bit color of an image, experiment with the JPEG Encoding Quality settings to determine how much compression an image can withstand. JPEG is a lossy compression (it removes information, which can't be restored), so make sure to use File, Save As to create the new

Arthur Steuer and Even Steven Levee, principals of i~potato production company, commissioned artist/animator Sharon Steuer to create the i-potato *logo for the cover of their pop-music CD and Web site. Steuer used Painter's Water Color tools, Brushes and Airbrushes variants to paint the image. Steuer created an animation of the eye blinking for the launching of the Web site (www.i-potato.net). She created the cels for the eye-blink in Painter, using a separate layer to draw each stage of the animation. So the animation would load quickly, her client chose to use only two of the three stages. (See a QuickTime movie with music that includes all three stages in Steuer's folder on the Wow! CD-ROM.) To read about creating a GIF animation step by step, turn to "Making a Slide Show Animation" on page 352.*

JPEG file with a different name, preserving your master file.

Creating a subdued background. Painter has tools for creating exciting backgrounds, but a busy, contrasty background can take attention away from the subject of the screen and overwhelm your audience. Here are two suggestions that will help you make a background more subtle: Turn down the contrast using Effects, Tonal Control, Brightness/Contrast, or desaturate the background (using Effects, Tonal Control, Adjust Colors) to call attention to brighter-colored content. To desaturate, move the Saturation slider to the left. Click OK when you see the look you want in the Preview window.

Adding movie stills and video to your page. You can open a movie in Painter and capture frames to use as static images or hot spots. And you can save a QuickTime or AVI movie using effective compression such as Cinepak, so it can be played within a Netscape or Internet Explorer browser.

Exporting a movie as a GIF animation. Painter makes it easy to add movement to your Web pages with GIF animations! You can open a QuickTime/AVI movie as a frame stack (or create your own animation in Painter) and export it directly from Painter as a GIF animation. Here are some tips to help you make a GIF animation that loads quickly and plays smoothly on your Web page: Make movies with a small frame size (such as 160 x 120). (Painter doesn't permit movies to be resized. So if you plan to import video into Painter, reduce the frame size in a video editor such as Adobe Premiere before opening it in Painter.) Use as few frames as possible. (You can use the Movie, Delete Frames dialog box to remove any unnecessary frames.) Reduce the number of colors—using black-and-white or just a few colors, for instance, will help to make a smaller animation file.

To save a completed frame stack as a GIF animation, choose File, Save As, Save Movie as GIF Animation. In the Save As GIF Options box, make the choices you need. To read about making a GIF animation step-by-step, turn to "Making a Slide Show Animation" on page 352. 🖌

WEB-FRIENDLY COLOR

Painter ships with several color sets built for Web graphics. To load a Web-friendly color set, open the Art Materials palette, click the right arrow on the Colors section bar and from the menu, choose Load Color Set. Navigate to the Painter 7 application folder and open the Color Sets folder. Select a Hexadecimal Color Set, the Netscape 216, the Macintosh default 256 or the Windows Default 256 Color Set and click Open.

SHRINKING A COPY

If you're doing detailed painting or retouching to be displayed on the Web at 72 ppi, you may want to create your art at a higher resolution so you can zoom in and paint the details. Then use Canvas, Resize to shrink a copy of your image down to 72 ppi. Sharpen areas that become soft (Effects, Focus, Sharpen).

Reducing Color Using Apply Screen

Overview *Choose an image; reduce color using Apply Screen; edit the color to make it Web-safe; export the image.*

CHER THREINEN-PENDARVIS / ORIGINAL PHOTO: CORBIS IMAGES

The original photograph with selection active and background sky made lighter

Choosing a Web-safe HTML color in the Select Screen dialog box on a Mac using the System 9 Color Picker

Choosing a Web-safe HTML color in the Select Screen dialog box using the Mac OS X Color Picker

The Apply Screen dialog box with preview showing the new color choices

REDUCING THE NUMBER OF COLORS is a frequently used method for making small files for faster downloading of Web graphics. To create this three-color image, we used Apply Screen—one of Painter's most efficient "color reduction" tools. It allows you to create images composed of only three colors without the anti-aliasing that creates many intermediate colors when it smooths edges.

1 Choosing a photo and making adjustments. Open an image that you want to convert to a three-color composition. In our first attempt to modify color using the Apply Screen function, the skiers merged with the background sky because the sky's value did not contrast enough with the skiers. We undid the Apply Screen, and before trying again, we isolated the sky by making a selection, and then lightened the sky. To make a selection of an area like the sky based on color, click on the area with the Magic Wand. To add areas of noncontiguous color to the selection, turn off the Contiguous checkbox in the Controls:Magic Wand palette; expand or shrink the range of colors by adjusting the Tolerance. (To read more about the Magic Wand, turn to page 132 in Chapter 4.) Then we increased the value within the selected sky using Brightness/Contrast (choose Effects, Tonal Control, Brightness/Contrast). After adjusting the Brightness, we chose Select, None.

2 Reducing color. To apply the color effect to your entire image choose Effects, Surface Control, Apply Screen, Using Image Luminance and choose a color by clicking the middle of the three color squares. In the color picker that opened, we settled on an aqua color, in addition to the black and white. (If you are using a Mac with System 8.0 or later featuring the updated Apple Color Picker, you can choose a Web-safe color at this point using the HTML Picker, and skip steps 3 and 4. If you have this option, check the Snap to Web color box, and select a color. In the OS X Color Picker, click on Name in the column on the left and when

The image showing active selection made with the Dropper and the Auto Select, Using Current Color dialog box

Close-up of the image with selection. The original aqua color shows dithering when viewed on a monitor with only 256 colors.

The Netscape Navigator 216 Color Set, showing the new aqua we used for the fill

Filling with the Web-safe color

Our settings in the GIF Options dialog box and the Color Set with three Web-safe colors

the Web Safe Color pop-up appears, choose a color.) If your computer does not have the HTML color option, choose a color to serve as a preview of the final effect. It doesn't have to be a Web-safe color. In step 3 you can replace it. We adjusted the Threshold sliders to bring out important details in the skiers' faces. The Threshold 1 slider controls the relationship between aqua (the middle color) and white (the color on the right); the Threshold 2 slider controls the amount of black (the left color).

3 Making a selection. Painter's Apply Screen dialog box does not let you directly apply color from a Web-safe color set. To replace our color with a Web-safe color, we first made a hard-edged mask. To make a hard-edged selection based on color, choose the Dropper and click on the colored area you want to mask. From the Select menu choose Auto Select, Using Current Color. Click OK; you'll see a selection marquee appear on your image.

4 Filling the selection with a Web-safe color. Now load the Web-safe Netscape Navigator 216 Color Set as follows: On the Art Materials palette's Colors section bar, click the right triangle to open the menu and choose Load Color Set. Navigate to the Netscape Navigator 216 Color Set. This set can be found in the Color Sets folder, in the Painter 7 application folder. Next, click on a Web-safe color that complements your design (we chose a bright aqua). Choose Effects, Fill With Current Color, and click OK.

5 Making a color set and exporting a GIF file. To preserve the Web-safe colors that you used in your illustration, export a GIF that uses a custom color set that contains the three Web-safe colors in your image. (This process is similar to setting up an Indexed Color palette in Photoshop.) Before you make the Color Set, open the Color Variability section of the Art Materials palette, choose "In HSV" from the pop-up menu and set the (± H), (± S) and (± V) sliders to 0. Now choose the Dropper tool and click on one of the three colors in your image. The Colors section of the Art Materials palette will display the color. In the Art Materials palette, click on the Color Set section bar to open the Color Set section, and click on the New Color Set button and choose Create New Empty Color Set from the pop-up menu. A very small Color Set title bar will appear. Click on the Add Color to Color Set button to add the selected color to the Color Set. Sample and add the two remaining colors by using the Dropper and the Add Color to Color Set button. To save your colors, click on the Library button in the Color Sets palette, then click Save, name the set and Save. (For more information about making color sets, turn to "Capturing a Color Set" on page 38, in Chapter 2.)

To export a GIF from Painter to use on your Web page, choose File, Save As, GIF. When the Save As GIF Options dialog box appears, under Imaging method, turn on Quantize to Nearest Color and choose the Color Set button. 👆

Posterizing with Web-Safe Colors

Overview *Open an image; load the Netscape Navigator 216 Color Set; posterize the image using the Color Set; retouch it using flat color fills and Painter's Web safe brushes; export the file.*

CHER THREINEN-PENDARVIS / ORIGINAL PHOTO: CORBIS IMAGES

1

The original photo

PHOTO: CORBIS IMAGES

2

The Netscape Navigator 216 Color Set

POSTERIZING CAN ADD AN INTERESTING GRAPHIC LOOK to a photo, and at the same time simplify color for faster downloading. We posterized the image above using Painter's Netscape Navigator 216 Web-safe color set so the color would not dither on most monitors. Then we exported our GIF file with color constrained by the color set.

1 Choosing a photo. We opened a 512-pixel-wide photo. Select a photo or an illustration with a simple background, such as this snowboarder image.

2 Posterizing using a Color Set. Begin by loading the Netscape Navigator 216 Color Set. On the Art Materials palette's Colors section bar, click the right triangle to open the menu and choose Load Color Set. Navigate to the Netscape Navigator 216 Color Set. This set can be found in the Painter 7 application folder, in the Color Sets folder. Now choose Effects, Tonal Control, Posterize Using Color Set. The command doesn't allow you to have complete control over how color reduction is performed, but it does automatically constrain all of the colors in the image to the Netscape 216-color palette and can be a real time-saver.

Making a selection with the Magic Wand

Painting with a Web-safe brush

To constrain our GIF to Web-safe colors, we turned on the Quantize to Nearest Color and Color Set buttons in GIF Options.

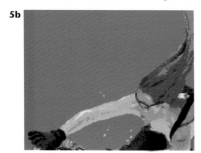

Detail of our final GIF shows no dithering when viewed using 256 colors.

3 Cleaning up the background. Posterizing with the Netscape Navigator 216 Color Set provided a close match for the important colors in our image (such as flesh tones), but it produced some distracting debris in the sky. We used the Magic Wand to select these areas. Click with the Magic Wand on the color you want to select. To select noncontiguous color, turn off the Contiguous checkbox in the Controls:Magic Wand palette. If needed, adjust the Tolerance slider in the Controls:Magic Wand palette. To read more about the Magic Wand, turn to page 132 in Chapter 4, "Selections, Shapes and Masks." After making the selection, we filled the area with blue sampled from the sky. To sample color in your image and fill as we did, choose the Dropper tool and click in your image. Then choose Effects, Fill, Fill With Current Color.

4 Touching up with a Web-safe brush. There was still some debris left after we applied the fill, so we painted the area using a "Web-safe" brush. To access the WebMedia Brushes, copy them from the Painter_CD2 CD-ROM to your Painter 7 application folder as follows: Begin by opening the Painter 7 Application folder then open the Brushes folder and the Painter Brushes folder. Now, insert the CD-ROM and open its Brushes folder. Select the WebMedia Brushes folder, and drag and drop it into the Brushes folder within the Painter 7 application folder. Now load Painter's WebMedia Brushes library by selecting Load Library from the bottom of the brush resource list on the Brushes palette. When the Load Library dialog box appears, click on Import, then click Open.

> ### WEB-SAFE BRUSHES
> Painter ships with a WebMedia brush library. The WebMedia Brushes use Grainy Edge Flat Cover and Grainy Flat Cover (two subcategories that incorporate aliased edges). The brushes are ideal for painting when you want to avoid the in-between colors that are generated during anti-aliasing.

Once the library was loaded, we chose the Calligraphic Winner brush variant of the W Thick-n-Thin brush. Then we used the blue, sampled from the sky, to paint over the remaining purple speckles. The sky was now a solid blue.

5 Exporting the image. You can export a GIF from Painter, while retaining Web-safe colors from the Netscape Navigator 216 Color Set chosen in step 2, as follows: Choose File, Save As, GIF, and when the Save As GIF Options dialog box appears, under Imaging method, turn on Quantize to Nearest Color, and under Number of Colors, choose Color Set.

This function works similarly to the indexed color palettes supported by Equilibrium DeBabelizer, Macromedia Fireworks and Adobe ImageReady that allow Web-safe colors to be preserved. Our final image is at the top of the previous page. 🖌

Making a Seamless Tile

Overview *Select an image; use the Kaleidoscope plug-in to make a tile; edit its color; test the tile; save the tile in JPEG format.*

PAINTER HAS SEAMLESS-TILE-CREATION TOOLS that are unequaled by other programs. To make this background for a Web site's welcome screen, we began by using the Kaleidoscope dynamic layer to create a symmetrical design based on a photo of palm trees. After making the seamless tile and testing it in Painter, we saved the finished image as a JPEG file for import into a Web page editor.

The original photograph of palm trees

1 Choosing an image. For this nostalgic background design, we chose and opened a 768 x 512-pixel image with gold-to-brown colors.

2 Using Kaleidoscope as a lens. As you move it over your image a Kaleidoscope dynamic layer distorts the underlying imagery into symmetrical designs that are ideal for perfect seamless tiles or fabric design. To make a Kaleidoscope layer, open the Layers section of the Objects palette by clicking the left triangle on the Layers section bar. Click the Plugins button at the bottom of the Layers section and choose the Kaleidoscope plug-in from the pop-up menu. When the dialog box appears, it will reflect the default size of 100 x 100 pixels. We typed 200 into the field to make a larger "lens." Use the Layer Adjuster tool to move the Kaleidoscope layer around your image until you find a "tile" effect you like. (To read more about dynamic layers, turn to Chapter 5, "Using Layers and Shapes.")

The image with Kaleidoscope dynamic layer

3 Making a tile image. Building a background by importing a single repeating tile into a Web page editor is much more efficient than importing an entire background image. That's because the smaller tile image downloads faster, and it can be repeated very quickly by the browser. Here's the quickest way to prepare your tile: With the Layers section of the Objects palette opened, choose the Layer Adjuster and select the Kaleidoscope dynamic layer by clicking on its name in the Layers section. To capture the Kaleidoscope imagery, convert the dynamic layer into an image layer by clicking the right triangle on the Layers section bar to open the pull-down

The new tile image

Lightening the color for a subdued look

Naming the pattern in the Capture Pattern dialog box

The Painter image filled with the Golden Palms pattern. The pattern can be found in the Palm Patterns library on the Painter 7 CD-ROM in the Wow! Items folder.

Saving the tile as a JPEG with Fair quality and a Smoothness setting of 5%

menu and choosing Convert To Default layer. Copy the layer (Edit, Copy), and then choose Edit, Paste into New Image.

4 Lightening the tile image. We lightened the new image to make a background that would not compete with text and other elements on the page by choosing Effects, Tonal Control, Adjust Colors. To lighten, move the Value slider to the right. Our setting was 121%.

5 Making a pattern. Select the entire tile image by choosing Select, All. Now you can capture the tile as a pattern and test its tiling in Painter. On the Art Materials palette, click the right triangle on the Patterns section bar to open the menu and choose Capture Pattern. When the dialog box appears, name your pattern. For a Rectangular tile with no Horizontal or Vertical Shift (like ours), leave the other settings at their defaults and click OK. (See Chapter 7 for more information about working with patterns.)

6 Testing the tile. To see the overall effect of your pattern in Painter, create a new 800 x 800-pixel document. Now choose Effects, Fill, and in the dialog box, click the Pattern button. Click OK to fill the new document with the pattern.

7 Exporting the seamless tile. At this point we saved our 200 x 200 pixel full-color file (File, Save). Always remember to keep your original file in a format that preserves its image quality, such as TIFF, RIFF or Photoshop. Because the audience for this site would be viewing its images using millions of colors, we didn't want to limit the colors. So we saved a copy of the tile in JPEG format, to preserve the 24-bit color depth. If you have Photoshop, Photoshop Elements or Fireworks, consider using one of these programs to save your file as a JPEG since they all allow you to see the file size as well as the quality. In Painter, you can save a copy of your file as a JPEG. Choose File, Save As, JPEG, and remember to add the proper file extension (.jpg) to its name. To make the image small, we chose the Fair setting, and we applied a Smoothness of 5% in the JPEG dialog box to soften the JPEG artifacts. Our final background (viewed in Explorer) is shown at the top of page 347. 🐾

BRACKETING TO COMPARE JPEG IMAGE QUALITY

Most designers export continuous-tone images for the Web using JPEG format. Often, a low JPEG setting will provide adequate quality and a tiny file size. To know for sure in Painter, test the file by "bracketing," or saving it using several different quality settings. Begin by opening the image you want to compress. To duplicate the image, choose File, Clone, and save it using the lowest quality setting (Fair). Name the file so you can compare results later. Select your original file, choose File, Clone again and save the second image using Good quality. Repeat the process twice more using High and Excellent quality settings. Close the images, and reopen to compare the results. (JPEG compression artifacts are not visible until an image is closed and reopened.)

JPEG settings: Excellent (top left), High (top right), Good (bottom left), and Fair (bottom right).

SOFTEN WITH SMOOTHNESS

When low-quality JPEG settings are used, square artifacts can appear in an image. The Smoothness setting in the JPEG dialog box can help to soften artifacts. Use Smoothness with care, however, because a setting that's too high can blur the image. A bonus: Smoothness can further reduce the size of the file.

Building an Image Map for a Web Page

Overview *Choose photos and other elements; fill with a patterned background; create layers and designate an image map in Painter; finish the HTML.*

1a

Setting up the file in the New dialog box

1b

Selecting the blue palm pattern

1c

The new file showing the pattern text

TO BUILD A PROTOTYPE WEB SITE for *Surf Nostalgia,* an ocean-related art and collectibles gallery, we used Painter to create a background pattern, graphics, and image map buttons for the index page (including some of the HTML code for the image map). We designed the site to be viewed with any browser and used our own site, http://www.pendarvis-studios.com, to develop the prototype.

1 Setting up the page. This step sets up the home page for the Web site. There are no absolute size restrictions on Web pages. They can be any length, because the viewer can scroll. We set up an 800 x 800-pixel file that would easily accommodate viewers' screens with resolutions of 1074 x 768 pixels and larger.

To test how the background pattern would look on the image, we filled it with a blue version of the golden palms pattern which was created step-by-step in "Making a Seamless Tile" on pages 347–348. (To load a blue version of the palm pattern, copy the Palm Patterns library from the Wow! Items folder on the Painter 7 Wow! CD-ROM to your Painter 7 application folder. Then choose Load Library from the bottom of the Patterns pop-up menu on the Patterns section of the Art Materials palette.)

For your prototype Web page design, create a new file. To see how your pattern will look as a background, fill the image by

2a

The Text settings in the Text section of the Objects palette

2b

The centered white text set on top of the filled background

2c

The settings in the Text section for the hard-edged shadow

2d

The shadow shows the color sampled from a dark area of the background.

choosing Effects, Fill, Fill With Pattern. The pattern will be removed from the file before the final export is done and a single pattern tile will be exported as a JPEG file to be repeated by the browser's tiling function for the finished page.

2 Creating a logotype and graphics. Using the Text tool with white as the current color, set large bold letters for a logotype. We typed "Surf Nostalgia" using the Reporter Two font and pressing the Enter/Return key after typing "Surf," to set the "Nostalgia" type on a second line. In the Text section of the Objects palette, we clicked the center button to center the type, then clicked the External Drop Shadow button to apply a solid, hard-edged shadow. The default color of the shadow is black. To change the shadow color (or other shadow settings), choose Shadow in the Settings For pop-up menu on the Text section. Using the Dropper tool from the Tools palette, sample a dark color from your image background, or click in the Color Ring in the Colors section's HSV triangle on the Art Materials palette. The shadow color will update automatically.

3 Completing the layout. Now that the title type is complete, choose the Layer Adjuster and drag the type into position. Open the other element files that you'd like to add to your page, including those that you want to use as button graphics. Then copy and paste them into the file with the background and type. Use the Layer Adjuster to position them. Painter's Rulers and Guides are helpful with positioning. To use the Rulers and Guides, choose Canvas, Rulers, Show Rulers. When the Rulers appear, click on a ruler to create a guide; you can drag an endpoint to reposition the guide. The Effects, Objects, Align command is also useful when positioning a series of images or text blocks. To read more about these useful tools, turn to Chapter 1, "Getting to Know Painter." (After the three images were pasted in, we set small text in the dark color used for the shadow under each image.)

4 Making the image map. Painter allows you to define an image file as an *image map* (a document that's divided into non-overlapping clickable regions, each of which lets you link to a different URL, or location on the Web). In the finished layout, target one of the button picture layers that will become a clickable region. (Our file included three layers that would each be designated as a clickable region.)

Now it's time to tell Painter what to include in the image map definition file (ours included the picture buttons, but omitted the tiled background layer; it would instead be tiled in the browser). For each layer you want to include in the image map, double-click the layer name in the Layers section to open the Layer Attributes dialog box. In the Name field, enter the name you want the layer to have on export. Use the checkbox to select WWW Clickable Map Region (the Region button will default to Rectangle Bounding

3

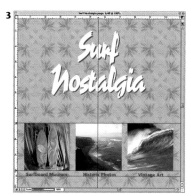

The in-progress layout with guides visible

4a

The "wave art" layer selected in the Layers section (left) and the Layer Attributes dialog box (right)

4b

Setting the Quality and Smoothness, then checking the Client Side Map File box to generate the map definition file for the client-side version of the image map

Box), and type into the URL field the URL you want to link to. Repeat for the other buttons.

Painter can create image map definition files for both server-side and client side image maps. We chose to create a client-side image map which would be more efficient when viewed using newer browsers because the instructions for client-side image maps are included in the HTML for the page. To export a map definition file for a client-side version of the image map, click the Client Side Map File box in the JPEG Encoding dialog box. (We chose the JPEG file format because of the art and photos present on the page and because most people in the site's viewing audience use 24-bit color systems.)

5 Finishing the HTML. Painter will make the map definition file for you—which lists the name of each region, defines its position using *x* and *y* coordinates and lists the URL it links to. Instructions for client-side image maps are downloaded with the file when it is viewed in newer browsers. For server-side maps, which are important for much older browsers, ask your service provider where the CGI script for image maps is stored and how to use it (CGI is an acronym for Common Gateway Interface, and CGI script is the external programming script used by the Web server). Check out these URLs on the World Wide Web to learn how to set up programming for client-side and server-side image maps: http://www.ihip.com/cside.html and http://www.ihip.com. You'll also need additional HTML programming to make the links work. A Painter-generated image map definition file text can be copied and then pasted into the html for the Web page. 🖌

FILE EXTENSION ALERT

When saving a copy of your image map file as a JPEG, make sure to delete the original RIFF file extension information from the file name by highlighting it and removing it by pressing the Backspace/Delete key. Leaving a remnant of the old extension in the name field may cause a problem when Painter attempts to create the image map description file.

Highlighting the file extension name, in preparation for deleting it for the export

5

The anatomy of one of the clickable regions in the client-side map definition file that Painter automatically generates

Making a Slide Show Animation

Overview *Choose images and resize them; create a new frame stack; paste each image into a frame; export the movie as a GIF animation.*

CHER THRIENEN-PENDARVIS

IT'S EASY TO ADD MOVEMENT to your Web pages using a slide show created as a GIF animation in Painter.

1 Preparing the images. Open several images that you want to include in your slide show. Resize your images to 72 ppi (choose Canvas, Resize, disabling the Constrain File Size box and entering a new size), then sharpen them (Effects, Focus, Sharpen). Save your resized and sharpened images under a unique name so that you don't accidentally destroy your originals. Keep the images open.

2 Making a new frame stack. To open a new frame stack, choose File, New and click the Movie button. Enter the dimensions and the number of frames you want to use. It's a good idea to make the movie a small size so that it will load and play quickly on your Web page. (We set up a 200 x 200-pixel frame stack with 3 frames.)

3 Pasting images into the frames. Activate the image you want in your first frame, choose Select, All (Ctrl/⌘-A), then copy it to the clipboard (Ctrl/⌘-C). In the new frame stack, the first frame should already be selected. Paste the image into the first frame (Ctrl/⌘-V), then drop it to the Canvas by pressing Ctrl/⌘-Shift-D. Because a layer sits on top of the entire frame stack, make sure that you've dropped it before advancing to the next frame. To advance the frame stack one frame, click the step forward icon on the Frame Stack palette (or press the Page Up key on your keyboard). Repeat the copy-paste-drop process to get the other images into the frame stack. (See Chapter 10 for more about working with frame stacks.)

4 Exporting the animation. To save the completed frame stack as a GIF animation, choose File, Save As, Save Movie as GIF Animation. Make sure to save your GIF animation under a new name so you don't accidentally replace your frame stack. (Painter will not open a GIF animation as a frame stack.) In the Save As GIF Options box, make the choices you need. (We chose 64 colors and Quantize to Nearest Color for the Imaging Method. Under Animation Options we chose a Frame Delay of 500 ms, Default Disposal Method and entered 3 times for the Loop.

1

Resizing an image to 200 x 200 pixels for the GIF animation

2

Setting up a new frame stack with three frames and 24-bit color

3a

Pasting an image into frame 1

3b

The Step Forward icon is circled here

4a

Saving the frame stack as a GIF animation

4b

Our settings in the Save As GIF Options dialog box

■ Art director **Ben Barbante** designed and illustrated *Efolio* for his Home page using a combination of Painter, Illustrator and Photoshop. He used Painter's Image Slicer to separate the picture into both GIF and JPEG files for optimal file compression, then he exported HTML code (including navigational buttons with JavaScript rollovers) and a GIF animation from Painter for the final page.

To begin the slicing and export process, Barbante opened the completed layered illustration, which included the efolio case with a light bulb (for the "off" state). He made a new layer and created a black screen on top of the light bulb as a place-holder, for the rollover "on" state. (Later, the "on" state graphic would be replaced by a GIF animation.) Then he hid the layer that would show the Mouse "on" state (the efolio with the black screen) by turning its eye icon off in the Layers section. He targeted the image canvas and chose the Image Slicer from the Dynamic Plugins menu on the Layers section of the Objects palette. In the Image Slicer, Barbante used the Horizontal and Vertical tools to divide the image, and used the Select tool to group some of the slices. Then using the Slice menu and the File Name field in the Image Slicer box, he named each slice that he planned to export and chose a compression method (File Type), choosing GIF

format to save slices with flat areas of color in the gray border outside the illustration, and JPEG format to save the slices within the illustration, which included airbrushed color gradations.

For most slices in the image, Barbante selected a slice that would not be exported and under HTML and JavaScript, he set the Rollover State to No Rollover. Next, he selected the efolio case slice that would be the Mouse "off" state, set the Rollover State to Mouse over-out and clicked the Export settings for Current Image State button. When the Export Settings dialog box appeared, he chose the Mouse out button, turned on Include JavaScript and clicked Export. He clicked OK in the Image Slicer, temporarily leaving the dialog box so he could turn on the hidden layer that would be the Mouse "on" state (when the cursor is over the button). He reopened the Image Slicer, selected the slice he wanted to export for the mouse "on" state and repeated the process he had used for the "off" state, but this time, he chose the Mouse over button in the Export Settings box. Painter saved the images and generated the JavaScript and the HTML.

For the final Home page, Barbante substituted a GIF animation for the "on" state image (the black screen). After slicing the image and creating the JavaScript rollover, he noted the exact pixel dimensions of

the mouse-over slice in the Image Slicer. He made a frame stack in Painter with five frames (featuring his illustration portfolio) using the exact dimensions of the efolio screen with the light bulb. He exported a copy of the frame stack as a GIF animation and gave it the exact name of the "on" image so the HTML would replace it in the Home page. The rollover displays the animated GIF when the cursor is placed over it. Barbante's Home page can be viewed at http://www.barbante.com.

Judy Miller, Web developer and artist for ForGET REALity Multimedia, designed and built graphics for the *Painter World Web site* using Painter, then exported the files to Macromedia Fireworks.

Miller made several seamless tiles by importing imagery, painting with brushes and applying special effects. She created the Painter World logo with Painter's type tools. After applying Surface Texture effects and beveling to the elements, she saved the tiles and logo as TIFF files and opened them in Fireworks. Miller assembled the banners in Fireworks and added other text and live effects to complete the banners, then she saved them as PNG files. The PNG files were assembled with other elements in Dreamweaver to create the pages.

For this prototype for the *Bloomers Floral Gift Shop* Web site, **Judy Miller** created an illustration of roses, a textured background and typography in Painter. Then she used the program's image map feature to export an image map file that she could incorporate into a Web page when assembling the site in Dreamweaver.

To begin, Miller created a textured pattern tile for the background in Painter, and exported it as a JPEG file which would be repeated by the browser to create the background. She began the roses in a source file by drawing a tight sketch. Then she created selections for areas of the roses (including individual petals) and saved them as masks. When painting the roses with the Fine Wheel Airbrush variant of Airbrushes, to keep the edges crisp (just like she would have used friskets in traditional airbrush technique) she used the selections to constrain the paint while she airbrushed. To paint inside and outside of the selections, she used the Draw Inside and Draw Outside buttons in the left corner of the Painter image window. Miller created the background behind the roses by layering color using the Artist Pastel Chalk and Oil Pastel variants of Dry Media, then blending areas with the Just Add Water variant of Liquid. To create the image map, Miller selected each type button area and converted it to an image layer by choosing Convert To Default Layer from the menu on the right side of the Layers section bar. Then for each layer in turn she opened the Layer Attributes dialog box by double-clicking the layer name, enabled the WWW Map Clickable Region button and assigned a URL in the Note field. When all of the clickable regions were designated, she saved the file in RIFF format for safekeeping. To export the image map, she chose File, Save As, choosing JPEG file format. In the JPEG Encoding dialog box, she enabled the Client Side File Map button and chose a Quality of approximately 60%, and then clicked OK.

■ **Judy Miller** developed the interface for the Flash-based Web site—*ForGET REALity Multimedia* using Painter. After the interface was built, she exported the files to Macromedia Fireworks to optimize them, then to Flash and Dreamweaver, where she assembled the site.

Miller imported the pillar shapes (which she had drawn in Adobe Illustrator) into Painter by choosing File, Acquire, Adobe Illustrator File. She converted all of the shapes into masks because she knew that she would need to load them numerous times as selections while she was painting the pillars. To convert each shape, she chose it in the Layers section of the Objects palette and chose Shapes, Convert to Selection. Then she saved the selection as a new mask by choosing Select, Save Selection. (See Chapter 4 "Selections, Shapes and Masks" for more about working with masks.)

The pillars were built using several layers. After adding a new layer (click the right triangle on the Layers section bar and choose New Layer from the menu), she loaded a selection for the pillars (Select, Load Selection) and filled the active selection with a custom stone pattern (Effects, Fill, Fill With Pattern). Then she blocked in the base colors with the Fine Wheel

Airbrush variant of Airbrushes using rich browns and black. So that she could efficiently paint inside and outside of the selections as she worked, she used the Draw Outside and Draw Inside buttons on the lower left of the Painter window. To paint the very fine details, she sized the Airbrush to a tiny size using the Size slider on the Controls:Brush palette, continually adjusting the size of the Airbrush as she worked.

Miller wanted to create a richer layering of color, so she added another new layer and airbrushed varied colors including rose and moss green. She set the Composite Method of this layer to Gel in the Layers section of the Objects palette. Then using the Opacity slider on the Layers section, she reduced its Opacity to 35%. Finally, Miller added yet another layer on top and using a pale blue, she carefully painted reflected light along the left sides of both pillars.

The central "backdrop" began as a photo of clouds taken by Miller with a digital camera from an airplane window. To add it to her design, she opened the source file, and copied and pasted the cloud image onto a layer in the interface composite file. Then she clicked on the new cloud layer and dragged it under the

pillars layers in the Layers section list, and carefully positioned it using the Layer Adjuster. Next, she added a new layer directly above the clouds layer and using the Digital Airbrush and black color, she painted a dark shadow along the top left side of the inner pillar to help the clouds recede into the design. She also added a very slight white highlight along the inside of the right pillar. She saved the image as a RIFF file in her Painter archive in case she needed to make changes later. Then she saved a copy as a Photoshop file for import into Fireworks.

In Fireworks, Miller added the company's logo graphics and type and used the program's slicing tools to segment the interface and to optimize the graphics. The final sliced file was saved as a PNG for import into Flash, where the logo was animated. Then the Flash movie was brought into Dreamweaver, where a new page was created with a frame set in order to house the Flash movie in the center of the page, regardless of screen resolution. This was used as an alternative to having the entire Flash movie open in a pop-up window the dimensions of the Flash movie.

■ When **Karen Dodds** was looking for something lively and hip for the launch of a Web site Dodds Design had developed for *Nicole's Shoes*, she commissioned **Susan LeVan** of LeVan/Barbee Studio to create a series of colorful on-off buttons.

LeVan began by choosing a saturated color palette from Painter's default color set, including warm oranges and yellows, accented by blues and greens. (Painter's default color set is composed of Web-safe colors.) LeVan applied colorful textures to the backgrounds using a variety of favorite textures from earlier versions of Painter (such as the Simple Texture library, located in the Paper Textures folder on the Painter_2CD CD-ROM). She applied the textures with Color Overlay, Using Paper and Hiding Power. LeVan drew the shoes, flower and face with the Scratchboard Tool variant of Pens. For the abstract elements, she drew shapes using the Pen tool (Tools palette) and filled the shapes with color. When she was satisfied with the arrangement of colored shapes, she merged the layers by selecting their names in the Layers section of the Objects palette and Grouping them, by clicking the Layer Commands button at the bottom of the palette, choosing Group from the menu and then choosing Collapse. To finish, she set the layer's Composite method to Gel.

■ Designer and artist **Debi Lee Mandel** created *DT-Car* and *DT-Space* (top), two proposed animated banners for the DigitalThink Web site (left), and two screens for the DuraFlame Web site, entitled *Campsite* (bottom).

Mandel began the banner animations by drawing the elements (the cars and buildings in *DT-Car* and the rocketship and planets in *DT-Space*) using the Pens variants, custom Brushes variants and Painter's frame stacks, finally adding the type with the Text tool.

For *Campsite*, she began by sketching in Painter with a custom "indigo-color crayon" (based on the Waxy Crayon variant) on a black background. Mandel began by painting elements for the animations (the comet and fire) using Painter's frame stacks. When she was pleased with the progression, she saved each frame stack as a GIF animation. After completing the crayon drawing, Mandel painted crisp-edged brushstrokes using flat color. To build up deep color saturation, she used custom Brushes variants with oval-shaped tips for a calligraphic feel.

■ Shawn Grunberger created this interactive map of *Hawaii* using Painter's Natural Media tools and effects. He used Painter's Image Slicer plug-in to divide the image into pieces that he could export from Painter with JavaScript rollovers. Because the irregularly shaped islands would be shown over a tiling background, he created two masks to achieve the transparency for each state. Grunberger opened the Painter RIFF file that contained the map elements. When making the file, he had saved two versions of the island images as two layer groups—"Islands On" and "Islands Off." The island name text labels were also organized in a layer group. Other elements were on separate layers. (For information about layer groups, turn to "Using Groups" in Chapter 5, on page 174.)

Before creating any slices, Grunberger set the File Type menu in the Image Slicer dialog box to "No export." Since all new slices inherit the settings of the first slice, this meant that all slices in the image would be set to "No Export" by default. He planned to export only the slices of the image that contained the islands and thus would have two different versions. Since most of the slices were open areas of the ocean, they wouldn't be exported, so using the "No Export" setting saved some time later. (Instead, the open ocean would be filled with a tiled background, that would be tiled in the browser, which would make the total size of the page and graphics smaller.) While Grunberger was setting up

the image slices, he also adjusted the position of the text captions, which had to fit within the slice boundaries.

To make a slice for the area with the four small closely associated islands, Grunberger selected and grouped them to create a single slice. (Grouping makes a single larger slice from multiple smaller slices in the grid.) To group the slices for the small islands, he chose the Select tool in the Image Slicer dialog box, clicked on the top left slice in the area he wanted to group and dragged the tool to the right and down to create a rectangular shape around the cels he wanted to combine. Later, he would make a separate image map for this area so it could include a hot spot for each island. He also grouped the large areas of the ocean that did not contain islands since they would not be exported at all.

When all of the slices were in place, he tested the HTML export of the sliced image table. In the Image Slicer dialog box, Grunberger set Rollover State to No Rollover for this test, because he wanted to check the image slice table in a browser before adding the complexity of rollover effects to the HTML code. Once he had exported the slices, Grunberger opened the HTML page in a browser. Now that the slices were ready, back in Painter, Grunberger set the final Image Slicer export. He set each of the island slices to GIF file type with 32 colors, as he had for the test, but this time with transparency. In the GIF Options dialog box he clicked the

Preview button to check the GIF Output Preview; the Preview revealed that the transparency worked correctly. He also set each of the island slices to a two-state rollover (Mouse over-out), and gave each island a URL pointing to the island's page on a NASA Web site. To export the images and code for two-state JavaScript rollovers, Grunberger did two separate export operations, one for each rollover state. (For more about exporting, see page 353.) When the settings were complete, he clicked OK and loaded the new HTML page into a browser to test, again. The map test was successful, but as exported from Painter, the map page didn't have a designated background color or background image. To add these instructions, Grunberger opened the HTML file in a text editor and modified the <body> tag to incorporate a tile (oceantile.jpg) he had designed and stored in the HTML folder. The process of applying a single tile using the browser's tiling function offers flexibility (the browser window can be resized to fill a large screen, with the ocean tiles covering the entire area). To complete this phase of the map production, Grunberger wrapped the HTML table in a <center> tag. This HTML tag ensured the map would always appear in the horizontal center of the page, regardless of the browser window size. The finished interactive map of Hawaii can be seen on the Web (http://beta.peachpit.com/wow/painter/map/part3.1/hawaii.html).

■ While working as the consulting Content Architect and Creative Director for the *TechView Consulting, Inc.* Web site, **Mario Henri Chakkour, AIA** used Painter to transform the original company logo into an image that looked like it had been drawn on a chalkboard.

He began the illustration by making a pencil drawing based on the already-existing company logo, using conventional pencil and paper. Then he scanned the drawing and opened the scan in Painter. Using the Effects, Tonal Control, Correct Colors, Curves dialog box, he adjusted the tonal range to bring out the texture of the pencil on paper and to "reverse" the values. After clicking OK to accept, he painted on the image. For

instance, to "stain" the illustration with color, he used the Felt Marker variant of Felt Pens, with which he could apply transparent color that would darken down to black. He also used the Eraser and Darkener variants of the Eraser to manipulate the values. Then, he added brushstrokes drawn with the Sharp Chalk variant of Dry Media.

To create the animated glows, Chakkour selected and copied tiny pieces from the image and noted the coordinates of each piece, using the width and height measurements in the Controls:Selection palette when he made each selection. Then he pasted the selection contents into a new file, by choosing Edit, Paste Into New Image and saved the images as

numbered PICT files. He opened them in Adobe After Effects, where he applied a Lens Flare filter over the Timeline, then he saved a copy of the animation, as a series of numbered PICT files, again in After Effects.

When the main image was complete, Chakkour saved it in Painter as a TIFF file, which he opened in Adobe Image Ready. In that program, he saved it as a JPEG file for export into a Web page editor. He also opened the PICT files for the animation in Image Ready and pasted each PICT into a frame, optimized the timing and color, then saved it as a GIF animation. When all of the graphic elements were complete, he assembled the page in Macromedia Dreamweaver.

■ While working with Wes Meador, the vice president and project director for MDHeal, Inc. **Mario Henri Chakkour** consulted as the creative director, illustrator and animator for the *MDHeal.com* Web site. The Web site incorporates several animations, including the man's face which turns, the hands on the keyboard and elements on the gate and statue.

To begin, Chakkour created all of the sketches, mockups, and conceptual drawings in Painter using a technique he calls "Digital Wet-on-Wet," as follows: He laid in the basic color and tones using the Sharp Chalk variant of Dry Media, then he blended with the Just Add Water variant of Liquid, switching back and forth between the Sharp Chalk and Just Add Water brushes as he developed the illustration elements. He often changed the size and opacity of the brushes as he worked, using the sliders in the Controls:Brush palette.

Once the basic elements were in place, he created digital "friskets" so that he could achieve a crisp-edged look when he painted, by drawing shapes with the Pen tool (Tools palette). Then he converted the shapes to selections and saved them as masks, so that he could use them to protect areas of the illustration as he refined the painting. Using a carefully planned approach, Chakkour refined the work with the Digital Airbrush variant of Airbrushes, the Sharp Chalk, Brushes variants and Water Color.

Chakkour created the animations using the same brushes. To create the moving head animation, he began with a copy of the file that without the sitting character. Working on a new layer, he painted the character sitting. Next, he painted a few heads in different positions, creating each one on its own layer, using the eye icon in the Layers section to turn visibility on and off as he worked. When they were complete, with the Pen tool, he drew a shape around each head, converted the shape to a selection (Shapes, Convert to Selection) and saved it as a mask. Then he copied and pasted each masked head into the main file, in turn, for all of the positions. (He also copied and pasted the layer that contained the whole figure.)

This gave him a painting with several layers floating in register. He saved the file in RIFF format using a unique name for his archive. Then he used the Crop tool to crop his file to include only the area he needed for the animated GIF. One by one, he opened the eye icon for each head layer to show it, then he flattened the file by choosing Drop All from the menu on the right side of the Layers section bar and he chose File, Save As, using a new name. With the saved file still open, he chose Edit, Undo (to undo the Drop All command), then opened the eye icon for another head layer, dropped it, chose Save As, and continued to repeat the process until he had several small files with the head in different positions, all in register. He saved copies of the animation files and the main illustration file in TIFF format and opened them in Adobe ImageReady. He assembled the animation files into the GIF animation and saved it as a GIF. He also saved a copy of the main illustration in JPEG format. Then he assembled the elements on the page using Dreamweaver.

12

PRINTING
AND
ARCHIVAL
CONCERNS

Wise Woman *is a part of the series*
Journey of the Spirit *by Dorothy Simpson
Krause. The image was printed on the
Roland HiFi Jet on Concord paper using
the Roland six-color pigmented ink set. The
35 x 28-inch print was printed in an edition of 20, coated with encaustic (beeswax)
and rubbed with pearlescent pigment.*

PAINTER AND CMYK TIFFS

Painter can open CMYK TIFF files,
but in doing so, it converts them to
RGB, Painter's native color space.
You can also save a CMYK TIFF
from Painter by choosing File, Save
As, selecting TIFF from the Format
menu and then clicking the CMYK
button in the Export Options box.

HOW WILL YOU PRESENT YOUR PAINTER ARTWORK to the world? Will it
be as a limited-edition digital painting, printed on archival paper by a
print studio or service bureau, then matted, framed, and hung on a
gallery wall? Or as an illustration in a magazine, where it's part of a
page layout that's output direct-to-plate, to printed on an offset
press? Or as a desktop color print? Or as part of a slide show? For each
of these and other output options, there are things you can do to prepare your Painter file so the output process runs smoothly. We hope
the tips that follow will help you as you plan your own project.

COLOR FOR PRINTING

Most types of printing involve the use of four-color process, or CMYK
(cyan, magenta, yellow, black) inks and dyes. Painter's native color
mode is RGB (red, green, blue), which has a larger color *gamut*
(range of colors) than the CMYK color model. (An illustration that
compares RGB and CMYK color gamuts is on page 10 in Chapter
1.) Although Painter doesn't let you specify CMYK color mixes as
Adobe Photoshop and some other programs do, it does allow you
to work in Output Preview mode, using only those colors within
the RGB gamut that are realizable in CMYK. You can also output
CMYK TIFF and EPS files for color separation directly from Painter.

Using Color Management. Before you turn a file over for output in a form that will be used for CMYK printing, consider using
Color Management with Output Preview. With this system you
can set up a monitor-to-printer calibration loop that will allow
you to see an on-screen approximation of how your printed image
will look. (A word of caution: There are many variables besides the
RGB-to-CMYK conversion that will affect how a color print will
look—for instance, the color cast of your particular monitor and

Click the Kodak Color Management icon to toggle between RGB and the Output Preview.

Setting up the Color Management dialog box to print a proof from our system to an Epson 2000P printer

EMBEDDED ICC PROFILES

Using Kodak Color Management provides a preview only, and makes no permanent changes to the file. To include an embedded ICC profile in a saved file (so the file will look the same when viewed in another program such as Adobe Photoshop), choose Canvas, Kodak Color Management and in the Color Management dialog box, click the Import/Export icon (the page), and choose a profile in the Advanced Import/Export dialog box.

The Advanced Import/Export Settings dialog box with a profile chosen for export

the color of your paper. Output Preview doesn't account for these factors.) Begin by choosing Canvas, Kodak Color Correction to open the Color Management dialog box. In the dialog box, choose an Internal RGB color space, a Monitor Profile and an Output Profile depending on whether you'll be outputting to separations or to a composite printer in your studio such as an Epson 2000P. When you perform a Painter Easy Installation, the program automatically installs a selection of Color Profiles into the Painter 7 application folder. You'll find more profiles in the Color Profiles folder on the Painter_2 CD CD-ROM. (If you don't see your monitor or printer profile in the list, it can often be obtained from the manufacturer.) To add profiles to your system, copy them from the Painter_2 CD-ROM as follows: Macintosh users should drag the profiles into the Painter 7 application folder. Windows users should copy profiles into the Windows\Color folder. The next time you launch Painter 7, the color profiles will be available in the Color Management dialog box.

To toggle between the broader-gamut RGB image and the Output Preview, click the Kodak Color Management icon above the right scroll bar. Remember to change the Color Management settings if you plan to print to another device. For more information about Painter's color management tools see "Color Management," in Chapter 21 of the *Painter 7 User Guide*.

Making CMYK conversions in another program. Some Painter artists prefer to work in the broader RGB color gamut and convert their finished images to CMYK in another imaging program such as Photoshop or Equilibrium DeBabelizer, because these programs allow more control of how the conversion is made. There are several good resources that give detailed explanations of color conversion using Photoshop, including the *Adobe Photoshop User Guide* and *The Photoshop 6 Wow! Book* and *Photoshop in 4 Colors* (these last two are from Peachpit Press). Some printing studios—for example, Cone Editions—prefer to receive RGB files from artists and make the conversion themselves using custom color tables they create in Photoshop especially for that image. (See "Making a Fine Art Master Print" on page 372 for an explanation of Cone Editions' process.) Check with your printer to work out a conversion method.

Writing EPS-DCS files from Painter. Many illustrators prefer to have control over the prepress process by ordering their own four-color film for illustrations that will be printed on a four-color sheet-fed press at a printing plant. Rather than an electronic file, they deliver the film separations and a laminated proof (a matchprint, for example) to the client. Whether you or someone else will be ordering the film, check with the operator who will be doing the output. He or she should be able to tell you the correct setup for the equipment that will output your job.

Detail of Winter/Spring, *by Pamela Wells. When making the fine art print of her image, Wells calibrated her computer system to the profile of the Iris inkjet printer at the service bureau she planned to send it to. Turn to page 311 in Chapter 9 to view the entire image.*

Bonny Lhotka created the digital file for Day Job *in Painter, by painting with brushes and using layers to composite several source files. Before printing the digital image, Lhotka prepared a one-of-a-kind surface using gold-and ochre-colored acrylics. She painted an abstract design on a nonporous surface to create a monotype that she could transfer to a piece of rag paper using a large roller. After drying and coating the surface of the monoprint with inkjet receiver to help it absorb the ink, she printed the image on top of it using an Encad NovaJet 3. A photograph of the final print is shown above.*

FINE ART PRINTING AT A SERVICE BUREAU

Many artists prefer to choose a service bureau or master printer who specializes in output for fine art printmaking. Rather than attempt to print an edition in their studio, they rely on fine art service bureaus for high-quality equipment—for instance, an Iris inkjet printer is not affordable for most artists. (Iris prints are accepted by many galleries and museums; they are no longer thought of as "experimental prints.") The expertise needed for a fine art print studio differs greatly from that of a commercial service bureau accustomed to making film and proofs for offset printing. Choose a printer who has experience working with artists and who understands archival and editioning issues. (See Appendix C for a list of service bureaus that specialize in working with artists.)

Printing digital watercolors with the Iris. Iris printers are special inkjet machines capable of producing images with luminous color and no visible dot, making the output desirable for fine art printmaking. The Iris sprays water-based CMYK dyes or pigment-based inks (similar to watercolors) through four extremely narrow nozzles. The paper or other substrate is taped to a rotating drum in the machine and sprayed with millions of droplets per second. Many fine art printers modify the Iris 3047 (the largest of the Iris printer line) so it can handle thicker substrates. Cone Editions and Nash Editions were among the first printers to pioneer this technique; they moved back the printing heads, allowing 400-lb. watercolor paper, canvas or metal to be taped onto the drum.

More large-format inkjet printers. Many more excellent choices are available for the artist who wants to order high-quality archival large-format prints of their work from bureaus. Some service bureaus offer prints from the Hewlett-Packard DesignJet 5000 CP series using the CP UV six-color archival ink set. These 1200 x 600 dpi printers can accept rolled watercolor paper and canvas and the largest model can print up to 60 inches wide. With these printers, sometimes images with very light, graduated tones can produce areas with tiny dots in a dither or scatter pattern. Printing on canvas can help hide these dots. Wilhelm Imaging Research Inc. reports that the HP DesignJet CP ink systems' UV inks will hold true color for 150+ years.

High-quality prints from large-format Epson printers are also available from some service bureaus. The Epson 7500 (24 inches wide) and the 9500 and 10000 (both 44 inches wide) are 1440 dpi inkjet printers that use six-color archival inks. They're capable of producing prints on a wide variety of media, including paper, canvas and posterboard with a thickness of up to 1.5 mm.

Large, high-quality prints from Roland printers are also available at service bureaus. The Roland HiFi Jet Pro has a resolution of 1440 dpi and uses an eight color archival ink set. The largest model can accommodate media widths to 64-inches.

Robert Manning of Supersample Corporation / Lilika Productions designed this scarf using Painter's brushes, special effects and pattern features. Then the image was printed on cotton twill fabric with a twelve-color Colorspan inkjet printer using Fiber Reactive dyes.

To check color and detail before printing on a Hewlett-Packard 2500CP with archival UV inks, Cher Threinen-Pendarvis proofed Forked Path *as an 8 x 10-inch Fujix Pictrography print. (Fujix Pictrography prints are described in "Outputting to a Digital Positive" on this page.) The final print was made at 15 x 17 inches on Arches cold-pressed watercolor paper and framed with UV-protective glass.*

LINE SCREEN AND RESOLUTION

When you're preparing files to be printed on an offset press, ask what line screen will be used for printing so you can begin your file with a high enough resolution (ppi) to accommodate it. A factor of 1.5 to 2 times the line screen is typical. For example, to accommodate a 150-line screen, set up your file with the dimensions you need at a resolution of 225 to 300 ppi.

Colorspan offers several large-format printers, even a model specifically designed to print fabric. Their Giclee Printmaker can accommodate media up to 35.5 inches wide and up to 3mm thick; it will print on almost anything that can be wrapped around the drum. The Giclee Printmaker uses eight-color light-fast dye inks.

Outputting to a digital positive. Major advances have been made in the area of direct digital photographic prints. In general, the three printing methods discussed below use a laser to image the digital file onto a photographic substrate.

Prints made from the Fujix Pictrography 3000 and 4000 (up to 12 x 18 inches) offer better registration and permanency and more natural color than a dye-sublimation print such as the Kodak XL7700 or 3M Rainbow. The Fujix uses a laser to image the digital file onto a "donor" sheet, which is then printed onto photographic paper using a single-pass, silver-halide printing process. The appearance and permanency (about 20 years) of the Fujix are similar to those of a photographic Cibachrome (C-print). Prints can be laminated with a coating that includes an ultraviolet inhibitor, extending their life further. Additionally, the Noritsu 2701 produces high-quality Cibachrome-like prints up to 12 x 18-inches.

The Cymbolic Sciences Lightjet 5000 also uses a laser, imaging the digital file to large-format archival photo paper and creating a continuous-tone print without visible dots, as large as 48 x 96 inches. Because the Lightjet 5000 uses 36-bit RGB color, the broad color gamut in these prints is comparable to that in photographic "R" prints. To prepare Painter files for the LightJet 5000, set up your file at its final output size, using a resolution of 150–200 ppi and save it as an uncompressed RGB TIFF file. The LightJet's software incorporates an interpolation algorithm that makes it possible to increase the resolution of the image while retaining its sharpness. Artist and photographer Phillip Charris often outputs his Painter-enhanced photographs using a Lightjet 5000, then carefully strips the print from its backing paper and mounts it on canvas.

Another recommended photo-slick, archival printmaking method is the Durst Lamda system. (Using a laser, it images to archival photo media, such as paper, color negative media or color reversal media.) It's also a 36-bit RGB system. The Durst Lamda 76 can print seamless 32-inch-wide images up to 164 feet long. Durst Lamda prints are reported to be lightfast for a minimum of 50

DYE-SUBLIMATION PRINTERS

Dye-sublimation printers such as the Kodak XL7700 and 8600PS and the 3M Rainbow offer continuous tone (no obvious dot pattern) and bright color. Many designers use dye sub prints for comps. However, they are very susceptible to humidity and can smear if rubbed. If you make dye-sublimation prints for a portfolio presentation, do not permanently store them in acetate sleeves—the trapped humidity can ruin the color in the print.

John Derry printed Capitola, *shown here as a detail, on an Epson 1270 six-color printer using Epson's archival ink set. Turn to page 380 in the gallery to view the entire image.*

A LENTICULAR SERVICE

Some service bureaus specialize in making lenticular signs. (A lenticular is an image that uses a lens to produce stereo 3D or video-motion-like effects as a transition is made from one image to another.) These companies (for instance, Durst Dice America, www.durstonline.com and Lenticular Development, www.lenticulardevelopment.com) can print a lenticular using an artist's files. They also offer proprietary software and training in the process.

INCREASING LONGEVITY

A few fine art printers (notably, Cone Editions and Nash Editions) have developed their own silk-screened coatings to protect Iris prints from fading. The coating merges with the ink on the substrate and doesn't change the appearance of the print. (Many ink sets developed for inkjet printers use water-soluble inks. Keep the print dry unless you purposely want to spot or mix the color with water.)

years. Some artists strip the prints, mount them on canvas, then finish them with glazes of UV-protectant varnish (such as Golden Varnish, described on page 365) to protect the print from humidity and to add a hand-finished look.

PHOTOGRAPHIC IMAGING OPTIONS

Many new technologies are available for Painter output at graphic arts service bureaus and photo labs that use digital equipment.

Imaging to transparencies using a film recorder. Small- and large-format film recorders are used to image digital files such as Painter artwork to transparencies ranging from 35mm to 16 x 20 inches. For output via a film recorder, images should be in landscape orientation (horizontal) to take advantage of the width of the film.

To avoid *pixelation* (a jaggy, stair-step look caused by lack of sufficient resolution) on transparencies generated by a service bureau's film recorder, here are some guidelines from Chrome Digital and Photodyne (San Diego) and The Digital Pond (San Francisco) for creating or sizing your files. Most professional-quality 35mm film recorders (such as the Solitaire 16 series) use a minimum resolution of 4,000 lines; for this resolution, your image should be 4,096 x 2,732 pixels (about 32 MB). The minimum resolution for 4 x 5-inch transparencies is 8,000 lines, requiring an 8,192 x 5,464-pixel (approximately 165 MB) file. For even more crispness, devices such as the Solitaire 16XPS will image at a resolution of 16,000 lines (a 16,384 x 10,928-pixel file, of approximately 512 MB). Two powerful film recorders used to create 4 x 5-inch, 8 x 10-inch and larger-format transparencies are the LVT (from Light Valve Technology, a subsidiary of Kodak) and the Lightjet 2080 (from Cymbolic Sciences, Inc.). Plan to create huge images (up to 15,000 x 18,000 pixels and approximately 800 MB) to take full advantage of the resolution capabilities of these machines.

Printing your images as Fujichrome. For fine art images, Fujichrome prints made from transparencies offer excellent detail and saturated color, and can be ordered with a high gloss. Prints can be made from 35mm slides or 4 x 5-inch transparencies. To print to the maximum size of 20 x 24 inches, a 4 x 5 transparency is recommended. The permanency of the Fuji print is 40–50 years, and this can be extended by adding a lamination with an ultraviolet inhibitor. Diane Fenster, a noted fine artist and photographer, produces much of her digital work as large-format Fujichrome prints.

FINE ART PRINTING IN THE STUDIO

Today, many exciting alternatives are available for artists who want to proof their images, or make fine art prints in their own studio using archival ink sets and papers.

Printing digital watercolors with desktop printers. Desktop inkjet printers can deliver beautiful color prints if they are set up properly. The affordable HP printers (such as the 1220c) and

Detail of Indigo, *an experimental Fresco print by Bonny Lhotka. To view the entire image, turn to page 385 in the gallery.*

Detail of Indigo, *an experimental Fresco print by Bonny Lhotka. To view the entire image, turn to page 385 in the gallery.*

PAPER-AND-INK COMBOS

The correct paper-and-ink combination can contribute to the greater longevity of your prints. Check out Henry Wilhelm's Web site, www.wilhelm-research.com for suggested paper-and-ink combinations.

Sometimes Philip Howe uses his digital paintings as templates for oil painting, as he did here for Profile. *Howe printed the digital painting onto canvas using an HP 2500 CP printer and archival inks. Then he painted over the entire image with oil paint. To see another of Howe's paintings using this technique, turn to the gallery on page 383.*

the Epson Stylus series (the 1280, for instance) are great printers not only for pulling test prints before sending images to an Iris, but also for experimental fine art prints. Most inkjet inks are water-soluble, so you can try painting into a print with a wet brush. There are a few exceptions, and the Epson 2000P is one. It ships with a six-color pigmented archival ink set and it produces beautiful water resistant prints, especially when used with Epson's Enhanced Archival Matte paper. These prints will accept acrylic paint without smearing or running. Although most desktop printers work best with slick paper, archival-quality cotton papers produce excellent results on some machines. For example, the Epson 1520 and 3000 print on thicker acid-free papers if you feed the paper manually. (Two papers to try are 80–120 lb. Arches cold-pressed watercolor paper and Rives BFK printmaking paper.)

New inks and substrates for desktop art prints. With the increased interest in desktop art-making, new inks and papers keep coming out. Henry Wilhelm has done important research regarding the longevity of different ink and substrate combinations. A comparison of color gamut and longevity with the different inks is available through Wilhelm Imaging Research, Inc., on the Web at www.wilhelm-research.com.

New inks with better longevity and waterproof characteristics are becoming available for many inkjet printers. For information about products for use with the Hewlett-Packard printers, check out www.hp.com; for information about Epson products, visit its company Web site at www.epson.com. Also, InkJet Mall (a sister company of Cone Editions) is another good resource for information and you can buy sets of archival inks (such as MIS) for several desktop printers; it's found on the Web at www.inkjetmall.com. Several other companies offer new archival inks sets for desktop printers. One of the most notable is Media Street, offering Generations Inks, found on the Web at www.mediastreet.com.

Several traditional art papers are now manufactured for digital printmaking—for instance, Somerset Enhanced, Concorde Rag and Orwell, all available from Cone Editions' Ink Jet Mall. Also check out Somerset photo-enhanced paper and other new papers on the Web at www.dygraphics.com. And there are many canvases available for use with inkjet printers. For instance, check out the artist-grade canvases available from Sentinel Imaging, located on the Web at www.inkjet.com, and the pure-white artist-grade-canvas from Dr. Graphix Inc. at www.drgraphix.com.

Inkjet receivers and protective coatings. To seal custom substrates (like handmade papers), so the ink will hold better, paint thin rabbit skin glue on to the substrate with a brush and dry it thoroughly. Then make your print.

You can treat prints yourself so the color will last much longer. Several protective coatings are available at your local art supply store, from Daniel Smith via mail order, or from Media Street on

Flint *by Dorothy Simpson Krause, includes elements collected during a journey to Tibet. After the collage was complete, Krause prepared the surface of the substrate (dimensionally stable spunbond polyester) for printing, by painting it with Golden Molding Paste. When the surface was dry, she added a coat of gel medium mixed with pearlescent pigment. To provide a receiver for the inks, she painted the substrate with rabbit skin glue, dried it, then compressed it by running it though a Coda laminator. The final print was made on a Roland Hi-Jet using the Roland pigmented six-color inks.*

IRIS PRINT AND MONOTYPE

Master printer David Salgado has developed a process that combines monotypes with Iris prints, using the 39 x 52-inch Mailänder flatbed hand-fed offset press at Trillium Press. After a mylar-coated aluminum plate is painted with lithography inks, the plate is mounted on the press and the press roller pulls ink from the plate to transfer to the Iris print. Depending on the image, seven to ten prints can be pulled in what is known as an *edition variée*. Some artists use an Iris print as a starting point, while others use cutout pieces of an Iris print as elements in collage work, then the collage is run through the press. Salgado feels they've just begun to discover the possibilities for this technique. Trillium has printed editions of artwork that have combined Iris printing, silkscreen, monotype and lithography in edition numbers of 50 and more.

the Web at www.mediastreet.com. One of our favorites is Golden MSA Varnish with UVLS (soluble with mineral spirits). Use a protective respirator and gloves for the process because the fumes from this coating are *very* toxic. To minimize contact with dangerous airborne particles, dilute the varnish and apply it with a brush. Golden Varnish is also available in a spray can, as is Krylon UV Protectant spray. Make sure to use a protective respirator when using the spray varnishes.

Caring for prints. After a UV-protective coating has been applied, treat your print as you would a watercolor and avoid displaying it in direct sunlight. Frame it using UV-resistant glazing (glass or Plexiglas) and preserve air space between the surface of the print and the glazing.

EXPERIMENTAL PRINTMAKING

In today's world of experimental printmaking, anything goes if it works with your vision of the image you're printing. For instance, many different substrates can be used successfully with inkjet printers; among the favorites are archival-quality papers with a high cotton content. Browse your local art store for Saunders handmade watercolor paper, Arches hot-press and cold-press watercolor paper, Rives BFK printmaking papers, and Canson drawing and charcoal papers. You can hand-feed these papers into a studio desktop printer, or request that a fine art print studio create an Iris print with paper that you supply. Fine art print studios often keep special papers in stock—Cone Editions, for instance, has hundreds of fine art papers on hand. Some print studios also print on canvas, film or metal.

<table>
<tr><td>**DIFFERENTIAL AGING**</td></tr>
<tr><td>If you plan to add another medium (such as acrylic or pastel) to a digital print, keep in mind that different pigments and dyes can age at different rates. So the strokes you carefully hand-work into the print may begin to stand out over time.</td></tr>
</table>

Mixing media. Prints from an Iris or another inkjet printer can be modified with traditional tools and fine art printing processes, such as embossing, intaglio and silkscreen. (Turn to page 368 to read about Carol Benioff's technique of overprinting a copperplate etching on top of an Iris print.) If you plan to hand-work an inkjet print with media such as pastels, pencils or oil paint—make the print on rag paper with enough body to hold together when you apply the traditional media to the print. Arches 140-pound watercolor paper and Rives heavyweight printmaking paper are good choices.

Making Translite transfers. The Translite transfer technique was pioneered by Jon Cone. First, a digital image is printed onto Translite film using an Iris printer. Then a piece of archival-quality paper (such as Rives BFK) is soaked in water, and when it is partially dry, the image is transferred from the Translite "plate" onto

Bonny Lhotka creates one-of-a-kind "monotype" substrates to use as unique surfaces in the printing of her digital images.

Detail of a sample certificate of authenticity. You'll find a PageMaker 6.5 file and a PDF of this sample certificate on the Painter 7 Wow! CD-ROM.

INKJET PRINT OR GICLÉE?

Some businesses in the fine art printmaking community have adopted the name Giclée (which can be loosely defined as *spray*) when referring to a fine art print made on a high-quality inkjet. Many artists who create their work digitally prefer to leave the Giclée term to the traditional fine art reproduction industry that originated it, thinking that it's important to maintain the distinction between an original print made from a digital painting or collage and a traditional reproduction. This is because each direct digital print has its own unique value and, in fact, is not a reproduction.

the dampened printmaking paper using an embossing press—producing a monoprint with softly graduated color.

Overprinting a digital file onto a monotype. To create a surface that she would later use for printing *Day Job* (shown on page 362), Bonny Lhotka created a one-of-a-kind monotype "plate" by applying acrylic paint onto prepared acetate. She laid a piece of rag paper onto the "plate" and used a custom-made 40-lb. roller to transfer the painted image onto the paper. After transferring, she lifted the paper off the "plate" and allowed it to dry. Then she used a Novajet inkjet printer to overprint the digital file on top of the monoprint. She believes that the overprinting process produces a broader range of color than is possible if the entire image is composed and printed digtially. The result is a print with more depth.

FINE ART EDITIONS FROM DIGITAL FILES

Some artists scan finished, traditionally created artwork and then print it on an Iris or another high-quality printer (such as an Epson 2000P or a Roland HiFi Jet). This process is actually *replicating* an original piece of work. However, when artwork *originates* as a digital file—using a program such as Painter—and is then output to a high-quality printer using an archival ink set, that print itself becomes an original. (Think of your Painter image as a kind of "digital printing plate" stored in your computer.)

Advantages of digital editions. Printing a digital edition has advantages over traditional, limited-run printing methods. Any number of multiple originals can be made from a digital file without loss of quality: The "digital plate" won't deteriorate. Also, the setup charge for the digital process is usually much less than when an edition is printed conventionally. And while an edition printed with traditional methods needs to be printed all at once, with digital editions, an artist may request prints from the fine art service bureau as needed.

Planning an edition. An edition should be carefully tracked and controlled, just as it would be if printed with traditional methods. It's wise to make a contract between the master printer and artist, stating the type of edition, the number of prints in the edition and that no more prints will be made. When an original is sold, the artist should give the buyer a certificate of authenticity that contains the name of the artist and the print, the date sold, the edition size, the print number, the number of artist proofs, the substrate, and any details of hand-working done on the print. Once the edition is complete, the artist should destroy the digital file, just as the screen would be destroyed after a silkscreen edition. (See "Making a Fine Art Master Print" on page 372.)

Combining Digital and Intaglio Printmaking

Overview *Make a print using a traditional printmaking method; scan the print; use the scan as a guide to create a colored image in Painter; output the digital file to an Iris printer; overprint the traditional print on top the Iris print in register.*

CAROL BENIOFF

Photograph of the copperplate etching. The composition is created in reverse.

Grayscale scan of the black-and-white intaglio print

CAROL BENIOFF'S INNOVATIVE PRINTMAKING method combines classic intaglio techniques with digital printing. An award-winning fine artist and illustrator, she has illustrated for magazines such as *Atlantic Monthly* and *Parenting*—and her work appears in the *CA Illustration Annual*. Currently she works with The Graphics Arts Workshop in San Francisco. One of the oldest artists' cooperatives in the United States, it has been in existence since the 1930s. To create *The Game*, a self-promotional piece, Benioff overprinted a copperplate etching on top of an Iris inkjet print made on Daniel Smith archival printmaking paper.

1 Making an intaglio print. Benioff planned the 6 x 7-inch copperplate knowing that she would be adding a dimension of colored imagery created in Painter. Using primarily a hard ground etching technique, she etched fine lines with a fine-point diamond stylus. When making a classic hard ground etching, an artist scribes lines into an acid-resistant coating, exposing the metal underneath. Then the plate is soaked in a acid bath to etch the drawing deeper into the plate. The acid-etched lines hold the ink, yielding warm, velvety black lines when printed.

Benioff rolled black ink onto the plate, working it into the lines with a cardboard dauber, then rubbed off excess ink with tarlatan (starched open-weave muslin). Next, she chose a piece of archival

The two images: A painted landscape (left), and a watercolor tint image to match the etching (right)

Photograph of the Iris print composite

Inking the plate (left) and making registration marks on a clear acetate sheet to help align the copperplate to the Iris print (right)

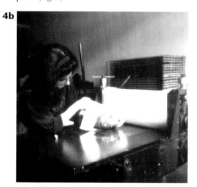

After lifting the press felts on the intaglio press, Benioff carefully pulled the finished print off the copperplate.

printmaking paper and soaked it, so it would absorb the ink better. After letting the paper partially dry, she made a print using an etching press.

When the print was dry, she scanned it and saved the scan to use as a guide to help develop two color images (described in step 2). Benioff's grayscale scan measured 2400 x 2800 pixels.

2 Creating color images and compositing. Open your scan, make a clone (File, Clone), and delete the contents of the clone (Select, All, and press the Backspace/Delete key). Now, turn on Tracing Paper (Ctrl/⌘-T). Using the scan as a guide, paint a colorful image that will complement your traditional print.

Benioff created two images: a painted landscape and a loose watercolor version of the etched composition. The landscape was designed to add dynamic tension to the composition. To begin the landscape, she sketched larger shapes with the Water Color brushes, then added details with the Chalk variants of Dry Media and Brushes variants. When the image was complete, she saved it for use later in the process.

To paint a second image, which would add colored tints to elements in the etching, she made a second clone of the scan, again deleting the contents. Using the scan as a guide, she painted a loose color composition with a custom Wash Camel Water Color brush.

Benioff composited the images in Photoshop by merging the second image with the first using the Image, Apply Image and the Multiply blending mode. To merge two color images in Painter, open both images and make the second image active. Select, All, Copy, and Paste it into the first image. In the Layers section of the Objects palette, choose a Compositing Method that complements your image.

3 Choosing paper for the print. To achieve a good ink impression of the copperplate, paper should be softened by dampening so that it will mold to the detail etched into the plate. This poses a problem when printing over an Iris print, because Iris prints bleed when wet. To resolve this problem, Benioff experimented extensively with different papers. She found that some very soft papers will soak through—even when you spritz the back of the paper to dampen it slightly—destroying the water-based Iris image. The paper she chose to print *The Game* (Daniel Smith archival printmaking paper) is fibrous enough to soften and swell when slightly moistened but thick enough that the dampness did not soak through to the inks on the front.

4 Overprinting the etching. After preparing the copperplate with ink, Benioff made an acetate template to register the image on the paper and plate. The elements in the Iris print needed to align perfectly with the copperplate, so she carefully traced the position of the figures and table onto the acetate. She aligned the template, the plate and the paper (Iris print) on the press bed and pulled the print. 🖌

Constructing a Lenticular Work

Overview *Build textured elements and layer them into a collage; set up multiple versions of the file for the lenticular; print the images on an inkjet printer; glaze the wood mat and embellish its surface.*

The handmade paper, the letterpress type block with the radio tower image and the tray filled with "lava"

The lava and paper elements with the Apply Surface Texture emboss added

An impression of the photo of sand and foam was embossed into the working image.

BONNY LHOTKA

"A LENTICULAR IMAGE SUSPENDS TIME, space and movement. It adds a level of ambiguity that engages the viewer's attention," says artist Bonny Lhotka. (A lenticular image is actually several images sliced into strips and alternated. A plastic sheet with a series of parallel lens strips, or lenticules, embossed into one surface is applied over the assemblage, so the different images are seen one at a time, as a viewer moves past the artwork.) To create *Ancient Echo*, Lhotka scanned elements, applied textural effects, then composited the source files into a collage. To build the lenticular, she created eleven variations of the file. As a viewer walks past *Ancient Echo*, the central portion of the image turns to black. At the same time, the background rotates through a rainbow of color shifts and the lower portion appears to recede. You may want to loosely follow Lhotka's process and also experiment with your own effects.

1 Preparing the source images. Lhotka chose squares of painted handmade paper from an earlier project, and a letterpress type block with a radio tower image. For one of the background layers, she built a surface using modeling paste and painted it with acrylics to look like lava. Lhotka scanned and touched up the source images. She created the rings in Painter and colored them with a gradient. To give the rings wire-like dimension, she used Glass Distortion.

2 Adding texture to elements. Lhotka likes to emulate the look of handmade paper, using Painter's Apply Surface Texture feature. For this work, she embossed several elements (including the lava and paper elements) with Apply Surface Texture Using Image Luminance and subtle settings.

The composite in progress

Printing the images

Preparing the transfer board

Mixing the gel and applying it to the board

Preparing to transfer the mat print

Burning the mat surface to crackle the glaze

3 Giving the colored fields texture. She wanted to add texture to more colored areas in the image. So she opened an original photo of beach sand and used Apply Surface Texture, Using Original Luminance to emboss the pattern of the foam and sand into her image. To ensure that the emboss effect will apply to your entire image, choose as your clone source an image with the same pixel dimensions as your working file. Make the image that you want to emboss active, target a layer you want to emboss and designate the clone source by choosing File, Clone Source. Choose Effects, Surface Control, Apply Surface Texture, Using Original Luminance.

4 Assembling the composite. After all of the elements were embossed with Apply Surface Texture, Lhotka copied and pasted the elements into Photoshop, where she completed the composite. After the image was finished, she created eleven different color variations of the central portion of the file, which would become the lenticular.

5 Processing and printing the lenticular. For the next step, Lhotka used SuperFlip software (available from www.flipsigns.com). Using a sophisticated mathematical formula, the software sliced the images into linear strips and reassembled them according to the specifications for the lenticular that Lhotka had chosen. When the assemblage was complete, Lhotka printed it on a Roland Hi-Fi Jet. The six-color printer uses a CMYKOG archival pigment set with saturated colors. After the interlaced image was printed, it was aligned with the lens.

6 Setting up a gel transfer for the glaze. When building the fine art mat for the lenticular, Lhotka chose Baltic birch. As she planned to pour liquid onto the wood, to prevent the wood from bowing, she temporarily attached a one-by-three-foot board to the back of the birch mat. To hold the liquid, she placed duct tape around the sides to make a tray. Then she made a gel: She dissolved rabbit skin glue in water, warmed it, and allowed it to return to room temperature, then added powdered pearlescent pigment to it. She used a strainer to remove undissolved colorant and large bubbles, then poured the mixture onto the wood.

7 Printing the image for the mat. Lhotka printed the image for the mat on Rexam white film. After printing, she transferred it to the gel on the wood. Placing the printed film on the gel caused the image to transfer immediately without pressure. When the gel dried, the image was permanently bonded into the wood.

8 Embellishing the surface of the mat. To give the glaze a crackled effect, Lhotka used a torch to burn the surface of the mat after it was dry. This caused the glue to bubble, creating a crackled glaze surface. The completed presentation of *Ancient Echo* measures 34 x 28 inches; the 28 x 22-inch center of the image with the 3D animated lenticular sits inside a one-half inch recession on the glazed mat board.

Making a Fine Art Master Print

Overview *Make a custom color conversion of a Painter image; choose a textured, handmade paper that will enhance the image; after a first, light printing, paint an iridescent polymer onto some areas of the print; print the image a second time; apply a UV-protective coating to the print; document the edition.*

1a

Cone at the Power Mac that's connected to the Iris system

1b

One of Cone's custom ink settings

JON CONE OF CONE EDITIONS PRESS has been making prints and editions for artists since 1980. In 1985, Cone Editions began using computers in printmaking, pioneering techniques such as digital gravure, digital silkscreen and various digital monotype techniques. The firm has made Iris inkjet prints since 1992 and has become a leader in Iris printing technology, sharing methods, materials and techniques with other fine art service bureaus.

When he makes a fine art Iris master print, Cone interprets the artist's image in a collaborative manner. Often the selection of a paper, a special color transformation or perhaps even an experimental printing method can enhance an image. Cone used all three of these to realize the Painter image above.

1 Resizing and converting the color mode. An image may need to be resized to take advantage of the Iris printer's resolution (300 dpi) and replication capabilities. The Iris achieves the look of a much higher resolution because of the way the ink sprays onto the paper. Although the optimal resolution for files that will be printed on the Iris is 300 ppi, the printer can interpolate resolutions of 150 ppi or 100 ppi to produce high-quality prints.

Cone prefers to use Adobe Photoshop for a monitor-to-output calibration loop. He has written a proprietary color transformation engine for Photoshop that he uses to convert images from RGB to CMYK. This interface also helps him calibrate the Iris, allowing the monitor to show a close approximation of the printed image. After converting this image, Cone used Photoshop's Image, Adjust, Curves

IRIS FACTS

The Iris printer's drum spins at 110 inches per second; up to 1 million droplets of ink per second are sprayed at 90 mph through each of its four nozzles. Using only cyan, magenta, yellow and black inks, it can simulate millions of colors.

2

Positioning the paper on the Iris drum

3a

Carefully painting the iridescent polymer coating on the print

3b

Drying the iridescent solution

4

Stopping the printer to show how the cyan, magenta, yellow and black inks are printed in sequence on the substrate

5

Using a silkscreen process to add a protective archival coating

dialog box to compensate for out-of-gamut blues that had been lost. (Since RGB has a broader color gamut than CMYK, out-of-gamut colors are dulled when an image is converted to CMYK.) The black plate was adjusted separately to bring out detail in the darkest areas of the image. Finally, a proprietary plug-in Iris format RIP (raster image processor) was used to save the image in a form that the Iris can use for printing.

2 Choosing a paper and setting up the Iris. Cone selected a sheet of heavy, handmade paper with a very soft, large surface grain and an exaggerated deckled edge that would complement the vivid color and lively brushstrokes in the image. He taped the paper to the drum of the Iris.

3 Printing, painting and drying. Cone used the Iris to print this particular image twice. For the first pass, he adjusted the ink tables in the Iris's RIP to print a faint version of the image. With the print still taped to the drum, Cone brushed an experimental iridescent solution (composed of titanium dioxide–coated mica and hydroscopic polymer) onto the lily only. Then he dried the hand-painted coating with a hair dryer.

4 Printing the image a second time. Cone loaded a new set of rich-printing color ink tables into the Iris's RIP and made a second printing pass. The transparent Iris inks adhered to the polymer coating on the lily as easily as they did to the uncoated paper; the iridescent polymer provided a subtle reflection, adding luminance to the lily.

5 Applying a protective coating to the print. Michael Pelletier, Systems and Production Manager for Cone Editions, applied a silkscreen coating of hindered amine light stabilizers (HALS) and ultraviolet absorbers (UVA) to the finished print. This solvent-based coating developed by Cone carries the protective additives deep into the printed image where they fully encapsulate the dyes, helping to produce what Cone Editions says is "the longest-lasting archival Iris print available today."

Documenting the edition. The artist now signs the finished print to make it the "right-to-print proof" against which future prints in the edition will be compared. After the artist has signed approval, an edition can be printed on demand while the image file is stored safely on CD-ROM at Cone Editions. A documentation sheet signed by both master printer and artist details the size of the edition, number of proofs printed, methods used and dimensions. Most importantly, it specifies that no other proofs or prints can or will be made. (After completing an edition, Cone destroys all copies of the image file.) Each print will bear a unique print identification number and will be signed and numbered in pencil by the artist.

Making an Archival Desktop Print

Overview *Scan a pen-and-ink drawing and a pencil drawing; use the scans as a guide to create a colored image in Painter; output the digital file to a desktop inkjet printer using archival materials.*

1

Benioff's pencil sketch (left) and pen-and-ink drawing (right)

2a

Blocking in color over the scanned pencil sketch using the Round Camelhair variant of Brushes

2b

Painting watercolor washes with the Soft Camel variant of Water Color

BY COMBINING A SCANNED PEN-AND-INK DRAWING with a colored painting created in Painter, Carol Benioff built the dynamic image *Flying Lesson*, which she printed on an Epson inkjet printer using an innovative combination of light-fast inks and archival paper.

1 Drawing, scanning and making a composite file. To begin, Benioff used a Cro Quill pen and India ink to draw a conventional pen-and-ink drawing on 11 x 14-inch Arches paper. She also drew a rough pencil sketch, (also on Arches paper) that would be used as a guide for the color work to be built in Painter. When the drawings were complete, she scanned them and saved the scans as TIFF files. Benioff's grayscale scans measured 3700 x 2775 pixels. Next, she opened both scanned drawings in Painter. With the ink drawing active, she chose Select, All (Ctrl/⌘-A), and copied and pasted the contents of the ink drawing into the pencil drawing scan, which produced a new layer in the Layers section

The image with the Water Color layer hidden (left) and with the Water Color layer visible (right)

3a

The Apply Lighting dialog box showing Benioff's custom "Soft Globe" light settings. The image before the lighting was applied (left), and after (right)

3b

With other layers hidden, adding watercolor to the branch and creature

3c

The short, overlapping brushstrokes added more texture to the flying figure and sky.

of the Objects palette. With the ink drawing layer active, she set its Composite Method to Multiply.

2 Painting with color. Working on the Canvas, Benioff began to add color to her image by painting with the Round Camelhair variant of Brushes, directly over the scanned pencil sketch. For smaller details, she switched to the Cover Pencil variant of Pencils and to add more texture she used the Nervous Pen variant of Pens. She continually switched between these three brushes as she established the color theme and the basic shapes and forms in the image, and she continually changed the size of the brushes as she worked, using the Size slider in the Controls:Brush palette.

Next, she painted watercolor washes on the sky and water using a custom Wash Camel brush and the Soft Camel variant of Water Color.

Choose the Wash Camel variant of Water Color and when you begin to paint, a new Water Color layer will automatically be created. Benioff painted light-colored washes using the Wash Camel, then she added deeper colors using the Soft Camel and fine details with the Simple Round Wash variant of Water Color.

3 Adding custom lighting and more watercolor. To create atmosphere and enhance the focal point of the image, Benioff applied a custom colored light to the Canvas. In the Effects, Surface Control, Apply Lighting dialog box, she chose the Plain Light and changed its Ambient Light Color to a light pink; she dramatically increased the Elevation so the light would be very soft, and she changed the orientation of the light to point it horizontally and to the left. (See "Adding Dimension With Lighting" on page 238 in Chapter 7 for more information about using Apply Lighting.)

Next, she added a new Water Color layer by clicking the Create New Layers button on the Layers section and choosing New Water Color layer. Using the ink drawing as a guide, she blocked in areas of color using the Soft Camel and a modified Wash Camel that incorporated less diffusion. And because she likes the bristle texture that it creates, she used the Dry Camel to paint more saturated colors using short, overlapping brushstrokes to build up subtle texture. Next, she targeted the first Water Color layer (on which she had painted the sky and water) and added deeper colors to it, using the Soft Camel and the modified Wash Camel brush. To create the vertical streaks, she used the Wet Bristle and a modified Wash Camel, enabling the Straight Line draw button in the Controls:Brush palette.

4 Completing the composite. Now that the watercolor brush-work was complete (so she could paint on the layer with other brushes), Benioff converted the sky Water Color layer to an image layer by choosing Convert To Default Layer from the menu on the right side of the Layers section bar. Then she added more detail to the entire image using the Cover Pencil, the Round

Facial details painted using the Simple Round Wash variant of Water Color and the Cover Pencil variant of Pencils

Detail of the final illustration with the opacity of the ink drawing layer reduced

Benioff's settings in the Color Management dialog box for the Epson 3000 and Museo paper

Camelhair brush and the Nervous Pen. So that the ink drawing would blend better with the image, she reduced its layer Opacity to 80% in the Layers section. Now that the image was complete, Benioff saved the composite image as a RIFF file for her archives and then saved a flattened copy of the file as an RGB TIFF for printing on an Epson 3000 inkjet printer.

5 Proofing and printing the image. For the print, Benioff chose Crane Museo paper, an archival printmaking paper that is manufactured to include a special coating created for use with inkjet printers.

For good results when printing on an Epson printer using Painter, make sure that you have Painter 7.1 loaded. (There was a bug in Painter 7.0 that caused images to print soft or slightly blurry and to subtly shift color when printing from Painter 7 to an Epson printer; printing to other printers was unaffected.) To check your software version, open your Painter application folder and click once on the application icon. Chose File, Get Info and note the version number of the software. You can download 7.1 from the Procreate Web site at http://www.procreate.com/go/painter_update/ and follow the directions to perform a clean install. Good results can also be achieved by opening the final RGB TIFF file in Adobe Photoshop and printing it from that program.

6 Setting up Color Management. Painter 7 offers Color Management controls that allow you to preview how your image will look when printed on a specific printer. To open the Color Management dialog box, choose Canvas, Kodak Color Correction. From the pop-up menu under the Internal Color Space icon, choose a profile that works best with your system. (Benioff chose Adobe RGB). To calibrate the display using your monitor's color profile, choose your monitor from the Monitor pop-up menu, then click the arrow that connects the Internal RGB profile to the Monitor icon. To make a color correction based on the printer's output profile, choose a printer from the pop-up menu under the Composite Printer icon (Benioff chose a custom profile that she had made for printing the Museo paper on her Epson 3000 printer with MIS inks), then click the arrow that connects the Internal RGB icon to the Composite Printer icon. (A custom ICC profile can be substituted for either of these choices, by copying it into the Color Profiles folder in the Painter application folder and then choosing it from the appropriate menu.) Now that the profiles are selected, save a new profile by clicking the + (Plus) icon and giving it a relevant name. Click OK to accept the changes and close the dialog box. To view the image with the Color Management setup and without, click the Output Preview button in the upper right corner of the Painter image window.

7 Printing the image. In the File, Page Setup dialog box, Benioff used the default setup for the Dot Gain and Screen

The Kodak Color Correction is turned off (top) and turned on (bottom).

The settings in the Epson 3000 Page Setup dialog box

Clicking the More Settings button to access the Advanced Settings dialog box

Selecting Superfine 1440, Photo Quality Inkjet, Error Diffusion and other choices in the Advanced Settings dialog box

Checking the settings a final time before printing

Gamma. Then, she chose File, Print and set up the Advanced Settings for use with her Epson printer as follows: In the Media Type pop-up menu, she selected the Photo-Quality Inkjet and selected the Color Quick Draw option. Then, she clicked the More Settings button to open the Advanced Settings dialog box and selected Super-fine 1440 from the Print Quality pop-up menu. (When Super-Fine 1440 is chosen, Micro Weave is enabled, but it's a good idea to also check the Super checkbox.) From the Half Toning pop-up menu, she chose Error Diffusion. She clicked on the Color Sync button and selected the ICC profile for her paper and ink she wanted to use. Then she clicked OK to accept the changes, and to return to the main Print dialog box. When all of the settings are completed, she clicked the Print button.

Benioff created Keep Your Legs Together, Don't Show Your Sex, *for her series,* The Unspoken Rules of Growing Up Female, *using similar techniques to those described on pages 374–377. She began the image by making two drawings: a sketch using pencil and paper and a second drawing using pen and ink. After scanning both drawings, she composited them in Painter and added colored brush work using various Water Color brushes, the Round Camelhair variant of Brushes and the Cover Pencil variant of Pencils. When the painting was complete, she saved a copy of the layered file in RGB TIFF format to flatten it. Then she printed the image on an Epson 3000 inkjet printer using the MIS archival ink set on Hahnmuelle paper that was manufactured for use with inkjet printers.*

■ When creating *Faccia*, **Laurence Gartel** combined his own photos with Painter brush work and special effects and conventional acrylic paint. He began the work by scanning a few of his photographs. Then he added acrylic paint to other photos and scanned them. He opened all of the scanned images in Painter and assembled them into a composition. He painted brushstrokes using the Smeary Round and Smeary Bristle Spray variants of Brushes. To blend areas of the image, he used Liquid variants. For instance, in the lower middle of the image, where the gray blends with the green, he created an interesting smudged texture using the Coarse Distorto variant of Liquid. To give the image the look of pools of water and levels of colorful translucency on the sides, he painted using Water Color brushes. To "lift" the black section of the face, he used the Bevel World dynamic layer effect. He used the Scratchboard Rake variant of Pens, creating a "mask" effect to the woman's face. When he was happy with the composition, Gartel printed the image on Epson Archival Matte paper using an Epson 2000P printer with Epson six-color archival pigmented inks. Then he painted over areas of the 13 x 19-inch print using acrylic paint.

■ **James Faire Walker** created *Global Coffee* (a member of his Color and Motion series) by collaging bits and pieces of his own digital photos, then painting brushstrokes and adding special effects. Walker loves the immediacy with which he can create an image—taking digital photos, opening them in Painter, pasting them into a collage, manipulating the pieces of photos on their own layers and then painting on the image with brushes. To color some of the photo pieces, he used Painter's Tonal Control effects, such as the Posterize feature. Then he added brush work, which was painted on transparent layers above the photo elements. He added the new transparent layers for the brush work by click-

ing the Create New Layers button on the Layers section and choosing New Layer. Then he painted using the Opaque Round variant and other Brushes variants to create colorful, loose strokes over and around the imagery of the coffee cups. To give the image depth and make the brush work layers stand out from the background, he applied soft drop shadows using the Create Drop Shadow command. As he developed the image, he proofed it in his studio on an Epson 3000 inkjet printer. The final 17 x 22-inch prints for the Global Coffee edition of 20 were printed on Somerset Radiant Velvet White paper on an Iris printer using the Pinnacle Gold archival ink set.

■ *Capitola* (top) and *Conch Shells* represent a new approach to image-making for artist **John Derry.** His purchase of a Sony DSC-F505 digital camera and the speed with which he could see the source images on screen opened some exciting possibilities.

To begin *Capitola,* Derry shot several digital photos of the colorful, quaint beachfront homes in Capitola, California. Back at the studio, he assembled the photos into a wide panoramic montage. He built the decorative border by copying embellishments from a few of the home fronts and assembling the pieces using layers. The panorama measures 24 x 3.7 inches.

Derry was walking along a beach in Belize when he spotted the inspiration for *Conch Shells.* He took several photographs of shells on a railing by the water. To create the watercolor run effect, he opened the image in Painter and added a new, empty layer by clicking the Create New Layers button on the Layers section

and choosing New Water Color Layer from the menu. Using the Runny Wash Bristle variant of Water Color and black paint, he loosely painted the rectangular area. Then he converted the Water Color layer to an image layer by choosing Convert To Default Layer from the menu on the right side of the Layers section bar. He then selected the Canvas (Ctrl/⌘-A) and chose Select, Float to cut it to a layer. He set the Composite Method of this layer to Screen in the Layers section, which dropped out the areas of the photo which were outside the black "mask" layer. When the composition was complete, he printed the 12 x 9.5 -inch image on his six-color Epson 1270 using Epson's archival ink set on sheets of Epson archival matte-finish paper. Derry has also printed his *Capitola* image larger on roll paper, taking advantage of the printer's ability to load a roll of 13-inch wide media, and print images up to 44 inches long.

■ In preparation for painting *Looking Toward Chasms*, **Cher Threinen-Pendarvis** made several color studies on location, carefully observing how light and atmosphere affect the color in highlights and shadows on the landscape forms and on the water.

Pendarvis's Downstream series (of which *Looking Toward Chasms* is a member) is inspired by breathtaking coastal views in California. Her series records favorite landscape features that are inevitably changing due to natural erosion. For this painting, Pendarvis began by making pastel sketches of the eroded cliff details and the overall

seascape, using Canson paper and pastels that she'd carried in her backpack. Later, back at the studio she created a new file in Painter. Using the Square Chalk and Soft Pastel variants of Dry Media and the Sanded Pastel Board texture, she sketched the composition. To build up layers of color interest on the hills, cliffs and water, she dabbed small strokes of paint on top using a small Round Camelhair brush. Then she blended areas of the cliffs, hills and water using the Grainy Water variant of Liquid. Pendarvis added lighter areas to the white water using the Square Chalk, then smoothed and blended color using the

Grainy Water. To add textured highlights to the beach and color interest to the cliffs, she lightly scumbled using the Square Chalk and Oil Pastel. To enhance the focal point of the composition and bring the foreground closer, she reworked the foreground cliffs and water using the Artist Pastel Chalk and the Oil Pastel using detailed, but expressive, loose strokes. Finally, to show movement in the water, she drew loose, swirly highlights on the water using the Artist Pastel Chalk and the Soft Pastel. The final image was printed on an Epson 2000P printer on 13 x 19-inch Epson Archival Matte paper using Epson's six-color pigmented archival ink set.

■ Artist **Judi Moncrieff** created *Traditions* (above) and *Generations* (right), two works in her series called *First Nation*, for a New York art exhibition. She began by taking photos of the people, artifacts and landscape surroundings at Spirit Days in Anchorage, Alaska. Spirit Days is a celebration of Native Americans from southeast Alaska to central and northern Alaska, and she had been invited to photograph people at the event. After the shoot, she used both Photoshop and Painter to create composite images from bits and pieces of many photographs, then added textures, more color and brushwork in Painter. "Nothing you see is real and, yet, *it is real*," says Moncrieff.

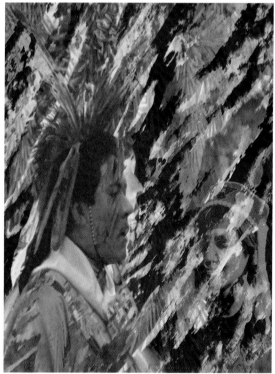

For the exhibition at the A.I.R. Gallery in SoHo, she created the main series as "one of a kind" (instead of members in an edition) because the images were presented using a complex printing, transfer and installation process that allowed Moncrieff to achieve a unique multidimensional look. To begin, the images were printed onto heat transfer paper on a Hewlett-Packard 2500CP with HP's pigment-based light-fast ink set. Then the resulting images on the heat transfer paper were applied to leather using heat and pressure. For the exhibition, the works were hung on the wall behind free-standing Plexiglas pieces on pedestals that were prepared with a black-and-clear image (printed onto a clear cling by the HP 2500 CP). Placing the Plexiglas elements one-half-inch away from the leather created a multidimensional effect.

■ *Heart of the Tree* is the second work in **Philip Howe's** series of angel paintings. It suggests that there is a life energy in everything and the ancient angel senses the old tree's history. Howe began the image by roughing out the concept in Painter—sketching and assembling finished drawings and photos from his archives into a composition. He turned the assemblage into an underpainting, using sepia-toned color, which he printed out on canvas to use as a base for working with oil paints. Then he printed the underpainting using a Hewlett-Packard DesignJet 2500CP printer, with Hewlett-Packard's archival ink set. To seal the canvas before painting on it, Howe used Liquin, which he had purchased from the Daniel Smith art store. The Liquin brought out rich values in the darker areas of the image and provided a good surface to paint over. When the sealer was thoroughly dry, he tacked the canvas up on the wall and applied oil paints over its entire surface. The tight, accurate underpainting allowed him to paint more loosely and concentrate on final effects. Howe used mostly wet-into-wet oil techniques, although he did let the image dry a few times, and painted translucent glazes over some areas of the canvas.

■ Fine artist **Dorothy Simpson Krause** created the collage *Primordial Fear* as the subject for a 35 x 28-inch lenticular. Krause assembled the image from six scanned objects and set each one up on its own layer: a photograph by Viola Kaumlen of a dramatic sky, a diagram of Babbage's computing engine, an early transistor, a photograph by Jan Doucette of the model Linda Serafin, a drawing of celestial alignments at Stonehenge and a compass.

Krause created several versions of the image, with elements in different positions, that would "animate" in the

lenticular. To make objects recede in space, Krause moved elements in small increments to the left. To make an object come forward in space, she moved it in small increments to the right. Greater increments and a larger number of steps created more depth. Krause saved eight "frames" as TIFF files. Then she used the Flip program to interlace the eight frames into vertical strips. She printed the interlaced image using a Roland HiFi Jet onto Roland PETG white film with Roland's six-color archival inks. Then she used a CODA laminator to apply the print to a plastic lenticular lens.

As a viewers moves past the completed image, they see one "frame" at a time and the image changes with each frame, creating the illusion of depth and movement. For instance, the transistor rises and sets (like a sun or moon) behind the woman, who is frozen with fear and does not move, the compass covering her face becomes a mask, and the lines of the azimuth and one circle from the Babbage diagram come forward in the picture plane.

■ *Indigo* is a 28 x 35-inch fresco transfer, and a member of **Bonny Lhotka's** *Heartland* series. The artist found inspiration for the work while visiting her hometown in Illinois in a unique store that had items left over from garage sales, the discarded possessions of everyday life. This mosaic of commonality inspired Lhotka, and she took many photographs while at the store. To create the image, she used the photos and also made scans of actual elements. For instance, she captured the position of a fragment of cheesecloth and her hand holding the marigolds. For another source image, she dyed the integra branches purple, and when they were dry, she laid them on a large-format Epson scanner and covered them with cheesecloth. When the collage was complete, she printed it

onto clear film with an Encad printer using the GO pigment ink set. Then she transferred the clear film print to a plaster fresco surface. (In her search for ways to apply her images to walls, Lhotka researched old masters' ways of creating gesso grounds and frescos. She made a fresco-like surface by applying a strained mixture of rabbit skin glue and calcium carbonate to a board.) When the fresco was nearly complete, she wanted to add a darker, metallic and iridescent look to the image's center (using a portion of the image she had printed earlier). So she coated a piece of translucent silver fabric with diluted rabbit skin glue (as an inkjet pre-coat), and when it was dry, printed the fabric on an Epson 3000 using Lysonic archival dye-based inks. Then she attached the print to the center of the fresco.

■ *Trnava Synagogue* was created by artist **Cynthia Beth Rubin** based on her own photographs taken while visiting the synagogue in Slovakia. "I am interested in how we can connect with the world beyond our own individuality, how we can connect with the past, and with each other living in the present," says Rubin. Although most of the compositing was done in Photoshop, Rubin used Painter extensively to bring out textures in the image and to enhance the color and lighting. She used the versatile Apply Surface Texture feature to add highlights and shadows to the forms of the Menorahs and all of the branches in the bottom of the work, making them look truly three dimensional. When the image was complete, she printed it on several surfaces using different devices. For instance, she ordered a 3M Matchprint on smooth vinyl (so that she could easily roll a print for shipping). She makes small prints in her studio on an Epson 1200 printer using Piezography inks and archival rag paper ordered from Jon Cone's inkjetmall.com. For an exhibition, she commissioned an Iris Print from Cone Editions that would be framed under UV protective glazing. She also ordered a larger print (which featured a richer color range) on photo-rag paper printed on a Roland inkjet printer using a six-color archival pigmented ink set.

■ Guardian IT commissioned **Fiona Hawthorne** to create *Large Busy Office* and *Night Meeting*—two paintings in a series devoted to the subject of international business. (Guardian IT does business continuity and disaster recovery by relocating work forces should there be a flood, fire, or even a hardware crash.) The purpose of the series was to enhance the work space, hopefully lifting the spirits of the relocated workforce, while at the same time showing that Guardian IT is involved with international business on a cutting edge level. Hawthorne began the project by drawing many developmental sketches on location with Painter's Scratchboard Tool (Pens), Pencils, Crayons and Brushes variants using a laptop computer with a pressure-sensitive tablet and stylus. Later, back at her studio, she scaled the images to a larger size and reworked them, adding finer details using various brushes. To add the Guardian IT logo to as many ties, mugs and computer screens as possible, she created a custom paper texture based on the Guardian IT logo and applied it using grain-sensitive brushes, such as the Chalk and Waxy Crayon variants of Dry Media. For more texture interest, she also pasted in a few bits of her own photos and painted over them so that they matched the paintings. The final images were output to a maximum 3 meters tall or 3 meters wide on a large format printer on pre-treated canvas, and then they were stretched on a wood frame.

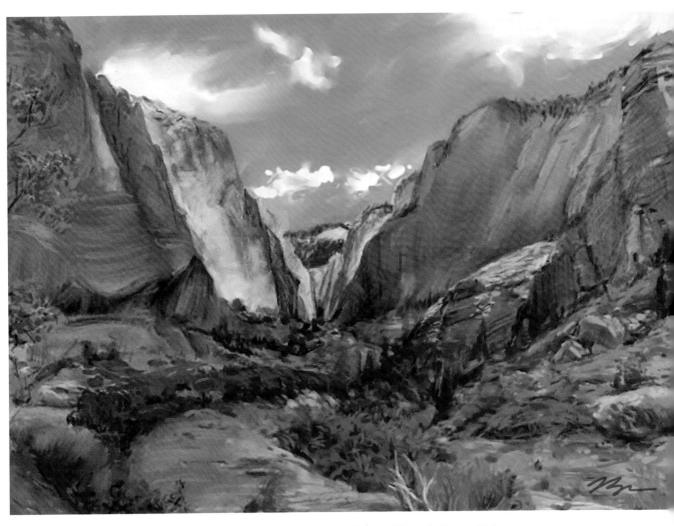

■ A traditionally trained artist, **Steve Rys** began *Zion National Park, Utah* by making conventional sketches using pencil and paper. While sketching, he referred to source photographs that he had taken on location. When he was happy with the sketch, he opened a new empty file in Painter and used brushes and a pressure-sensitive tablet and stylus to develop a color study. He sketched using the 2B Pencil variant of Pencils and the Calligraphy variant of Pens. To build the large masses of color, he used the Round Camelhair variant of Brushes, continually varying the size of the brush to achieve an expressive feeling with dynamic movement. As he developed the basic color theme and forms, he began with the lightest colors and then gradually built up darker tones. To blend areas, he used the Just Add Water variant of Liquid, also varying the size of the brush, adding more color with Round Camelhair when needed, for the look of wet paint. The final image was saved as a 240 ppi RGB file in TIFF format and was printed on a Roland Hi-Fi Jet inkjet printer using an archival six-color ink set on Concord Rag Bright White watercolor paper, which was manufactured with an inkjet receptive coating. The print was then sealed with a Krylon overcoat spray to protect the inks and paper from moisture and to increase the lightfastness of the print.

■ **Chet Phillips** created these larger-than-life-size vehicle graphics (top and middle left) for *Dallas Photo Imaging*, using the Scratchboard technique described on page 196. To make sure the three images would fit the truck exactly, he used a full-size template of the Suburban's shape (provided by the service bureau) to plan each panel. He created individual panels for the driver's side, passenger's side and the truck's back. Phillips built the original files at a resolution of 65 ppi; each file was over 100 MB. When the illustrations were complete, they were output on Dallas Photo Imaging's Idanit inkjet printer onto Avery fleet graphic vinyl with adhesive backing, then attached to the truck.

■ As the principal and creative director for Cinco de Mayo Design Studio, **Mauricio Alanis** conceived and built the *Shouting Bucket* vehicle graphics (bottom left) for Abigarrados, a service bureau in Monterrey, Mexico, which specializes in large-format printing. Using Painter, he created a layered image that included the paint can photo, the circular shapes around the can image and the exploding paint. To give the paint more realistic dimension, he added a semi-transparent layer of Liquid Metal brushstrokes. To add to the relief, he used Apply Surface Texture with Image Luminance. The final 65 ppi image was output onto adhesive-backed vinyl media using a large-format inkjet printer, and mounted on the Abigarrados van.

Appendix A
Images on the *Wow!* *CD-ROM*

These vendors provided photos or video clips from their collections for the Wow! CD-ROM *in the back of this book.*

Artbeats
Volumes of backgrounds and textures, including Wood and Paper and Leather and Fabric; sizes to 16.5 MB; Reel Textures, a collection of 40 animated backgrounds

Corbis Images
Extensive collection of royalty-free images, available on CD-ROM or online. Business, lifestyle, nature, backgrounds and more; sizes to 32MB.

Fabulous Fonts
Volumes 31–36 (e.g. Friz Quadrata Book, Corroded Rust and Vidigris; Shelley Volante, Gold and Platinum); picture fonts in sizes to 2.6 MB, designed by John Dismukes and Jo-Anne Redwood of Capstone Studios

Digital Wisdom
Body Shots: One volume of photographs shot with twelve models in various business situations against a white background; sizes to 4 MB

Image Farm
Volumes including Arizona Desert, Berlin Walls, Cottage and Country, Real Rock, Streets of London, and Industrial Backgrounds and Objects; high quality photographic textures and backgrounds; sizes to 18 MB.

Mediacom
Adclips: One volume (2 CDs) of video clips including Recreation, Corporate, Historical, Lifestyles, Wildlife; sizes to 320 x 240 pixels

Getty Images / PhotoDisc
85,000 images downloadable from the Web; over 190 thematic CD-ROM discs; including Signature Series; Object Series (with clipping paths); Fine Art series and Background Series discs; sizes to 28.5 MB

PhotoSpin
Premiere Series and Photo Objects (images with masks); sizes to 25 MB; 50–100 images per disc

Visual Concept Entertainment
Pyromania 1, 2 and Pyromania! Pro:
3 volumes of digitized video of explosions,
fireworks, smoke, and other incendiary
displays; sizes to 640 x 480 pixels

Appendix B Vendor Information

IMAGE COLLECTIONS

Artbeats, Inc.
1405 N. Myrtle Road, Ste. 5
Myrtle Creek, OR 97457
541-863-4429 541-863-4547 fax
www.artbeats.com

Corbis Images
15395 S.E. 30th Place, Ste. 300
Bellevue, WA 98007
800-260-0444 425-641-4505 fax
www.corbisimages.com

Digital Wisdom, Inc.
300 Jeanette Drive, Box 2070
Tappahannock, VA 22560
800-800-8560 804-443-9000
804-443-3632 fax
www.digiwis.com

Fabulous Fonts
c/o PhotoSpin
4030 Palos Verdes Drive North, Ste. 200
Rolling Hills Estates, CA 90274
310-265-1313 888-246-1313
310-265-1314 fax
www.photospin.com

Image Farm, Inc.
490 Adelaide Street West, Suite 301
Toronto, ON
Canada M5V 1T2
800-438-3276 416-504-4163 fax
www.imagefarm.com

Mediacom
9210 Arboretum Pkwy. Ste. 150
Richmond, VA 23236
804-560-9200 804-560-4370 fax

Getty Images / PhotoDisc
701 North 34th Street, Suite 400
Seattle, WA 98103
800-528-3472
877-547-4686 fax
www.gettyimages.com

PhotoSpin
4030 Palos Verdes Drive North, Ste. 200
Rolling Hills Estates, CA 90274
310-265-1313 888-246-1313
310-265-1314 fax
www.photospin.com

Visual Concept Entertainment
P.O. Box 921226
Sylmar, CA 91392
818-367-9187 818-362-3490 fax
http://www.vce.com

HARDWARE

Apple Computer, Inc.
800-767-2775

Hewlett-Packard / *Desktop color printers*
16399 West Bernardo Drive
San Diego, CA 92127
858-655-4100
www.hp.com

Epson America / *Desktop color printers*
P.O. Box 2854
Torrance, CA 90509
800-289-3776 800-873-7766
www.epson.com

Wacom Technology Corporation
Drawing tablets
1311 SE Cardinal Court
Vancouver, WA 98683
800-922-6613
sales@wacom.com

INKS AND SUBSTRATES

Charrette Corporation / *Substrates and Inks*
800-367-3729
www.inkjet.com

Dr. Graphix Inc. / *Substrates*
www.drgraphix.com

Epson / *Substrates and Inks*
www.epson.com

Hewlett-Packard / *Substrates and Inks*
www.hp.com

ilab Corporation, Inc. / *inks for Epson, Iris and Novaget*
P.O. Box 1030
Atkinson, NH 03811
603-362-4190 603-362-4191 fax
www.ilabcorp.com

InkjetMall / *Substrates and Inks*
P.O. Box 335
148 Main Street
Bradford, VT 05033
802-222-4415 802-222-3334 fax
Contact: Sarah Lyons

Luminos Photo Corporation / *inks for Epson and other printers*
P.O. Box 158
Yonkers, NY 10705
800-586-4667 914-965-0367 fax

Media Street / *Substrates and Inks*
888-633-4295
888-329-5991 fax
www.mediastreet.com

TSS Photo / *Substrates and Inks*
801-363-9700 801-363-9707 fax
www.inkjetart.com
www.tssphoto.com/sp/dg/

Wilhelm Imaging Research, Inc. / *Ink and paper longevity information*
P.O. Box 775
Grinnell, IA 50112-0775
515-236-4222 fax
www.wilhelm-research.com

SOFTWARE

Adobe Systems / *After Effects, Dimensions, GoLive, Illustrator, PageMaker, Photoshop, Premiere*
345 Park Avenue
San Jose, CA 95110
800-833-6687

Auto F/X / *Photographic Edges*
31 Inverness Parkway, Ste. 270
Birmingham, AL 35242
205-980-0056
www.autofx.com

procreate / *Painter 7 KPT Effects, Knock Out 2*
1600 Carling Avenue
Ottawa, ON
Canada K1Z 8R7
800-772-6735
www.procreate.com

Macromedia / *Director, Dreamweaver, FreeHand, Fireworks, Flash*
600 Townsend Street, Suite 310-W
San Francisco, CA 94103
800-989-3762
415-252-2000

Appendix C
Fine Art Output Suppliers

These bureaus specialize in making large format prints for fine artists, using the Iris inkjet and other printers. More are listed on the Wow! CD-ROM.

Cone Editions Press / *Fine Art Prints*
P.O. Box 51
17 Powder Spring Road
East Topsham, VT 05076
802-439-5751 802-439-6501 fax
Contact: Sara Larkin

Chrome Digital / *Fujix Pictrography prints; film recorder output*
858-452-1588

Color Reflections / *Durst Lamda and Fujix Pictrography prints; film recorder output*
www.colorreflections.com

Dallas Photo Imaging *LightJet 5000 prints; vehicle graphics*
3942 Irving Boulevard
Dallas, TX 75247
800-852-6929 214-630-4351
www.dpitexas.com

Digicolor / *Iris fine art prints*
Seattle, WA
206-284-2198

Digicolorado / *Iris fine art prints*
610 South Lipan Street
Denver, CO 80223
303-777-6720

Digital Output Corp. / *Hewlett-Packard DesignJet CP prints; Iris fine art prints*
2121 5th Avenue
San Diego, CA 92101
619-685-5800
619-685-5804 fax
www.digitaloutput.com

Durst Dice America / *Lenticular prints*
16 Sterling Road
Tuxedo, NY 10987
914-351-2677

Electric Paintbrush / *Iris fine art prints*
Hopkinton, MA
508-435-7726

Foto 1 Imaging / *LightJet 5000; Fujix Pictrography prints*
800-761-3686
www.foto1.com

High Resolution / *Iris fine art prints*
Camden, ME
207-236-3777

Imagestation / *Iris fine art prints*
Kihei, HI
808-536-1718

Lenticular Products / *Lenticular prints*
www.lenticulardevelopement.com

Nash Editions / *Iris fine art prints*
Manhattan Beach, CA
310-545-4352

Paris Photo Lab / *Iris fine art prints*
Los Angeles, CA
310-204-0500

Photodyne / *Hewlett-Packard DesignJet CP prints; film recorder output*
7012 Convoy Court
San Diego, CA 92011
858-292-0140

Photoworks / *Noritzu prints; Cibachrome*
858-755-0772

River City Silver / *LightJet 5000 prints*
800-938-2788

Salon Iris / *Iris fine art prints*
Vienna, Austria

Trillium Press / *Iris fine art prints; monotypes; silk screen*
91 Park Lane
Brisbane, CA 94005
415-468-8166
415-468-0721 fax

Urban Digital Color / *Iris fine art prints*
San Francisco, CA
415-626-8403

Appendix D
Contributing Artists

Mauricio Alanis
c/o Cinco de Mayo
5 de Mayo Pte., Monterrey, N.L.
Mexico, 64000
malanis@mail.cmact.com

Ben Barbante
1176 Key Avenue
San Francisco, CA 94124
415-657-9844

Laurel Becker

Carol Benioff
2226 11th Avenue #4
Oakland, CA 94606
510-533-9987

Richard Biever
117 N. Frederick
Evansville, IN 47711
812-437-9308

Kathleen Blavatt
4261 Montalvo Street
San Diego, CA 92107
619-222-0057

Ray Blavatt
4261 Montalvo Street
San Diego, CA 92107
619-222-0057

Athos Boncompagni
web: http://go.to/athos
e-mail: athos@libero.it

Marc Brown
2786 South Monroe
Denver, CO 80210
303-758-9411

Jeff Burke
8755 Washington Boulevard
Culver City, CA 90232
310-837-9900

Michael Campbell
MCC@michaelcampbell.com

Steve Campbell
1880 Fulton #5
San Francisco, CA 94117
415-668-5826
campbell12.home.mindspring.com
campbell12@mindspring.com

Karen Carr
www.karencarr.com

Mario Henri Chakkour, AIA
703-317-1923
www.chakkour.com
mario@chakkour.com

Phillip Charris
27184 Ortega Highway
San Juan Capistrano, CA 92675
949-496-3330

Gary Clark
823 Lightstreet Road
Bloomsburg, PA 17815
717-387-1689

Stephen Crooks
scrooks@earthlink.net

James D'Avanzo
(11/2/73–5/28/96)
Family of James D'Avanzo
1446 Jennings Road
Fairfield, CT 06430
203-255-6822

Linda Davick
4805 Hilldale Drive
Knoxville, TN 37914
615-546-1020

Jack Davis
1315 Belleview Avenue
Cardiff, CA 92007
619-944-7232

Michela Del Degan
mdegan@infinito.it

John Derry
St. Louis, MO
pixlart@mac.com

Eduardo Diaz Juliano
kaffa@retemail.es

Ellie Dickson
185 West End Avenue #3L
New York, NY 10023
212-724-3598

Matt Dineen
1465 Dougmar Road
Santa Cruz, CA 95062

John Dismukes
949-888-9911
www.dismukes.com

Mary Envall
1536 Promontory Ridge Way
Vista, CA 92083
760-727-8995

Grace Ferguson
2226–11th Avenue
Oakland, CA 94606

John Fretz
707 S. Snoqualmie Street, #5D
Seattle, WA 98108
206-623-1931

Laurence Gartel
P.O. Box 971251
Boca Raton, FL 33487
561-477-1100

Kerry Gavin
154 East Canaan Road
East Canaan, CT 06024
203-824-4839

Steven Gordon
136 Mill Creek Crossing
Madison, AL 35758
256-772-0022

Rhoda Grossman
rhoda@dnai.com

Shawn Grunberger
415-552-0367
shawn@deepstorm.com

Francois Guerin
33 Rue Alexandre Dumas
75011 Paris, France
0-11-331-43-73-36-62

Kathy Hammon
bouchedoree@wanadoo.fr

Andrew Hathaway
805 Page Street
San Francisco, CA 94117
415-621-0671

Fiona Hawthorne
47 Barlby Road
London W10 6AW, UK
++44 (0)20 8968 8889
fionahawthorne@dsl.pipex.net

Brent Houston
brenthouston@earthlink.net

Philip Howe
12425 68th Avenue SE
Snohomish, WA 98296
425-385-8426
dooder1@aol.com

Geoff Hull
4054 Cartwright Avenue
Studio City, CA 91604
818-761-6019

Aleksander Jensko
www.aljen.de
www.kreaftwerk.com
aljen@mac.com

Donal Jolley
c/o Studio 3.0
1506 Black Spruce Court
Lilburn, GA 30047
770-923-6480

Ron Kempke
217-278-7441

Rick Kirkman
11809 N. 56th Drive
Glendale, AZ 85304
623-334-9199

Dorothy Simpson Krause
P.O. Box 421
Marshfield Hills, MA 02051
781-837-1682
www.dotkrause.com

Ted Larson
7718 Corliss Avenue North
Seattle, WA 98103
206-525-0588
theoneson@earthlink.net

John Lee
2293 El Contento Drive
Los Angeles, CA 90068
213-467-9317

LeVan/Barbee
LeVan/Barbee studio
P.O. Box 182
Indianola, WA 98342
www.bruckandmoss.com

Bonny Lhotka
5658 Cascade Place
Boulder, CO 80303
303-494-5631

Michele Lill
2503 Kieffer Court
Valparaiso, IN 46383
219-531-4728
lill@netnitco.net

Keith MacLelland
27 Lanark Road #7
Brighton, MA 02135
617-734-2428
keith@yourillustrator.com

Debi Lee Mandel
530-886-8910
www.catsprite.com

Robert Manning
Supersample Corporation
Lilika Productions
212-414-1680 212-414-1681 fax
meglartin@aol.com
www.supersample.com

Janet Martini
4857 Biona Drive
San Diego, CA 9211
619-283-7895

Craig McClain
9587 Tropico Drive
La Mesa, CA 91941
619-469-9599

Pedro Meyer
1333 Beverly Glen #1004
Los Angeles, CA 90024
pedro@zonezero.com

Judy Miller
31 Martin Drive
Fall River, NS
B2T 1E7 Canada
902-861-1193
judy@creativeartist.com

Judi Moncrieff
(10/25/41–4/06/01)
Family of Judi Moncrieff
122 North 83rd Street
Seattle, WA 98103

Brian Moose
P.O. Box 927
Capitola, CA 95010
831-425-1672

Wendy Morris
4876 Orchard Avenue
San Diego, CA 92107
619-222-5044
wendydraw@aol.com

Richard Noble
899 Forest Lane
Alamo, CA 94507
510-838-5524

Louis Ocepek
1761 Pomona Drive
Las Cruces, NM 88011
505-522-0427
505-646-7550

John Odam
2163 Cordero Road
Del Mar, CA 92014
858-259-8230

Corinne Okada

Dennis Orlando
116 West Norton Drive
Churchville, PA 18966
215-355-1613 215-355-6924 fax
dorlando@voicenet.com

Cris Palomino
1457 Bellevue Avenue
Los Angeles, CA 90026
elektralusion@elektralusion.com
http://www.elektralusion.com

Chet Phillips
6527 Del Norte
Dallas, TX 75225
214-987-4344
www.chetart.com

David Purnell
c/o New York West
8145-100th Street W
Lonsdale, MN 55046
507-744-5408

Arena Reed
617-945-2754
arena@visualarena.com
www.visualarena.com

Mike Reed
1314 Summit Avenue
Minneapolis, MN 55403
612-374-3164
mikelr@winternet.com

Cindy Reid
cindy@reidcreative.com

Dewey Reid
dewey@reidcreative.com

Cecil Rice
5784 Salem Terrace
Acworth, GA 30102
770-974-0684

Lew Robinson
Photography and Digital Imaging
310-837-7009

Cynthia Beth Rubin
85 Willow Street
New Haven, CT 06511
http://CBRubin.net

Peter Mitchell Rubin
c/o Production Arts Limited
310-915-5610

Steve Rys
12051 256th Avenue
Trevor, WI 53179
262-862-7090
http://www.rysdesign.com

Chelsea Sammel
P.O. Box 30132
Oakland, CA 94604-6332
510-628-8474

Don Seegmiller
c/o Saffire
734 East Utah Valley Drive
American Fork UT 84003
801-847-1400
don@saffire.com

Nancy Stahl
470 West End Avenue
New York, NY 10024
212-362-8779

Sharon Steuer
205 Valley Road
Bethany, CT 06524
203-393-3981

Don Stewart
Greensboro, NC
336-854-2769
don@donstewart.com
www.donstewart.com

Jeremy Sutton
415-626-3871
jeremy@portrayals.com
www.portrayals.com

S. Swaminathan
P.O. Box 1547
Capitola, CA
408-722-3301

Margaret Sweeney
12939 Indian River Drive #6
Sebastian, FL 32958
561-388-2620

Jean-Luc Touillon
jean-luc.touillon@wanadoo.fr
jasiu@lafactory.fr

Lorraine Triolo
8755 Washington Boulevard
Culver City, CA 90232
310-837-9900

Stanley Vealé
zetar@yahoo.com

Pamela Wells
136 Verdi Avenue
Cardiff, CA 92007
760-632-8495

James Faure Walker
88 Greenwood Road
London E8 1NE, UK
jamesfaurewalker@compuserve.com

Hiroshi Yoshii
1-2-13-304, Tamagawadai, Setagaya-ku
Tokyo 1580096, Japan
tel/fax 81.3.5491.5337
hiroshi@yoshii.com

Appendix E
Reference Materials

Here's a sampling of recommended references for both traditional and digital art forms.

ART BOOKS

Art Through the Ages
Fifth Edition
*Revised by Horst de la Croix
and Richard G. Tansey*
Harcourt, Brace and World, Inc.
New York, Chicago, San Francisco,
and Atlanta

The Art of Color
Johannes Itten
Van Nostrand Reinhold
New York

**Drawing Lessons
from the Great Masters**
Robert Beverly Hale
Watson-Guptill Publications
New York

Mainstreams of Modern Art
John Canaday
Holt, Reinhart and Winston
New York

Printmaking
Gabor Peterdi
The Macmillan Company
New York
Collier-Macmillan Ltd.
London

The Natural Way to Draw
Kimon Nicolaides
Houghton Mifflin Company
Boston

The Photographer's Handbook
John Hedgecoe
Alfred A. Knopf
New York

TypeWise
*Kit Hinrichs
with Delphine Hirasura*
North Light Books
Cincinnati, Ohio

COMPUTER IMAGERY BOOKS

Creating Killer Web Sites
Second Edition
David Siegel
Hayden Books
201 West 103 Street
Indianapolis, IN 46290

Elements of Web Design
Second Edition
*Darcy DiNucci with Maria Giudice and
Lynne Stiles*
Peachpit Press
Berkeley, CA

Deconstructing Web Graphics
Second Edition
Lynda Weinman and Jon Warren Lentz
New Riders Publishing
Indianapolis, IN

Designing Web Graphics 3
How to Prepare Images and Media
for the Web
Lynda Weinman
New Riders Publishing
Indianapolis, IN

Non-Designers Web Book
Robin Williams and John Tollett
Peachpit Press
Berkeley, CA

The Illustrator 9 Wow! Book
Sharon Steuer
Peachpit Press
Berkeley, CA

The Photoshop 6 Wow! Book
Linnea Dayton and Jack Davis
Peachpit Press
Berkeley, CA

PUBLICATIONS

Communication Arts
Coyne & Blanchard, Inc.
410 Sherman Avenue
Palo Alto, CA 94306

Design Graphics
Design Editorial Pty. Ltd.
11 School Road
Ferny Creek
Victoria 3786 Australia

EFX Art and Design
Roslagsgatan 11
S-113 55 Stockholm, Sweden
+46-8-15 55 48 +46-8-15 55 49 fax

Electronic Publishing
Ten Tara Boulevard, Fifth Floor
Nashua, NH 03062

Graphis
Graphis US, Inc.
141 Lexington Avenue
New York, NY 10016

How
Ideas and Techniques for Graphic Design
104 Fifth Avenue
New York, NY 10011

Print
RC Publications
104 Fifth Avenue
New York, NY 10011

Step-by-Step Graphics and
Step-by-Step Electronic Design
Step-by-Step Publishing
6000 Forest Park Drive
Peoria, IL 61614

Index